Aviation Investment

Aviation Investment uniquely addresses investment appraisal methods across the key industries that make up the aviation sector, including the airports, air traffic management, airline and aircraft manufacturing – or aeronautic – industries. This practice-oriented book presents methods through realistic case studies. It covers both economic appraisal, or cost-benefit analysis, measuring the value of projects to society, and financial appraisal, valuing projects as cash generators.

This substantially expanded second edition covers in greater detail the treatment of environmental emissions, paying particular attention to climate change. It addresses the treatment of Market-Based Mechanisms (MBMs), including cap and trade systems like ETS and offset systems like CORSIA, and compares them to environmental taxes. It also addresses the adjustments needed to measure the foreign exchange generating value of projects, relevant in the presence of trade barriers. The new edition includes two new project types. One is airport relocations, perhaps the most complex type of airport projects, where the economic case is often more nuanced than may be apparent. The second is the re-introduction of supersonic travel.

Aviation Investment offers all aviation sub-sectors a single-source reference, bringing together the theoretical background of the economic appraisal literature and aviation investment in practice. It is written in a style that is accessible to non-academic professionals, using formulae only where strictly necessary to enable practical applications, and benefits from the substantial practical experience of the author.

Doramas Jorge-Calderón is an economist at the European Investment Bank, the EU project financing bank, based in Luxembourg. He appraises investment projects mostly in the aviation sector in Europe and in countries throughout the world with which the EU has development cooperation agreements. He was previously with economic consultants NERA in London working on regulatory and competition projects. He holds a PhD in transport economics from the University of Leeds and has written a number of papers in academic journals on air transport economics and investment appraisal.

'There are many manuals and cookbooks for the evaluation of investments but surprisingly not one focusing on Aviation. Doramas Jorge-Calderón has made an impressive attempt to fill this gap. The book will be the natural reference guide for those evaluating aviation investments. In addition, the book will be useful for those teaching courses in applied welfare economics at universities and business schools.'

Per-Olov Johansson, Stockholm School of Economics, Sweden

'This is an excellent book on aviation investment. The book is soundly and clearly written by an author with a thorough theoretical background and deep knowledge of the aviation industry. I have learned and enjoyed reading this book and highly recommend it to anyone interested in the aviation industry or in investment evaluation.'

Ginés de Rus, University of Las Palmas de Gran Canaria and University Carlos III de Madrid, Spain

Aviation Investment

Economic Appraisal for Airports,
Air Traffic Management, Airlines
and Aeronautics

Second Edition

Doramas Jorge-Calderón

Routledge
Taylor & Francis Group

LONDON AND NEW YORK

Second edition published 2021
by Routledge
2 Park Square, Milton Park, Abingdon, Oxon, OX14 4RN

and by Routledge
52 Vanderbilt Avenue, New York, NY 10017

Routledge is an imprint of the Taylor & Francis Group, an informa business

© 2021 Doramas Jorge-Calderón

First edition published by Ashgate 2014

British Library Cataloguing-in-Publication Data
A catalogue record for this book is available from the British Library

Library of Congress Cataloging-in-Publication Data
Names: Jorge-Calderón, Doramas, author.
Title: Aviation investment : economic appraisal for airports, air traffic
management, airlines and aeronautics / Doramas Jorge-Calderón.
Description: Second edition. | Abingdon, Oxon ; New York, NY :
Routledge, 2021. | Includes bibliographical references and index.
Identifiers: LCCN 2020034888
Subjects: LCSH: Aeronautics, Commercial--Economic aspects. | Aeronautics,
Commercial--Capital investments. | Airports--Economic aspects. | Air traffic
control--Economic aspects. | Airlines--Economic aspects.
Classification: LCC HE9782 .J67 2021 | DDC 387.7/1--dc23
LC record available at https://lccn.loc.gov/2020034888

ISBN: 978-1-138-03663-5 (hbk)
ISBN: 978-1-315-17845-5 (ebk)

Typeset in Bembo
by MPS Limited, Dehradun

To my father.

Contents

3   The basic framework

4   Airports

Tables

Figures

Preface to the Second Edition

Since the first edition of this book was published, two developments have substantially changed the policy and institutional landscape within which aviation investment takes place. Firstly, the dramatic growth of the so called environmental, social, and governance (ESG) considerations in private sector production. Managers that had traditionally focused on shareholder value are now asked to pay attention to value to society as well. Economic (also called socio-economic) appraisal measures societal value. The first edition discussed the relevance of economic appraisal beyond guiding public sector investment. Of most immediate relevance to managers may well be that economic appraisal measures full value, beyond project revenues, to project users and customers. Less immediately apparent is that by measuring how an investment project adds or subtracts value to society and by identifying winners and losers, economic appraisal helps the private sector chart the future direction of public policy and the extent of likely government interventions.

There are concerns as to whether managers are well equipped conceptually to understand the societal value of their operations. MBAs teach financial appraisal but rarely socio-economic appraisal. ESG appraisals frequently follow a scorecard or multi-criteria framework which, besides consisting of ad hoc criteria, is disconnected from the concept of value that managers understand well.

The key tool for socio-economic appraisal is societal cost-benefit analysis (CBA). It is not a new technique. The cash-flow appraisal of an investment is a constituent part of CBA. Cash flow analysis measures the value of the investment project to suppliers of financial capital. CBA broadens the measure of value to that accruing to society at large, including also non-financial costs and benefits. The mechanics to estimate the two measures of value are the same, they both follow the logic of opportunity cost, and the calculation of economic value yields also financial value.

The worked appraisal examples in this second edition continue to emphasise the interplay between financial and economic, or societal, value, including the role of government policy in shaping the relationship between the two. New appraisal examples deal with an expanded set of issues concerning the environment, land use and value, regional accessibility, and trade.

The second development that has changed the policy and institutional landscape of aviation investment since the publication of the first edition is closely related to the first one. It is the rise in public and political concerns about climate change, and the accompanying policy initiatives to address it. In 2016 most countries signed the Paris Agreement (PA), within the United Nations (UN) Framework Convention on Climate Change. The PA has since been leading to policy initiatives addressing production and consumption throughout the economy, aimed at lowering economy-wide emissions of greenhouse gases (GHG).

In aviation, so far the policy tool of choice to 'internalise' GHG emissions consists of what are known as market-based mechanisms (MBM). The UN is promoting the Carbon Offsetting and Reduction Scheme for International Aviation (CORSIA), whereby airlines operating routes linking signatory countries would need to buy GHG offsets. CORSIA begins its pilot phase in 2021, as this second edition goes to print. In Europe, airlines were included in the EU Emissions Trading System (ETS) in 2012. ETS is a cap-and-trade mechanism whereby carriers are required to buy GHG emission allowances on flights within the European Economic Area. Concerns about the effectiveness of ETS due to the low price of allowances in the mid 2010s have partly dissipated as prices have increased lately. They are expected to increase further through the 2020s. However concerns remain, prompting calls to introduce carbon taxes to supplement MBMs.

Aviation investment projects may therefore encounter carbon price in a number of ways: offset mechanisms; cap and trade mechanisms; as an externality; and perhaps as a tax. They will also face situations where the market price of carbon in MBMs would be lower than the reference social-cost of carbon, perhaps leading to taxes supplementing MBMs. Chapter 2 of this second edition addresses the different implications of MBMs and taxes for investment appraisal, extended in the appendix to the chapter. Chapter 5 addresses the implications of combining MBMs with taxes, illustrated through an aircraft acquisition project.

It is worth highlighting also three other novelties in this edition. First is the appraisal of airport relocations. As urban population grows, the value of urban land close to city centres increases, and with it the opportunity cost of airport sites. Proximity to urban areas also constrains the ability of airports to expand capacity. While airport relocation projects are relatively infrequent, they still appear with some regularity and tend to be very large, high profile projects with long gestation periods. In economic terms, the case for relocating an airport involves balancing the land value released by vacating the existing site, the costs of accessing the new site and the differing incidence of externalities between the two sites. Chapter 4 includes an illustration of one such appraisal.

Second is the role that the flows of foreign exchange associated with an investment project play in the desirability of the project for society. Aviation can generate and use substantial amounts of foreign exchange. This becomes an important consideration for the investment case both in poorer countries where foreign exchange can be scarce, but also more broadly wherever there are significant barriers to trade. Economic appraisal techniques to deal with foreign exchange scarcity were developed in the 1960s and 1970s by academia, multilateral development banks (primarily the World Bank), and other multilateral organisations like the UN and the Organisation for Economic Cooperation and Development (OECD). In the 1980s and 1990s these techniques fell into disuse, for two reasons. Firstly, the Bretton Woods system was abandoned in the 1970s, easing constraints on access to foreign exchange, at least for those countries that could print currencies that were generally accepted internationally. Secondly, the latest round of globalisation, backed by a process of trade liberalisation. This process arguably began in the 1980s, accelerated with the collapse of the communist block at the turn of the 1990s and culminated with the creation of the World Trade Organisation (WTO) in 1994. It meant that trade barriers were curtailed and with them price distortions at 'borders', reducing the size of the adjustments resulting from the referred techniques.

Yet, all along that process of globalisation, nations have continued to run into balance of payment problems by issuing debt in currencies that they cannot print and by not managing well those liabilities. Most visible were the Latin American Debt Crisis of the 1980s, culminating in the Tequila Crisis of 1994, followed by the Asian Crisis and Russian default in the second half of the 1990s, the collapse of the Argentine currency board in the early 2000s, and the balance of payments problems of some Euro area countries in the early 2010s. There were also many other lower profile instances of IMF assistance throughout the period, as well as of bilateral assistance between countries. All this implies that large capital investment projects could well be implemented and operated in conditions of tight foreign exchange constraints while, in the case of aviation projects, involving themselves substantial foreign exchange flows.

In addition, more recently, protectionism and trade barriers have been making a comeback in the international scene. The combination of foreign exchange scarcity and rising protectionism bring back into relevance the appraisal techniques that reflect foreign exchange scarcity. They are illustrated through an air traffic management project in Chapter 5.

Finally, while climate change looks bound to prove, and rightfully so, an overarching policy theme for many years to come, one cannot forget the underlying case for aviation and its value to society. Aviation reduces the cost of travel and of shipping products between destinations, where travel time is a substantial part of that cost. The weight of travel time in the generalised cost of transport grows with distance. As long distance air travel grows throughout the world and as incomes rise, the cost bill to the world economy of person-hours spent in long distance travel would be ever growing, and with it the willingness to pay to reduce it. With the cessation of Concorde operations, aviation not only stopped but actually took a step back from its historical trend of increasing speed. However, the aeronautical industry has not forgotten the case for speed. It is arguably only a question of time before the commercial case for a return to supersonic travel becomes evident. But besides immediate business case considerations, industrial policy may well prompt, in any case, government financial support for such a project. Chapter 7 on the aeronautical industry proposes how to build the socio-economic case for investing in re-introducing supersonic travel.

In completing this second edition I have benefited from what I have learnt from many people. Naming them individually would produce too long a list, while any attempt at being concise would unfairly leave many individuals out. I would like to thank my colleagues in the various directorates of the European Investment Bank (EIB) and in other international financial institutions and European institutions. Promoters in the aviation industry financed by the EIB are the primary source of my knowledge of industry practice. Many thanks to all of them. Trade bodies in the industry produce sound, informative research and constitute an excellent means to follow the pulse of the industry. On the academic side, the German Aviation Research Society (GARS) and collaborating research and educational institutions are playing an important role in promoting debate and research on aviation economics. Nongovernmental organisations have been increasingly vocal about the aviation industry in the last few years. Their views and work are highly appreciated. I trust this tome will be useful to them as well.

I would like to make a special mention to the engineers in the Projects Directorate of the EIB who have appraised aviation projects with me since the publication of the first edition of this book. They include, in first name alphabetical order, Elena Campelo, Stéphane Petti, Stephen O'Driscoll and Tiago Lopes.

Professor Per-Olov Johansson kindly commented on some of the new sections of this second edition. Any remaining errors are mine. Also mine are the views and opinions expressed, which are not attributable to any of my affiliations. In particular, the views expressed here are not necessarily those of the EIB.

My gratitude also goes to the publishing team at Routledge, in particular to my editor, Guy Loft. And a big thank you to my family for putting up with me dedicating a significant part of my 'time off' over the last two years to producing this second edition.

Preface to the First Edition

Aviation has significant advantages over alternative transport modes. The ability to offer fast, reliable services, largely independently of geographical obstacles, means that the degree to which it improves accessibility worldwide cannot be matched by other transport technologies, so that aviation has become a very distinctive source of value. As a result, society and the economy at large benefit through the widening of the scope of markets, fostering the generation of wealth and the enriching of lifestyles. Today, aviation is a necessary component of commercial and cultural activity. Without it, the functioning of modern societies and economies as we know them would be fundamentally altered.

Because of the strong competitive advantage as a sector, particularly for long-distance passenger travel, aviation investments can be very profitable. Whereas some sub-sectors within aviation, notably airlines, have a mixed reputation with private investors, the underlying competitive advantage of aviation means that there are pockets of strong pricing power. Economic regulation to cap prices is frequent, as is, increasingly, discretionary taxation to raise revenues for governments. Moreover, whereas it is already a very large industry, aviation is expected to continue growing, probably doubling in size over the next 15 to 20 years. Much is made, and rightly so, about aviation not paying for its full environmental cost. Still, the distinctiveness of the aviation product is such that making aviation pay fully for its environmental cost would only marginally affect its viability.

Despite strong value generation, competitive advantage, and high growth rates, substantial amounts of resources can also be wasted in unviable investments in both the private and public sectors. Aviation is a capital-intensive sector, where investments can involve large sums of money and where debt tends to account for an important share of the financial structure of industry operators. High financial gearing underscores the need for sound investment decisions, as both gains and losses are leveraged. Bad, large, leveraged investments can be instrumental in putting private companies or local economies in severe financial hardship. Beyond financial considerations, bad investments represent a waste of resources that society could deploy in other, more productive activities. Conversely, good, large, leveraged investments can help generate substantial profits and transform local economies for the better.

Private sector investments are generally appraised through standard business plans, including estimates of the financial return and present value of the investment, a financing plan, and a risk assessment. However, transport operations are characterised by taxes, subsidies, and externalities – both positive and negative. Also, situations of monopolistic competition, when combined with price regulation, can result in substantial non-monetised user benefits. As a result, financial analysis cannot be expected to measure the total private value generated by investments, or their viability for the economy at large. Financially profitable operations may reflect financial transfers among stakeholders and protection to certain operators rather than genuine value generation. Conversely, financial losses can mask projects that are still worth carrying out because of the non-monetised value they generate. Therefore, governments are unlikely to rely on financial appraisals alone, often requiring cost-benefit analyses – also called economic appraisals – in order to evaluate the underlying economic viability of investments for society at large.

All too often, the private sector is only interested in cost-benefit analysis as a marketing tool to help make a case to the government for a project, generally involving government financial support or protection from competition. Otherwise it deems economic appraisal a largely academic exercise with little or no relevance for the business case of the project. This reflects the general misunderstanding among transport managers of what an economic appraisal conveys. At times, managers putting forward the results of economic appraisals emphasise elements such as the jobs created by the project, the expenditure by tourists and other benefits to the wider economy, and savings on environmental emissions.

In reality, even when any such alleged benefits are legitimate (e.g. jobs are a cost, not a benefit; and expenditure by tourists is not a benefit) they tend to be a small proportion of project benefits. The actual benefits to both the private sector and society at large tend to be much more immediate and relevant to the operator. By removing distortions, taking into account the most immediate externalities (in practice most other alleged externalities tend not to be legitimate), and measuring non-monetised user benefits, an economic appraisal unveils the value of the sustainable competitive advantage of an operation, its pricing power, and the risks that may hide behind market distortions. In addition, the mechanics of calculating the full economic returns of a project informs the demand forecasts used in the financial analysis. For the private sector investment analyst, financial and economic analyses complement each other. Financial appraisal constitutes the building block from which to start building the economic appraisal. In turn, the economic appraisal gives a comprehensive picture of the intrinsic viability of the investment, yielding important information to the private investor regarding profit potential and sources of risk. For the public sector investment analyst, the economic appraisal is the central test on which to base the investment recommendation.

This book combines standard methods of financial, cost-benefit (i.e. economic), and real-option analyses, and applies them to the appraisal of the financial and economic viability of aviation investments. Also, it highlights the relevance of economic analysis to private-sector financial appraisals, applying cost-benefit analysis to sectors where it is used more rarely, including airlines and aeronautics.

The term 'investment' is used in its economic sense: that is, the assignment of resources to produce capital, where capital is any asset, physical or not, used to produce useful goods or services. The book deals primarily with physical capital assets, including airports, air traffic management (ATM) infrastructure, aircraft, and aircraft manufacturing plants, but also with intellectual capital, including research into aircraft technology. In so doing, it deals with an array of different conditions regarding technology and competition, as follows:

- Airports: infrastructure operations with a substantial component of sunk costs, operating as monopolies or under monopolistic competition, but which are becoming increasingly competitive;
- ATM: infrastructure operations often in a position of natural monopoly;
- Airlines: a capital-intensive industry in the service sector, with low barriers to entry and exit and limited scope for product differentiation, which make its markets very competitive;
- Aerospace: a high-tech manufacturing sector with heavy up-front investments in product development, operating under oligopolistic or monopolistic competition.

The book is aimed at public and private sector analysts concerned with appraising the financial and economic case for aviation investments, as well as to students of air transport and of applied investment appraisal. It assumes at least some training in economics. It is written using the easiest possible language but takes for granted basic knowledge of standard financial appraisal techniques and provides only short explanations of general economic appraisal topics, which are well documented in the literature.

Similarly, the book also illustrates the use of real option analysis, always including a step-by-step calculation process, but leaving justification for real options to other sources. Whereas real options are geared towards conditions of uncertainty, the book does not deal with risk analysis or management, as there is no feature in aviation that raises sector-specific issues. The techniques used in other sectors apply to aviation and the reader is referred to a well-supplied market of project risk management references.

Air transport demand forecasting and cost estimation are not discussed as they are fully covered in the applied transport economics and transport planning literature, so that to discuss then here would simply duplicate material available elsewhere. Instead, the focus is on methods of measuring investment returns, which the literature covers extensively for other modes of transport, particularly land transport modes, but less so for aviation.

The book is structured in two broad parts. The first runs from Chapter 1 to Chapter 3 and includes the conceptual framework (or theoretical background) that underpins the measurement of returns from the financial and the economic points of view. The introductory Chapter 1 provides a brief overview of the difference between financial and economic profitability, highlighting the links between them. Chapter 2 identifies the benefits of aviation projects, which fall into three groups: first, the drivers of customer value, which determine consumer surplus in the economic appraisal, which in turn underpins competitive advantage, on which any financial profitability must rest; second, external effects, which are also an important driver of economic returns and can be interpreted as signals of regulatory risk in the financial analysis; and third, the wider economic benefits of investments, a fertile source of invalid reasons to justify bad investments. The first part of the book concludes with Chapter 3, which introduces the basic theoretical framework underpinning the benefit measures.

The second part of the book consists of four chapters that address each of the aviation sectors in the subtitle of the book. Chapter 4 addresses airports, including investments to accommodate passengers and those aimed at accommodating aircraft. Chapter 5 addresses air traffic management, including investments aimed at expanding the airspace aircraft movement capacity and those aimed at improving flight efficiency. These two chapters cover, therefore, the basic infrastructure sectors of air transport. Infrastructure operations tend to be government owned; when privatised, they are normally subject to economic regulation. Included in these two chapters are four sections addressing investment issues that arise with private sector involvement (labelled 'involving the private sector'). The issues they cover include identifying when there is room for private sector participation in the investment process and when there is only justification for a management contract; differences that regulation may make to the outcome of the investment; and the relevance of pricing policy in affecting incentives and outcomes. In addition, Chapter 4, section 5, addresses the incentives to overinvest in infrastructure, which is left out of the list of private sector issues because it may also apply to the public sector.

Chapter 6 addresses airlines, usually the most competitive of the aviation sectors. Because of the extent of competition, the role for economic analysis is more limited. However, it still plays a role, particularly when addressing inter-modal competition and when estimating the value of air transport to society. In addition, options on aircraft tend to be present in airline aircraft purchase programmes, mostly due to the high degree of uncertainty regarding future market and competitive conditions. The chapter discusses the circumstances under which options are valuable, and how to value them. Chapter 7 addresses the aeronautical sector, also a competitive industry, but generally imperfectly so due to high entry barriers and sunk costs. The imperfectly competitive nature of the sector calls for special considerations in the appraisal process. Also, as with airlines, uncertainty gains relevance again, in this case via the prospects of technological innovation. Here the uncertainty and risks involved are usually a motivation for government intervention in financing such investments, which again call for the tools of economic appraisal. Finally Chapter 8 offers some concluding remarks regarding possible additions to the various appraisal methods discussed.

A book that applies welfare economics tools to practical decisions concerning the building of physical assets and the launching of programmes naturally benefits from influences from a range of fields. I am deeply grateful to Professors Ginés de Rus and Per-Olov Johansson, who kindly read an early draft. Their comments contributed to the improvement of the economics underpinning the book. Thanks also to Stephen O'Driscoll, the current European Investment Bank (EIB) in-house airports engineer, for comments on technological issues in the chapter on airports. Likewise, I should mention other colleagues at the Projects Department of the EIB with whom I have appraised aviation investment projects over the years, including in particular Klaus Heege, Alan Lynch, and Bernard Pels. I owe to them an appreciation of project conception and planning through the vantage point of aeronautical, civil, and systems engineering. I would also like to thank the many professionals in promoters of aviation projects financed by the EIB with whom I have worked. I have learnt from them many of the practicalities of conceiving and implementing capital investment programmes across the various industries that constitute civil aviation.

In the book I touch upon a number of regulatory and competition issues. My exposition doubtlessly benefited from what I learned during my time at National Economic Research Associates, particularly from Ian Jones (now a UK Competition Commissioner). Thanks also to a number of anonymous referees. Many of their views are reflected in the final product.

I am also grateful to Guy Loft, my commissioning editor, and to Emily Ruskell, from Ashgate, for managing the publishing process so brilliantly, as well as to Helen Varley for her most valuable editing input.

Any remaining errors or omissions are mine. So are the opinions expressed in the book, which do not necessarily reflect those of the EIB or any other institution.

List of Abbreviations

ALRMC	Airlines' Long-Run Marginal Cost
AMEC	Airline Marginal Environmental Cost
ANSP	Air Navigation Service Provider
AS	Aircraft Size
ASK	Available Seat-Kilometre
ATM	Air Traffic Management
CAGR	Cumulative (or Compounded) Annual (or Average) Growth Rate
CBA	Cost Benefit Analysis
CCD	Continuous Climb Departures
CDA	Continuous Descend Approaches
CORSIA	Carbon Offsetting and Reduction Scheme for International Aviation
DCF	Discounted Cash Flow
ERR	Economic (internal) Rate of Return
ETS	Emissions trading system (of the EU)
EU	European Union
FAA	Federal Aviation Administration (of the United States of America)
FRR	Financial (internal) Rate of Return
GC	Generalised Cost
GDP	Gross Domestic Product
GHG	Greenhouse Gas
HSR	High Speed Rail
IATA	International Air Transport Association
ICAO	International Civil Aviation Organisation
IRR	Internal Rate of Return
LRMC	Long-Run Marginal Cost
MBM	Market-based mechanism
MEC	Marginal Environmental Cost
MR	Marginal Revenues
MTOW	Maximum Take-Off Weight
NPV	Net Present Value
OPD	Optimised Profile Descent
Pax	Passengers
PV	Present Value
R&D	Research & Development
RDI	Research, Development and Innovation
ROA	Real Option(s) Analysis
ROV	Real Option Value
RPK	Revenue Passenger-Kilometre
SCF	Standard conversion factor
SER	Shadow exchange rate
VoT	Value of Time
WACC	Weighted Average Cost of Capital

1 Introduction

1.1 Reasons to invest in aviation

There are three main reasons to invest in aviation and these are common to all modes of transport. They are:

1 Reducing the time it takes to transport a person or freight from one place to another (including time-saving by reducing congestion and increasing on-time departure).
2 Reducing the cost, in terms of resources used, of moving a person or freight from one place to another.
3 Improving the safety of a journey by reducing the risks inherent in physical transportation.

Comfort and quality of service are additional sources of value in transport, but are rarely in themselves a reason to invest. Instead, they tend to accompany some combination of the three main reasons. Also, time can be considered a resource, implying that the first reason should be included in the second one. But time is such an important driver of value that it is usually considered separately.

Private sector operators develop their competitive strategies by focusing primarily on the first two reasons, and value the returns on their investment through a financial appraisal. The third reason is mostly relevant for promoters in countries with very poor transport conditions. Public sector investors also base their investment decisions on the very same criteria, although they widen the scope of benefits and costs beyond monetised private flows to include non-monetised private flows, as well as flows to third parties including, ultimately, society at large. Such an exercise constitutes an economic or socio-economic investment appraisal.

The private and public perspectives on investment – the financial and the economic, respectively – are mutually complementary in two respects. First, private financial benefits and costs offer a first approximation to economic benefits and costs. Indeed, the financial appraisal is a subset of the economic appraisal, constituting a partial look at the flows associated with a project.

Second, the economic benefits of an investment takes a broader perspective at the sources of value, offering the private sector investor clues about untapped sources of revenue; and economic costs signal potential risks arising from market distortions and badly defined property rights. These issues are explored in section 1.2 of this chapter.

However, the distinction between financial and economic returns is often saddled with confusion, opening the doors to abuse. For example, the projected positive financial profitability of an investment may be touted as proof of the soundness of a project. However, what is advertised as a financially viable investment may in fact not reflect social value or a competitive advantage at all, but rather transfers from other stakeholders. After all, operators and investors may try to influence public policies in order to protect their competitive positions by erecting barriers to competition and, more generally, distorting markets, in extreme cases turning a financially non-viable project into a viable one. In such situations an economic appraisal would show that the proposed investment would be wasteful, despite the positive financial return. A second example is when politicians, for electoral reasons, may want to justify devoting public money to financially loss-making investments with arguments about all sorts of wider benefits to the local economy. On closer examination, a proper economic appraisal may show that many of the alleged wider economic benefits are invalid.

Besides the three fundamental reasons to invest in transport – including time and cost savings and safety improvements, as mentioned above – investment appraisal analysts are continuously confronted with myriad other reasons put forward to justify investments. Some of these reasons are ultimately invalid, but come mixed with elements of the three valid reasons set out above, making it hard to distil the extent to which an investment creates value, and the extent to which it constitutes waste and abuse. Arguments put forward may include the following:

- This investment will open up our region and lead to new economic activity and industry. This is a valid rationale insofar as it is reflected in the three fundamental reasons. Unfortunately, it tends to open the gates to all sorts of claims to benefits that are in fact mostly invalid. Examples of the resulting waste include newly built airports that remain virtually empty after opening and which end up constituting a sink of regional resources, the exact opposite of the original intention.
- This is the latest technology. The fact that a project introduces the latest technology does not make it necessarily a good investment. There may be a case for keeping the technology alive, but that does not imply its deployment. An example was the Concorde supersonic aircraft.
- And this technology will improve safety. In aviation, the safety argument has been used over the years all too often as an excuse to preserve market power (with the accompanying economic rents) and to justify transfers. Safety does not justify any expenditure, regardless of the cost. Expenditure

on safety has to be set against the value of the expected safety improvement, and investments argued for on safety grounds in circumstances where operations already meet international safety standards tend to have other motivations.

- It will create jobs and the multiplier effect will generate more economic activity in the area. Many of the jobs 'created' may be crowded out from other activities. Moreover, loss-making investments also 'create' jobs and unleash multiplier effects. Contrary to frequent popular discourse, jobs and multipliers are not in themselves a sound reason to invest.
- We will bring more tourists. Whether this is a good reason or not will depend on the cost of bringing those tourists, and the added benefits the tourists generate.
- We need to increase market share. Many businesses have gone bust making wasteful investments in their chase for market share rather than profit. The history of the airline industry is full of examples of defunct airlines that had expanded too fast in the quest for market share.

There are also more clearly invalid reasons for investing that are easier to spot in advance:

- We must operate that route because an airline like ours has to be seen flying that route. Such routes are usually found on the route maps of nationalised airlines.
- Our neighbours have it, so we must have it. Very often politicians will push to supply locally what a nearby region or city already has, independently of whether there is a case to have it in the neighbouring location but not in the proposing politician's constituency (or, indeed, in neither of them).
- Visitors must be impressed when they arrive in our country. The funds used to impress the visitors come at the expense of other items that society may demand more urgently.

And even:

- Passengers get the feeling of an amusement park attraction when they see this project. It may well be that the promoter is subject to rate of return regulation, and the motive of the project at hand is to inflate the regulatory asset base of the promoter. In such cases, financing the project with debt can boost the return on equity of the promoter.

To conclude, sound financial returns and arguments with popular appeal are no guarantee that the investment will be worthwhile. The ultimate case is based on saving time, reducing costs, and improving safety in ways that ensure that the benefits outweigh the costs. A project with a positive financial return and a negative economic return is likely to be fully dependent on political patronage.

1.2 Financial and economic returns

The financial appraisal of an investment project involves estimating revenues and costs, including financing costs. Such an estimate constitutes the backbone of any standard business plan. In this regard, there is nothing exceptional in the mechanics of conducting the financial appraisal of an investment in the aviation sector, or in transport in general, relative to a project in any other sector. To simplify, the financial appraisal as presented in this book ignores considerations regarding the capital structure of a project. The focus is on whether the financial resources invested in a project as a whole generate a sufficient cash return to the promoter. Projects can be thought of as being 100 per cent financed with equity capital.

The financial return of a project is a subset of the wider economic returns of the project. Under very specific circumstances the financial return equals the economic return. When markets are competitive, are free from distortions such as taxes, subsidies or price regulations, when there are close substitutes for all goods and services, when an investment project is too small relative to the size of the economy to significantly alter prices, and property rights are well defined, prices reflect the benefits of an additional unit of output produced and costs reflect the resource cost of producing that unit. Private sector investors, in following expected revenues and costs in making investment decisions, will make investments that are in line with maximising not only private profit but also social welfare. That is, the investor will inadvertently be part of the proverbial 'invisible hand' whereby the pursuit of private interest leads to an allocation of resources that is socially desirable.

In such circumstances, the financial appraisal of a private sector investment analyst would be sufficient to decide whether the investment should be made from the point of view of society at large, without any need for a public sector economist to carry out any other viability test. However, in reality, prices are often distorted, property rights are not always well defined, and substitutes may be imperfect, giving certain operators a degree of market power. These three distortions are addressed in turn in the following paragraphs.

Firstly, prices may not reflect full resource cost because of the presence of taxes, subsidies, or regulations such as minimum wages or price caps in markets for inputs or outputs. A tax on an input, for example, means that the promoter will pay for the resource cost (the opportunity cost) of the input, plus a transfer (the tax) to the government. The price the promoter pays for the input overestimates the cost of the input to society, and therefore, as far as society is concerned, this price cannot be taken as the basis for making a sound allocation of scarce resources since the taxed input would tend to be consumed less than would be socially desirable. A subsidy on an input would have the opposite effect. Similarly, price regulation, such as price ceilings or floors, may imply that the price does not reflect the scarcity of the input. Prices may instead reflect a market outcome that over- or under-supplies the good.

Secondly, when property rights are not well defined, a market transaction involving a buyer and a seller may interfere with the rights of a third party that does not voluntarily take part in the transaction. These impacts to third parties are called 'externalities', in the sense that they are external to the parties that voluntarily agree to a transaction. In the case of aviation the main examples of potential externalities concern the environment, including emissions of greenhouse gases, air-polluting particles, and noise. When the property rights of third parties are well defined, the parties involved in the transaction will also have to pay, via taxes or direct compensation, to the third parties affected by the transaction.

It should be noted that effects on third parties may not only be negative. Projects can have positive external effects, such as knowledge spillover effects from investments in research and development (R&D), although in aviation these do not seem to be large (Niosi and Zhegu, 2005). There can also be beneficiary price effects, as when a project is large enough to affect the price of one of its inputs in the presence of cost economies in the production of that input. The higher demand for of the input brought about by the project would lower the price of the input, yielding productivity gains to other firms, which are unrelated to the project but also use that input.

Finally, when the products supplied by competitors are not close substitutes, consumers can experience a cost in switching from one producer to another. In such situations, if supply is lumpy (i.e. there are indivisibilities) competitive markets may not work well to address supply shortages, giving incumbents an element of pricing power that can be abused. An example may be an airport (supply is lumpy: capacity cannot be doubled at short notice) that is a monopolist in a city, and users have as an alternative another airport two hours' drive away (constituting a switching cost). The monopolist airport could adjust prices in order to try to convert all of the cost of switching into extra revenues (extracting rents through market power).

In recognition of this monopoly power, the prices offered by the airport (aeronautical charges) are often regulated by the government, leaving such switching costs un-monetised. The switching costs represent a resource use (time to drive to the alternative airport and operating cost of the vehicle to reach that other airport), so much so that the airport user would be willing to pay in order to avoid it. Such willingness to pay, however, remains unregistered by the revenues or costs of the project, and therefore ignored in a financial appraisal. Whereas they are un-monetised, the switching costs measure consumer willingness to pay – over and above existing prices (aeronautical charges) – to continue using the airport, before switching to a competing service. Switching costs constitute, therefore, a measure of the competitive advantage of the airport, that is, how much customers value the distinctive characteristics of the service offered by the operator (in this case consisting largely of location, or proximity) over and above those of its competitors and, therefore, how much extra they would be willing to pay to the airport before switching to the next best competitor (Jorge-Calderón, 2013).

An economic appraisal aims at quantifying the three distortions mentioned above, and incorporates them in the calculation of project returns. It attempts to work through price distortions, inefficient property rights, and unobserved willingness to pay, in order to register the full, undistorted value of resources used by the project and the actual full extent of benefits produced by it. It is, in other words, an attempt to estimate the net benefit of the investment to society (where value to society is largely reflected by the use of the facility) when the presence of market imperfections leaves the estimate of financial return incapable of answering that question. Fortunately, the tools of economic appraisal are very apt for application to transport projects, including aviation. The standard technique for economic appraisal is cost-benefit analysis (CBA).

The literature on CBA is well developed, often extending to application to transport projects.[1] Table 1.1 below summarises the main differences between financial and economic appraisals. While it is merely a summary table, it gives a flavour of where to pay attention in order to avoid frequent sources of confusion in the calculation process. Chapters 2 and 3 discuss some of the issues that merit special attention in the context of aviation projects. Section 1.3 of this chapter deals with the discount rate and the related subject of risk and uncertainty. These are topics that are not particular to aviation, and this introductory chapter merely outlines the treatment they are given in the book.

The result of an economic appraisal informs the public sector investor about the economic viability of a project for society, independently of its financial returns. In addition, the linkages between financial and economic analysis include four elements that are of particular relevance to the private sector investor, as follows:

- As is mentioned above, by measuring non-monetised benefits to users, the CBA is effectively estimating the monetary value of the competitive advantage of an operation. It is an indication of the pricing power of the facility, over and above what existing prices are appropriating. The government may also look to that non-monetised benefit as a potential target for arbitrary taxes, that is, taxes meant purely to raise revenues rather than to correct price inefficiencies.
- The non-observed consumer surplus constitutes a gauge to estimate traffic that may be generated by an investment project. In this respect, the calculations involved in the economic appraisal of the investment become an input into the traffic forecast to be used in the financial appraisal.
- Differences between financial and economic costs point to possible determinants of competitive advantage that are within the power of the government to alter. For example, by conducting an economic appraisal an operator may be able to identify the cause of any abnormal traffic disparity between competing airports as being due to price distortions rather than to any inherent competitive disadvantage of the local operation.
- Finally, non-internalised external costs may signal a risk of future tax or regulatory action by the government. A topical example is how emissions

Table 1.1 Financial and economic calculations of return on investment: differences and linkages

Item	Financial calculation	Economic calculation	Linkages
Objective	Concerned with cash flows and benefits to the private investor	Concerned with full resource use and value created to society	Sharp differences between the two may indicate: i desirability of financial government assistance; ii untapped revenue potential and the need for price regulation; or iii non-apparent costs
Revenues	Main source of benefits	Important source of benefits	An operating loss may hide value created to society that could only be monetised at prices that may be politically unacceptable
Operating and investment costs	Main source of costs	Main source of costs	Differences point to market distortions that may affect the competitiveness of the operation
Non-monetised user benefits	Ignored, but points to potential sources of untapped revenues	Important (sometimes main) source of benefit	A key measure of competitive advantage and potential revenue generation
Taxes	Important source of outflows	Can constitute transfers or internalisation of externalities	Can be the reason why costs differ in the financial and economic appraisals and why profit underestimates social returns
Non-monetised externalities	Ignored	Important source of costs	Non-monetised externalities signal risks of future government intervention
Subsidies	Important source of benefits	Almost always a transfer. Can also be an internalisation of a positive externality	An insufficient financial return matched by a positive economic return justifies the granting of subsidies
Interest on loans	Important source of outflows and risk (ignored here)	A transfer between owners of financial capital	Not significant

(Continued)

Table 1.1 (Continued)

Item	Financial calculation	Economic calculation	Linkages
Discount rate	Weighted average cost of capital	Social discount rate or, in its absence, yield on long-term government bond	Differences between the two are due to different abilities to bear risk by private and public sectors, distortions in financial markets, and government ethical considerations (mostly ignored in this book)

of greenhouse gases (GHG), a long neglected social cost of aviation, has irrupted into the financial cost structure of the industry. In the case of concessions, the investor may feel reassured by the contractual framework of the project. But contracts are a social construct, changeable if there is sufficient political benefit in so doing. Project lives spanning 20 years and more leave plenty of room for changes of government and in government policy. The magnitude of any external costs should be a measure of the extent of the risk the operation faces.

1.3 Discount rate, risk, and uncertainty

The rate of discount applied to estimate the present value of benefits and costs may vary between the financial and the economic analyses. The private sector financial analysis would be made with the (private) weighted average cost of capital (WACC). This is determined by the opportunity cost of equity financing, the cost of debt financing of the promoter, the promoter's capital structure, and the riskiness of the project. These variables are relatively easy to observe.[2]

On the other hand, benefits and costs in the economic appraisal are discounted with the social discount rate, which at the most fundamental level depends on the social rate of time preference, the expected growth rate of the local economy, and the rate of diminishing social marginal utility of income. These factors are much more difficult to measure than the components of the WACC in the financial analysis. In addition, if the size of a project is sufficiently small relative to the size of the national economy, the risk premium on the social discount rate should be removed. The estimate of social discount rate would also have to correct for taxes and other distortions in the financial markets and would need to internalise inter-generational externalities. The result is that, in practice, estimating social discount rates can be a very cumbersome exercise. Unless the government publishes official social discount rates, the analyst may be better advised to rely on the real interest rate of the traded government debt security with the longest duration available as a proxy. The yield of such a security determines, after all, the marginal cost of financing of the state for long-term investment in the country.[3]

Since these issues are not specific to air transport, are widely discussed in the financial and economic appraisal literature, and are largely empirical or project-specific, the issue is sidestepped in this book by assuming a 5 per cent discount rate on all cases whether financial or economic.[4] The subject is only briefly revisited in the discussion of economic analysis of aeronautical projects in Chapter 7.

A presentational advantage of using the same discount rate for financial and economic profitability is that the cash and non-cash magnitudes become easier to compare. This is useful, since some of the non-cash benefits and costs used in the economic but not in the financial appraisal are relevant for private investors, for example, consumer surplus. Having consumer surplus valued at a lower discount rate in the economic than in the financial appraisal may confuse private sector analysts into believing that consumer surplus is higher relative to financial profitability than it really is. For this reason, when re-viewing the economic viability of investments, it may be useful for private investors to carry out the parallel exercise of discounting financial and eco-nomic returns with the same discount rate in order to gain a more realistic picture of the financial potential of the investment.

When the appraisal is based on net present value (NPV) rather than the internal rate of return (IRR), the discount rate would normally already in-corporate the risk premium. Alternatively, the NPV can be estimated with the risk-free discount rate, and the reported NPV of a project would then be the risk-weighted expected value of the NPV, resulting from the probability distribution of NPV estimates.[5] This would be the normal procedure to follow in IRR-based appraisals, given that risk does not enter directly into the IRR calculation. The estimation process would usually involve three steps:

1   Performing a sensitivity analysis to see what variables have the potential to cause project profitability to diverge from the estimated central case.
2   Estimating the risk-weighted expected rate of return. The resulting figure would constitute the central case, or base estimate, of project returns.
3   Estimating the probability that a project would perform below the threshold profitability below which it becomes undesirable. Deciding on both the minimum accepted level of profitability and the maximum tolerated probability of returns dipping below the threshold is a managerial decision, informed by the performance of the project relative to the risk-reward profile of other investments in the sector and in the wider economy.

The mechanics of performing a risk analysis are not specific to aviation and are well documented in specialist sources.[6] Therefore this book does not illustrate risk analysis. The related issue of uncertainty, which arises where there is in-sufficient evidence to perform a standard risk analysis, is also covered in specialist sources on real options analysis (ROA).[7] However, in cases when there is substantial uncertainty ROA can become central to the investment appraisal. The use of ROA is illustrated in the sector chapters of this book, in two cases, including the valuation of options on aircraft, in Chapter 6, section 2, and the appraisal of innovative aeronautical projects in Chapter 7, section 7.2.

1.4 Additional considerations

The project examples in this book show a number of simplifications in order to ease the presentation and help the reader focus on key appraisal issues. The main ones include the following:

- The estimations assume no residual value. There is no hard and fast rule about residual value estimation. Any estimate is heavily dependent on the circumstances surrounding a project and the nature of the facility or technology, and ultimately rests on analyst judgement. The exception is the case of airline fleet replacement, where older aircraft are assumed to be sold.
- Long-term demand forecasting can be an elaborate process, constituting a field in itself that is outside the scope of this book. The cases illustrated in this book tend to rest on normal long-term magnitudes common in the industry.
- Prices are averaged per customer. This book does not address pricing structure, as this would entail entering the realms of industrial organisation and regulatory policy further than is already done. Any investment appraisal would have to reflect the specific regulatory circumstances of the promoter; and the investment analyst should be mindful of the implications of price regulations on investment incentives. By way of illustration, Chapter 5, on Air Traffic Management, includes an example of the types of implications that pricing policy may have for the investment decision.
- For promoters that are subject to price regulation, price adjustments tend to take place at regular intervals along the life of the project, as dictated by the terms of the applicable regime of economic regulation. The examples used in this book instead assume constant prices throughout the life of the project, consistent with any applicable regulated rate of return.
- Prices are assumed to be in real terms, that is, where inflation has been deducted.
- Taxes are simplified, applying only to inputs and outputs, rather than to profits or property. The main purpose is to illustrate the treatment of taxes on economic appraisals, rather than the effects of specific tax regimes.
- Public funds are assumed to come with no additional marginal cost resulting from the tax wedge or any other loss of efficiency.
- Finally, whereas the methods presented in the book apply to both passenger and freight transport, the presentation focuses on the passenger segment. Still, the book refers to the freight segment whenever the discussion raises issues of particular interest for freight transport.

Notes

1 See Boardman et al. 2018 and Campbell and Brown 2016. For a more advanced presentation see Johansson and Kriström 2015. For more detailed treatment of transport, de Rus 2010.

2 For more on the estimation of WACC refer to textbooks on project or corporate finance. An accessible source is Brealey et al. 2017.

3 The difficulties about what social discount rate to use can be partly sidestepped by focusing the evaluation on the internal rate of return rather than the net present value. Still, the discount rate is eventually necessary to decide on whether the estimated return makes the project acceptable.

4 Textbooks on CBA normally cover the social discount rate and its relation to market rates. Accessible sources include Boardman et al. 2018, Campbell and Brown 2016 and de Rus 2010.

5 Note that estimating a risk-weighting expected NPV from the probability distribution of NPV outcomes when the NPV has already been calculated with a risk-adjusted discount rate would amount to double-counting risk.

6 For a practical guide see, for example, Vose 2008. For a summarised presentation see European Commission 2014.

7 An accessible source is Kodukula and Papudesu 2006. More technical presentations include Dixit and Pindyck 1994 and Trigeorgis 1996.

2 Identifying benefits

2.1 Air transport as an intermediate service

Economics considers air transport, and transport services in general, as intermediate services, that is, services that are used not as ends in themselves but as a means to some other ulterior consumption or production. This means that economics assumes that no one flies for the sake of flying, but to reach another location for commercial purposes, visit a friend or relative, sightsee, or migrate. The implication is that transport is treated as a cost, and the passenger is understood as wanting to minimise the cost of moving from one place to another.

The cost of transport consists not only of the ticket price but also of all other elements that constitute an effort which the passenger would want to minimise. These can be summarised in the following three categories:

1 The time taken to travel from A to B.
2 The operating cost of travelling, namely the full cost of the airline ticket, which would tend to include the cost of all infrastructure, including airport and ATM charges, and the operating cost of the access and egress time taken to complete the door-to-door cycle.
3 The risk that the user takes in embarking on a trip. The cost is reflected in the user's willingness to eliminate or reduce the risk of an accident. Normally this is deemed negligible, but not in regions with poor infrastructure or services.

These three elements apply to both passenger and freight transport. In addition, in the case of passenger transport, there is a growing practice in transport appraisals to include willingness to pay to avoid discomfort, but empirical evidence in this area for aviation is less well established. The three cost categories are addressed in turn.

2.2 Travel time

2.2.1 Measures of travel time

An immediate, observable component of travel time is door-to-door travel time. This would include the time to access the airport, or access time; the time spent in the airport being processed into the plane, or the departing passenger processing time; the time in the aeroplane, or flying time; the arriving passenger processing time in the airport; and the time taken to journey from the airport to the final destination, or egress time. This full sequence of door-to-door travel time, which is strongly dependent on location factors and infrastructure conditions, is already predetermined at the time the passenger buys the airline ticket.

But the passenger also experiences two additional time costs, or delays before buying a ticket. Firstly the difference between the passenger's preferred departure time and the actual time when a flight is available. This time, known as frequency delay, is reduced by increasing flight frequency. Then there is the delay that occurs when the desired departure flight is full. This delay will vary directly with load factor: the higher the load factor, the higher the likelihood that the passenger will have to travel in a different flight than the preferred flight. This delay is called stochastic delay. The summation of the frequency and stochastic delays is called the schedule delay.[1] This is a delay that is controlled by airlines when they set their schedules and their load factor targets.

Any investment in air transport capacity will affect some combination of door-to-door travel time and schedule delay. In practice, stochastic delay will largely depend on airline pricing and load factor policies, which fall within the realm of airline operations planning and are rarely affected by investments on infrastructure or equipment. This is especially the case in competitive airline markets, where any unaccommodated traffic resulting from high load factors by an airline may be picked up by competing airlines. The relevance of other travel time components for valuing investments will become evident in the remainder of this book. Investments aimed at enhancing passenger handling capacity will tend to affect door-to-door travel time, whereas investments aimed at increasing aircraft movement capacity will tend to affect frequency delay.

Travel time also applies to air freight. Cargo forwarders will use air transport to the extent that it pays to save time versus operating costs, such as in perishable products, or high-value manufacturers integrated in just-in-time logistic chains. The principles underlying the appraisal of time benefits for freight and passenger traffic are the same.

In practice, time-savings are often the main determinant of the benefits from aviation investments. In order to attach a value to the benefit arising from delay savings it is necessary to know how much the passengers are willing to pay for time-savings.

2.2.2 The value of time

Travellers are willing to spend money to save time to the extent that the time used in travelling could be used for other productive or leisure activities. How much a passenger is willing to spend to save time is called the 'money value of time', or simply the 'value of time'.

The intuition behind the valuation of time can be illustrated with a simplified example. Assume a person is offered a choice of two travel options, Mode 1 and Mode 2, to go from A to B. With Mode 1 it would take the person four hours to get from A to B and cost EUR50; Mode 2 would take one hour and cost EUR110. All other factors are equal. The person must decide whether it is worth paying EUR60 (the difference between the two ticket prices) to save three hours (the difference between the time taken between the two modes). If the answer is yes, it implies that the person's value of time is at least EUR20 per hour (EUR60 divided by three hours), meaning that the traveller is willing to pay at least EUR20 in order to save an hour. If the answer is 'no', then the traveller's value of time is less than EUR20.

Studies of value of time gather evidence on many such choices to compute statistically significant monetary values, normally expressed in currency units per hour. The value of time is determined by many variables. A key one is income, or productivity, with a direct relationship between either and the value of time. The cases presented in this book assume that the value of time grows on average at 2 per cent per year, in line with the assumed growth in income per capita.[2]

Other factors include trip purpose. Generally, working time, leisure time, and commuting time are valued differently, with evidence showing higher willingness to pay for working travel time. Appendix A2.1 to this chapter includes a schematic presentation of the analytical framework linking the various time values with productivity.

Value of time research is widespread and many estimates are available in official government guides and the academic literature. A widely known example is HEATCO (2006), a research project sponsored by the European Commission, which finds an average value of time in the European Union (EU) for airline business travellers of EUR32.80 per hour and EUR13.62 for long-distance leisure travellers, both at 2002 prices. Wardman et al. (2016) offers a more updated European survey, finding values of time for business trips that range between EUR40–60 per hour for the largest European countries. The latest available guidance from the US government at the time of writing (US Department of Transportation 2016) was for USD 63.20 per hour for business trips and USD 36.10 per hour for personal trips.[3] It should be noted that studies and guides include also estimates and guidance regarding margin of error.

The willingness to pay for time-saving in the cargo sector derives from elements such as perishability of the product, value-to-weight or value-to-volume ratios of the product, and the time sensitiveness of just-in-time production chains. Estimates on the value of time for air freight are difficult to come by, let alone estimates disaggregated by product perishability. Widely used transport appraisal guides do not address it, limiting time value to the most common surface based transport modes (see, for example, HEATCO 2006, and France Stratégie 2013). Limited evidence would suggest an average value of an order of magnitude of EUR200 per tonne per hour.[4] There is also some indirect evidence from the trade literature.[5]

2.3 The money cost of travel

2.3.1 The 'out of pocket' money cost of travel

The money cost of travel involves the 'out of pocket' money price that the traveller or shipper pays for the door-to-door journey. This includes the operating costs and any return on capital for all operators involved in the door-to-door transport chain, including the airline, and whichever means of transport the passenger or shipper uses on the airport access and egress journeys. Normally, payments to infrastructure providers are included in the ticket price, but if they are not, they should also be included in this category.

Whether in passenger or freight air transport, together with the time invested in the journey, the money cost to the traveller or shipper constitutes the key parameters in shaping the decision of the transport user on what routing to take, whether to divert to an alternative transport mode, and whether the trip is made at all.

When making an economic appraisal, however, there are additional considerations to take into account, due to the frequent presence of distortions in the money cost of travel.

2.3.2 Distortions to the money cost of travel

The money prices the traveller pays may not reflect the opportunity costs of the resources employed in producing the transport services purchased. Taxes, subsidies, externalities, and imperfect competition can result in prices diverting from resource opportunity costs, in which case the economic appraisal will need to make adjustments to observed money prices.

Figure 2.1 illustrates the case of a tax on an input. The supply curve of the input is depicted by S+t, including a unit tax equal to t over the tax-free cost of the input. S would correspond to the distortion-free supply of the good, reflecting the input's opportunity or economic cost p_e. The tax causes an undersupply of the good equal to $q_{e1}-q_1$. Let us say that the project causes demand for the input to increase from D_1 to D_2, shifting quantity demanded from q_1 to q_2. The observed price remains constant at p+t, which would be the cost that the project promoter uses in the calculation of the financial returns of the project. However, this financial cost disguises a welfare gain, resulting from an increase in the supply of an under-supplied good, equal to

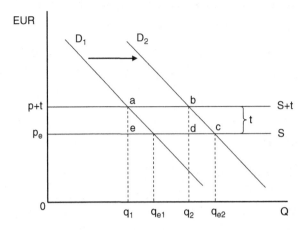

Figure 2.1 Effect of a tax on the money cost and economic cost of an input.

area abde, which is transferred to the government through the tax on the input. An economic analysis would have to deduct that welfare gain from the observed input costs q_1abq_2, resulting in an economic cost of the input equal to q_1edq_2. This alternative price reflecting economic costs is called the 'shadow' or economic price of the input, to distinguish it from the out of pocket, observed, or market price.

As is implied by Figure 2.1, economic cost considerations are of no relevance to the passenger, who will make the travel decision following observed out of pocket money prices, independently of how distorted those prices are. Therefore, when conducting the economic or the financial appraisal of an investment, consumer behaviour is inferred from out of pocket prices and not from shadow prices. So the economic analysis would use the quantities observed in the financial analysis, which are, after all, the actual quantities of goods supplied to the project, but would value them at p_e, rather than p+t.

The most common adjustments involve energy costs, should energy taxes apply, and labour costs. Taxes and net social security contributions can be viewed as transfers and would then be removed from costs, to produce the shadow price of labour, or the 'shadow wage'. The last section of this chapter includes a fuller discussion of employment issues.

Subsidies would have the opposite treatment to that of a tax. In the financial analysis a subsidy constitutes an income for the project or a saving to investment or operating costs. In the economic analysis that apparent income or cost saving is recognised as a transfer of resources from the government to the project, and as such must be added back to costs.

Developing countries may witness a wider set of distortions, including, for example, capital controls and wide price differences between formal and informal sectors. Shadow prices are well covered in the economics literature, and the reader is referred to those sources for a fuller discussion.[6]

Finally, it is worth pointing out that whereas such adjustments are not necessary for the estimate of financial return, they still offer useful information relating to the financial return of a private investor. They point to areas where government policy may be inefficient and arbitrarily affect travel choice. They may point to areas of potential future changes in government policy with adverse or favourable implications for market prices.

2.4 Accident risk

People are willing to pay to reduce the risk of serious injury or loss resulting from accidents. Likewise, freight forwarders buy insurance against loss of or damage to a shipment. In addition, accidents incur medical and legal costs, as well as loss through damage to equipment and property. Transport projects therefore generate benefits if they bring about reductions in accident risk, safety improvements being a legitimate component of any transport project appraisal. However, for normal aviation investment projects in countries with well-developed institutions, such benefits are very small relative to other benefits.

Project benefits resulting from reduced accident risks can accrue in two respects. The first is through the improvement of safety conditions within the existing transport mode. In countries with well-developed institutions, aviation operations are not allowed to take place if they do not comply with safety standards, and such rules leave the risk of death or serious injury very low. In this respect, the case for an aviation investment aimed at bringing a facility to meet safety standards does not depend on the benefits of increased safety. If the investment is not made, the facility cannot operate at all. Therefore, the investment decision will depend on whether the necessary investment cost to meet safety standards leaves the facility still viable or not.

Ironically, therefore, in practice the value of safety is of no (direct) relevance in the appraisal of investments aimed at improving safety. Instead, the economic analysis of safety measures becomes relevant in deciding what the safety standards should be. In that case, the analysis would enter the field of economic appraisal of policy, not of economic appraisal of investment projects. Once a policy is set, safety standards will determine project design characteristics and costs, and through such costs affect individual project viability. In this respect, safety-related costs and benefits are always (indirectly) present in project appraisals.

The second respect in which safety benefits can accrue to projects is in situations when a project causes the shifting of traffic between modes, which, while meeting regulatory safety standards, have different safety records. Road transport has generally a higher accident rate per passenger-kilometre than air or rail. Road transport does not, however, provide a suitably close substitute for air transport. The closest substitute, although for short-haul trips only, would be high-speed rail. But the safety record of high speed rail is not dissimilar to that of air transport.

Road transport becomes relevant for air transport appraisals mainly when passengers switch between airports by road. But there again, assuming normal driving conditions, the benefit that aviation projects generate by avoiding road accidents is a small proportion of the broader benefits of the project. This is illustrated in the discussion of a greenfield airport, in Chapter 4, section 4.1.

Therefore, safety generally plays a minor role in justifying air transport investment.[7] In projects with a weak institutional framework, where international safety standards are not met for air and other transport modes, investments in safety gain a higher prominence among project benefits. Such situations, however, are not covered in this book.

2.5 Externalities

2.5.1 An overview

As seen in the preceding section, user prices can be distorted through mechanisms such as taxes and subsidies. However, they can also be distorted by failing to reflect costs imposed on parties not directly involved as consumers or producers in an air transport project. As already introduced in Chapter 1, section 1.2, ultimately this is due to poorly defined property rights. In any free market, the production and sale of any good or service is the result of the free trading decisions of the direct participants in the transaction, namely the consumer's decision to buy, and the producer's decision to sell. Such decisions are based on the costs and benefits perceived by each of the two parties, and will depend on such participants finding the transaction mutually beneficial.

Welfare economics argues that transactions are worthwhile to society when they result in a net gain to social welfare, which occurs when the value of a good or service to the consumer is higher than the value of the resources used up in its production. When both parties involved in the transaction freely agree to transact, the transaction can be expected to be beneficial to society, that is, to result in an improvement in social welfare.

But the transaction may result in costs to third parties that are not involved in the decision to use or supply the service. Such parties may not have a legal entitlement to claim compensation for the cost or damage incurred. Examples may include people who have to endure aircraft noise, or who must be relocated to allow the building of airport facilities. Indeed, the 'third party' may consist of large parts of the world population, which may experience costs from global warming resulting from greenhouse gas emissions.

Advanced societies increasingly grant de facto property rights by means of compensation, taxes, and other restrictions on production or consumption in order to ensure that the primary participants in the transaction – the buyer and the seller – include costs to third parties in their decision to transact. Examples include fuel taxes (not applicable generally to commercial aviation at the time of writing), requirement to buy emissions rights, and noise-related landing charges at airports. When that happens, third party, or 'external', costs are said to be 'internalised'. The resources raised can be used to finance compensation such as installing double glazing in properties affected by noise, financial payments for relocation, or investing in carbon-capturing sectors such as forestry. The result is that whereas the transaction takes place only if it is mutually beneficial to the buyer and the seller, the economic calculation involved in the trading decision includes costs to third parties, so that the transaction can be taken to constitute a welfare improvement for society. Sections 2.5.2 and 2.5.3 below discuss emission taxes and rights (including both trading and offsets) in more detail, including their treatment in economic appraisals.

In cases where externalities are internalised, the financial return of an investment already includes the external costs. Moreover, the amount of goods consumed and produced will reflect such costs. Assuming there are no other distortions, the financial return of the project also reflects the economic return.

However, when externalities are not internalised, the financial analysis does not reflect externalities. Hence, the economic appraisal of the investment should include the external costs as additional to the financial calculation. This will rely on the availability of data on relevant shadow prices for the externalities concerned. The main environmental externalities of aviation include greenhouse gases, contrails, noise and air particles. The academic literature offers many estimates, but academic papers tend to offer location-and method-specific results. It is therefore more prudent to use studies that amalgamate results from a number of papers. European Commission (2019) offers a comprehensive view including also the different modes of transport.[8]

It should be noted that since quantities produced and consumed will not be affected by such external effects, consumption and production will be higher than if such costs had been internalised. The resulting economic costs would tend to be of a greater magnitude than when they are internalised.

The economic analysis is playing a dual role. It helps the public sector planner measure the actual returns to society of the project. And it helps the private sector analyst by pointing to areas of risk for the promoter regarding future government intervention. However, whereas the economic analysis identifies the risk and measures the potential cost, the actual cost to the promoter of an eventual government intervention to internalise the external cost would depend on the precise policy instrument the government decides to apply.

This raises a possible scenario of government intervention aimed at other objectives, but resulting in similar outcomes as intervention aimed directly at internalising an externality. This may occur with items such as arbitrary air passenger charges levied uniquely for money-raising purposes. If the result of the arbitrary charge is raising the price of airline tickets by an amount at least as large as that which would result from internalising an existing externality, as far as the economic analysis is concerned the air passenger charge may fully offset the effects of the externality.

It is worth highlighting that externalities do not concern only costs, but can also constitute benefits, such as when an aviation project helps alleviate road transport congestion, or creates knowledge that can be used in other industries.

Also, beyond externalities, aviation investments can bring about benefits to third parties through price effects on secondary markets. Aviation services can generate substantial economic activity in the region where they are located and enable the exploitation of economies of scale for certain products. As discussed below in section 2.7.3, these are valid indirect economic benefits to be attributed to a project.

When an aviation project benefits third parties through externalities or indirect benefits, aviation investors may enlist the third parties likely to benefit from the project to support the investment. This is another significant piece of project information generated by an economic appraisal that may be important to management, and which is not captured by the financial appraisal.

2.5.2 *Emission taxes*

Commercial aviation is generally exempt from taxes on aircraft fuel, although they apply on some jurisdictions. Another area where taxes may apply is aircraft noise. This section discusses how such taxes may be treated in an economic analysis, using aviation fuel as an example. The externality could then refer to emissions of greenhouse gases (GHG), causing external damage through climate change, or emissions of other fuel-related particles causing health risks. The example here is narrowed to refer to damage related to climate change.

A tax on aviation fuel can be represented through Figure 2.2, which is a modified version of Figure 2.1, both dealing with an input. Say that this time the market input is that of airline services supplied for package holidays. A tourism development causes demand for package holidays to increase (not shown in the graph), which in turn causes demand for air travel to increase

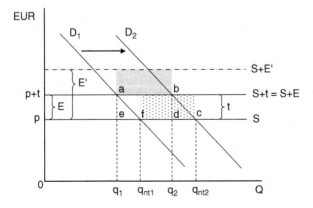

Figure 2.2 Internalising an externality with a tax.

from D_1 to D_2. Schedule S represents the supply of air services. The growth in demand causes total trips to increase along the horizontal axis.

Unlike the case on Figure 2.1, assume now that there is an environmental externality E, whereby each passenger carried causes a cost to society equal to tax t. We can think of E as the damage, or cost, each additional passenger imposes on the rest of society by emitting climate-change-inducing GHG. With the tax, the the supply curve in the airline market would be S+t which is equal to S+E. The total ticket price, including the tax, for the additional air travellers would be rectangle abq_2q_1.

Following the logic of section 2.3.2, where taxes constitute transfers, abde would be a transfer to the government and edq_2q_1 revenues accruing to the airlines, net of tax t. Transfers are deducted from input costs. Airline revenues edq_2q_1 would measure the resource cost of the airline input to the package holiday product, representing the full societal economic cost of the input, and p the societal marginal cost. But this time there is also a marginal environmental cost to society E, meaning that the project yields a cost to society equal to abde, which is also a resource cost to society and must be added back as costs in the economic appraisal.

Assume now a second situation, whereby there is no tax t but the environmental externality E remains. The supply curve perceived by the customer, or faced by the market, is S. Then the starting quantity of air travel would be q_{nt1} (where nt stands for 'no tax') rather than q_1, and the increase in demand from D_1 to D_2 would make traffic grow to q_{nt2}, as the new market equilibrium would be point c, rather than b. The environmental damage caused by that growth in traffic would be equal to the area of the dotted rectangle.

Now the financial analysis would see airline revenues to be $fcq_{nt2}q_{nt1}$, which would also correspond to an apparent economic cost since there is no tax. But we would need to add the externality E, not reflected in revenues, bringing total resource cost back up to airline revenues $fcq_{nt2}q_{nt1}$ plus the dotted area.

Comparing these first two situations (pollution with tax versus pollution with no tax), note that the effect of the tax is to make passengers pay for the environmental cost they cause to society. The resulting quantity of air transport following the tax is q_2, the same as if passengers otherwise paid the cost of the externality they cause, that is, if they faced supply curve S+E, rather than S. In the first situation the out of pocket price, gross of tax, constitutes also the economic price. The tax is no longer a transfer that needs to be deducted from costs in the economy appraisal. While in the second situation, where there is no tax, the economic cost of pollution needs to be added to the market price, to come up with the full social cost of air travel. The situation with the tax constitutes an internalised external cost, while the situation without the tax constitutes an external cost.

There could also be a third, middle ground situation: we are back in the case where there is a tax t but the environmental damage per passenger is E' rather than E. The tax does not reflect the full environmental cost of emissions. There is an excess environmental cost measured by the area of the shaded rectangle.

In terms of calculation steps, in this third case the financial analysis would see abq_2q_1 as airline revenues gross of tax t. To estimate societal economic cost the analyst would deduct abde, the taxes paid to the government from the price of the input (i.e. the airline ticket), and then add the externality – not reflected in revenues – which is also equal to abde plus the area of the shaded (not dotted) rectangle. An equivalent calculation of economic cost would be to take the revenues gross of taxes, that is area abq_2q_1, and add the area of the shaded rectangle, the excess externality not reflected in the tax.

Two key messages flow from these three scenarios. First is that the societal resource cost of air travel is the revenues net of tax t to the airline plus the environmental cost imposed on society. Taxes may not be equal to marginal pollution costs – indeed the taxes may not target pollution at all but may be simply there to raise revenues for the government. Therefore, when the appraisal includes both taxes and emissions, the analyst must know both the marginal cost of pollution (E) and the marginal tax rate (t). We will see in the next section that in the case of market based mechanisms there may not be a need for the analyst to know the marginal cost of pollution.

Second, besides raising revenues for government, taxes, by increasing the price paid by the passenger and hence affecting the total amount of traffic, can also bring the level of air travel back to the level that would take place if passengers actually paid for pollution, thereby improving the economic efficiency of air transport.[9] Whether the tax actually targets pollution or is simply there to raise revenues for the government, the implications for the economic efficiency of air transport and project appraisal are the same: resulting market prices are efficient and there is no need to make any additional adjustment.

Finally, it is important to note the implications for carbon footprinting. Whether there are taxes or not, the effect of the project would be to increase emissions, and do so proportionally to the growth in traffic. The carbon footprint increases both for the air transport sector and for the world (or society) as a whole by the same amount. All the tax does is make sure that the amount of air travel that takes place is valued by society at least as highly as the resource cost of air travel to society (which includes the costs of operating an airline plus the environmental cost), fulfilling a prerequisite for economic efficiency. But, while emissions would be higher without the tax, taxation does not preclude total societal emissions from increasing.

To summarise and frame the presentation, remember that the economic appraisal of a project measures the social value and cost of changes produced by the project for society as a whole, relative to the without project scenario. When a project increases total societal emissions, the project causes total social costs to increase. Meanwhile taxes on inputs overstate the opportunity cost of the input (excluding pollution). In the computation of the social value of the project, the net result on project value of a change in a taxed, polluting input would depend on how the tax and the pollution compare. If the tax rate equals the social cost of pollution, the net effect of polluting is zero, since the cost of pollution equals the extent to which the tax overstates the (before pollution) opportunity cost of the input. If the tax is lower than the cost of pollution, then the analyst must include the difference as the net economic cost of the project. In the hypothetical case that the tax on pollution was higher than the cost of pollution, by polluting the project would produce a net benefit to society.

The picture changes in the next section, addressing an alternative way of internalising externalities, whereby as a result of the project emissions by the air transport sector would grow but, crucially, not the emissions of society as a whole. This changes the treatment of the price (instead of tax) paid by the emitter in the computation of the social value of the project. Subsequently, section 2.5.4 includes very simple numerical examples of the calculation of economic value under both mechanisms.

2.5.3 Emissions trading and offsets

As an alternative to environmental taxes, externalities can also be internalised by requiring the polluter to abate the pollution. Polluting and abatement can be done by separate entities, by means of use and issuance of rights to pollute, rights that can be traded in a market. Two such market-based mechanisms (MBM) to tackle pollution are in operation in international aviation, each falling in a separate category. The most global of all is Carbon Offsetting and Reduction Scheme for International Aviation (CORSIA), promoted by ICAO, which is an 'offset' scheme. The other is the EU's Emissions Trading System (ETS), which is a 'cap and trade' scheme.

We address these two systems generically. Under offset systems (like CORSIA) airlines are required to buy offsets (called 'units' in the case of CORSIA) ultimately supplied by projects that capture carbon, such as, say, carbon sequestration by digging carbon underground or capturing carbon by planting trees. The total number of tonnes emitted can grow, but since they are offset, the net emissions remaining in the atmosphere is zero, making airlines carbon-neutral.

Cap and trade systems work differently. The authority governing the system sets a cap in the total carbon emissions that can be released to the environment per year for all sectors included in the MBM. In the case of EU ETS at the time of writing these include mainly energy generation, industry, and airlines. Participants in the MBM are allocated a pre-specified number of emission permits (called 'allowances' in ETS) each year. For an airline to grow its emissions it must buy permits from other MBM participants, whether airlines or, say, an energy generator. For the energy generator to be able to sell a permit but continue producing, say, electricity, it must invest in other electricity generating technologies that do not emit GHG and hence do not require the permit.

The above are generic descriptions of the two mechanisms. Like in any market, rules can be applied to alter its functioning. There are many possibilities, including combining the systems. For example, while in pure cap and trade systems there is no room for market participants to issue offsets, the EU ETS cap and trade system allows the limited issuance of offsets. There is no technical reason why offsets could not be given freer access, blurring the line between cap and trade and offset schemes.

As far as economic appraisal is concerned, the analyst may deal with projects where airlines may have to buy rights to emit on some markets – and possibly under different MBMs – and not in others. At the extreme, notionally, a European aircraft may perform a return flight within the EEA in the morning, requiring the purchase of ETS allowances, followed by a return flight to a CORSIA signatory non-EU country at midday, requiring the purchase of offsets, and to a CORSIA non-signatory country in the evening, where emissions may not be internalised at all. Also, the carbon market prices may differ across different MBMs at any one time. Moreover, the carbon market prices of MBMs may well differ from estimates of the social cost of carbon – the estimated social cost imposed by the pollution, labelled E in Figure 2.2 in section 2.5.2 above.

The treatment of MBM prices in financial appraisals is straightforward: the market price, the cash outflow, is the cost of polluting. But this market price may be different from the social cost, raising the question of how the analyst should price emissions within MBMs in economic appraisals. As we will see, in generic cap and trade or offset mechanisms, the economic cost of the emission by the project is also determined by the MBM price, so long as this price is above EUR0.

Cap and trade systems are effectively tradable quotas. It could happen that the number of permits available, the cap, is higher than the quantity of permits demanded, making their price zero. Likewise, in offset schemes, notionally, if capturing GHG was costless (implying there is no externality), the market price of offsets would be zero. In such circumstances, under either MBM, nothing must be given up in order to pollute. When instead the permit price is above zero, the right to emit is scarce – that is, it has an opportunity cost, measured by the market price of the permit. And in MBMs that opportunity cost is the cost of someone else giving up the emission (in cap and trade schemes) or abating the emission (in offset schemes). Note that in the without project scenario that someone else neither gives up nor abates the emission. Therefore the project, when compared to the without project scenario, does not impose any net increase in emissions to society.

In other words, the social cost of carbon measures the cost of society emitting an extra tonne of carbon. Since no extra tonne of carbon is emitted in net terms, the social cost of carbon does not apply. What applies is the cost of ensuring that there is no extra tonne of GHG emitted, which is the MBM price. This result is presented graphically now.

The presentation starts with the measure of societal cost where a cap and trade system results in a EUR0 price of emission right. This is followed with societal cost when the price of the emission right is positive. In this latter situation the conclusions for cap and trade also apply to offset schemes. The equivalence between the two MBM systems is presented in more detail in Appendix A2.2 to this chapter. For a more formal presentation of the analysis see Johansson (2015 and 2016) or Jorge-Calderón and Johansson (2017).

Figure 2.3 represents the market for emitting CO_2 as perceived by airlines. The horizontal axis is a composite input of fuel F and emissions. The analysis takes the point of view of airlines, with homogeneous fuel, so that there is a fixed proportions relation between fuel and emissions. This assumption is relaxed in Appendix A2.2.

The price p along the vertical axis represents the private cost of emitting a tonne of CO_2. Q represents the annual quota, or cap, on emissions. When the cap Q is met (or the quota filled) the supply curve becomes completely in-elastic (i.e. vertical), as no further emissions are possible for industries operating within the cap. Before Q is reached, the price of allowances is EUR0, so that the supply curve for emissions alone would run along the horizontal axis.

Demand curve D_1 represents a situation where demand for emitting CO_2 is well below Q. The private cost of burning fuel at p_1 consists of the fuel cost p_f only. Along the vertical axis, c_s corresponds to a low social cost of carbon emissions, over and above the price of fuel, while c'_s represents an alternative, high social cost of carbon scenario.

Say that a growth in demand for air travel brought about by an investment project (we can think of the same package holiday example as in the preceding section 2.5.2) causes demand for emissions to grow from D_1 to D_2. The quantity of the fuel-emission composite input grows from q_1 to q_2. Since at such levels of demand emission permits are given out for free, the private cost of consuming fuel does not change ($p_1 = p_2$), and is made only of the price of fuel. The total private cost of the increase in the demand for fuel consists of

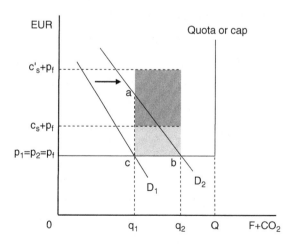

Figure 2.3 Economic cost of emissions under a cap and trade system where the cap is not met.

area cbq_2q_1. Meanwhile, under the scenario with the low social cost of carbon c_s, the societal cost of such an increase in the fuel-emissions composite would be this private cost plus the light shaded area. If instead the social cost of carbon is c'_s, the social cost would also include the darker shaded area.

So far, the treatment of externalities in the financial and economic appraisal is therefore exactly the same as in the case of no internalisation that we saw when discussing environmental taxes in section 2.5.2. The private cost is the price of fuel and the societal cost is the price of fuel plus the cost of the externality.

The private value added by consuming more of the fuel-emissions composite is given by the consumer surplus of the emitter, measured by triangle abc. In the case of a low social cost of carbon c_s, the externality (area of the lighter shaded rectangle) looks broadly of a similar magnitude to the private value added area abc. The net social value of the increase in air transport demand is therefore expected to be approximately EUR0.

By contrast, in the case of the high social cost of carbon c'_s, the total shaded area (lighter plus darker areas) is greater than the area of triangle abc. The externality caused by emitting is therefore higher than the private value added. Under the c'_s scenario therefore, in the absence of any other external benefits, the growth in air travel demand would result in a net societal loss.

The situation changes markedly once demand for the fuel-emission composite meets the cap Q and the price of allowances becomes positive. This is illustrated in Figure 2.4. Demand is initially at D_1, and the price of emitting is at p_1. This is made of the cost of fuel p_f, plus the cost of emission allowances ($p_{a1} = p_1 - p_f$). The project causes demand for air transport to grow from D_1 to D_2. The result is that the price of allowances increases from p_{a1} to p_{a2}.

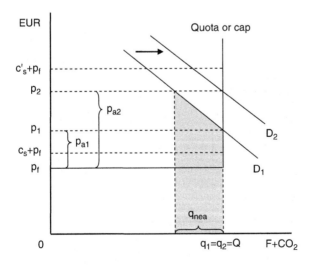

Figure 2.4 Economic cost of emissions under a cap and trade system where the cap is met.

Note that the total, societal amount of emissions does not increase, remaining at Q. This aspect is crucial in understanding the difference in the treatment of taxes and of MBMs in economic appraisals. Remember that the marginal social cost of carbon measures the damage caused on society by emitting one extra tonne of carbon. Say that the marginal social cost of carbon is at c'_s. This cannot represent the social cost of the emissions of the project since, when comparing the project to the without project scenario, the project results in no extra emissions for society as a whole. Without the project, demand would have stayed at D_1 and the total amount of emissions would have remained at Q, the same as with the project.

This is not to say that emissions by air transport do not grow. The total amount of new emissions by air transport is q_{nea} along the horizontal axis. But total emissions do not grow for society as a whole. In the absence of the project, all those q_{nea} emissions would have been emitted by other sectors. Air transport substitutes other sectors as emitters, paying those other sectors to give up emissions. This is known in the MBM literature as the 'waterbed' effect, in reference to the fact that pressing one area of a waterbed does not change the total volume of water held in the waterbed, it only displaces the water to some other area.

Within a cap and trade system then, the opportunity cost of air transport emitting is the payment required by those other sectors to stop emitting – that is, to incentivise them to sell their emission permits to airlines. This would be measured by maximum willingness to pay by those other sectors to emit, represented by the shaded area in Figure 2.4. This is calculated by multiplying the amount of GHG emissions concerned q_{nea} by the average of the price of emissions allowances with and without the project $((p_{a1} + p_{a2})/2)$. By being paid at least the value measured by that area, those other sectors find it worthwhile either to continue producing but switching to a cleaner technology or to cease producing altogether.

With MBMs therefore, so long as the permit price is above zero, the permit price measures both the financial and the economic costs of polluting. There is no need to adjust for any difference between the permit price and the social cost of carbon, as done for taxation, discussed in section 2.5.2.

These conclusions also apply should the cap in the cap and trade MBM be too tight. Say that the social cost of carbon is c_s rather than c'_s, while the project remains with the same effect of pushing up the price of permits from p_{a1} to p_{a2}. The price paid by allowances is higher than the social cost of emissions, and the project pushes it even higher. One may be tempted to price the emission at c_s. But still, the opportunity cost of the airlines emitting additional carbon remains the value of carbon (willingness to pay to emit carbon) to the sectors that willingly sell the emission permits to the airline, measured by the price at which that sale takes place.

The project would be operating under too tight an MBM cap. But the cap does not change with the project – it is rather an exogenously set regulation imposed on the project that holds whether the project takes place or not. This is a critical condition for defining the appropriate pricing for emissions in economic appraisals, and is discussed further in section 2.5.4 below.

The results are equivalent when dealing with an offset scheme, rather than a cap and trade scheme. Section 2.5.4 next includes very simplified numerical examples of how the computation of economic value of polluting would work under each MBM, alongside a similar example for the tax mechanism discussed in section 2.5.2 above. Appendix A2.2 to this chapter goes into more detail on the graphical representation of how the two MBMs – cap and trade and offsetting – would work to yield the same implications for CBA.

2.5.4 Stocktaking and practical considerations

The implication of the discussion on taxes and MBMs so far for emissions pricing in projects could be summarised as follows. What is important for deciding on the economic price on emissions is not the emissions of the project in themselves but the effect of the project on total societal emissions. To the extent that a project increases societal carbon emissions, the economic cost of emissions is the social cost of carbon. To the extent that the project does not result in a net increase in carbon emissions, the economic cost of the emissions is the cost of ensuring that net carbon emissions do not increase.

Some simple numerical examples could be helpful. With emissions taxes, the net emissions of the project correspond to societal emissions, and the act of emitting in itself brings about a welfare gain or loss to the extent that the tax differs from the social cost of carbon. So, say that following a project an airline emits 3 million tonnes of CO_2 in year t (the 'with project' scenario) and that in the absence of the project it would have emitted 2 million tonnes in the same year t (the 'without project' scenario). The net societal increase in emissions by the project in year t would be 1 million tonnes. Say that the social cost of carbon is EUR50 per tonne of CO_2. The project would imply a net cost to society of EUR50m (=1 m tonnes × EUR50) in year t, acting to decrease project value. If the airline is subject to a carbon tax of EUR50 per tonne, the project would imply an increase in EUR50m in the tax bill for the airline. Ignoring pollution, input taxes are transfers and therefore are deducted from input costs in economic appraisals. Therefore the project would be 'overestimating' input costs by EUR50m, which need to be deducted from costs, thereby increasing project value by EUR50m. In the computation of net project value, the EUR50m tax will show up as an increase in value and the EUR50m social cost of pollution as a decrease in value. The net effect of polluting would be EUR0 (=EUR50m – EUR50m).

If the emissions tax was instead EUR30 per tonne of CO_2, the 'overestimation' of input costs would be EUR30m. In net terms the act of polluting would then be a decrease in project value of EUR20m (=EUR30m – EUR50m). If the emissions tax was higher than the social cost of carbon, say EUR60 per tonne, then the act of polluting would work towards increasing the value of the project by EUR10m (=EUR60 – EUR50).

Regarding MBMs, the economic cost is the price of the permit or offset certificate. Starting with cap and trade systems, the project would result in an increase in emissions by the promoter by 1 million tonnes, which means that the promoter would have to buy 1 million additional 1 tonne emission permits. These permits are sold to the promoter by another operator which, in the 'without project' scenario would have consumed them itself. By selling them to the project promoter the operator would decrease its emissions by 1 m tonne. Therefore the project does not result in a net increase in emissions for society as a whole. Since society does not see emissions 'with project' increase relative to emissions 'without project' scenario, the cost of the net increase in emissions is EUR0 (=0 tonnes × EUR50). Meanwhile the permit price is an input cost to the project airline which, in economic terms, measures the value foregone in the sector selling the emissions to the airline. It does not matter whether the price of the permit is above or below the social cost of carbon. Both the financial and economic cost of emitting is the price of the permit whether – assuming for illustrative purposes the same magnitudes as the tax above – this is EUR30, EUR50, or EUR60.

In the case of an offsets MBM, the seller of offsets assumes the equivalent role to that of the seller of permits in an MBM cap and trade system. The project increases emissions by 1m tonnes and needs to buy 1m offset certificates. The offsetting counterparty increases the production of offsetting certificates by, say, planting additional trees, that would not have been planted without the airline project. The net result is that society does not see a net increase in emissions. The price of the offset certificates constitutes both the financial and economic costs. It is the economic cost because, in a competitive offsets market, it measures the resource cost incurred by the offsetting counterparty in, following the example, planting more trees.

That is, to sum up, the project bears both financially and economically the cost of ensuring that carbon emissions do not increase for society as a whole and, if they do increase, the extra emissions are priced at the social cost of carbon.

In practice, when appraising under MBMs, it is crucial therefore to determine whether the project does indeed result in net societal emissions increasing or not. This rests on the design and operational integrity of the particular MBM at hand. For example, in the case of the EU ETS the EU introduced a Market Stability Reserve in 2015, where any excess emissions allowances (as emissions permits are known in EU ETS) are banked or stored. In 2018 additional rules were introduced whereby after certain conditions are met, banked allowances would be permanently eliminated from the system, implying a reduction in the cap.[10] This opens the possibility for the cap, in contrast to being exogenously set, as has been assumed in the presentation of generic cap and trade systems, to become, at least partially, endogenous to changes in demand for allowances. This implies that projects, by acting on demand for emissions, could affect the cap and with it total societal emissions. Following the waterbed analogy, the waterbed would become punctured, at least partially and for a limited period of time. If so, any change that a project causes on the cap, by constituting a net change in societal emissions, should be priced at the social cost of carbon in economic appraisals, while the rest of the emissions would be priced at the permit price. Appendix A2.3 offers a graphical analysis of this result. A formal presentation can be found in Johansson (2020).

The analyst then would need to estimate the extent to which the project could be expected to alter the cap. Unfortunately, at the time of writing in 2020 the literature on how to measure this effect, specific to the EU ETS, is only emerging.[11] Until the validity of methods becomes resolved a workable assumption would be to adopt the 'small project' assumption, whereby the MBM would not produce meaningful changes in the cap, and treat the MBM as generic. Still, the analyst would be well advised to test project viability with the social cost of carbon rather than the permit price. In any case, over long-lived projects, it is reasonable to assume that MBM regulators would behave efficiently and regulate towards making the MBM price converge with the social cost of carbon over time.

Another issue to bear in mind with cap and trade system is referred to as 'leakage'. This consists of economic activity relocating outside the geographical area of the cap and trade regime to avoid paying the permit price. Say a polluting factory in country A falls within the cap and trade system in that country. The factory wants to expand but expects the permit price to increase in the future. If the higher permit price would leave production with the existing technology unprofitable, the two options it has are either switch to a cleaner technology or relocate to country B where there is no pollution tax or MBM and export from country B to country A. Say that an airline in country A wants to expand capacity and happens to buy its permits from the factory. If the factory decides to switch technology the cap and trade system is fulfilling its role of capping emissions: the expansion of capacity by the airline would not cause a societal increase in emissions. If the factory instead relocates to country B, then the airline expansion would not be resulting on a societal cap in emissions.

There are two provisos to this situation. Firstly, the factory, by relocating and falling outside the MBM, would stop receiving or bidding for permits in subsequent years, so ultimately in future years the airline would be buying permits from some operators that stay within the MBM. Second, airlines do not know what operators they are buying permits from, so the project analyst does not know whether it is causing some operator to relocate. For this reason what matters is whether there is a regular 'leakage rate' from the MBM. If it is well known that an MBM has a leakage rate of, say, 3 per cent, it would mean that 3 per cent of permits bought would not result in a parallel reduction in societal emissions. Those 3 per cent of emissions would have to be priced at the social cost of carbon, rather than the permit price. On the other hand, persistent leakage rates are likely to be addressed through policy, such as imposing import carbon duties to countries that do not price emissions.

Still, in the case of aviation, addressing such leakage may be harder to remedy. For example, routes within country A would be subject to cap and trade system but routes between countries A and B would not. Services from A to a tourist destination in A would have emissions priced while routes from A to tourist destinations in B would not. Other things being equal, airline tickets to the tourist destination in country A would be more expensive as passengers would pay for emissions. But note that policy context does not change with the project. Instead, for project appraisal what matters is the difference made in the 'with project' versus the 'without project' scenarios. As will be seen in Chapter 3, projects tend to lower user generalised cost of transport relative to the 'without project' situation. Such generalised cost will normally grow with time in the 'without project' scenario due to growing congestion without a capacity expansion. So, lack of capacity expansion in tourist destination A would result in more tourists from A switching to holidaying in tourist destination B. A project to expand capacity in A would bring some of that traffic back from B to A, and with it reduce leakage. What matters for project appraisal is the difference that the project makes.

Finally, another theme is integrity of the systems, namely whether the laws are policed and observed. This is particularly important in offset systems, where the production of offsets should be incremental for emissions to be actually offset.

2.6 The generalised cost of transport

The total, or societal, generalised cost of transport adds up all the costs involved in transportation for the user and for society at large. A distinction is normally made for the subset of costs that are borne by the user and which therefore determines travel behaviour, called the 'behavioural generalised cost'. The total generalised cost would also allow for any subsidies, externalities, and other distortions. In this book the term 'generalised cost' is used to refer to behavioural generalised cost for reasons explained later in this section. Subsidies, externalities, and other distortions are included in the analysis separately. An example of (behavioural) generalised cost calculation is included in Chapter 4, section 2.1, and a simplified example distinguishing between behavioural and total generalised cost in Chapter 6, section 6.3.

As is explained at the beginning of this chapter, transport is an intermediate good, and the transport consumer will try to minimise the cost incurred in travelling between points A and B. As far as the user is concerned, the value of an investment in a transport facility will be measured by the extent to which it reduces the generalised cost of the user when making the trip. In making a travel decision, transport users will consider all options available: transport modes such as boat, rail, car, or air, and within air, all routings, operators, and alternative departure and arrival airports available. Indeed, if the option yielding the least generalised cost is deemed too high, the prospective passenger will decide not to travel.

The measure of time included in the generalised cost of travel would normally be the door-to-door travel time plus the frequency delay. Whereas frequency delay is harder to measure than door-to-door travel because it depends on subjective departure time preferences, it is still an important driver of traveller behaviour and willingness to pay. Lack of sufficient departure frequency can be a reason to travel through alternative airlines, airports, and modes of travel, or not to travel at all. However, frequency delay becomes relevant to investment appraisal in situations where the project affects departure frequency, otherwise similar delays with and without the project means that the frequency delay cancels out in net terms. For the reasons mentioned in section 2.2 above, stochastic delay is left out of the analysis. An example of dealing with frequency delay is included in Chapter 4, section 4.7.

Another component of generalised cost would be discomfort and the willingness to pay to avoid it or minimise it. The higher ticket price of business class seats is not an adequate measure because it mixes comfort issues with ticket flexibility. Also, frequent flier programmes introduce principal-agent issues. Evidence for willingness to pay for comfort factors and service attributes is emerging.[12] However, the evidence so far is mixed, and additional research would be required before estimates can be incorporated reliably as a welfare consideration. Over the last two decades there has been a growing application of stated preference techniques to model air travel demand, enabling the study of variables that had been harder to model with revealed preference techniques.[13]

As a factor to weigh on the decision to invest in air transport at all, comfort really is relevant on short-haul trips where the traveller faces competing transport modes. On long-haul trips, where the only choice is air transport, comfort conditions with and without the project are on average the same, and comfort becomes an issue of inter-airline competition, rather than one of whether to invest in air transport at all. Still, even on short-haul trips the level of comfort offered by airlines and high-speed rail is comparable, and choice of travel mode tends to be made largely on travel time and money cost. That is, any net benefit contributed by comfort issues is likely to be dwarfed by other components of generalised cost.

Turning to the total, or societal, generalised cost, in addition to allowing for subsidies and externalities, it would use economic or shadow prices to measure the scarcity of resources (see section 2.3.2 above), instead of out of pocket prices. In this sense, the total generalised cost can be thought of as the economic generalised cost, as it would measure the actual resources used up by the traveller, to distinguish it from the subset of costs that would constitute the user or behavioural generalised cost described above, which corresponds to costs incurred by the traveller. The mechanics for calculating investment return would vary slightly depending on the measure of generalised cost used. Using the total, societal or economic generalised cost would still require an estimate of the user generalised cost in order to make demand projections. As mentioned above, this book focuses on behavioural generalised cost. It links generalised cost to observed demand, making the appraisal exercise more intuitive and the financial appraisal easier, and enables the use of the same generalised cost measure in both the economic and financial analyses. The economic analysis then makes the necessary adjustments to the financial analysis to include all other effects. This permits in turn to discriminate the effects of the project across individual societal variables.

Table 2.1 sums up the components of generalised cost as will be used through this book. It is important to highlight that, as will become evident, for investment appraisal the relevant magnitude is the change in generalised cost brought about by the project relative to those costs that users would face without the project, rather than the absolute generalised cost.

2.7 Wider economic benefits

Analysis of economic returns from transport investments often include among project benefits items such as multiplier effects, tourist expenditure in the local economy, job creation, and increases in the value of land. They constitute secondary markets (where the primary market is the transport market that the project addresses) and include all markets that will feel the impact of the project. All these effects are intuitively appealing and often reflect actual benefits of the investment. However, there are two problems affecting their inclusion in the economic analysis of the investment. First, many of them double-count benefits already picked up by savings in the generalised cost of travel. And second, whereas some may measure actual benefits, they do not measure incremental benefits and do not take into account the alternative use of resources in the absence of the project and, therefore, do not constitute appropriate measures to guide investment decisions.

Ultimately, the standard economic appraisal techniques – focusing on changes to full or economic generalised cost of transport, measuring inputs at opportunity costs, and including externalities, as set out in the chapters that

Table 2.1 Components of generalised cost of transport as used in this book

Cost item	Usage
Travel time: door to door	Included
Travel time: frequency delay	Included
Money cost of travel	Included
Safety	Included, but significant mostly in situations where travel conditions are particularly unsafe
Comfort	Excluded, effect deemed to be relatively small
Externalities	Excluded from generalised cost but added to the economic analysis as additional costs
'Shadow price' adjustments to observed prices	Excluded from generalised cost, but included in the economic appraisal as a separate adjustment

follow – measure the full benefit of the project to the local, national, and world economies. Consideration of secondary markets is the exception rather than the norm, as is explained below.

The rationale behind this conclusion rests on the economic information that prices reveal under different market circumstances regarding competition and distortions. The discussions that follow apply to all economic appraisals in transport and other sectors. They are not particular or specific to air transport. Therefore this section includes only a brief summary of the key arguments. The reader is referred to the specialist literature for a more detailed treatment.[14]

2.7.1 Prices reflect marginal valuation and opportunity costs

The valuation of a user for a good or service is revealed by the user's willingness to pay for them. Looking at the economy as a whole, at a given point in time consumers will spend their income on the combination of goods and services they prefer most (that is, that maximises their utility). Inter-temporally, they will borrow or save according to their preferences for present over future consumption and the prevailing interest rate. Meanwhile, producers will compete to produce with the most efficient available technology to satisfy customer requirements, and through competition will end up supplying their products at normal profits (which will be equal to the risk-adjusted interest rate). That is, consumption and production in the whole economy are solved simultaneously to yield the combination of goods and services most valued (welfare maximising) by consumers, for a given state of technology and resource availability.

When this happens, any observed pattern of consumption and production reflects marginal consumer preferences (including valuations of the range of products available) and marginal production costs (that is, price equals marginal cost). For any additional good or service to be produced, it must be marginally more desirable than the alternative use of resources, and it will be produced with a normal profit. Hence that marginal unit produced must be valued at the margin, namely as its observed money price.

According to such reasoning, in a competitive market, without distortions, the observed financial profitability of a given investment project reflects normal risk-adjusted profits resulting from efficient production and the price at which the output is sold reflects marginal valuation. Therefore, in such market circumstances the financial profitability of the project is taken as a fair reflection of economic profitability.[15]

This is the underlying assumption that is applied to those sectors that are deemed highly competitive, such as airlines and, perhaps to a lesser extent, aeronautics. In reality, markets in those sectors still present some distortions, mostly taxes, subsidies, and distortions on secondary markets. The investment appraisal will need to make adjustments, as will be shown in the cases examined in later chapters, but the financial and economic returns will tend to be relatively close.

2.7.2 *Differences in generalised cost reveal value*

Unlike the airline and the aeronautical sectors, the supply of infrastructure services tends to be far from highly competitive. Indivisibilities in capacity provision mean that marginal increases in capacity may be lumpy, giving rise to both sunk and fixed costs. This means that infrastructure operations will exhibit strong cost economies and minimum efficient scales that render the sector prone to monopolistic outcomes. Therefore, when an airport suffers congestion, the alternative airport may be some non-trivial distance away. In those circumstances, the user will experience costs in switching to the alternative airport, possibly involving additional hours of travel. The switching cost to the user is measured by the difference in the generalised cost of transport between the alternatives, and the user will be willing to incur it to the extent that the user still values the trip highly enough. The switching cost therefore reveals consumer surplus available from using the preferred airport.

In other words, the cost of switching from facility A to B measures the additional value that A is creating to the user relative to B. To illustrate, say airport A is congested and does not have airline seats left to the desired destination. The user has to drive to an alternative airport B located two hours drive away, incurring an additional generalised cost of, say EUR60, relative to the generalised cost experienced when travelling through A. Then, those EUR60 measure the user's additional willingness to pay for additional capacity at airport A, and therefore measures the (incremental) value that airport A offers.

Users can consist of passengers or shippers. For freight shippers, the transport will almost always be a component of a production chain. In the case of passengers, trip purpose can either be leisure or business. For leisure users, the generalised cost is an element of the total valuation of the final good (say, a holiday). The leisure traveller's willingness to pay to avoid switching costs will ultimately depend on how much the traveller values the holiday.

For business or work-related travel, as for freight, the ticket price is an input cost in the production chain. Businesses will be willing to incur the cost to the extent that it ultimately produces a good which is valued by the final user sufficiently to make the trip worth it. This same consideration also applies to the willingness to devote paid worker time to travelling. The value of the time invested in travelling must ultimately reflect the value of the output produced as a result of that trip. That is, a business will invest the time of its workers in travelling to the extent that it is profitable to do so. And the worker's revealed value of time (in other words, the amount the firm will be willing to pay to save worker travelling time) will reflect the value of the output that that worker could have produced with that time, that is, the worker's time opportunity cost. In short, working value of time will measure the opportunity cost of output foregone and, by implication, the money valuation of the time savings yielded by a transport project will reflect the amount of additional output enabled by the project.

The implication of the above is that the savings in generalised cost that a project grants to local businesses reflect the value that the airport generates to the local economy in terms of enabled additional production. This implies that, in economic appraisals, savings in user generalised costs already reflect production benefits in the local economy, so that adding additional benefits to firms would constitute double counting. There is an exception to this conclusion, though, discussed in the next section.

2.7.3 Secondary markets

Primary markets reflect value on the secondary market when two conditions are met. Firstly, the secondary market is free of distortions. Second, the magnitude of changes in the primary market brought about by the project are calculated with long run demand elasticities. The demonstration of this result would be lengthy and the reader is referred to, for example, Boardman et al. (2018) for an introductory presentation and to Just et al. (2004) for a more detailed, technical presentation. The extent of the additional project-related value gain or loss in a secondary market is related to the size of the distortion. So, a project that brings about an expansion of production in a secondary market that is, say, taxed, would produce benefits additional to those reflected in the primary market, measured by the tax rate, in a fashion equivalent to that illustrated in Figure 2.1 above. Likewise, if the secondary market is subsidised, the project will bring about additional costs through a higher subsidy bill.

Taxes, subsidies, quotas and externalities are relatively easy to observe. Distortions related to imperfect competition less so. This is illustrated with the help of Figure 2.5. Let us assume that the secondary market in question consists of engine lubricants and that the market for lubricants is free of distortions. An airport project will cause the demand for lubricant products to increase in the

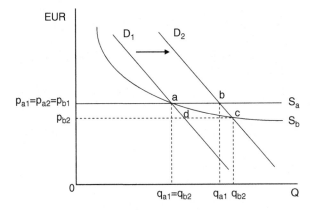

Figure 2.5 Effects of a project on secondary markets.

local economy. The market for lubricants is large – so that economies of scale have been exhausted – and the market is competitive, with the marginal cost (and supply) curve as depicted by S_a. The increase in demand for lubricants brought about by the project is illustrated by the shift from D_1 to D_2, increasing the quantity of lubricants demanded from q_{a1} to q_{a2}, but this has no impact on prices, which remain the same before and after the project ($p_{a1} = p_{a2}$). There is no impact on marginal costs either and suppliers of lubricants continue making normal profits. The implication is that the scarcity of lubricants in the local economy is left unchanged by the project. The project has no knock-on effect on the local economy that affects the welfare of third parties, other than through distortions such as taxes or externalities associated with the lubricants market.

Assume instead that the market for lubricants is small, still enjoying economies of scale, and that the project brings about a substantial increase in market size, allowing suppliers to exploit economies of scale. This would be the situation illustrated by the marginal cost curve S_b in which despite the absence of taxes, subsidies, or externalities, the declining cost curve signals the likely presence of imperfect competition.[16] This situation is likely to take place in projects that are large relative to the size of the local economy. The project shifts demand from D_1 to D_2, causing quantity demanded to increase from q_{b1} to q_{b2}, but now the price of lubricants in the local market falls from p_{b1} to p_{b2}.[17] The airport, the airlines operating from the airport, and other suppliers of airport services will enjoy a lower price of lubricants than was the case before the project. This constitutes a primary market benefit which will show in the standard calculations of financial returns (the airport) and the economic returns (the airport, airlines, and eventually passengers) of the project.

However, other users of lubricants in the local economy (for example, factories and road hauliers unrelated to airport activities) will also enjoy lower prices. The project has made lubricants less scarce in the local economy. This brings about a welfare gain in the secondary market equal to the area p_{b1}–a–d–p_{b2}, which the financial analysis will ignore, but which the economic analysis will have to include as a knock-on benefit of the project to a secondary market (the local lubricants market).[18] This production benefit is not picked up by valuations of gains in consumer surplus of project stake-holders in the primary market and would have to be added as an extra benefit to the local economy.

The effect of the project on a secondary market could also be adverse. In cases of decreasing returns to scale, implying an upward supply curve, the project will increase prices in the secondary market, bringing about a knock-on welfare loss to the local economy that must be subtracted from the economic returns of the project.[19]

In practice, though, value gains or losses through distorted secondary markets are normally small relative to those in the primary market. Moreover, they can be both positive and negative. A pragmatic take for practice is that these effects cancel out and that the analyst should only account for special cases where the project is expected to have a significant effect on a secondary market that is substantially distorted. They should be ignored otherwise.

An alternative technique to deal with distorted secondary markets would be computational general equilibrium (CGE). This is a technique that estimates the effects of policies or very large projects in the economy as a whole, by modelling the entire economy. It is computationally more burdensome than CBA, but it does model all of the key markets in the economy. On the other hand, most CGE models are designed to measure national income. They therefore tend to leave out elements specific to cost-benefit analysis such as changes in consumer surplus and externalities.[20] There is no reason though why a CGE model could not be developed to include these variables. Indeed, at the moment the multinational C-Bridge project is seeking to do that by developing a CGE model compatible with CBA.[21] There should be interesting developments in this area over the next few years. In principle, they should be most helpful for very large projects in highly distorted economies.

2.7.4 *The value of land*

Among aviation projects, airports in particular are substantial land users. Land therefore becomes an important input to the projects and, as will be seen in Chapter 4, land value can drive the rationale for a project. As an input market, land is a secondary market in project appraisal and the same considerations introduced in the preceding section 2.7.3 above apply. The primary (air travel) market would reflect value changes in the secondary, input (land) market other than any distortions in the secondary market. The most frequently found such distortion in the case of land would be land taxes, including also capital gain taxes.

There is a close relationship between the value of property and its proximity, or accessibility, to desirable locations, such as a city centre, a high-quality residential area, a beach, or a centre with economic activity. Improvements in transport services in an area enhance the accessibility of the area. Airport projects, like any other transport infrastructure development, tend to increase the value of land in their vicinity. The exception would be those areas affected by negative externalities of a project which, in the case of airports, consist mostly of those areas below noisy landing and take-off paths.

The extent to which a transport facility is desirable will be reflected in the amount of traffic the facility processes. People and firms will relocate to an area close to an airport to the extent that they or their clients use the airport, and their willingness to pay for property in the new location will be commensurate with how much they value the improved accessibility supplied by the airport. Improved accessibility can be measured through savings in generalised cost of transport enabled by the airport.

So, users who value proximity to the airport will relocate to the airport vicinity and will be willing to push property prices up to the present value of its expected savings in generalised transport costs. Meanwhile, local residents in the vicinity of the airport who do not value proximity to the airport by as much will sell their properties to those who value such proximity to the airport. In effect, those selling their property are appropriating the buyers' capitalised value of the improved accessibility to the airport. The increase in the value of the property therefore constitutes a transfer, rather than a generation of value additional to the savings in generalised cost of transport produced by the project. The implication is that including land price increases resulting from a transport investment as a benefit of the investment will double-count benefits that are already being included in the analysis through savings in generalised transport cost.

The result that changes in land prices resulting from a project can consist of the capitalisation of the changes in generalised costs can turn into a useful tool for the project analyst. In a hypothetical project where there is poor data on both the value of time and the origin of trips to the airport (that is, where it is not possible to compute savings in generalised transport costs resulting from the project), changes in the value of land can be taken as a surrogate measure of the accessibility benefits brought about by the project.

Just as increases in land prices measure capitalised benefits, falls in land prices measure capitalised losses. It is mentioned above that aircraft noise can bring about a decline in property prices in affected areas. Such a decline would be a surrogate measure of the noise externality, and not an additional cost to a monetised measure of noise externality in an economic appraisal.

The investment analyst should proceed with care in gauging the expected increase in land prices resulting from a project. If the analyst is appraising a project after it has been announced to the general public, it may well be that land prices already reflect at least part of the expected benefits of the project.[22]

2.7.5 Multiplier effects

Economic appraisals through cost-benefit analysis, just like financial appraisals, measure the value generated by allocating resources to one particular use (the project), relative to another use (the without project scenario). Income multiplier effects resulting from expenditures in project inputs and from project outputs do not take part of appraisals of economic viability. This is because had the funds been invested in their alternative use they would also have caused multiplier effects. Any expenditure will generate multipliers. Even projects that both lose money and generate a net welfare loss will still generate multipliers.

The net difference that the project will make to income and welfare consists of net monetised and non-monetised value generated, which is what cost-benefit analysis measures. Multipliers are the domain of impact studies, which describe the effects of a project on the local economy, but do not address the question of whether the project generates a profit or a net welfare improvement over and above the opportunity cost of inputs.[23]

2.7.6 Job creation

Another common source of error in economic appraisals is the treatment of employment. Whereas job creation is good and is welcomed, it is very common to cite job creation as a justification for an investment project. On the other hand, there is no need to explain to business people that labour constitutes a cost. Labour is a scarce productive resource. Occupying a worker in a project precludes other businesses from employing that worker. Therefore, subject to the frequent distortions in labour markets (such as taxes, social security contributions, and restrictive labour market laws), salaries reflect the opportunity cost of labour, a scarce service.

The opportunity cost of labour can be illustrated with a simple example that reminds us that countries become richer when a task can be done with less labour input (increasing labour productivity), freeing labour resources for other tasks. If society can make a B-747 fly with three pilots (two in the cockpit plus one in reserve) instead of four (three in the cockpit plus one in reserve) society will be richer because it can create a service (flying a B-747) with fewer resources (labour input), releasing a pilot to operate other flights.

However, whereas labour is an input, as we saw above in section 2.3.2, input costs can be distorted due to the presence of taxes or subsidies. In the calculation of economic returns, labour taxes and social security contributions should be deducted from the money labour costs to estimate the shadow price of labour. In that sense, there is a 'benefit' to using labour inputs in a project in the form of a deduction from project costs of what is in fact a transfer to the government or to a social security fund.[24] Such a 'benefit' works out to a lower input cost, rather than a net benefit.

In addition to taxes and social security contributions, shadow wages can also correct for additional distortions to the labour market, such as high unemployment benefits, the existence of minimum salaries, and rigid labour market laws that may result in unemployment.[25]

Appendix A2.1: Productivity and the value of time

When travelling for work, the time spent travelling can be most immediately valued by referring to hourly earnings. But to operate within a more complete framework for valuing travel time savings, including travelling during both leisure and working time, it is necessary to embed time valuation into consumer theory. The framework is also to allow for distortions caused by taxation. There are various models to embed time into microeconomic theory. For a review of these models, including their evolution through time, see Jara-Díaz (2007).

What follows here is a graphical representation of a generic model. Individual models may differ from this generic model in matters of detail in various ways. The intention is for the reader to understand how the various categories of time values that analysts will find when appraising air transport projects fit into the broader set of prices and magnitudes relevant for the appraisal. A central one is labour productivity, which explains much of the differences in time values that project analysts will encounter across countries.

Figure A2.1 represents the labour market. The horizontal axis measures the total number of hours available. It could be thought of as hours in an average day, month, or year. Likewise, the axis could represent an individual, a segment of population, or indeed the population at large. There is a minimum hours set aside for vital needs, such as sleep and so on. This would determine the maximum amount of working hours, as represented by the long-dashed, vertical line. Once personal preferences are set, the decision as to how much of the remaining hours are split between working and leisure would depend on the wage rate. The wage rate itself would be the result of the supply and demand for labour, together with any distortions present in the labour market.

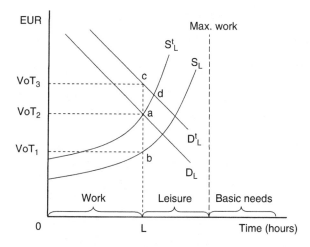

Figure A2.1 Labour productivity and the values of time.

This appendix illustrates distortions through taxes. Other distortions frequent in the labour market are a minimum wage and involuntary unemployment.

S_L represents the after tax labour supply schedule. The supply of labour would depend on the preferences of individuals as to how much they are willing to trade work for leisure. Generally, as the salary increases the quantity of working hours supplied will go up, hence the upward sloping S_L curve. As people work longer hours, the marginal utility of the remaining leisure hours increases. Therefore the S_L schedule becomes steeper as more hours are worked and there are fewer remaining hours of leisure. S_L^t corresponds to the supply of labour before tax, where t would represent tax on salary income. Full labour compensation should also include fringe benefits, but for simplicity these are excluded from the presentation as a separate item. The reader could think of them as being present in hourly, net of tax compensation.

Meanwhile the demand for labour schedule D_L is downward sloping, displaying a decreasing marginal product of labour as more hours are worked. The first few working hours are dedicated to the most productive tasks and are therefore highly valued. As more hours are worked, they are dedicated to less productive output, decreasing the willingness to pay for such additional work.

Companies would hire additional workers to the extent that the marginal value product of labour (that is, labour productivity) equals the salary demanded by workers, gross of personal income tax. This corresponds to point a in Figure A2.1. If there are additional taxes paid by the employer that vary with employment, then the demand for labour by employers will not measure the full marginal product of labour, which would also include the taxes paid by the employer as a result of the additional labour input. Schedule D_L^t represents this full, or social, marginal product of labour. In other words, how much society values the marginal work effort.

Therefore, hour worked L along the horizontal axis would produce value to society equal to the distance cL. Of this, bL accrues to the employee as after-tax salary. Distance ab accrues to the government as tax on salary income, paid by the employee. Finally, distance ca is paid by the corporation as tax resulting from the employment of labour hour L. It is being assumed that the corporation operates in a competitive market with no distortions other than the tax. The corporation therefore makes a normal profit that just covers its cost of capital. Employment by a company that operates in an uncompetitive market, generating super-normal profits, would yield additional value, which would be represented graphically by a further wedge between demand and supply of labour at point a.

In terms of value of travel time savings, let us assume first that the passenger views time spent travelling as a cost and does not derive any utility from it. The traveller (as opposed to the employer) would be willing to pay to avoid an hour spent travelling the same amount of money as would be willing to pay to enjoy an extra hour of leisure. This amount would be measured by the amount of (after tax) salary that would be needed to compensate the traveller from giving up an hour of leisure. That is, the marginal value of time (VoT) for someone working L hours would be equal to the hourly after tax salary bL, equal to VoT_1 on the vertical axis, which becomes the value of time when travelling for leisure.

When that passenger travels for work, the trip must pay for the salary, gross of income tax, incurred by the company employing that person. The relevant marginal product of labour for the employer would be that which the corporation can generate net of corporate tax. The willingness to pay to save one hour would then be aL, equal to an hourly value of time of VoT_2. This is the main reason explaining why time values are higher when the trip motive is work rather than leisure.

This willingness to pay of the employer for reducing employee travel time drives the decisions by the employer as to the means of travel of the employee. Say the employer of a passenger considering to travel on airline route A is willing to pay EUR50 to save one hour of employee travel time. Another airline route (or mode of transport) B is EUR30 cheaper but the trip takes one hour longer. Then the employer would be happy to pay for the employee to travel via A rather than B. Since such value of time measure explains passenger behaviour it is referred to as a *behavioural* value of time. This would correspond to VoT_2 on the graph. However, the value to society of the labour output lost by travelling would not be just the EUR50. Such societal measure would also need to include the corporate taxes paid by the employer in devoting employee time to the trip. The *social*, or *economic*, value of time would then be VoT_3.

In principle, therefore, economic appraisals should use two values of working time simultaneously. Firstly, VoT_2 to explain business passenger behaviour, that is, to estimate the private or behavioural generalised cost of travel with and without the project and with it to estimate changes in traffic. And secondly, VoT_3 to place a societal value on the increase or decrease of travel time with the project relative to the without project scenario, through estimates of the total, or societal, generalised cost of travel. In practice, though, appraisals use a single working value of time for both behavioural estimation and societal valuation. Corporate taxes that vary with employment may not account to much or are taken to be related to capital rather than labour. Meanwhile, for leisure trips, VoT_1 would constitute both the behavioural and societal value of time.

Note that VoT_1 measures labour productivity as appropriated by the worker, VoT_2, labour productivity as experienced by the corporation, and VoT_3 labour productivity as measured by society. As an aside, assume that there are no corporate taxes, so that schedule D_L represents both corporate and societal demand for labour. The schedule intersects the (income taxed) supply of labour at point a. At that market equilibrium, VoT_2 represents both societal labour productivity and labour productivity (marginal value product of labour) as perceived by the employer. Assume now that there is a positive productivity shock, due to, say, a transfer of knowledge from some other economy, causing an increase in demand for labour, shifting D_L upwards to D^t_L, while continuing to assume that there are no corporate taxes. The new labour productivity, following the productivity shock, would be measured by the distance between point d and the horizontal axis. Projecting horizontally from point d to the vertical axis we will see that the value of time would increase, up from that implied by the pre-shock market clearing point a.

This outcome illustrates that in more productive, higher income economies, the values of business travel time are normally higher than in less productive, lower income economies. Likewise, projecting vertically from point d downwards towards the horizontal axis we will see that that projection would intersect schedule S_L at a higher point, relative to the vertical axis, than b. That is, in more productive economies, the value of travel time on leisure trips is also higher than in lower income economies. Still a word of caution is required for air travel in lower income countries. These economies often portray dual economic systems with marked differences on labour productivity between the two, or otherwise have a more skewed income distribution than higher income countries. Air travel in such lower income countries would be used by the segments of the population with higher income. Therefore, there may be less difference in the values of time for aviation between upper and lower income countries than would be suggested by per capita national income measures.

As mentioned at the beginning of this appendix, the travel time model presented here is generic, and put together to illustrate the underlying rationale for differences in travel time value. Detail can be added. For example, the model assumes that travelling (in the sense of in-vehicle time) is not in itself a particular source of utility or disutility. If a person enjoys travelling, the willingness to pay to save travel time would be lower. When that person flies on holidays, the willingness to pay to save one hour of flying time would be less than VoT_1 in Figure A2.1. The opposite would happen if a person dislikes travelling. A complete estimate of the value of leisure travel time would require valuing also the alternative uses of leisure time (see Jara-Díaz, 2007, for a review of the various theoretical models). Another factor loosening the link between the value of leisure travel time and personal income is that, on an average household, some leisure travel is conducted by household members that do not generate income, further lowering willingness to pay to save time. As a result of all these factors, guidance often includes a wedge between personal income and leisure travel time value. As an example, the US Department of Transportation (2016) values personal (i.e. leisure) air travel time at 70 per cent of earnings.

Likewise, when travelling for work, if people can take advantage of in-vehicle time to work, the willingness to pay to reduce travel time would be lower than VoT_2. At the extreme, notionally, if a person is as productive while travelling as while in the office, the value of travel time savings would be EUR0. These circumstances illustrate why ultimately the analyst, when appraising projects, must often rely on direct estimations of values of time, derived from actual behaviour through revealed preference studies or from surveys through stated preference techniques. Reference to hourly earnings could be a fall-back, indirect approach to estimate values of time, when no direct estimates are available.

In other modes of transport, planning and appraisal studies often make a difference between waiting time and in-vehicle time. For urban transport, it is often necessary to substitute the working-leisure trip purpose dichotomy by a working-commuting-leisure trichotomy. Also, given the differences in speed of different modes of transport, the choice of mode of transport is itself a means for travellers to reveal their willingness to pay to save time. It is therefore common to see differences in estimated values of time across transport modes.

For aviation, further differentiation may be introduced by adding categories such as airport processing time, in-vehicle (or flying) time, access and egress time, etc. In the presence of congestion at peak times in a given facility, there may also be a case to draw a difference between, on the one hand, the value of delay to passengers that still travel through the same facility but divert to travel at less preferred departure times and, on the other hand, to passengers that rather than travelling at a less preferred time, divert to an alternative transport mode or an alternative airport. These two forms of traffic diversion are introduced in Chapter 3.

For simplicity though, a single, average value of time is used throughout the book. Appraisals that focus on specific service attributes like, say, reducing waiting time in security checks, may conduct time valuation studies that target specific components of travel time. Transport operators and authorities may conduct tailored time valuation studies for a variety of purposes apart from investment appraisal, such as formulating marketing or competitive strategies, valuing service quality, planning, or supporting a case before the competition authorities.

Appendix A2.2: Cap and trade and offsetting schemes compared

A2.2.1 Introduction

This appendix presents in more detail how generic market-based mechanisms (MBM) to internalise emissions would operate. The presentation in the chapter focused on permits in cap and trade systems (the terms permits and allowances are used interchangeably). This appendix extends the presentation in two directions. Firstly, it goes beyond the tradable permits market to include the permit buying and permit selling markets as well. Taking the selling market to be the electricity generating market, it explores the consequences of the market displaying an inelastic demand curve versus a more normal downward sloping demand curve. Secondly, it illustrates offset schemes, including also upstream and downstream markets. The appendix modifies the graph for the permits market to leave it only as the market for permits, rather than the composite of emissions and fuel of Figures 2.3 and 2.4. This is because the presentation in this appendix includes different sectors among which the fuel causing the GHG emission may differ, and with it the fuel-emissions ratio in the composite measure. The horizontal axes in the various relevant figures now measure tonnes of CO_2 rather than a composite measure of fuel and emissions. The vertical axis in the figure representing the permits market now includes measures net of fuel cost for both emission permits (or offsets) and the social cost of carbon.

Both the cap and trade and offset schemes are represented with the same Figure A2.2.

A2.2.2 Cap and trade

Quadrant a) in Figure A2.2 represents a growth in demand for airline services (or air travel) through a shift in the demand schedule from D_{a1} to D_{a2}. Supply for airline services excluding permits is represented by supply curve S_{axp} ('a' stands or airline, 'x' for exclusion, and 'p' for permit). When airlines are not required to buy emission permits, the shift in demand for air travel would not cause a change in the price of airline tickets.

In contrast, supply curve S_{aip} represents the airline supply curve including permits (where 'i' stands for inclusion), which become a required input for airlines. The curve is upward sloping because the higher the number of permits required the higher their price. When demand is at D_{a1} the price of airline tickets is p_{a1}, which includes the permit price p_{p1}. The shift in demand to D_{a2} increases the price of airline tickets from p_{a1} to p_{a2}, due exclusively to the increase in the price of permits from p_{p1} to p_{p2}.

Airlines acquire their emission permits on the permits market, represented by quadrant b) of Figure A2.2. The permits market experiences the growth in airline demand (D_{a1} to D_{a2} in quadrant a)) as a shift in demand for permits from D_{p1} to D_{p2}. This results in the price of permits increasing from p_{p1} to p_{p2}. Notice the difference in the vertical axis between this quadrant b) and the vertical axis in Figures 2.3 and 2.4. Quadrant b) represents only the permits market, whereas the vertical axes in Figures 2.3 and 2.4 include also the associated fuel price.

The growth in demand for air travel leaves total societal emissions unchanged at Q, on the horizontal axis in quadrant b). The amount of permits bought by airlines to accommodate the growth in air travel demand is equal to the distance between points c and d along the horizontal axis in quadrant b). These permits used by the airlines are sold by some other GHG emitting sectors which, as the permit price increases from p_{p1} to p_{p2}, find it financially worthwhile to either cease production altogether or to continue producing but by switching to a technology that does not emit GHG. For these other sectors, the path describing the permit price-quantity combination at which the switching takes place is represented by the section in the demand curve D_{p1} linking points a to b in quadrant b). The permits bill paid by airlines, measured by the area of the shaded trapezoid in quadrant a), measures the size of the transaction in euros, which is mirrored by the shaded trapezoid in quadrant b).

Sellers of permits can come from any of the sectors included in the cap and trade scheme, including as well other airlines. But since D_a consists of total demand of permits by the airline sector as a whole, the illustration assumes that the airline sector is a net buyer of permits. Let us assume for simplicity that all permit sellers come from coal energy generation, represented in quadrant c).

In the absence of a tradable emission permits scheme, coal energy generators would have a supply curve depicted by S_{cxp} ('c' meaning coal, 'x' exclusion and 'p' permits). By introducing permits, the coal energy supply curve becomes S_{cip} (where the 'i' stands for inclusion). As with airlines in quadrant a), the supply curve is upward sloping because greater production of coal-generated energy would require the purchase of ever pricier emission permits. The growth of demand for permits by airlines (quadrant a)), and the resulting increase in the price of permits (quadrant b)), is perceived by the coal energy generating market as an exogenous upward shift in the supply curve from S_{cip1} to S_{cip2} (quadrant c)). This shift is explained fully by an increase in the price of permits from p_{p1} to p_{p2}, and results in the price of energy generated with coal to increase from p_{c1} to p_{c2}, alongside a reduction in the quantity of energy generated with coal from q_{c1} to q_{c2}. The amount of permits involved in this reduction in coal energy generation corresponds to the amount of permits cd along the horizontal axis in quadrant b), which in turn corresponds to the permits associated to the increase in air transport output from q_{a1} to q_{a2} in quadrant a). Note that the units in the horizontal axis of each of these three graphs differs: quadrant a) would measure, say, million tonne-kilometres (tonne referring to aircraft payload, not GHG emissions); quadrant b) would measure, say, thousand of 1-tonne permits (tonne referring to GHG emissions); and quadrant c) would measure, say, megawatt-hours.

The area of the shaded trapezoid in quadrant c) would measure the value of the lost coal-generated energy, caused by the higher price of emission permits. It also measures the total revenues of the coal energy sector from the sale of the emission permits. That is, it has the same area, in euros, as the shaded trapezoid in quadrants a) and b). Indeed, this is the key conclusion in this section, namely the value of the emission permits bill paid by the airlines equals the loss in value associated to coal energy generation. [26]

This could well be the final outcome as far as energy production is concerned. Should there be no substitute to coal for energy generation, the increase in supply of air transport would involve a reduction in energy generation (where energy is understood to be, say, electricity or heat, rather than aviation kerosene). Fortunately, energy generation normally has other substitute technologies to coal (and assuming there are no national policies protecting the coal industry). Quadrant d) depicts the market for renewable energy. It could be viewed either as the aggregate supply curve of renewable energy technologies or, more abstractly, as a single source of renewable energy. The important condition is that such renewable energy source does not require the purchase of emission permits. [27]

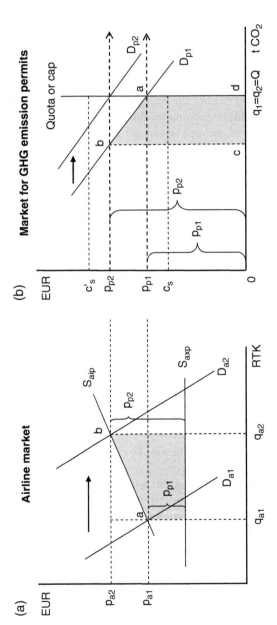

Figure A2.2 Market adjustments with cap and trade and with offset systems.

(*Continued*)

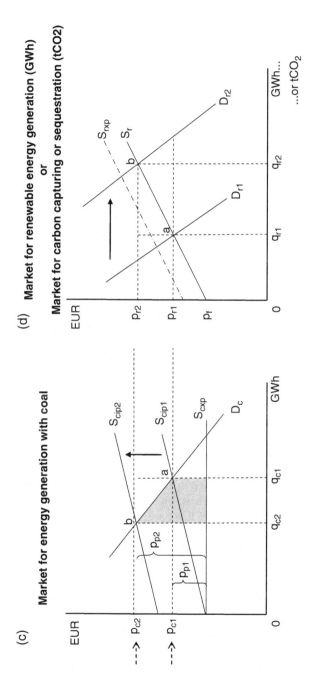

Figure A2.2 (Continued)

The market for renewable energy generation is depicted with an upward sloping supply curve S_r, as each additional amount of energy generated involves ever more expensive capacity, implying diminishing returns at a given state of technology. The diagram in quadrant d) represents the state of the world at a given period in time, within which the increase in demand for aviation depicted in quadrant a) takes place. Longer term, technological change would shift downwards or flatten the supply curve. Even looking at the renewable energy market narrowly from the aviation perspective, the expectation that aviation would grow the demand for emission permits over the long term would incentivise investing in improvements in renewable energy technology, flattening the long term supply schedule S_r over time.

The increase in the price of energy generated by coal from p_{c1} to p_{c2} taking place in quadrant c), brings about an increase in demand for substitutes, in this case renewable energy, represented in quadrant d) as an outward shift in the demand curve for renewable energy from D_{r1} to D_{r2}.[28] This shift in the demand curve causes an increase in the quantity of renewable energy produced from q_{r1} to q_{r2} and an increase in its price from p_{r1} to p_{r2}. Note that the increase in price of renewable energy would also have consequences in turn for coal-generated energy, since they are substitutes both ways. The various curves in the various quadrants of Figure A2.2 are then to be thought as general equilibrium outcomes, once all price adjustments related to the initial change in demand for air transport have taken place.[29]

For completeness, area $abq_{r2}q_{r1}$ under the supply curve S_r in quadrant d) measures the resources that would need to be mobilised in order to deliver new energy into the market. It reflects area $baq_{c1}q_{c2}$ in quadrant c), consisting of the value of coal energy production foregone inclusive of the cost of GHG emissions. However, note that it has been assumed that all of the additional permits required by air transport associated with a growth in air travel demand from D_{a1} to D_{a2} (in quadrant a)) are supplied by coal energy. Should permits for sale come into the market from a broader set of productive sectors, such as energy generation through petroleum, gas, or the petrochemical industry – each one represented by a separate quadrant c), it would be the summation of the areas equivalent to $baq_{c1}q_{c2}$ in all of these sectors that would measure the gross value of generation foregone in these sectors. Still, the shaded area in quadrant b) would reflect the GHG-related resource cost of all of these sectors on aggregate.

Likewise, there could be more than one renewable energy technology, each one with their own equivalent to quadrant d). If so, each of these d) quadrants would only partially reflect the resource implications in the aggregate of c) quadrants. It would be the aggregate of all of the renewable energy sectors that would reflect the production foregone in all of the aggregate c) quadrants. There is no need to look at these sectors though. The net value foregone in other GHG emitting sectors with the growth in air travel is reflected in the permits market in quadrant b).

A2.2.3 *Offsets*

The requirement for airlines to buy GHG offsets turns such offsets into an input in the production of air transportation by airlines, just as is the case with permits.[30] Both permits and offsets constitute equally rights to emit. In the case of cap and trade schemes, the quantity supplied of the input (or rights) at hand is fixed ex ante, so that the use of the input by the airline requires another user to give up using that unit of input. Instead, with offsets the quantity of the input is not fixed. The airline buys the offset from another sector that issues such right to emit by capturing an equivalent amount of GHG. The supply of offsets can be expanded or contracted, while not altering the outcome that emissions are offset.

For all practical matters, the marginal net societal emission in both MBM systems – cap and trade and offsets – is the same, namely zero. But the mechanics are different. In the case of cap and trade schemes, airlines pay to substitute other users of GHG, whereas in the case of offsetting the airline pays for an increase in the supply of offsets.

At its simplest, say that there is a sector that produces carbon sequestration as its sole output, such as companies capturing and storing GHG underground on sinks that have been previously exploited to generate energy, regardless of carbon capturing possibilities. We will subsequently see the implication of a sector for which carbon capturing may be a by-product of some other production. An example would be forestry for wood production.

In the case of offsets, the polluter buys directly, through a market, from the offsetting sector. The graphical representation would involve considering only quadrants a) and d) in Figure A2.2. Quadrant b) does not apply since there is no formal or explicit cap. Meanwhile quadrant c) does not apply either since the transaction between the airline and the producer of offsets does not necessarily imply that there is a substitute to offsets production that would see its demand or supply schedules shift with the change in price of offsets.

The offsetting mechanism would then work through the graphical representation as follows. Starting in quadrant a), the increase in demand faced by airlines is represented by a shift in the demand curve from D_{a1} to D_{a2}. The supply curve in the airline market without a requirement to buy offsets is represented by S_{axp} – the same as without a requirement to buy permits – discussed in section A2.2. When airlines need to buy offsets, the supply curve would be S_{aip}, which is upwards sloping since each additional tonne of GHG that needs offsetting would involve an increasingly expensive offset.[31] This is reflected in quadrant d), representing the market producing the GHG offsets, by the upward sloping supply curve S_r. The increase in demand for offsets by airlines causes an outward shift in the demand for offsets from D_{r1} to D_{r2}. The increase in price in quadrant d) from p_{r1} to p_{r2} corresponds to the increase in the price of emission rights from p_{p1} to p_{p2} in quadrant a). That is, as far as airlines is concerned, offsets and permits are equivalent.

The total bill for offsets paid by airlines would be equal to the area of the shaded trapezoid in quadrant a). This would be equal to the income received by the offsetting sector from the sale of offsets, corresponding to area of trapezoid $abq_{r2}q_{r1}$ in quadrant d). The key message is that the economic cost of buying offsets is reflected in the sale price of offsets, just as the economic cost of buying emission permits through a cap and trade scheme are reflected in the price of permits. For a marginal change in demand for permits or offsets, the economic price can be taken to be their spot price. For a larger, non-marginal change in demand for permits or offsets, the economic price would be the average of their initial and final prices.

Consider now sectors that supply offsets as byproducts like, say, wood production. Abstract momentarily quadrant d) from the rest of Figure A2.2, and assume it describes the market of wood harvesting. The supply curve of trees would be the dash-dotted S_{rxp}. There is then a regulatory change creating a market for offsets in which tree growers can participate by selling offsets while their plantations are capturing GHG – that is, until the trees are cut for wood selling. This could be represented graphically as akin to the tree-growers receiving a subsidy, shifting the supply curve for tree growing down to S_r.

Mathematically, the supply of wood and offsets would be in fixed proportions, and dependent on both the price of offsets and the price of wood. Returning to viewing quadrant d) as the market for offsets only, the supply curve S_r would be subject to upwards or downwards shifts through a decrease or increase in the price of wood, for factors unrelated to the offsets market.

Appendix A2.3: Valuation of emissions with an endogenous cap

Phase 4 of the EU ETS includes the possibility that allowances (permits) that enter the market stability reserve (MSR) may be permanently cancelled. Projects or policies that contribute to moving allowances into, or prevent allowances from leaving, the MSR would help shift the cap. From the perspective of economic appraisal the cap ceases to be exogenous and becomes endogenous to the project or policy under appraisal. As mentioned in section 2.5.4, developing a formula to estimate the number of allowances by which a project or policy could be expected to shift the cap is still in the early stages and is outside the scope of this appendix. Rather, this appendix identifies graphically the economic cost of allowances that shift the cap. Johansson (2020) offers a formal exposition.

Take a project that cuts demand for emissions relative to an alternative technology. In a future aviation context this could consist of an airline renewing its fleet and considering an element of electrification. The appraisal of the electrification project would consist of comparing hybrid electric aircraft (the 'with project' scenario) relative to an alternative, same vintage, all kerosene aircraft (the 'without project' scenario). Figure A2.3 represents the effects of the project on the market for emission permits under three alternative

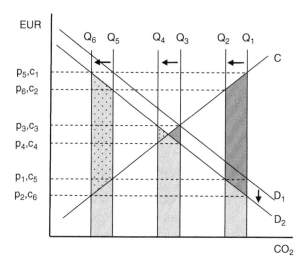

Figure A2.3 Economic cost of shifting the cap in a cap and trade scheme.

initial caps, represented by vertical schedules Q. The project would shift demand for emissions from D_1 to D_2. Schedule C represents the social cost of carbon. Ideally, the cap would be set at, or as close as possible to, the interception of schedules D and C. With such a cap the permit price would reflect the social cost of carbon.

Assume instead a cap that is too loose, like Q_1, set at a level of emissions much higher than that indicated by the intersection of schedules D and C. Assume initially that the rules governing the cap and trade scheme are such that the cap is exogenous. The shift from D_1 to D_2 would cause the price of emissions to fall from p_1 to p_2. The area of the lightly shaded trapezoid would constitute the permits bill saved by the project to the promoter. These permits are made available to other permit users, so that the trapezoid measures also the value of additional production elsewhere in the economy made possible by the airline requiring fewer permits. More precisely, it measures the willingness to pay elsewhere in the economy for those permits as determined by the marginal value product of those permits. The private cost savings to the airline constitutes also a societal benefit through increased production elsewhere in the economy. Meanwhile emissions with and without the project remain unchanged at Q_1. The societal value of the permits released by the project is thus measured by the light shaded area alone. Since there is no change in societal emissions, the social cost of carbon, at c_1, does not enter the calculation of societal value.

Assume alternatively that the rules of the cap and trade system are such that the cap is no longer exogenous and is instead endogenous to the project. Moreover, as an extreme scenario, assume that all of the permits released by the project would translate into a permanently reduced cap. This means that the cap would shift from Q_1 to Q_2, leaving the price of permits the same both with and without the project, unchanged at p_1. If so, the light shaded area would still constitute a project benefit, consisting of savings in the permits bill to the project promoter. However, there is now also a reduction in total societal emissions, valued as the area under schedule C and between schedules Q_1 and Q_2. This implies an additional societal benefit from reducing the cap equal to the area of the darkly shaded trapezoid. The value of this additional benefit would be the difference in the social cost of carbon, reflected in c_1 and c_2 along the horizontal axis, and the permits bill saved to the promoter as measured by the lightly shaded trapezoid.

Take now an alternative starting point for the cap, set at Q_3, where the cap should be on efficiency grounds, at the intersection of schedules D and C. Assuming to start with that the cap is exogenous, the project would lower the price of allowances from p_3 to p_4. The lightly shaded area – including both the un-dotted and dotted portions – would measure the value of the savings to the airline from the project, equal to the increase in production to sectors that use the permits released by the airline. As the demand schedule D shifts, the cap becomes slightly loose, leading to a small loss of efficiency equal to the darkly shaded triangle formed within schedules C, Q_3, and D_2. This efficiency loss would represent small imperfections likely to accompany the practical workings of any mechanism and could be ignored in appraisals. The social cost of carbon, at c_3 does not enter the calculation since there is no difference in societal emissions with and without the project.

If instead the cap was endogenous, the project would reduce the cap from Q_3 to Q_4, keeping the permit price constant at p_3, while the social cost of carbon falls from c_3 to c_4. The light shaded area, including both the dotted and un-dotted portions, would measure the savings in the permits bill to the airline. The small, lightly shaded dotted triangle formed by the schedules D_2, C and Q_4 would measure a small loss in efficiency, or deadweight loss resulting from a cap slightly more restrictive than would be efficient. As with the dark green triangle to its right, this small cost could be ignored.

The conclusion from the analysis of this second cap location scenario (Q_3 and Q_4) is that where the cap is efficiently set, the savings in permit costs (the permits bill) caused by the project for the promoter represent a close approximation to the social benefits of the project in terms of reduction of emissions. Whether the cap is exogenous or endogenous would make little or no difference.

Finally, take the hypothetical example of too tight a cap, represented by Q_5. Under an exogenous cap system, the project would reduce the permit price from p_5 to p_6, producing a savings equal to the area of the shaded trapezoid – including both the dotted and un-dotted parts – between schedules Q_5 and Q_6. The savings in the permits bill to the airline measures the increase in production elsewhere in the economy, thereby constituting both a private and societal benefit. The social cost of carbon remains constant at c_5 and does not enter the calculation since total societal emissions do not change with or without the project, remaining as determined by Q_5.

Under an endogenous cap the project leaves the price of permits constant at p_5 and the cap shifts from Q_5 to Q_6. This time the dotted portion of the trapezoid would constitute a welfare loss to society. The project would cause a decrease in production, valued at the shaded area (both dotted and un-dotted), out of which only the un-dotted portion of the shaded area constitutes a saving in resource cost (the emissions). The dotted portion would constitute a net loss of value to society which, under competitive conditions, would consist of loss of consumer surplus. This exemplifies a situation where the societal losses from avoiding emissions are greater than the societal cost of the emissions avoided. Another way of viewing this is by, conversely, considering a loosening of the cap from Q_6 to Q_5. The un-dotted shaded area would measure the cost of this shift in terms of increase in emissions, while the dotted area the additional value generated through gains in consumer surplus.

In terms of implications for appraisal, the most likely scenario for a system with an endogenous cap would be that described by caps Q_1 and Q_2. Indeed the rationale for making a cap endogenous is to tighten it and bring it closer to its efficient level (around Q_3 and Q_4). The analysis in this appendix then shows that when appraising a project with a loose, endogenous cap, any proportion of permits that are allocated from or to alternative production should be valued at the permit price, while any permits that could be expected to be – or prevented from being – withdrawn, should be valued at the social cost of carbon.

Notes

1 See Douglas and Miller 1974.
2 The relationship between income per capita and value of time comes hand in hand with the relationship between income per capita and labour costs. In principle, labour costs should also grow with income per capita, increasing the unit costs of a project. On the other hand, growth in income per capita generally implies growth in labour productivity, decreasing unit costs. The important thing for the investment analyst is to bear in mind that when making assumptions about growth in the value of time over the lifetime of a project, the analyst should also make assumptions about growth in labour costs and productivity. If the analyst assumes that value of time grows in real terms over time, but assumes that labour costs do not, the analyst is implicitly assuming that there are sufficient productivity gains to compensate for the growth in labour costs. See also Appendix 1.
3 The DoT recommends equal values of time for high-speed railway and air travel. It revises its estimates regularly in line with total hourly earnings in the US economy. The value of time for business travel is set at 100 per cent of total hourly earnings for all transport modes. For personal travel it is set at 70 per cent of total hourly earnings for air and high speed rail and at 50 per cent for other surface modes.
4 de Jong (2007), studying shippers and carriers in the Netherlands with stated preference techniques, reports a value of EUR 132.24 per tonne per hour, corresponding to a full freighter aircraft value of EUR 7,935 per hour for 2002. The study does not specify the reference or average aircraft size. In a subsequent, updated study (de Jong et al., 2014), using also stated preference techniques with a Dutch sample, the authors

report a value for a full freighter aircraft of EUR13,000 per hour, a 64 per cent increase relative to the previous estimate, without reporting a value per tonne. Assuming the same percentage increase as for the full aircraft, it would suggest a value, rounding, of EUR216 (=132 × 1.64).

5 Hummels and Schaur (2013), for example, approaching time as a trade barrier, finds a time cost per day equivalent to a 0.6 to 2.1 per cent ad valorem tariff. Other similar studies include Nordas 2006 and Hummels and Nathan Associates 2007.

6 See, for example, de Rus 2010 and Campbell and Brown 2016 for an introduction; and Londero 2003 for a fuller treatment.

7 See Chapter 4, section 4.1.

8 For a broad discussion of air transport and the environment see Daley 2010.

9 Such taxes, when targeting pollution, are known as Pigouvean taxes. The reader is referred to any introductory microeconomics or public economics textbook for a fuller presentation of these.

10 European Union (2018) includes the legislation and Bruninx et al. (2019) offer an analysis of the likely effects.

11 See Perino (2018) and Perino et al. (2019) for a proposed formula. A debate on the appropriateness of the suggested formulation is emerging, see Rosendahl (2019) and Perino (2019).

12 See, for example, Tsafarakis et al. 2018, Jiang and Zhang 2016, Hess et al. 2007, Ling et al. 2005, Lu and Tsai 2004, and Coldren et al. 2003. The literature of valuing service quality attributes overlaps with that of brand loyalty, augmented by the widespread presence of frequent flier programs in the airline industry. See Dolnicar et al. 2011 as well as the already referred Jiang and Zhang, 2016.

13 See Garrow 2010.

14 See, for example, Boardman et al. 2018 and de Rus 2010. A more in depth, technical analysis can be found in Just et al. 2004. For a broader treatment of transport investment in economic development see Banister and Berechman 2001. The reader should bear in mind the distinction to be made between the appraisal of economic viability, which measures changes in welfare, and impact analysis on income or employment, regardless of the net effect on welfare. See below, sections 7.5 and 7.6.

15 See Varian 1992 for a formal proof. Note should be taken that in a project appraisal context income to production factors have an opportunity cost. Therefore in a perfectly competitive economy marginal projects would tend to have an economic net present value of zero.

16 Note that Just et al. (2004, Chapter 9) find that primary markets also reflect value in secondary markets in the presence of decreasing or increasing marginal costs in the secondary market, although their presentation assumes fully vertically integrated producers, which is not the case here. In turn, the illustration here implicitly assumes some element of collusion. It abstracts from the implications of the declining marginal cost curve for the structure of the secondary (i.e. lubricants) market. With increasing returns to scale the market will not be perfectly competitive. Instead there would be some alternative, less efficient structure such as monopoly or possibly some form of co-operative oligopoly. In turn, this could have additional implications for the estimation of welfare changes resulting from the project, depending on the extent to which the cost savings are passed on to users or appropriated by the producers of lubricants. This illustration only introduces generically the types of situations where a project may have welfare implications for secondary markets.

17 This assumes that cost savings in lubricant delivery are passed on to users of lubricants. The conduct of the suppliers of lubricants may be different, with implications for the extent of welfare changes, as suggested in footnote 16. Note, however, that even if lubricant suppliers appropriate all of the cost savings, their increase in profits constitutes

a welfare gain. Other things being equal, such a gain in welfare would be less than the corresponding welfare gain had the market for lubricants enjoyed marginal cost pricing.

18 Area p_{b1}–a–d–p_{b2} also includes lubricants usage by the airport without the project. Care must be made not to double-count this benefit.

19 Care must be made not to mix a welfare loss with an increase in producer surplus that may accompany such a scenario. Just et al. (2015) show that with full vertical integration the value effects of a project or policy on a secondary market are reflected in the primary market.

20 Examples of such studies in the aviation sector are, to the knowledge of the author, centred on the airports sector. Notable examples include London and Sydney, both of which performed both CBA and CGE studies. For Sydney, the relevant studies of the Sydney Aviation Capacity Joint Study are Ernst & Young (2012a and 2012b) for CBA and CGE, respectively. For London, the relevant studies are Airports Commission (2015a and 2015b) for CBA and CGE, respectively. The Airports Commission makes it clear that the results of its CBA and CGE studies are not additive (Airports Commission, 2015b and 2015c). Mackie and Pearce (2015) review the London studies, offering insights into the type of issues likely to arise when relating CGE and CBA results. For the purposes of project decision making on economic case grounds, Mackie and Pearce favour relying on results from CBA with ad hoc adjustments in distorted secondary markets (what they call a CBA+ approach), over CGE results. The author shares this conclusion, at least until CGE is made compatible with CBA.

21 Reports and code are being made available at the project website: http://c-bridge. ulpgc.es/.

22 The possibility that land prices start to increase before a project is announced to the public should not be ruled out, particularly in conditions of poor institutional quality.

23 See Crompton 2006 for a discussion of misuses of multiplier effects within a travel context.

24 A less orthodox but perhaps more pragmatic approach would be to view labour taxes and social security contributions as necessary payments for the good functioning of society, like paying fire insurance for buildings. That would save the analyst from having to estimate shadow wages. In any case, such adjustments are rarely of sufficient magnitude relative to other project costs to make a significant difference to the outcome of an investment appraisal.

25 See Londero 2003.

26 For a more general analysis of the welfare implications of vertically and horizontally related markets with price changes see Just et al. (2004).

27 If there were no substitutes to coal for energy generation, so that the demand curve D_c would correspond to the demand for (non aviation) energy, demand in quadrant c) would be less elastic than if there were substitutes. The conclusion as to the interpretation of the shaded area under the supply curve would remain unchanged though.

28 Products A and B are substitutes when an increase (decrease) in the price of A causes an increase (decrease) in the demand – understood as an outward (inward) shift in the demand curve – of B, and likewise for the demand for product A regarding the price of product B. Product B is a complement of the demand for product A when an increase (decrease) in the price of A causes a decrease (increase) in the demand – understood as an inward (outward) shift in the demand curve – of B, and likewise for product A regarding the price of product B. Coal energy and renewable energy are substitutes. The former requires a GHG permit as an input and the latter does not. Airlines also require GHG allowances as an input and compete for them with coal generated energy. In sum, airlines and renewable energy are both substitutes in production to coal-generated energy, while airlines and renewable energy are complements in production. Note though that these conditions rely on the presence of the emissions MBM.

29 For a more developed analysis of the various welfare effects involved the reader is referred to Boardman et al. (2018) and, for a greater degree of detail still, to Just et al. (2004).
30 Airlines use offsets as inputs, just as they use permits under a cap and trade scheme as inputs. The offset producing sector may compete with other offset producers to supply such inputs to airlines and to other industrial sectors that use offsets as an input.
31 As in the case of cap and trade, the presentation assumes constant technology in the offsetting sector. A longer term perspective would incorporate technological change and would result on a different supply curve profile.

3 The basic framework

Introduction

Aviation investment projects may be classified into two broad categories: landside and airside. Landside investments would involve projects that enhance the capacity of the system to process passengers or tion, in terms both of quantity and quality. Airside projects are those that expand the capacity to handle aircraft, in terms of number of aircraft movements or aircraft size or take-off weight.

This chapter introduces the underlying conceptual models used to evaluate the returns of investments in airside and landside projects.[1] It also discusses issues that arise when building the 'with project' and 'without project' scenarios for appraisals.

3.1 Landside investments

Landside investments concern the quantity of passenger and freight throughput in the air transport system, and the quality (or level) of service offered to those transport users. This section of the chapter discusses passenger transport, but the framework applies equally to freight transport.

The market for air travel can be modelled as described in Figure 3.1. The graph presents the case of an airport, but could also be used to describe airline and air traffic management (ATM) investments.

For a certain region, g_0 is the generalised cost to the average traveller of using the local airport; this is referred to from now on as 'the airport'. The generalised cost to the same travellers of using the immediate alternative means of transport would be g_1. This alternative could be another airport located outside the region. Note that the fact that the generalised cost to the customer differs between the alternatives implies that the market is characterised by product differentiation. At the extreme, when the product differentiation is very large, the situation would be akin to a monopoly. The current situation therefore does not reflect perfectly (or highly) competitive market conditions. The implication of this issue for scenario-building is discussed in section 3.3.2 below.

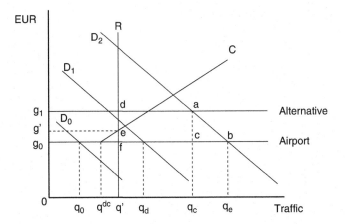

Figure 3.1 Demand and supply in landside capacity provision.

The analysis proceeds by considering the demand for which the airport represents the preferred means, or node, of travel. When demand conditions faced by the airport are as described in schedule D_0, traffic at the airport would be q_0. The airport can accommodate all passengers with an average generalised cost of g_0. As demand grows the demand curve shifts rightwards. At some point it will reach design capacity q^{dc}. From that point onwards, further demand growth will cause congestion in the terminal, creating time costs to travellers in the form of higher passenger processing times, greater likelihood of departure delays, or forcing them to travel at less preferred times. As demand grows, the cost to the average traveler will also grow, as denoted by schedule C.

Airports differ on the level of congestion they allow for in their design capacity. Generalised cost g_0 is taken to reflect the passenger processing time, and hence the level of congestion deemed acceptable and targeted by the governing bodies of the airport. The models in this book take congestion costs to mean costs imposed on passengers through the additional passenger processing time above that implied by the airport design capacity. They constitute therefore a measure of excess congestion.[2]

The airport will generally establish a certain capacity level beyond which it will begin rationing capacity and negate airlines additional check-in desks, larger boarding gates, or slots. This rationing is depicted by schedule R, taking place at a throughput of q' passengers, who would experience a generalised cost of g'. The difference in money terms between g' and g_0 along the vertical axis measures the cost of congestion to the average passenger using the airport when the airport is at capacity rationing stage.[3]

Should the airport choose not to ration capacity, as demand grows, shifting the demand schedule rightwards, airport throughput would increase beyond q', making the airport increasingly congested. At some point, congestion, and the accompanying passenger generalised cost, would reach a point where the average passenger would be indifferent between using the airport and the alternative means of travel. This situation would be depicted by the intersection of the curves C and 'Alternative', where the latter describes the generalised cost to passengers (for which the project airport is the preferred choice) of diverting to the alternative means of travel. Generally, this would consist of an alternative airport from which to access air travel, but for shorter routes it may also mean alternative surface modes of inter-city transport, such as rail. At that point, the generalised cost experienced by the average traveller would be g_1.

Returning to the rationing scenario, as demand grows beyond D_0, there is a discontinuous one-off jump of generalised cost between g' and g_1 caused by rationing. This would imply that there is some traffic that would be willing to travel through the airport if there was capacity available, but for which the cost of diverting to the alternative means of travel, at g_1, is too high. Such potential traffic will therefore not travel, and consists of *deterred* traffic. By the time demand conditions are as described by schedule D_1, such deterred traffic is measured by the difference between q_d and q'.

As demand continues to grow, once D intersects the 'Alternative' schedule to the right of R, there will be traffic that uses the alternative travel means at a generalised cost of g_1, even though it would have preferred to travel through the airport, at generalised cost g_0. This traffic is called *diverted* traffic. By the time demand grows to D_2, traffic at the local airport would be q', but there would also be substantial local traffic diverted to the alternative travel means $(q_c - q')$ and deterred traffic $(q_e - q_c)$; the latter is also called *generated* traffic.[4]

For all practical purposes, R can be taken to be the de facto capacity of the airport, which would exceed design capacity. R is the capacity at which diversion starts to take place. This is obviously a simplification, at least until traffic reaches g_1. An alternative would be to allow for diversion to take place continuously from much lower capacity than design capacity. This would involve using mathematical functions to represent increasing marginal costs up until g_1. The approach followed in this book instead splits traffic into traffic types and assigns an average cost to each type. While using an increasing marginal cost function would be theoretically neater, using average costs is simpler to work with as a practitioner, making 'back of an envelope' calculations easier to perform, a task that practice requires frequently. The alternative approaches should produce very close results. Any difference between the two would apply only to the transition until marginal costs increase to g_1.[5]

A project to expand total airport capacity beyond q' would produce benefits to three categories of passengers. First, it would save existing traffic (passengers that would use the airport both with and without the project) the cost of congestion $(g' - g_0)$, equivalent to area g'efg$_0$. Second, it would save diverted traffic $(q_c - q')$ the additional generalised cost incurred in using the alternative means of travel $(g_1 - g_0)$, equal to the area dacf. And third, it would accommodate generated traffic $(q_e - q_c)$. Such generated or deterred traffic would include passengers ranging from those who were just about to accept that they would incur g_1 to those who just about accept g_0; the latter category of passenger is called the 'marginal traveller'. Demand schedule D_2 depicts the declining reservation price (i.e. the maximum willingness to pay) of each subsequent passenger. The welfare gain to these passengers from the project would be equal to area abc, measured by the expression $((q_e - q_c) \times (g_1 - g_0))/2$, equal to half the benefits per passenger that would have accrued to the same amount of diverted passengers. The division by 2 is an approximation to the actual welfare gain, which would ultimately depend on whether the demand curve between points a and b in Figure 3.1 is actually a straight line. Such an approximation is called the 'rule of a half'.[6]

As is mentioned at the beginning of this section this same model can be applied to the case of an airline. If the airline has a monopoly on a route, the analysis can be replicated conceptualising the airline in place of the airport. The 'Alternative' would then represent either an alternative airline offering the same city pair but with an intermediate connection, or the road, rail, or sea transport modes. If instead the airline competes with other airlines also offering direct services on the route, the alternative would become other airlines offering alternative, less convenient departure times, or fewer departure frequencies. If the competing airlines offer schedules of comparable quality, the generalised costs become very close, products are less differentiated and the situation becomes close to perfect competition.

Table 3.1 illustrates numerically the framework with a hypothetical project to expand the capacity of an airport from 5 million passengers to 10 million. Columns a and b in Table 3.1 total 10 million passengers each. The 5 million passenger figures in column a correspond to q^{dc} in Figure 3.1, consisting of the maximum amount of passengers that can be handled at the desirable level of service or congestion (so, $q^{dc} = 5$ m passengers). Take D_2 in Figure 3.1 as the future demand curve that the airport will face once traffic reaches the additional design capacity supplied by the project, so that q_e corresponds to 10 million passengers. As mentioned, such design capacity measures normally include already an element of congestion, the extent of which depends on the minimum level of service (or maximum level of congestion) that the airport governing bodies targets as *desirable*. Therefore, congestion experienced when traffic exceeds q^{dc} should be understood as excess congestion over and above the congestion deemed desirable, the latter being determined by the targeted level of service.

Without the capacity expansion project, traffic at the airport could still grow substantially beyond 5 million passengers without experiencing diversion. Such diversion would take place once the demand schedule intersects point d in Figure 3.1. Let us say that diversion starts once traffic reaches 6.7 million passengers per year, corresponding to q' in Figure 3.1 (so, q' = 6.7 m passengers, and $q' - q^{dc} = 1.7$ m passengers). Using standard transport planning terminology, such 6.7 million passengers corresponds to 'existing' or 'normal' traffic, consisting of the amount of traffic that can be expected to travel

Table 3.1 Traffic types with and without project for a hypothetical airport capacity expansion project

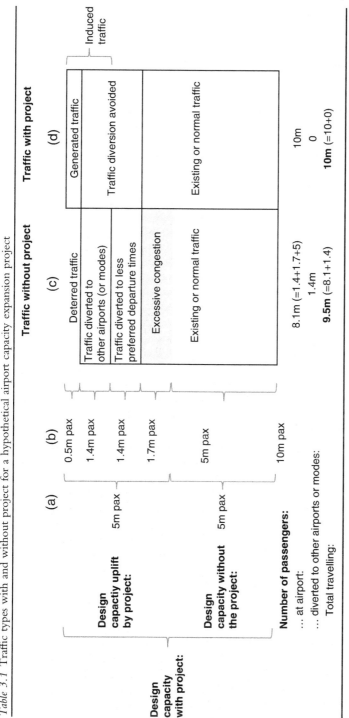

through the airport either with or without the project at the minimum *acceptable* level of service (that implied by schedule R in Figure 3.1).

Any additional traffic beyond 6.7 million per year will incur diversion, which can take two alternative forms. First, substantially altering the travel time at which passengers can actually travel relative to their preferred travelling time (diversion in time). And second, travelling through alternative means, either another, less preferred airport or another transport mode (diversion in mode).[7] Let us say for simplicity that such diverted traffic is split equally between those diverting in time while travelling from the project airport, and those diverting to alternative travel means, with 1.4 million passengers each. Table 3.1 includes these figures in column b, reflected also in column c. Once demand grows over time to reach D_2, the aggregate of both types of diverted traffic corresponds to $q_c - q'$ in Figure 3.1 (that is, $q_c - q' = 2.8$ m passengers). Once demand is at that level, there would also be $q_e - q_c$ of generated passengers. Recall that q_e corresponds to the 10 million passenger design capacity of the airport, implying that generated traffic would be 0.5 million passengers ($q_e - q_c = 0.5$ m passengers).

The effects of the capacity expansion project can be visualised in Table 3.1 by comparing columns c and d. Table 3.1 assumes that traffic in the system is already at 10 million passengers. That is, it corresponds to the situation in Figure 3.1 when demand is at D_2 and q_e reaches 10 million passengers. Then, summing up, for 1.7 million out of 6.7 million of existing traffic the project would eliminate congestion costs. The project would also avoid the cost of diversion to a total of 2.8 million passengers. In addition, it would generate 0.5 million passengers. Remember the terminology that traffic generated by (i.e. 'with') the project can also be depicted as traffic 'deterred' by the absence of (i.e. 'without') the project.

In terms of the total travel market, the difference in total trips without and with the project is only the 0.5 m passengers of generated (deterred) passengers with (without) the project. During the year when the airport with the project would see a traffic of 10 million (third to last row of column d) in Table 3.1, the 'without project' scenario would see the airport having a traffic of 8.1 million (third to last row of column c). Many of these 8.1 million passengers would be incurring a higher generalised cost than the g_0 (in Figure 3.1) that all passengers would experience 'with the project': 1.7 million passengers would be incurring excessive congestion (g' in Figure 3.1) and 1.4 million would be incurring diversion to a less preferred travel time (g_1 in Figure 3.1).

The benefits of the project consist then of avoiding these higher generalised costs, avoiding diversion costs (also of g_1) to another 1.4 million passengers to other less preferred travel means, and avoiding the costs associated to traffic deterrence (equal to $(g_1 - g_0)/2$) to 0.5 million passengers.

It is worth noting in passing that the difference in traffic at the airport with (10 million) and without (8.1 million) the project, can be referred to as 'induced' traffic. This is made up of both traffic diverted to other travel means and generated traffic.

In practice, the analysis depicted in Figure 3.1 can be applied to estimate project returns when there is sufficient permanent differentiation in product attributes between the alternatives, with corresponding differences in generalised costs. This usually involves airports competing with other airports or other transport modes, or air navigation service providers (ANSPs) serving airlines that can choose different routes with alternative ATM service providers, which may happen mostly on long-haul trips. When the competitors offer similar products, so that the generalised costs offered to users do not differ much among competitors, the outcome approaches perfect competition, in which case, as discussed in Chapter 2, section 2.7.1, the benefits of the project would be the financial returns after correcting for any price distortion. The corollary of this discussion is that the difference between g_0 and g_1 measures the degree of competitive advantage (in terms of granting the customer additional value) granted by the project to the promoter, in a way that promoter revenues cannot measure. Measures of competitive advantage are illustrated in project examples analysed later in the book.[8]

Likewise, the analysis is valid for freight transport. For most freight categories, however, the room for product differentiation through generalised cost is somewhat narrower than for passengers, especially in terms of choice of departure and arrival airports. This is because users may have lower values of time and be less sensitive to departure time and in-vehicle time, although much difference could be expected across product categories.

In terms of inter-modal competition in freight, air transport as a whole can still develop definitive competitive advantages. The more perishable the good the higher the willingness to pay for time savings and, hence, the greater the responsiveness to time differences. In extreme cases, some industries such as year-round intercontinental delivery of fresh flowers can only be viable through air transport. In such cases, the absence of air transport would imply that deterred traffic would consist of the local flower export business as a whole. The benefits to the local economy can be substantial (more on this in section 3.3.3 below).

3.2 Airside investments

Airside investments aim at increasing the number of aircraft movements or the size of aircraft a system can process. These outcomes constitute two sources of benefits. First, an increase in the capacity to handle aircraft movements implies an increase in departure frequency. This has the effect of reducing the frequency delay – or the time the average passenger or freight shipper has to wait until the next departing flight – and hence the behavioural or user's generalised cost of transport. Relevant investments include building a new runway or taxiway in an airport, or increasing the capacity of ATM through, say, investing in ATM equipment to enable reduced vertical separation.

The second source of benefit arises from enabling the operation of larger aircraft, which brings about improvements in operating costs because larger aircraft are cheaper to operate on a per-seat basis. These types of investments would apply exclusively to airports. There is no ATM equivalent to this second benefit, as smaller, propeller aircraft tend to be slower, requiring more ATM capacity. That is, there is an inverse relationship between aircraft size and ATM capacity requirements, and a direct relationship between aircraft size and airport capacity requirements. Still, ANSPs can influence aircraft size by constraining airspace flight movement capacity.

However, there is often a trade-off between the two sources of benefit. Airlines, for example, when replacing or expanding capacity, weigh the extent to which the new capacity should take the form of more aircraft or larger aircraft. Emphasising more aircraft would enable greater departure frequency and more direct destinations to be offered, improving the quality of the airline's schedule; whereas emphasising larger aircraft creates the potential for cheaper tickets; it may also have some comfort advantages.[9]

The decision of airlines and airports are not independent. In deciding on fleet composition, airlines need to consider constraints on airport capacity. For example, constraints on the availability of slots at their hub airports mean that airlines are forced to tilt their decision towards greater aircraft size, rather than greater departure frequency. Similarly, airports that expand capacity tend to take into account the capacity requirements of the fleets of the main airlines serving the airport, which may require adjusting terminal, apron, taxiway, and runway sizes.

Considering airlines and airports together, the trade-off between aircraft size and departure frequency is depicted in Figure 3.2. The downward-sloping FD curve represents the marginal frequency delay, which decreases with flight frequency. The monetary value of the frequency delay is measured along the left vertical axis. For a given number of seats supplied,

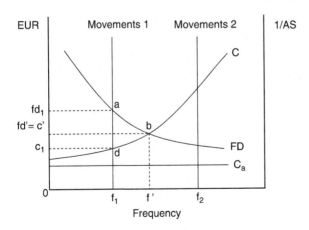

Figure 3.2 Costs in airside capacity provision.

frequency delay varies directly with average aircraft size (AS) – that is, for a given number of seats, the larger the aircraft size the lower the departure frequency and the higher the frequency delay. Therefore, the FD schedule increases (decreases inversely) with aircraft size, as depicted on the right vertical axis.

The horizontal C_a schedule represents the marginal cost to the airport of adding an extra flight, assuming constant returns to scale to provision of airside capacity. The C curve represents the total cost, including both airport and aircraft costs. It is upward-sloping because, for a given number of seats, as frequency increases the average size of aircraft decreases, increasing per seat costs since smaller aircraft have higher unit costs.

The vertical Movements 1 and Movements 2 schedules represent frequency capacity of the system before and after airside expansion, respectively. The Movements 1 schedule can be thought of as the departure frequency capacity of the airport with only one runway, equal to f_1, and Movements 2 as the frequency capacity adding a second runway, higher at f_2. The 'Movements' schedules can also represent two airspace capacity levels, before and after equipment enhancement.

When airside capacity is at Movements 1 and departure frequency is constrained at f_1, the marginal benefit of adding a departure frequency is fd_1 on the left vertical axis. This is higher than the marginal cost of decreasing aircraft size, equal to c_1. By expanding airside capacity to Movements 2, flight frequency would increase to f', which would be accompanied by a decrease in aircraft size. At that point the marginal benefit of improving frequency delay is equal to the marginal cost of decreasing aircraft size (fd' = c'). The benefit of expanding airside capacity from Movements 1 to Movements 2 would be equal to the area abd.[10]

3.3 Scenario-building

Investment appraisals aim at measuring what producers and – when the appraisal is economic – consumers and society at large gain as a result of an investment, relative to what could be expected to happen should the investment not take place. That is, project benefits and costs are measured in incremental terms. Investment appraisal therefore relies on building at least two scenarios. First, the project, or 'with project' scenario, describing what is expected to happen regarding key input and output variables during the implementation and operation of the project. And second, the counterfactual or 'without project' scenario, including assumptions about what could be expected to happen should the project not be carried out. The degree of competition in the market where the investment project takes place plays a central role in building the scenarios. A high degree of competition would imply that competitors would tend to offer similar products to those offered by the project promoter, restricting the options of the promoter in the 'without project' scenario. If instead, competition is feeble or practically nonexistent, the project promoter has greater discretion and the analyst would have to make assumptions about the 'without project' scenario in two respects: the behavior of the promoter; and the amount of available capacity in the market from close substitutes should the project not be carried out.

This section of the chapter addresses these issues in turn. Beforehand, however, it deals with another issue that is the subject of much variation in scenarios built up in project appraisal in practice, namely: whose benefits and costs are accounted for? Are they those of the world at large, the nationals of a particular country, or local residents? The results of an investment appraisal will differ if particular groups are not accounted for, or if the benefits of some groups are given greater weight.

3.3.1 *Whose benefits and costs?*

Financial appraisals include promoter income and costs and consider all users regardless of their provenance. Economic appraisals should include benefits and costs from all users and non-users affected by a project, including competitors, regardless of their provenance. The analysis then answers the question whether the project constitutes an efficient allocation of resources and, therefore, whether the world would be better off with the project.

Sometimes economic appraisals are conducted paying attention to who benefits, who pays and who loses. Decision-makers may have distributional objectives, may be concerned with benefits to locals or nationals, or may be particularly interested in revenues from non-residents.[11] There is not necessarily anything methodologically wrong with such appraisals, so long as the analyst and the decision-maker are aware that the appraisal is more concerned with distributional issues than with economic efficiency. In addition, when such distinctions among stakeholders are made, building scenarios that totally exclude groups who are deemed not relevant may create confusion in the calculation process by, for example, making the measurement of capacity utilisation more difficult. It is generally a better approach to consider all stakeholders in the estimation process and then attribute different weights to the benefits and costs of different groups.

The analyst should be aware that by disregarding costs and benefits to specific groups, the appraisal exercise runs a risk of reaching counterproductive outcomes. In particular, aviation projects enjoy cost economies through capacity utilisation (economies of density), vehicle or facility size (economies of scale), and joint service to different traffic categories, such as passenger and freight (economies of scope), as well as network benefits to passengers (range of departure frequency and destinations in hub-and-spoke networks). In such contexts passengers exert positive externalities on each other and it is erroneous to assume that subtracting the benefits of one traffic category leaves the benefits to other categories unchanged. For example, an air route from A to B may enjoy a departure frequency of four flights a day with low costs per seat through use of larger aircraft only because traffic density is increased by connecting passengers from other destinations and of other nationalities. Without those connecting passengers the route may sustain a lower departure frequency and higher unit costs (through use of smaller aircraft), reducing the welfare of origin – destination users from A and B.

This book follows a 'world economy' viewpoint in the construction of scenarios, ignoring issues of provenance or distribution, as is done in traditional financial appraisals, and following the standard tenets of welfare economics.

3.3.2 Degree of competition

The need to build an ad hoc counterfactual scenario in investment appraisal is governed by the competitive conditions that characterise the market where the investment project takes place. The degree of competition ranges from a perfectly competitive market, where the number of competitors is or can be very large, to a natural monopoly, where there can be only a single viable producer. In between these two extremes there is a continuum array of possibilities of market conditions, for which industrial organisation (or industrial economics) offers a number of generic models, such as duopoly, oligopoly, and monopolistic competition. These models are built from premises about issues such as barriers to entry, cost economies, synergies, and product differentiation, among others.[12]

It is very rare to find either perfectly competitive markets, where producers readily substitute each other at no cost to the consumer or to society, or natural monopolies that have no substitutes at all. Moreover, in practice there is always some degree of product differentiation, if only because of brand image. For investment appraisal purposes, the issue is one of judging the degree of competition in the market where the investment project takes place. The key judgement to make is whether, in the absence of the project, there are other firms (existing or potential entrants) that would be able to supply the market at the same or very similar conditions as the promoter. If the answer is yes, the project can be considered to be carried out in competitive markets. In that case, there is no need to build an ad hoc counterfactual, since in the absence of the project, some competitor would supply the consumers otherwise supplied by the promoter, and do so at the same, or very similar, quality and price. In effect, the counterfactual is simply the opportunity cost of the resources invested in the project.

If instead the answer is no, then in the absence of the project the consumer is dependent on the conduct of the promoter. The consumer has either no alternative supplier, or would experience switching costs to access the closest substitute, involving a loss of welfare. In such a case the analyst must make assumptions about what supply conditions the market would face should the promoter not carry out the project, meaning that the analyst must design an ad hoc counterfactual scenario. Building a counterfactual scenario would involve two critical dimensions: the actions assumed by the promoter should the project not be carried out; and the assumed capacity available in the market from close substitutes should the project not be carried out. These two issues are treated in turn in the next two sections of this chapter: 3.3.3 and 3.3.4.

Table 3.2 summarises the generic competitive situations that the analyst is likely to find when appraising aviation projects. Whereas the table is self explanatory, three issues may merit further explanation. First, note that it does not really matter whether the underlying competitive structure resembles more a perfectly competitive market or an oligopoly. In either case, should the project not be carried out, the market will be supplied by another competitor. In the case of perfect competition this would occur either through established players or through new entrants. In the case of oligopoly it would be by existing players expanding production.

The second issue follows from the first. The fact that under sufficiently competitive conditions substitutes are available in the primary market has implications also for the impact of the project on secondary markets, whether vertically or horizontally related. If it is assumed that without the project the same or a similar product would be supplied anyway, no effect on secondary markets can be unambiguously attributed to the project. As will be seen, this is particularly relevant for the aircraft manufacturing sector, which tends to be competitive. There, the output – namely, the aircraft – is operated in a (vertically related) secondary market – the airline market – which may be subject to distortions, such as externalities. It is legitimate to attribute such externalities in the secondary market to a project (which takes place in the primary market) if the project affects perceivably the conditions in the primary market, which in turn affects the conditions in the secondary market, leading to more externalities. For example, if an aircraft manufacturing project affects prices in the primary market, and hence affects the total number of aircraft sold, there will be more aircraft in operation and more external costs in the secondary market as a direct consequence of the project. But if the primary market is sufficiently competitive, so that in the absence of the project other aircraft makers would take up the production otherwise carried out by the project promoter, no changes can unambiguously be attributed to the project in the secondary market, including external costs.

Note that the issue refers to whether the project distinctively affects output (or prices) in the secondary market, an issue discussed in Chapter 2, section 2.7.3 This is a related issue to that of adjusting prices from secondary markets affecting directly the primary market, such as taxes on inputs to the project, discussed in Chapter 2, section 2.3.2.

Third, where the promoter has market power – meaning monopoly situations and, to a lesser extent, under monopolistic competition – refraining from carrying out investments may involve serious consequences to the local economy. For example, preventing a remote location from accommodating growing demand for air transport services by denying it additional airport capacity may disrupt the economic development of the region. This issue is discussed below in section 3.3.4, but it is worth highlighting at this stage that such scenarios are sometimes

Table 3.2 Competitive conditions and scenario-building in investment appraisal

Degree of competition	Key characteristics	Instances in aviation	Treatment in investment appraisal
Perfect competition	• Many competitors • Many potential entrants and no barriers to entry • No product differentiation and no pricing power by any firm • Profitability kept at opportunity cost of capital	• Airlines in dense route between uncongested airports • Inter-hub competition on intercontinental markets • suppliers of standardised components in aeronautics	• No need to define ad hoc counterfactual • Secondary markets remain unaffected by project • Lack of project has no wider consequences
Oligopoly	• Few participating firms • Little or no product differentiation • High entry barriers but incumbents keep each other in check • Higher profitability than in perfectly competitive market	• Large airlines competing within a hub • Manufacturers of 'industry workhorse' aircraft models • Airports on a multi-airport city	• No need to define ad hoc counterfactual • Secondary markets remain unaffected by project • Lack of project has no wider consequences
Monopolistic competition	• Differentiated product gives company market power in market segment • Entry possible but may be costly • Company enjoys monopoly rents while there is no entry, although demand curve reflects competition from differentiated products	• Airline offering 'low-cost' services from a distant airport • Aircraft manufacturer on niche aircraft segment • Airports in nearby cities with overlapping catchment areas • ANSPs on alternative routes	• Need to define ad hoc counterfactual • Secondary markets may be affected by project • Continued lack of project may involve non-extreme wider consequences

(Continued)

Table 3.2 (Continued)

Degree of competition	Key characteristics	Instances in aviation	Treatment in investment appraisal
Monopoly	• Only one firm in the market • Competitive entry de facto impossible • The firm sets price and quantity to maximise profit, unless subject to government regulation	• Sole airport on remote island • Sole air service to remote location • Approach or domestic ANSP • ANSP serving large areas of oceanic airspace	• Need to define ad hoc counterfactual • Secondary markets may be affected by project • Continued lack of project may involve extreme assumptions

erroneously used in situations where there is de facto competition, even if the facility at hand, say the local airport, may be perceived as a local monopoly. Many subsidised airports are better closed down than expanded (with subsidies) if there is adequate surface transport to alternative airports. Shutting down the airport may actually help the local economy by saving it unnecessary subsidies.

The same logic underlies the often used (and erroneous) arguments of impacts on the local economy as a justification for building local airports. If sufficiently good air services are available to airports in nearby cities, there is a good chance that the local airport (despite its apparent local monopoly position) will constitute a wasteful investment. Many of the benefits registered by the project would constitute transfers from the alternative, nearby facility. The key is to define well the competitive environment. The sole service provider in town may still be engaged in monopolistic competition with service providers in neighbouring locations.[13]

3.3.3 Counterfactual behaviour by the promoter

The previous section of this chapter discussed how a sufficient degree of competition does away with the need to define an ad hoc counterfactual scenario describing what would happen in the market if the promoter did not carry out the project. Where competition exists, so long as the project is sufficiently profitable, competitors will carry out the project if the promoter fails to do so. Where competition is sufficiently imperfect to grant the promoter a large degree of market power, promoter behaviour in the absence of the project is not forthcoming. Defining an ad hoc counterfactual scenario is necessary in order to compare the project with what could be expected to occur without it. There are three basic types of such ad hoc counterfactual scenarios regarding promoter behaviour, as follows:

1   Do nothing: This assumes that the counterfactual to the project is that no investment takes place at all and, hence, that the capacity will gradually deteriorate, reducing the future ability of the facility to accommodate traffic. This type of 'without project' scenario is suitable for projects that consist of facility rehabilitation.
2   Do minimum: The 'without project' scenario assumes that there will be sufficient investment to keep the existing capacity operational. It is a suitable counterfactual for capacity expansion projects. The investment analysis would compare the project against making the necessary investments to keep installed capacity operational for the full life of the project.
3   Do something (else): The 'with project' scenario is already a 'do something' scenario. A 'do something (else)' scenario would consist of an alternative approach to meet the objectives of the project. It is therefore an appropriate counterfactual for analysing project options, once it has been recognised that 'something' must be done. For example, an airport might expand capacity by building a second terminal or by

expanding an existing terminal. A cargo airline might replace an ageing fleet of freighters by buying new freighter aircraft or by converting passenger aircraft into freighters.

A common source of error in scenario-building involves mixing counterfactuals 1 and 2. This might happen when a management team confronts the question 'do we expand capacity?' and then carries out the investment analysis by comparing the project against a 'do nothing' scenario, instead of a 'do minimum'. By setting 'do nothing' as the counterfactual to the project, the question that management is really asking is 'do we expand the airport or do we let it slowly degrade?' which is not the same as 'do we expand the airport or keep capacity at current levels?' If what management mean to ask is the latter question, but they define the analysis through the former question, they will tend to overestimate the returns of the capacity expansion, which may lead them to take a wrong decision, probably by overinvesting.

The third type of counterfactual refers to what is often known in planning as 'options analysis', not to be mixed with real options analysis in economics. Depending on what the remit of the analyst is, it may not be enough to compare a project against a 'do nothing' or 'do minimum'. The analyst may be asked to check whether there are better project alternatives (the other options) that would maximise value for the company or for society. In competitive situations, not following the best alternative opens the way for a competitor to adopt it and develop a competitive advantage.

3.3.4 Counterfactual capacity

Passenger behaviour in the 'without project' scenario will be determined by how much alternative capacity is available – both from the promoter and from substitutes – and under what conditions. When markets are competitive, the answer is straightforward: in the absence of the project, competitors would supply a similar amount of capacity, and at similar price and quality conditions, to what the promoter would supply with the project. However, when competition is poor, the amount of capacity available in the market should the project not take place may not be obvious. And yet, knowing the counterfactual capacity is necessary for the analyst to estimate both diverted and generated traffic. This gives raise to two potential problems. The first is that it is not always possible for the analyst to be certain about available capacity without the project. When that is the case it is quite likely that the analyst will have to contemplate the possibility that, at some point in the project life, any counterfactual capacity would entail much poorer generalised cost conditions. This leads to the second problem, which is that even when the capacity conditions in the alternative scenario are known but are much inferior to those supplied by the project, the analyst may be forced to make extreme assumptions in the 'without project' scenario, which would involve difficult to quantify knock-on effects on the local economy.

To illustrate the discussion that follows, let us return to Figure 3.1 above and assume that it consists of an airport project. Generated traffic is $q_e - q_c$, and diverted traffic $q_c - q'$. Say that the difference in generalised cost between the 'with project' and 'without project' scenarios consists of two hours of traveller time for the average passenger. That is, the difference between g_1 and g_0 on the vertical axis of Figure 3.1 is accounted for by two hours worth of passenger time alone. In the case of an airport, those two hours can refer to the additional time incurred by driving to the alternative airport, or to the average delay to an alternative, less convenient departure time at the project airport. To simplify, it is also assumed that this remains the case per passenger for the entire life of the project, which is why the schedules relating generalised cost g to traffic are horizontal.

Such a scenario carries with it an implicit assumption, which becomes increasingly artificial as one looks further into the future within the project lifespan. The implicit assumption is that there is sufficient existing capacity in the airport where the project will take place (the project airport), and/or in the alternative airport, to accommodate all diverted traffic throughout the life of the project. In reality, this may be so only in very particular circumstances involving substantial overcapacity during off-peak periods at the project airport and/or in the alternative airport. Traffic diverted to the alternative airport in the 'without project' scenario will use up capacity at the alternative airport that was originally planned for traffic in the more immediate catchment area of that airport. At some point in the future, the growing traffic diverted from the project airport to the alternative airport will bring forward in time any need for capacity increase at the alternative airport. Therefore, a realistic 'without project' scenario may involve assuming capital investments in the alternative airport a few years into the project life. Such an assumption would be in line with the underlying assumption in economic appraisal that 'life continues' in the absence of the project: the economy continues to invest in capacity to adjust to the circumstances without the project. This brings us into the conundrum that the 'without project' scenario may involve an investment equivalent to that in the 'with project' scenario at the project airport, but at an alternative airport and possibly further into the future. In effect, the investment appraisal then becomes a planning appraisal where the investment is not questioned, what is being appraised is rather whether it is better for the investment to take place through the project under consideration or through some other operator.

The conundrum is all the more puzzling for traffic which in the 'without project' scenario is diverted to inferior off-peak flight times within the project airport. At one point there will be no capacity left at inferior times. The 'without project' scenario would reasonably have to include investment in additional capacity. That is, the alternative to the project would be the project itself. Alternatively the 'without project' scenario would soon imply extravagant assumptions.

To see this, let us consider the case where there is no alternative airport, and where the existing airport has substantial market power. A hypothetical extreme case would be a remote island with a single, highly congested airport. Here, the alternative to air transport would be much inferior – say an eight-hour flight would have to be substituted by a week-long ship voyage. The delay experienced by diverted traffic (to inconvenient flight schedules) will grow longer over time as the airport faces growing demand and congestion. As a result, a growing share of traffic in the 'with project' scenario will constitute traffic generated by the project, rather than diverted traffic. This is illustrated in Figure 3.3, which restates Figure 3.1, leaving the now non-applicable 'alternative' generalised cost schedule in the background as an intermittent dash-and-dot line. Figure 3.3 also introduces an alternative exponential cost line C_{exp}, depicting exponentially growing delays as the airport gets increasingly congested even during less preferred travelling times (off-peak would no longer be a valid description as the airport will tend to become equally busy throughout the day). Finally, for clarity Figure 3.3 also removes demand curve D_1.

In Figure 3.1 traffic generated with the project (or deterred without the project) was $q_e - q_c$, and diverted traffic $q_c - q'$. Now, in Figure 3.3, assuming that the generalised cost experienced by travellers relates to traffic as depicted by schedule C, generated traffic grows its share of project traffic to $q_e - q_{c2}$. In the 'without project' scenario, if rationing is implemented as depicted in schedule R, an amount of traffic equal to q' could be expected to travel at reasonable times, experiencing a generalised cost of g', and $q_{c2} - q'$ traffic will experience diversion to less than preferred departure times, causing their generalised cost to increase to g_2. Perhaps more realistically, the schedule delay and associated diversion costs will grow exponentially as depicted by schedule C_{exp}, with traffic experiencing increasingly higher costs as available flight times are pushed into more inconvenient times. Deterred (or generated) traffic would grow to $q_e - q_{c3}$, and diverted traffic would diminish to $q_{c3} - q'$. Soon, thereafter, as C_{exp} tends towards verticality, additional demand for air travel will be deterred from travelling altogether and the costs imposed on travellers will be ever-growing.[14]

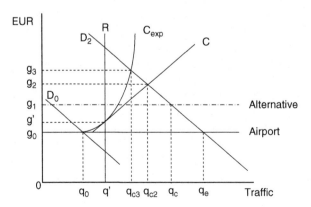

Figure 3.3 Alternative counterfactual capacity conditions in the presence of market power.

An ever-rising generalised cost g up the vertical axis in the 'without project' scenario will imply extravagant assumptions in the investment appraisal exercise. Denying an area access to highly demanded airport capacity when alternative transport means are much poorer – as tends to be the case in medium- to long-haul air passenger transport – would eventually start preventing local firms from generating economies of scale and prompt industry relocation. The 'with project' and 'without project' scenarios would have to assume differential knock-on effects on the local economy, affecting productivity and income levels.[15] The costs of the 'without project' scenario become very large, dwarfing any costs of carrying out the project, leaving virtually any airport project, however costly, worthwhile. Quantification of benefits and costs both to users and to the local economy becomes difficult, rendering the exercise highly speculative.

The analyst faces two possibilities then. One is to use consumer surplus on the primary market as a first approximation to benefits which will be, in any case, enormous and which is likely to render any reasonable project as economically viable. The second is trying to estimate the dislocation caused to the local economy. The exercise is complex because of the many sectors involved and the computational difficulty of attempting to estimate the effects on each of them. The exercise would necessitate a change in estimation method towards computable general equilibrium (CGE), modeling the regional economy.[16] Either way, a key point to take note of is that, in such an exercise, most of the traffic growth with the project will constitute generated traffic.

In practice though, appraisals in circumstances where the facility is vital for the local economy are likely to consist of comparisons of project alternatives. The exercise then becomes one of planning, about project conception and timing, rather than of seeking to determine whether a project should take place at all.

3.3.5 Producer surplus

This section briefly addresses three issues regarding producer surplus that are the source of frequent confusion. The first is that when dealing with the producer surplus of a project, the analysis does not measure promoter profitability as a whole, but the incremental profits that result from the project. That is, the difference between the profits that the operator makes with the project and the profits that the operator could be expected to make in the absence of the project. So it is possible for an airline, say, to make a bad investment in aircraft, one that generates losses, while the airline remains profitable. The link between the appraisal of the investment project and the wider profitability of the airline is that, other things being equal, the negative returns shown in the investment appraisal exercise will bring about a lower degree of profitability to the airline as a whole, following the implementation of the project, relative to the profitability the airline would have achieved had the project not been carried out.

The second issue relates only to the economic profitability of the project, not to the financial profitability of the promoter. When looking at society at large, the incremental profits to take into account are both those of the project and those of the alternative service that users would have used had the project not taken place, regardless of whether that alternative service were run by the promoter or by an alternative operator. So, if one investment project simply switches traffic from one service to another (diverted traffic) and the profits of both services are equal, total producer surplus, as far as society is concerned, remains unchanged. On an economic appraisal, only profits arising from generated (or deterred) traffic, that is, traffic that would not travel at all should the investment project not take place, amount to a net gain in producer surplus, and hence in social welfare. Profit from diverted traffic would cancel out.

Finally, the analyst must be careful to distinguish between a producer surplus gain that results from added capacity and one that results from increased prices. Price changes involving supernormal profits constitute welfare transfers between consumers and producers; they also generate deadweight losses. Such a situation will be illustrated in Chapter 7, section 7.1.2, discussing investments in the aeronautical sector under conditions of monopolistic competition.

3.3.6 Conclusion

When carrying out an investment appraisal, the analyst should first identify the competitive nature of the market concerned. The key assumption to make is whether in the absence of the project there are other firms that would be able to supply the market at similar conditions – as measured by the generalised cost of transport – as the promoter. If yes, there is no need to build an ad hoc counterfactual scenario. The counterfactual is simply the opportunity cost of the resources invested in the project. If instead the promoter enjoys a degree of market power, the alternative to the project may involve costs to the consumer and the supply conditions must be defined. The counterfactual scenario would have two dimensions: the actions of the promoter without the project, and the capacity conditions available in the market to the user without the project, by the promoter or by other operators. Regarding the counterfactual line of action of the promoter, the analyst must see that the type of action chosen, whether 'do nothing', 'do minimum' or 'do something (else)' matches the purpose of the project and, hence, the question that the analysis is aiming to answer. Each of those types of counterfactual is suitable for rehabilitation, capacity expansion and evaluation of alternatives, respectively.

When the alternative to the project is much inferior to the project in terms of generalised cost, the gain in consumer surplus in the primary market alone will render almost any conceivable project viable. The without project scenario in any case becomes highly speculative. Fortunately in such situations the appraisal is likely to consist of a planning exercise, comparing project options and timing, rather than of establishing whether a project is needed at all.

Notes

1 A formal presentation of the models that follow is available in Jorge and de Rus 2004.

2 Congestion begins happening at peak hours. As congestion grows the number of hours per year when the airport experiences congestion increases. Following the traditional IATA terminal design criteria, most airports plan for level of service C (IATA 2004). It is not infrequent to find airports that target the higher level of service B, and less frequent to find airports that target the lower level of service D. In the revised IATA-ACI design criteria (IATA-ACI 2014, further updated in IATA- ACI 2019, see Renner and Wielgus, 2015, for a summary), airports now target an 'optimum' level of service, which corresponds approximately to the former IATA level of service C. Design capacity therefore can involve different targeted degrees of congestion, specific to the airport under appraisal. In addition, airports also vary on the degree to which in practice they allow service levels to differ from their targeted standards.

3 This congestion cost is incurred by the users of the facility. However, in network industries, like air transport, underperformance in one node may cause disruption in other nodes, generating further costs to users elsewhere in the network. Any such costs caused by the project under appraisal should be incorporated into the calculation of economic returns. Notionally, they can be treated as the project affecting costs on secondary markets, discussed on section 2.7.3 of Chapter 2. The magnitude of the delay is project specific and relies on models of the network surrounding the airport. The US FAA has long recognised the relevance of system-wide delay propagation (see FAA 1999) and has been pursuing innovative research in this area (see FAA 2010). However, the evidence is so far very much focused on delays to aircraft rather than to passengers. The two may differ because passenger missed connections may mean that delays to passengers may be longer than delays to aircraft. Since this book is focused on costs to passengers, and investment analysts would find evidence on costs to passengers hard to come by, the issue is ignored from the project examples. However, as evidence on passenger delays emerges in the future, it is a cost item that should become conventional on economic appraisals in aviation. See note 8 on section 4.1 of Chapter 4 for a tentative illustration.

4 Traffic ($q_e - q_c$) is deterred in the sense that it is deterred from travelling by the absence of the project, and it is generated in that it travels only because of the project. The terms 'deterred' and 'generated' can be used interchangeably.

5 Beyond g_1 all additional passengers would simply divert to the alternative airport or transport mode. The same g_1 cap would also apply to passengers that, without the project, still travel from the project airport but are diverted to much less preferred departure times. They would not experience a higher cost than g_1 in travelling from the project airport, otherwise they would divert to the alternative airport or mode.

6 Formally, by 'rule of a half' is meant the whole trapezoid area dabf, even though it is only generated traffic that is divided by half. Presumably the reason is that the formula for the area of a trapezoid used to measure the welfare gain jointly to existing, diverted, and generated traffic uses a division by a half. A related issue is whether welfare gains to diverted traffic should be divided by 2 or not, which will depend on the extent to which diverted traffic can be considered as existing traffic. It is common in the literature to find that diverted traffic is also divided by half (see World Bank 2005). However, that is generally justified where diversion occurs because of a lowering in the relative generalised cost between the transport modes between which diversion occurs, but not when it is a result of removing a capacity constraint. In the current context, the term 'diverted' is used for air transport traffic that uses alternative airports as a less preferred choice because of lack of capacity in the project airport. For short-haul routes, such diverted traffic may also use modes that are available to the user at a generalised cost no greater than that of conducting the trip through an alternative airport. Diverted traffic that results from a constraint in capacity would have used the airport just as existing traffic does, had there been sufficient capacity available. There is

no reason to divide by half the surplus of such traffic, since their gain in welfare from the project is as high as the welfare gain for existing traffic. In practice, since such distinctions among traffic categories are generally very demanding in terms of passenger data, a pragmatic alternative would be to treat diverted traffic as homogeneous by assuming that diverted traffic shares common characteristics besides an average value of time, such as location relative to the two airports, implying that marginal and average cost of diversion are equal for that traffic category, removing the need to divide by 2 the welfare gain to diverted traffic.

7 This concept of diversion is not to be confused with the concept of diversion used by Eurocontrol, for which diversions are flights that land on airports different from those where they were scheduled to land (see Eurocontrol 2018).

8 For airports see Chapter 4, section 4.2; and for airlines see Chapter 6, section 6.3. For a discussion of the link between generalised cost, competitive advantage, and valuation, see Jorge-Calderón 2013.

9 There is some evidence that passengers attach a comfort value to larger aircraft. See, for example, Coldren et al. 2003 and Ghobrial 1993. However, as is argued in Chapter 2, section 2.6, comfort issues are ignored. More generally, Ussinova et al. 2018 offer a succinct literature review of studies addressing the departure frequency vs. aircraft size trade-off and offer insights into competitor reaction.

10 Note that by building the second runway there would be – at least initially – excess runway capacity. While this may well be the welfare maximising option, generally traffic growth means that capacity is eventually filled. Supplying facilities that operate at less than full capacity stems from technological indivisibilities in production functions.

11 Distributional considerations and the use of distributional weights is a frequent topic of debate in the economic appraisal literature. See Florio 2014 for a comprehensive presentation. The closely related issue of whose benefits and costs to count at all in the appraisal is known as the issue of *standing* in the economic appraisal literature but is less frequently addressed. See Johansson and de Rus 2019.

12 See any textbook on industrial organisation, for example Belleflamme and Peitz 2015 or Martin 2010.

13 The conceptual tools of industrial organisation used for defining markets, which are central to the practice for competition policy, may be useful to the analyst in understanding competitive conditions in the market where the investment takes place. See Belleflamme and Peitz 2015, Motta 2004 or, for a very accessible guide, Fishwick 1993. Marketing references also offer valuable insights. See in particular Lambin and Schuiling 2012.

14 In such a case, when computing total user costs, making a distinction between traffic experiencing a generalised cost of g' and traffic experiencing a generalised cost of g_3, is largely circumstantial, depending on scheduling practices and how the 'without project' scenario is defined. An alternative way to frame the scenario would be to view the C or C_{exp} schedules not as marginal delay but as average delay schedules, in which case the distinction disappears. After all, should such a scenario materialise, airlines lucky enough to have slots at the most desirable hours of the day will tend to respond to demand pressure by increasing the price of air tickets for flights at those preferred hours, appropriating any consumer surplus available. In that case, the increased profitability of the airlines will constitute a welfare transfer from the passengers to the airlines.

15 In graphical terms, the situation could be illustrated with the analysis in Chapter 2, section 2.7.3. The demand curve faced by multiple secondary markets in the local economy in the 'without project' scenario would fall to the left of where it would fall in the 'with project' scenario, implying higher prices on multiple goods and services to the local population.

16 See Forsyth 2006.

4   Airports

Introduction

This chapter addresses the economic appraisal of airports, putting in practice the concepts introduced in Chapters 2 and 3. It also illustrates a number of economic policy issues that manifest themselves in the economics of investment. The sequence of project types begins with a greenfield airport in section 4.1, followed in section 4.3 by a terminal capacity expansion, which builds on the greenfield airport case. Airside capacity projects are illustrated through the appraisal of enlarging an existing runway in section 4.6 and adding a new runway in section 4.7. Finally, section 4.9 addresses airport relocation.

Policy issues are introduced in self-contained sections alongside these project examples. The policy issues are not necessarily specific to each type of project. Rather, they are introduced whenever the results of a case invite discussion. Three of the policy sections concern the suitability of private sector involvement in infrastructure investment, including identifying when there is room for such involvement (sections 4.2 and 4.4); and how the regulatory framework affects the incentives the private sector operator faces in the investment decision (section 4.8). The latter case is linked to the generic incentive to overinvest brought about by rate of return regulation, discussed in section 4.5.

Whereas the focus of the case presentations is on illustrating estimation processes, and it is not the intention of the book to arrive at any policy recommendation, the numbers used in the examples are realistic. However, they do not relate to any specific real-life project.

4.1 A greenfield airport

Town A and its conurbation have experienced significant population and income growth following the discovery of mineral deposits just over a decade ago. Population is currently around 200,000, with an average income per capita of EUR15,000 per year. Town A has no airport and locals use the nearest airport, which is in town B, about two hours' drive away. Given the already sizeable and growing population, and the distance to town B's airport,

Table 4.1 Estimating traffic-generating potential of town A

	Year	1	20	30
(1)	Population CAGR since year 0		1.2%	1.2%
(2) from (1)	Population	200,000	253,887	286,052
(3)	Income CAGR since year 0		2.0%	2.0%
(4) from (3)	GDP/capita (EUR)	15,000	22,289	27,170
(5) from (4)	Cummulative income growth		49%	81%
(6)	Income elasticity of demand		1.4	1.4
(7) from (5) and (6)	Trips/capita	1.5	2.5	3.2
(8) = (2)×(7)	Trips	300,000	639,919	916,471
(9) = (8)×2	Passenger throughput	600,000	1,279,838	1,832,942
(10) from (9)	Throughput CAGR since year 0			3.8%

the local authorities wondered whether they should develop a local airport and hired airport planners to estimate local demand and propose an airport project.

The planners began by estimating the potential air transport demand generation in the area, depicted in Table 4.1. They surveyed demand in the country, estimated the catchment area, built econometric models, and found out that at that income level, the region should generate about 1.5 trips per inhabitant, or 300,000 trips in total per year. Local economic forecasts assumed that the population would continue to grow at a compound annual growth rate (CAGR) of 1.2 per cent per year; so that in 20 years' time the population would grow to 254,000 and in 30 years to 286,000.

The planners expected the income elasticity of demand going forward to be 1.4, meaning that a 10 per cent growth in income would bring about a 14 per cent increase in the propensity to travel. Studies showed that income per capita was expected to grow at 2 per cent per year over the long term. This would imply that over 30 years, real incomes would grow some 81 per cent to just over EUR27,000. Such income growth, combined with an income elasticity of 1.4, would mean that propensity to travel would rise by 114 per cent to 3.2 trips per inhabitant per year.[1] The result of this would be that in 30 years, town A would generate almost 920,000 trips per year. Since each trip involves a departure and an arrival, the airport would see a throughput of 1.83 million passenger movements. The resulting compound annual average growth rate of traffic in the period is 3.8 per cent per year.

In parallel to the desk exercise of the traffic generation capacity, the planners undertook surveys of actual travellers and found that the number of passengers from town A using town B's airport each year was around 300,000, implying 600,000 passenger movements per year. This was the same round figure which they had estimated through the desk exercise. The planners were surprised by this result, which was higher than expected, since the observed traffic estimated by the survey would exclude deterred traffic (or traffic that would be generated by the town A airport project). Something in the demand mix of town A made it a stronger generator of traffic than expected, probably attributable to the export

Table 4.2 Estimating deterred (or generated) traffic in town A

	Generalised cost (GC) with diversion			
(1)	Avg. flight duration	hours	1.5	
(2)	Avg. one-way air ticket price	EUR	200	
(3)	Passenger processing time	hours	1.5	
(4)	Access/egress time	hours	2.25	
(5)	Access/egress operating cost	EUR	20	
(6)	VoT	EUR	15	
(7) = (2) + (5)	Total money cost	EUR	220	
(8) = ((1) + (3) +(4)) × (6)	Total time cost	EUR	78.75	
(9)	Air safety cost	EUR	1	
(10)	Access-egress safety cost	EUR	3.6	
(11) =(7) + (8) + (9) + (10)	**GC with diversion**	EUR		**303.35**
	Net cost of diversion			
(12)	Access/egress time	hours	2	
(13) = (6) × (12)	Access/egress time cost	EUR	30	
(14)	Access/egress operating cost	EUR	15	
(15)	Access/egress safety cost	EUR	3	
(16) = (13) + (14) + (15)	Total savings	EUR		48
(17) = (11) - (16)	**GC without diversion**	EUR		**255.35**
(18)	GC elasticity			-1.2
(19) = ((17)/(11)) – 1	Relative change in GC			-15.8%
(20) = (18) × (19)	**Deterred/Generated traffic**			**19.0%**

sector playing a larger role in the local economy than the national average. Therefore it was deemed advisable to increase the traffic estimate for the airport, adding an estimate of deterred traffic. The estimation of deterred traffic was made by comparing the private (or behavioural) generalised cost of transport with and without project, then estimating the impact of their difference on traffic using standard demand elasticities. The calculation is summarised in Table 4.2.

The survey found that the average duration of flights taken by air travellers from town A through the airport at town B was 1 hour and 30 minutes (i.e. 1.5 hours). The average one-way air ticket paid was EUR200. Time spent at the airport at both ends of the route also averaged 1.5 hours. It took on average 2 hours and 15 minutes (i.e. 2.25 hours) to access airport B from A, at a cost of EUR20 per trip. Studies carried out for transport planning for the regional economy saw that the average airport user travelling on business would be willing to pay about EUR20 to save an hour, and the average leisure traveller about EUR10. Surveys also showed that air transport trip purpose in the region was 50 per cent business and 50 per cent leisure, so the average value of time was EUR15. The safety costs of travelling by air were estimated to be EUR1.[2] Diversion occurred mostly by car and local transport planning parameters of road accident rates and willingness to pay for safety resulted in a cost of safety per passenger of EUR3.6 per one-way trip.[3] With those parameters, the generalised cost was estimated at EUR303.35 per one-way trip.

With an airport in town A, access and egress time to the airport would take 15 minutes, instead of the 2 hours and 15 minutes taken to reach airport B, and would cost EUR5 instead of EUR20. The shorter distance by road would also mean that the road safety cost would fall to 60 cents. Therefore the savings to generalised cost by using airport A instead of B were estimated at EUR48 per one-way trip and the generalised cost of travelling through airport A would be EUR255.35 per one-way trip. This constitutes a saving of 15.8 per cent in generalised cost of travel, which at a demand elasticity of −1.2 would translate into an estimate of traffic currently being deterred by the lack of an airport in town A of 19 per cent of observed traffic. Therefore, should the airport in town A be opened at the time of estimation, traffic at the airport would be the 600,000 passenger trips currently diverted to B, plus 19 per cent of generated traffic, or an additional 114,000 passenger trips per year, bringing total traffic to 714,000 passengers per year.[4]

Given traffic projections, the planners proposed an airport with a capacity for 1.2 million passengers per year, sufficient to accommodate both current and expected demand for the next 20 years.[5] The planners estimated that the airport would cost EUR280 million to build. Land was relatively expensive as the airport was to be located close to town A, some 7 kilometres away. Land expropriation would cost EUR100 million, bringing cost to EUR380 million.[6] The existing access road was deemed sufficient to handle the expected increase in road traffic. However, a small suburban community would be affected by noise, so that the investment would need to include EUR20 million to install double glazing in buildings. All in all, the investment would add up to EUR400 million.

Regional politicians were keen to have an airport. However, the cost was large and the government had other pressing needs, including a large hospital. Airport consultants had said that an airport of that size would at best be marginally profitable and that the government should expect the airport to be a net financial liability over the foreseeable future. On the other hand, they pointed out that the airport would improve the accessibility of the regional economy, decreasing costs to businesses, encouraging visits by non-residents, and improving leisure options for local residents.

The government wondered whether the airport should be built and commissioned a financial and economic analysis of the investment to help it make a decision. Table 4.3 presents the results of the analysis, including all construction years (years 1 to 4), the first year of operation, and selected years through the life of the airport.

The first step would consist of estimating the financial returns of the project, based on total cash consumed and generated. Revenues would come from two broad sources. First, aeronautical activities, which would include charges per passenger movement, ground handling for aircraft and passengers, and aircraft landings, parking, and servicing. A comparison of charges with those of other airports in the country showed that they could add up to an average of EUR6 per passenger. The second source would be non-aeronautical activities,

Table 4.3 Financial and economic returns of a greenfield airport project

		PV/Year	1	2	3	4	5	10	15	20	25	29
	FINANCIAL RETURNS											
(1)	Airport passenger capacity	(thousand)	0	0	0	0	1,200	1,200	1,200	1,200	1,200	1,200
	Passenger throughput											
(2)	with project	(thousand)	0	0	0	0	829	999	1,203	1,450	1,596	1,596
(3)	without project	(thousand)	0	0	0	0	0	0	0	0	0	0
	Operating cashflows (after tax)											
(4)	with project	(EUR m)	-40.0	0.0	0.0	0.0	0.0	-4.1	-3.9	-3.5	-2.9	-2.4	-2.4
(5)	without project	(EUR m)	0.0	0.0	0.0	0.0	0.0	0.0	0.0	0.0	0.0	0.0	0.0
(6)=(4)-(5)	Net benefit	(EUR m)	-40.0	0.0	0.0	0.0	0.0	-4.1	-3.9	-3.5	-2.9	-2.4	-2.4
(7)	Capital investment	(EUR m)	354.6	100.0	100.0	100.0	100.0						
(8)	Subsidy	(EUR m)	0.0	0.0	0.0	0.0	0.0						
(9)=(6)-(7)+(8)	Net cash flow to operator	(EUR m)	**-394.6**	-100.0	-100.0	-100.0	-100.0	-4.1	-3.9	-3.5	-2.9	-2.4	-2.4
	Operator FRR		N/A										
(10)	Government financial flows	(EUR m)	89.8	15	15	15	15	2	3	3	4	4	4
(11)=(9)+(10)	Operator + government flows	(EUR m)	**-304.8**	-85	-85	-85	-85	-2	-1	0	1	1	1
	Private and Government FRR		N/A										

(Continued)

Table 4.3 (Continued)

ECONOMIC RETURNS

		PV/Year	1	2	3	4	5	10	15	20	25	29
Diverted passengers												
(12) with project	(thousand)		600	623	646	671	0	0	0	0	0	109
(13) without project	(thousand)		600	623	646	671	697	839	1,011	1,219	1,469	1,705
Deterred passengers												
(14) with project	(thousand)		114	118	123	127	0	0	0	0	151	324
(15) without project	(thousand)		114	118	123	127	132	159	192	231	279	324
Cost of diversion												
(16) = (12) ×time cost time cost with project	(EUR m)	70.0	17.6	18.7	19.8	20.9	0.0	0.0	0.0	0.0	0.0	5.6
(17) = (13) × time cost time cost without project	(EUR m)	548.8	17.6	18.7	19.8	20.9	22.2	29.5	39.2	52.2	69.5	87.3
(18) = ((12) – (13)) × other costs op & safety costs of diverted pax	(EUR m)	214.0	0.0	0.0	0.0	0.0	12.5	15.1	18.2	21.9	26.4	28.7
(19) appropriated by operator	(EUR m)	0.0	0.0	0.0	0.0	0.0	0.0	0.0	0.0	0.0	0.0	0.0
(20) = – (16) + (17) + (18) – (19) Net benefit to user	(EUR m)	692.8	0.0	0.0	0.0	0.0	34.7	44.6	57.5	74.2	95.9	110.5
Cost of deterrence												
(21) = 0.5 × (14) × time costs time cost with project	(EUR m)	15.7	1.7	1.8	1.9	2.0	0.0	0.0	0.0	0.0	3.6	8.3

(Continued)

(22) = 0.5 × (15) × time costs	time cost without project	(EUR m)	52.1	1.7	1.8	1.9	2.0	2.1	2.8	3.7	5.0	6.6	8.3
(23) = 0.5 × ((14) - (15)) × other costs	op. & safety costs of deterred pax	(EUR m)	17.0	0.0	0.0	0.0	0.0	1.2	1.4	1.7	2.1	1.1	0.0
(24)	approapriated by operator	(EUR m)	0.0	0.0	0.0	0.0	0.0	0.0	0.0	0.0	0.0	0.0	0.0
(25) = - (21) + (22) + (23) - (24)	Net benefit to user	(EUR m)	53.4	0.0	0.0	0.0	0.0	3.3	4.2	5.5	7.0	4.2	0.0
	Cost of congestion												
(26)	with project	(EUR m)	43.0	0.0	0.0	0.0	0.0	0.0	0.0	6.0	7.9	9.6	10.4
(27)	without project	(EUR m)	0.0	0.0	0.0	0.0	0.0	0.0	0.0	0.0	0.0	0.0	0.0
(28) = - (26) + (27)	Net benefit	(EUR m)	-43.0	0.0	0.0	0.0	0.0	0.0	0.0	-6.0	-7.9	-9.6	-10.4
(29)	Gross producer surplus airport B	(EUR m)	25.0	0.0	0.0	0.0	1.4	1.4	1.7	2.1	2.5	3.0	0.0
(30) = (11) + (20) + (25) + (28) - (29)	Economic flows (ex externalities)	(EUR m)	**373.5**	-85.0	-85.0	-85.0	-86.4	34.9	46.0	54.5	71.5	88.9	101.5
	ERR without externalities		**11.8%**										

(*Continued*)

Table 4.3 (Continued)

		PV/Year	1	2	3	4	5	10	15	20	25	29
Externalities												
From land transport diversion												
(31) = ((13) - (12)) × GHG cost	greenhouse gas	(EUR m)	19.7	0.0	0.0	0.0	0.0	0.8	1.1	1.6	2.2	3.1	3.8
(32) = ((13) - (12)) × noise cost	noise	(EUR m)	11.9	0.0	0.0	0.0	0.0	0.7	0.8	1.0	1.2	1.5	1.6
(33) = ((13) - (12)) × air pollution cost	air pollution	(EUR m)	17.8	0.0	0.0	0.0	0.0	1.0	1.3	1.5	1.8	2.2	2.4
(34) = ((13) - (12)) × safety cost	safety cost	(EUR m)	11.9	0.0	0.0	0.0	0.0	0.7	0.8	1.0	1.2	1.5	1.6
(35) = (31) + (32) + (33) + (34)	Total	(EUR m)	61.3	0.0	0.0	0.0	0.0	3.2	4.1	5.1	6.5	8.2	9.3
From generated air transport												
(36) = ((15) - (14)) × GHG cost	greenhouse gas	(EUR m)	58.5	0.0	0.0	0.0	0.0	3.1	4.3	6.0	8.4	5.3	0.0
(37) = ((15) - (14)) × noise cost	noise	(EUR m)	5.7	0.0	0.0	0.0	0.0	0.4	0.5	0.6	0.7	0.4	0.0
(38) = ((15) - (14)) × air pollution cost	air pollution	(EUR m)	3.8	0.0	0.0	0.0	0.0	0.3	0.3	0.4	0.5	0.3	0.0
(39) = ((15) - (14)) × safety cost	safety cost	(EUR m)	0.6	0.0	0.0	0.0	0.0	0.0	0.0	0.1	0.1	0.0	0.0
(40) = (36) + (37) + (38) + (39)	Total	(EUR m)	68.5	0.0	0.0	0.0	0.0	3.8	5.1	7.0	9.6	6.0	0.0
(41) = (35) - (40)	Net external effect	(EUR m)	-7.2	0.0	0.0	0.0	0.0	-0.5	-1.1	-1.9	-3.1	2.2	9.3
(42) = (30) + (41)	Project net economic flows	(EUR m)	366.2	-85.0	-85.0	-85.0	-86.4	34.4	45.0	52.7	68.3	91.1	110.8
	Project ERR		11.6%										

including revenues from retail activities in the terminal, car parking and renting of property on the airport site. Estimates showed that non-aeronautical activities could generate EUR2 per passenger net of cost of merchandise sold.

Row 1 in Table 4.3 shows the design capacity of the airport. Forecasted throughput is included in row 2. The airport would have sufficient capacity to absorb all of the traffic that town A is forecasted to generate during the first few years of operation. Traffic would reach design capacity by year 15 and by year 25 capacity would start being rationed. Rows 4 to 9 show revenue and cost calculations. The net cash flow shown in line 9 includes operating revenues minus operating costs and capital investment.

The project would not be financially viable. Discounted at 5 per cent, the yield of long-term government bonds, it would have a negative present value of EUR394.6 million. If the project were discounted at the capital cost of the private sector, estimated at around 8 per cent, it would be even less appealing to the private sector. Therefore the project would not be carried out by the private sector without financial assistance provided by the government.

Should the project be operated by the public sector, total financial returns would include also the taxes collected on inputs and outputs. In town A, the tax rate applying to all revenues and costs, including taxes on energy, sales, etc., as well as social security contributions were fixed at a 15 per cent rate. The resulting tax revenue is included in row 10. Adding tax revenues to operating revenues would still leave the project with a strong negative financial value, as shown in row 11. Moreover, from the point of view of the public sector as a whole, much of the tax revenues would constitute transfers from revenues from airport B. However, airport B falls outside the remit of local authority A, the local authority considering to build airport A, and local authority A disregards financial flows of other local authorities.

Despite the negative financial returns, the project would produce benefits to the local economy, improving the accessibility of local population and local firms, potentially improving the productivity of the local economy. The extent to which this would happen would on average be measured by how much firms and the local population would be willing to pay for the accessibility benefits. This would in turn depend on their willingness to pay for time, which as discussed above was estimated to average EUR15 per hour. Also as commented above, income per capita in the regional economy was expected to grow by 2 per cent per year and this would be a good approximation to the growth over time in the willingness to pay for time.[7]

Following the surveys conducted, diverted traffic would amount to 600,000 passengers per year and would grow in the future as depicted in row 13. Diverted traffic would travel for 2 hours to town B, incurring time costs, vehicle operating costs and safety costs as depicted in rows 16 to 20. Deterred traffic – potential passengers who do not travel because the generalised cost is too high – with and without the project is shown in rows 14 and 15, respectively. The difference between the two measures will constitute traffic generated by the project. So during the first year of operation, in year 5, the airport would generate 132,000 new one-way passenger trips. In year 25, as the airport would get increasingly congested, lack of airport capacity would mean that traffic would start being deterred with the project. In year 29 the project would not generate any traffic, meaning that all traffic flying through the airport would have travelled through airport B, had airport A not been built. The user welfare gain created by generated traffic (or, in other words, net deterred traffic avoided) is estimated in rows 21 to 25, making use of the 'rule of a half', as discussed in Chapter 3, section 3.1.

Congestion in airport A would become evident from year 15, once traffic exceeds design capacity, as indicated in rows 1 and 2. From there on, service quality at the terminal would diminish, and additional traffic would mean longer queues, waiting times and flight delays. The cost of this congestion is estimated to be around 15 additional minutes of throughput time per passenger and is shown in rows 26 to 28. It is assumed that there is ample capacity in the alternative airport, so no congestion cost is incurred in the 'without project' scenario.[8]

It was seen in the financial appraisal that the local government disregarded the financial effects of the project on region B.

Any private promoter will also follow the same approach. In the economic appraisal, looking at net resource use for the economy at large, all welfare changes need to be included regardless of where they are incurred. Any gross producer surplus (net income plus taxes) that airport B would have generated without the project needs to be subtracted from project benefits. It is assumed that airport B was generating a total of EUR2 per passenger in net producer surplus and tax revenue to the government. This applies only to diverted passengers and the resulting monetary value is included in row 29.[9]

The estimate of economic returns takes into account all monetised effects on the primary market, as picked up in the financial appraisal. Since airport revenues are measured net of taxes, tax revenue has to be included as it constitutes a payment by the user to the promoter that the promoter in turn transfers to the state. Likewise, since both the operating and capital expenditure costs of the airport are measured gross of taxes, tax revenue to the government arising from such items has to be deduced from resource costs and added as a transfer of benefits to the government.[10] Therefore the measure of financial flows to be used in the economic appraisal is as depicted in row 11. Adding to this resource flow both the diversion cost avoided by the project, measured by row 20, the consumer surplus of generated traffic, measured by row 25, and subtracting both the congestion incurred by users of airport A, depicted in row 28, and the reduction in gross producer surplus of airport B, in row 29, widens the measure of resource flow to include welfare changes incurred by the airports and their users, whether monetised or not. It can be seen that the airport generates a net welfare gain of EUR373.5 million, despite the strong negative financial returns depicted in row 11.

To complete the estimate of economic return, the analysis needs to include welfare changes to parties not taking part directly in the production or consumption of air transport. The nature of externalities varies depending on traffic type, whether it is generated or diverted. Generated traffic constitutes traffic that would not have travelled without the project and that travels as a consequence of the project. If the passenger paid in full for all external costs of air transport, that is, if all external costs were internalised, there would be no need to make any further adjustments to the economic analysis. Instead, in this case it is assumed that non-internalised environmental costs of air travel include external costs per passenger trip of EUR20 for greenhouse gas (GHG) emissions, EUR3 for noise and EUR2 for air pollution.[11] This could reflect a situation where, say, all airline tickets flying to and from the airport include an environmental tax that falls below the social cost of carbon by EUR20 per tonne. Another possible scenario could be one where there are no environmental taxes and instead a proportion of services operate within an MBM and others do not. The EUR20 is then an average cost across all passengers, reflecting the externality caused by passengers flying on services outside the MBM. The marginal cost of GHG emissions is assumed to grow at an average annual rate of 3 per cent, as the cost of additional emissions increases with GHG concentration. In addition, there will be a cost of 30 cents imposed on the rest of society through accident risks.[12] The resulting external costs are measured in rows 36 to 40 in Table 4.3.

Note that it would not be correct to assign such external costs of air transport to diverted traffic, as diverted traffic travels by air in the 'without project' scenario as well, hence such costs cannot be attributed to the project. For diverted traffic, the environmental externality to include would be the external costs inflicted on third parties as a consequence of the diversion. In this case, these would include external costs of the additional road transport necessary to access airport B. Planners estimated that such costs include on a per passenger basis, EUR1 for greenhouse gases (again growing at 3 per cent per year), EUR1 for noise, EUR1.50 for air pollution and EUR1 as safety costs.[13] Since such costs would be avoided by the project, they represent a project benefit and are included in rows 31 to 35.

The net external impact is included in row 41 and it is added to the private flows to estimate the overall net economic flows of the project, included in row 42. The economic net present value of the project is EUR366.2 million and constitutes an economic return on investment of 11.6 per cent. The local government deems that such returns are sufficient to warrant the construction of the airport. However, the strong negative financial return raises the question of how to finance it.

4.2 Involving the private sector (1): no room for capital investment

The results of the project appraisal exercise in Table 4.3 show that the local government of town A faces a potentially viable investment for the economy, producing a sound economic return, but which would yield a strong negative financial return.

The economic analysis shows that most of the value of the project consists of benefits to diverted traffic, totalling EUR692.8 million, as shown in row 20 of Table 4.3. In addition, there is also the EUR53.4 million in willingness to pay of generated traffic, shown in row 25. Such consumer surpluses measure the competitive advantage that the airport would have against airport B, in the market for air travellers from region A. One possibility for raising money to help finance the project would be for the airport to appropriate part of that surplus. This could be done by raising aeronautical charges.

The average revenue per passenger (also known as passenger yield) of the airport assumed in the estimation of project viability in Table 4.3 is EUR8, consisting of EUR6 in aeronautical yield and EUR2 in non-aeronautical yield. The estimation of savings in private generalised cost in Table 4.2 shows that the average passenger would value the proximity of airport A by up to EUR48. That constitutes the upper boundary for an increase in aeronautical charges, since with such an additional charge passengers would be indifferent to whether they travel through airport A or airport B. Planners surveyed other airports elsewhere and found that aeronautical yields of EUR20 were possible. The local government believed that it would be politically feasible to increase aeronautical yields to EUR22, which with non-aeronautical yields at EUR2 would triple passenger yield to EUR24.

The effect of the pricing policy is depicted in Figure 4.1. The generalised cost to the traveller of travelling through airport A before the increase in airport charges is g_0. The generalised cost of travelling through the alternative airport is g_1, which is EUR48 higher than g_0. By increasing the aeronautical yield by EUR16 to EUR22, the generalised cost of travelling through airport A increases to g_p. The airport sees net operating revenues (i.e. operating

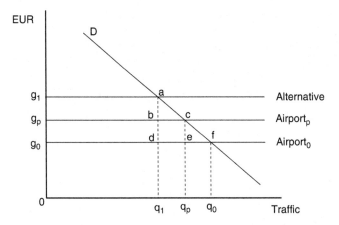

Figure 4.1 Effects of increasing airport aeronautical charges on user and airport surpluses.

revenues minus operating costs) increase by the area $g_p ceg_0$. This is a transfer of surplus from passengers (consumer surplus) to the airport (producer surplus). Because of the increase in prices, traffic falls from q_0 to q_p, which would take the form of lower generated traffic than would be the case without the increase in aeronautical charges.

The effects of increasing aeronautical charges on project returns are shown in Table 4.4. The price increase will result in a small fall in traffic, as depicted in row 2. By year 15, for example, passenger throughput will be about 60,000 lower than with the lower charges. This fall in traffic consists of fewer generated passengers (or more deterred passengers). The higher revenues would reduce substantially the negative return to the operator, increasing the net present value of the investment from a negative EUR394.6 million to a negative EUR212.5 million, as shown in row 9 of Tables 4.3 and 4.4. The higher revenues will also mean higher taxes, as shown in row 10 of both tables. Even so, the project will still have a negative financial worth of EUR92.8 million to the local government, assuming that the local government operates the airport. That figure would constitute a transfer of money from the taxpayer to the airport user, which is now much smaller than the EUR304.8 million that would be the case without the increase in charges.

The loss of welfare to the airport user is registered in row 20 for diverted traffic and row 25 for generated traffic. Note that the economic value of the project before externalities falls slightly from EUR373.5 million to EUR364.9 million, as shown in rows 30 of tables 4.3 and 4.4, respectively. The corresponding economic returns fall from 11.8 per cent to 11.6 per cent. There has been a small loss of welfare because some of the traffic generated by the project has now been deterred by the higher airport charges. The loss in economic welfare corresponds to the area cfe in Figure 4.1. However, once externalities are taken into account, the increase in charges actually increases economic value, as depicted in row 42. This is because all of the negative externalities of the project are due to generated traffic, which is reduced by the higher charges. The increase in aeronautical charges can be viewed as a surrogate taxation of externalities, bringing about an improvement in social welfare. Ultimately, however, because the airport project still makes a loss, the broader net effect of the increase in prices is to reduce the transfer of wealth from taxpayers to airport users.

Despite the increase in price, the private sector would not be interested in the project. Whereas aeronautical charges could be increased further, the local government deems it politically unfeasible. The government would still need to operate the project and will expect to incur a financial loss with a present value of EUR92.8 million after additional tax revenues generated by the project, as shown in row 11.

An attempt to privatise the project would require a transfer of welfare from the public to the private sector. Assuming the private sector demanded a return of at least 8 per cent on the investment, the necessary government subsidy would need to amount to EUR258.9 million in present value terms, which

Table 4.4 Financial and economic returns of the greenfield airport project with higher aeronautical charges

		PV/Year	1	2	3	4	5	10	15	20	25	29
FINANCIAL RETURNS												
(1)	Airport passenger capacity	(thousand)	0	0	0	0	1,200	1,200	1,200	1,200	1,200	1,200
	Passenger throughput											
(2)	with project	(thousand)	0	0	0	0	785	946	1,139	1,373	1,596	1,596
(3)	without project	(thousand)	0	0	0	0	0	0	0	0	0	0
	Operating cashflows (after tax)											
(4)	with project	(EUR m)	142.1	0.0	0.0	0.0	0.0	6.8	9.2	12.2	15.9	19.8	19.8
(5)	without project	(EUR m)	0.0	0.0	0.0	0.0	0.0	0.0	0.0	0.0	0.0	0.0	0.0
(6) = (4) - (5)	Net benefit	(EUR m)	142.1	0.0	0.0	0.0	0.0	6.8	9.2	12.2	15.9	19.8	19.8
(7)	Capital investment	(EUR m)	354.6	100.0	100.0	100.0	100.0						
(8)	Subsidy	(EUR m)	0.0	0.0	0.0	0.0	0.0						
(9) = (6) - (7) + (8)	Net cash flow to operator	(EUR m)	**-212.5**	-100.0	-100.0	-100.0	-100.0	6.8	9.2	12.2	15.9	19.8	19.8
	Operator FRR		**N/A**										
(10)	Government financial flows	(EUR m)	119.7	15	15	15	15	4	5	6	7	8	8
(11) = (9) + (10)	Operator + government flows	(EUR m)	**-92.8**	-85	-85	-85	-85	11	14	18	23	27	27
	Private and Government FRR		**N/A**										

ECONOMIC RETURNS

		Unit	Total										
Diverted passengers													
(12) with project		(thousand)		600	623	646	671	0	0	0	0	0	109
(13) without project		(thousand)		600	623	646	671	697	839	1,011	1,219	1,469	1,705
Deterred passengers													
(14) with project		(thousand)		76	79	82	85	0	0	0	0	58	216
(15) without project		(thousand)		76	79	82	85	88	106	128	154	186	216
Cost of diversion													
time cost with project	(16) = (12) × time cost	(EUR m)	70.0	17.6	18.7	19.8	20.9	0.0	0.0	0.0	0.0	0.0	5.6
time cost without project	(17) = (13) × time cost	(EUR m)	548.8	17.6	18.7	19.8	20.9	22.2	29.5	39.2	52.2	69.5	87.3
op & safety costs of diverted pax	(18) = ((12) – (13)) × other costs	(EUR m)	214.0	0.0	0.0	0.0	0.0	12.5	15.1	18.2	21.9	26.4	28.7
appropriated by operator	(19)	(EUR m)	190.2	0.0	0.0	0.0	0.0	11.1	13.4	16.2	19.5	23.5	25.5
Net benefit to user	(20) = – (16) + (17) + (18) – (19)	(EUR m)	502.6	0.0	0.0	0.0	0.0	23.6	31.2	41.3	54.7	72.4	84.9
Cost of deterrence													
time cost with project	(21) = 0.5 × (14) × time costs	(EUR m)	9.4	1.1	1.2	1.3	1.3	0.0	0.0	0.0	0.0	1.4	5.5

(*Continued*)

Table 4.4 (Continued)

			PV/Year	1	2	3	4	5	10	15	20	25	29
(22) = 0.5 × (15) × time costs	time cost without project	(EUR m)	34.7	1.1	1.2	1.3	1.3	1.4	1.9	2.5	3.3	4.4	5.5
(23) = 0.5 × ((14) - (15)) × other costs	op. & safety costs of deterred pax	(EUR m)	11.7	0.0	0.0	0.0	0.0	0.8	1.0	1.2	1.4	1.1	0.0
(24)	appropriated by operator	(EUR m)	20.8	0.0	0.0	0.0	0.0	1.4	1.7	2.0	2.5	2.0	0.0
(25) = - (21) + (22) + (23) - (24)	Net benefit to user	(EUR m)	16.2	0.0	0.0	0.0	0.0	0.8	1.1	1.6	2.2	2.1	0.0
	Cost of congestion												
(26)	with project	(EUR m)	36.1	0.0	0.0	0.0	0.0	0.0	0.0	0.0	7.5	9.6	10.4
(27)	without project	(EUR m)	0.0	0.0	0.0	0.0	0.0	0.0	0.0	0.0	0.0	0.0	0.0
(28) = - (26) + (27)	Net benefit	(EUR m)	-36.1	0.0	0.0	0.0	0.0	0.0	0.0	0.0	-7.5	-9.6	-10.4
(29)	Gross producer surplus airport B	(EUR m)	25.0	0.0	0.0	0.0	1.4	1.4	1.7	2.1	2.5	3.0	0.0
(30) = (11) + (20) + (25) + (28) - (29)	Economic flows (ex externalities)	(EUR m)	364.9	-85.0	-85.0	-85.0	-86.4	33.9	44.7	58.7	69.5	89.3	101.9
	ERR without externalities		11.6%										

Externalities

	Formula											
From land transport diversion												
greenhouse gas	$(31) = ((13) - (12)) \times$ GHG cost	(EUR m)	19.7	0.0	0.0	0.0	0.8	1.1	1.6	2.2	3.1	3.8
noise	$(32) = ((13) - (12)) \times$ noise cost	(EUR m)	11.9	0.0	0.0	0.0	0.7	0.8	1.0	1.2	1.5	1.6
air pollution	$(33) = ((13) - (12)) \times$ air pollution cost	(EUR m)	17.8	0.0	0.0	0.0	1.0	1.3	1.5	1.8	2.2	2.4
safety cost	$(34) = ((13) - (12)) \times$ safety cost	(EUR m)	11.9	0.0	0.0	0.0	0.7	0.8	1.0	1.2	1.5	1.6
Total	$(35) = (31) + (32) + (33) + (34)$	(EUR m)	61.3	0.0	0.0	0.0	3.2	4.1	5.1	6.5	8.2	9.3
From generated air transport												
greenhouse gas	$(36) = ((15)-(14)) \times$ GHG cost	(EUR m)	40.8	0.0	0.0	0.0	2.0	2.9	4.0	5.6	5.3	0.0
noise	$(37) = ((15)-(14)) \times$ noise cost	(EUR m)	3.9	0.0	0.0	0.0	0.3	0.3	0.4	0.5	0.4	0.0
air pollution	$(38) = ((15)-(14)) \times$ air pollution cost	(EUR m)	2.6	0.0	0.0	0.0	0.2	0.2	0.3	0.3	0.3	0.0
safety cost	$(39) = ((15)-(14)) \times$ safety cost	(EUR m)	0.4	0.0	0.0	0.0	0.0	0.0	0.0	0.0	0.0	0.0
Total	$(40) = (36) + (37) + (38) + (39)$	(EUR m)	47.8	0.0	0.0	0.0	2.5	3.4	4.7	6.4	6.0	0.0
Net external effect	$(41) = (35) - (40)$	(EUR m)	13.6	0.0	0.0	0.0	0.7	0.6	0.4	0.1	2.2	9.3
Project net economic flows	$(42) = (30) + (41)$	(EUR m)	378.4	-85.0	-85.0	-86.4	34.6	45.3	59.1	69.6	91.5	111.3
Project ERR			11.8%									

could take various forms, including a 73 per cent grant on investment costs, or some combination of grants, tax rebates, and subsidies to operating costs. None of this would change the economic returns of the project since it would constitute simply a transfer from the public sector to the private sector.

For the project to be worthwhile outsourcing to the private sector, the differences in efficiency of building and operating the project between the private sector and the public sector would have to be substantial. Otherwise the financial return to the private sector will just largely reflect the subsidy. Generally, under such circumstances, private sector involvement in the investment is not justified. Any private sector involvement would instead be through a management contract to operate the airport, minimising or eliminating any upfront capital investment by the private sector and hence minimising transfers from the taxpayer.

This situation is most frequent. Small airports that charge standard levels of aeronautical charges are loss-making, but are economically justified because of non-monetised benefits and are left to the government to develop and operate. There is a rationale for private sector investment in small airports in situations where incomes in the catchment area are very high, increasing user willingness to pay for saving time. In such situations the airport can command high aeronautical charges which, combined with the potential for higher non-aeronautical yields, may constitute investment opportunities with sound financial prospects.

4.3 Terminal capacity expansion

The years following the opening of the airport in town A, the local economy went on to grow faster than had been expected, bringing about faster traffic growth at the airport. It soon became clear that the new airport would become fully utilised earlier than anticipated. At the originally expected 3.8 per cent growth rate in traffic, the airport terminal would reach design capacity of 1.2 million passengers by year 16, some 12 years after opening. Thereafter it would have continued being able to accommodate additional traffic with some congestion. Deterred traffic would become evident by year 24, and traffic diversion by year 27. Following such projections, it was expected that additional terminal capacity would have to be operational by year 25, some 21 years after the opening of the airport.

Instead of the expected 3.8 per cent growth rate, traffic went on to grow at 5.2 per cent per year. By year 10, passenger throughput was already 1.1 million and the revised demand projection was for traffic growth to average 5 per cent per year over the foreseeable future. Under such projections, the airport would reach design capacity within the next couple of years. Traffic rationing would begin to be evident earlier than expected, traffic deterrence would become evident by year 18, and diversion by year 20.

The airport operator wished to have new capacity in place by year 18 and began preparatory studies for a new terminal, with a view to starting construction no later than year 14. The project would consist of expanding terminal capacity by an additional 1.2 million passengers per year, bringing the total capacity of the airport to 2.4 million passengers. Construction would begin in year 14 and conclude in year 17. Total investment would be EUR100 million, incurred in equal shares across the four-year construction period. Note that this investment, needed to accommodate an additional 1.2 million passengers, is much smaller than the greenfield investment of EUR400 million that would also accommodate 1.2 million passengers. Much of the infrastructure capacity developed at greenfield stage, including the runway, apron, tower, and access roads, will be sufficient to operate the expanded terminal facility. Since the additional investment is smaller in the expansion stage than in the greenfield stage, but the amount of incremental traffic accommodated is the same in both stages, the returns on investment can expected to be stronger in the expansion stage than in the greenfield stage. Such returns will reflect a mixture of economies of scale and density.

The results of the estimation of financial and economic viability are displayed in Table 4.5. Traffic would reach design capacity of 2.4 million passengers by year 26, some 9 years after opening the expanded facility. Thereafter additional traffic would cause congestion, eventually leading to capacity rationing and deterred traffic by year 32, followed by traffic diversion by year 34, some 17 years after the expanded facility would be opened.

The new project would generate a positive financial return since, unlike at greenfield stage, the present value of the additional operating profits is higher than the investment cost of the project. For the operator the project has a net present value of EUR37.7 million (row 10) and a financial return of 7.1 per cent. The government will see additional tax revenues with a present value of EUR53.2 million (row 15). The combined financial value of the project to the operator and the government is 90.9 million (row 16), or a combined financial return of 9.6 per cent.

The economic return is calculated using the same procedure as in the greenfield case, adjusting the 'without project' scenario to include the existing airport capacity in town A and adding a measure of consumer surplus appropriated by the airport from captive traffic (row 34). This is traffic that would have used airport A regardless of whether the project is carried out, that is, total traffic minus deterred and diverted traffic. Such captive traffic was obviously not present at greenfield stage. For ease of comparison with the greenfield case, surplus appropriated by the operator for diverted and deterred traffic is calculated taking as a baseline an airport passenger yield of EUR8, the same baseline as in the greenfield case. Since the passenger yield is EUR24, the initial capacity expansion scenario already displays surplus appropriation by the promoter. In the case of captive traffic, surplus appropriation is EUR0 because the yield of EUR24 also applies to the 'without project' scenario where there is no capacity expansion.

Costs associated with diverted traffic once more constitute a key determinant of the economic returns of the project (row 22). Note that the analysis

Table 4.5 Financial and economic returns of the terminal capacity expansion project

		PV/Year	14	15	16	17	18	25	30	35	42
FINANCIAL RETURNS												
Airport passenger capacity												
(1) with project	(thousand)		1,200	1,200	1,200	1,200	2,400	2,400	2,400	2,400	2,400
(2) without project	(thousand)		1,200	1,200	1,200	1,200	1,200	1,200	1,200	1,200	1,200
Passenger throughput												
(3) with project	(thousand)		1,374	1,443	1,515	1,591	1,671	2,351	3,000	3,192	3,192
(4) without project	(thousand)		1,374	1,443	1,515	1,591	1,596	1,596	1,596	1,596	1,596
Operating cashflows (after tax)												
(5) with project	(EUR m)	430.0	16.6	17.8	19.0	20.2	17.4	28.3	39.1	42.7	42.7
(6) without project	(EUR m)	303.7	16.6	17.8	19.0	20.2	20.6	20.6	20.6	20.6	20.6
(7) = (5) − (6) Net benefit	(EUR m)	126.3	0.0	0.0	0.0	0.0	-3.2	7.7	18.5	22.1	22.1
(8) Capital investment	(EUR m)	88.6	25.0	25.0	25.0	25.0					
(9) Subsidy	(EUR m)	0.0	0.0	0.0	0.0	0.0					
(10) = (7) − (8) + (9) Net cash flow to operator	(EUR m)	**37.7**	-25.0	-25.0	-25.0	-25.0	-3.2	7.7	18.5	22.1	22.1
(11) Operator FRR		**7.1%**									

Ref	Item	Unit										
(12) = (5) − (8) + (9)	Private value of airport with project	(EUR m)	341.4	−8.4	−7.2	−6.0	−4.8	17.4	28.3	39.1	42.7	42.7
	Government financial flows											
(13)	with project	(EUR m)	179.1	10.4	10.7	11.0	11.3	8.5	11.4	14.1	14.9	14.9
(14)	without project	(EUR m)	125.9	10.4	10.7	11.0	11.3	7.5	7.5	7.5	7.5	7.5
(15) = (13) − (14)	Net revenue	(EUR m)	53.2	0.0	0.0	0.0	0.0	1.0	3.9	6.6	7.3	7.3
(16) = (10) + (15)	Operator + government flows	(EUR m)	**90.9**	−25.0	−25.0	−25.0	−25.0	−2.2	11.6	25.1	29.4	29.4
	Private and Government FRR		**9.6%**									

ECONOMIC RETURNS

Ref	Item	Unit										
	Diverted passengers											
(17)	with project	(thousand)		0.0	0.0	0.0	0.0	0.0	0.0	0.0	206.9	1,590.6
(18)	without project	(thousand)		0.0	0.0	0.0	0.0	0.0	490.6	1,067.1	1,802.9	3,186.6
	Deterred passengers											
(19)	with project	(thousand)		0.0	0.0	0.0	0.0	0.0	0.0	0.0	430.3	605.4
(20)	without project	(thousand)		0.0	0.0	0.0	0.0	74.6	264.1	337.1	430.3	605.4
	Cost of diversion											
(21) = (17) × time cost	time cost with project	(EUR m)	92.9	0.0	0.0	0.0	0.0	0.0	0.0	0.0	9.2	81.4

(Continued)

Table 4.5 (Continued)

			PV/Year	14	15	16	17	18	25	30	35	42
(22) = (18) × time cost	time cost without project	(EUR m)	470.3	0.0	0.0	0.0	0.0	0.0	17.9	43.1	80.4	163.2
(23)= ((17) - (18)) × other costs	op & safety costs of diverted pax	(EUR m)	157.6	0.0	0.0	0.0	0.0	0.0	8.8	19.2	28.7	28.7
(24)	approapriated by operator and gov.	(EUR m)	140.1	0.0	0.0	0.0	0.0	0.0	7.8	17.1	25.5	25.5
(25) = - (21) + (22) + (23) - (24)	Net benefit	(EUR m)	237.3	0.0	0.0	0.0	0.0	0.0	18.9	45.2	74.3	84.9
	Cost of deterrement											
(26) = 0.5 × (19) × time costs	time cost with project	(EUR m)	34.6	0.0	0.0	0.0	0.0	0.0	0.0	0.0	9.6	15.5
(27) = 0.5 × (20) × time costs	time cost without project	(EUR m)	73.1	0.0	0.0	0.0	0.0	1.2	4.8	6.8	9.6	15.5
(28) =0.5 × ((19) - (20)) × other costs	op. & safety costs of deterred pax	(EUR m)	18.8	0.0	0.0	0.0	0.0	0.7	2.4	3.0	0.0	0.0
(29)	appropriated by operator	(EUR m)	33.3	0.0	0.0	0.0	0.0	1.2	4.2	5.4	0.0	0.0
(30) = - (26) + (27) + (28) - (29)	Net benefit	(EUR m)	38.5	0.0	0.0	0.0	0.0	0.7	3.0	4.4	0.0	0.0
	Cost of congestion											
(31)	with project	(EUR m)	124.2	5.2	5.5	5.9	6.3	0.0	0.0	15.4	18.1	20.8
(32)	without project	(EUR m)	111.8	5.2	5.5	5.9	6.3	6.5	7.4	8.2	9.1	10.4
(33) = - (31) + (32)	Net benefit	(EUR m)	-12.3	0.0	0.0	0.0	0.0	6.5	7.4	-7.2	-9.1	-10.4
(34)	Surplus appropriated from captive traffic	(EUR m)	0.0	0.0	0.0	0.0	0.0	0.0	0.0	0.0	0.0	0.0
(35)	Gross producer surplus airport B	(EUR m)	17.5	0.0	0.0	0.0	0.0	0.0	1.0	2.1	3.2	3.2
(36) = (11) + (25) + (30) + (33) - (34) - (35)	Economic flows (ex externalities)	(EUR m)	479.9	-25.0	-25.0	-25.0	-25.0	4.9	39.9	65.4	91.5	100.8
	ERR without externalities		19.6%									

Externalities

		(EUR m)							
From land transport diversion									
$(37) = ((18) - (17)) \times$ GHG cost	greenhouse gas	470.6	0.0	0.0	0.0	20.5	51.8	89.8	110.5
$(38) = ((18) - (17)) \times$ noise cost	noise	26.3	0.0	0.0	0.0	1.5	3.2	4.8	4.8
$(39) = ((18) - (17)) \times$ air pollution cost	air pollution	17.5	0.0	0.0	0.0	1.0	2.1	3.2	3.2
$(40) = ((18) - (17)) \times$ safety cost	safety cost	2.6	0.0	0.0	0.0	0.1	0.3	0.5	0.5
$(41) = (37) + (38) + (39) + (40)$	Total	517.0	0.0	0.0	0.0	23.1	57.5	98.3	118.9
From generated air transport									
$(42) = ((20) - (19)) \times$ GHG cost	greenhouse gas	88.9	0.0	0.0	2.5	11.1	16.4	0.0	0.0
$(43) = ((20) - (19)) \times$ noise cost	noise	6.3	0.0	0.0	0.2	0.8	1.0	0.0	0.0
$(44) = ((20) - (19)) \times$ air pollution cost	air pollution	4.2	0.0	0.0	0.1	0.5	0.7	0.0	0.0
$(45) = ((20) - (19)) \times$ safety cost	safety cost	0.6	0.0	0.0	0.0	0.1	0.1	0.0	0.0
$(46) = (42) + (43) + (44) + (45)$	Total	100.0	0.0	0.0	2.9	12.5	18.2	0.0	0.0
$(47) = (41) - (46)$	Net external effect	417.0	−25.0	−25.0	−2.9	10.7	39.3	98.3	118.9
$(48) = (36) + (47)$	Project net economic flows	**896.9**	−25.0	−25.0	2.0	50.6	104.7	189.8	219.7
	Project ERR	**22.2%**							

assumes that diverted traffic consists of traffic that is forced to make alternative travel arrangements, in this case travelling by car to the nearest alternative airport – the airport in town B, as in the greenfield case – and travelling by air through it. In practice there may be other alternatives, as discussed in Chapter 3, section 3.1. Some travellers may divert to an alternative transport mode to the final destination, although in the case of air transport this would be limited to short-haul traffic.

Likewise, traffic could be diverted to less busy travel times. In particular, once a terminal reaches capacity and airlines are not able to secure slots at preferred times, they may schedule additional capacity at less preferred times. In such cases a demand analysis would have to establish whether this new, less convenient schedule is more attractive to the passenger than travelling through an alternative airport or transport mode. Surveys from passengers can help to shed light on the pattern of passenger behaviour at any airport. However, as far as the calculation of economic benefits is concerned, the additional generalised transport cost the passenger would incur by diverting to the alternative airport constitutes an upper limit to the generalised cost that the passenger would be willing to incur by alternative forms of diversion. That alternative cannot involve a higher generalised cost than travelling through airport B, or else the traveller would travel through airport B.

To the extent that the diverted traveller decides to wait and travel through the airport at a time different from the preferred time, the passenger would generate revenue and operating costs at the project airport. This means that, as far as the financial analysis is concerned, the difference in operating cash flows between the 'with project' and 'without project' scenarios would be smaller than if the passenger diverts to an alternative airport (or transport mode), reducing the financial return of the project. The extent to which the economic (as opposed to financial) return would be affected would depend on the producer surplus assumed in the alternative airport (row 35).[14]

The project generates a strong return of 19.6 per cent before externalities, much higher than in the greenfield case, reflecting the cost efficiencies enjoyed by more efficient use of the airside. Including externalities, the economic return improves even more. This is because the negative external effects created by generated traffic (row 46) are far outweighed by the additional external costs created by land transport used by diverted traffic (row 41). The environmental benefit is larger than in the greenfield case because the real price of carbon is higher, as it is assumed that carbon price would increase by 3 per cent per year in real terms. This is not a necessary result of airport projects. For any project, whether there is a net environmental cost or benefit would depend largely on the means of transport used by diverted traffic. For example, if diversion to the alternative airport is effected by train, which can be far less polluting than road transport, the environmental benefits of avoiding traffic diversion will be smaller and the environmental performance of the project would deteriorate. The result reported here serves only to illustrate that the net environmental impact of an airport is not necessarily negative. Moreover, recall that it has been assumed in section 4.1 above that there is either an environmental tax lower than the social cost of carbon or that MBMs only apply to a portion of traffic. If the tax reflected the social cost of carbon or if MBMs covered all of the traffic in the airport, there would not be an external environmental cost from the project.

The finding of a positive net environmental benefit illustrates the desirability of internalising the external costs of aviation. Even partially internalising environmental costs is better than nothing. Still, making the users of any transport mode pay for the mode's full external costs yields the most economically efficient outcome. If airline users paid for their external costs in full, the economic returns of airport investments would improve, as any non-internalised environmental cost from generated traffic (rows 42 to 44) would disappear.

4.4 Involving the private sector (2): room for capital investment

As is discussed above, unlike the greenfield project the expansion project is profitable, as the expansion exploits economies of scale and density, including the more intensive operation of installed airside infrastructure. In addition, the overall airport now generates a positive financial return and is sellable to private investors as a whole without the need for subsidies or concerns about transfers from the public to the private sector.

The net present value (NPV) of the airport without the project is EUR303.7 million (row 6). For ease of reference, the analysis ignores expenditure in any refitting that the existing terminal may require. The sale may be made conditional on capacity expansion, even though the private sector would have an incentive to carry out such expansion anyway, because of its expected positive financial return. A private sector operator content with a minimum real return on investment of 5 per cent would be willing to pay the government up to EUR341.4 million for the airport (row 12), invest the EUR100 million over the four years required to carry out the terminal expansion project, and generate a 5 per cent return on the total EUR441.4 million invested. The value of the airport to the private sector would be lower should the risk-adjusted return demanded by the private sector be higher. If, for example, the 7.1 per cent project return represented also the minimum return demanded by the private sector for both the project and the airport as a whole, the value of the airport would be EUR327.4 million, calculated by discounting the cash flows in row 12 by 7.1 per cent instead of 5 per cent.

Private sector involvement could occur either by an outright sale of the airport, combined with economic regulation if it is judged that there is insufficient competition to check a potential abuse of market power; or by granting a concession for the whole or parts of the airport for a predetermined period.[15]

For the public sector, the decision to involve the private sector would depend on government budgetary considerations, and on the extent to which any higher cost of capital of the private sector relative to that of the public sector could be expected to be outweighed by a more efficient project implementation by the former. The decision for the private sector to get involved would rest on whether the expected financial returns are sufficient to compensate for the risks included in the competitive, regulatory, or contractual frameworks defined by the model of privatisation put forward by the public sector.

In the perhaps simpler case of an outright sale of the airport, government revenues from privatisation would consist of the up to EUR341.4 million from the sale of the airport (row 12), plus future tax revenues from inputs and output over the life of the project, with a present value of EUR179.1 million (row 13). This is EUR53.2 million higher than the EUR125.9 million the government would raise without the project (row 15). Should the private sector succeed in generating efficiency gains over the life of the project, and should the government decide to pass on some of those efficiency gains to consumers through lower airport charges, tax revenue would decrease through lower input taxes, but increase through any additional traffic generated by the lower charges. Beyond government revenues, however, the lower costs to passengers will bring about a net welfare gain to society, including higher productivity for local businesses, reflected by gains in consumer surplus. Should the airport remain in public sector hands, the project would be worth EUR90.9 million to the government (row 16), namely the summation of EUR37.7 million to the (in such a case, public sector) airport operator, plus the EUR53.2 million net gain in tax revenue.

4.5 The incentive to overinvest

The significant difference between the financial return and the economic return before externalities in the terminal expansion example of Table 4.5 signals a potential for additional revenue generation by the airport. Such potential is measured by non-monetised consumer surplus from diverted traffic (row 25), but not from generated traffic since the level of charges that would appropriate all consumer surplus from diverted traffic would eliminate any generated traffic. In addition, there is potential consumer surplus to be extracted from captive traffic, that is, traffic that would fly from the airport without the project. One way of tapping such revenue would be by increasing charges. But under conditions of economic regulation this avenue would be blocked.[16] Moreover, the regulatory regime will normally include scheduled revisions in charges in order to pass at least part of any efficiency gains on to customers.

One other way of tapping such a consumer surplus would be by overinvesting, or overbuilding. Under a regulated rate of return, profits can be raised by increasing the amount of capital that is remunerated at that rate of return. This incentive to overinvest is called the 'Averch–Johnson effect'[17] and it is illustrated in this section.

Let us assume that the government and the private sector agree to a rate of return on investment of 7.1 per cent – the return arrived at in Table 4.5. The private sector operator could put forward a number of ways to increase investment. It could argue that the traffic forecasts are too conservative, as proved to be the case during the planning of the greenfield project. It could also propose a particularly ostentatious design that would appeal to the public, and in doing so incentivise local politicians to support it. It could also try to convince the authorities to aim for a higher quality of service target than used so far.

Let us assume further that the outcome of such lobbying is to double the size of the airport terminal project, one that would supply additional capacity for 2.4 million passengers per year, instead of the 1.2 million passengers initially envisaged. The new, larger expansion would bring the total capacity of the airport to 3.6 million per year, instead of 2.4 million. The investment cost would double from EUR100 million to EUR200 million, and operating costs per passenger in the larger terminal at opening will be 20 per cent higher than in the smaller terminal, due to the lower traffic density.

Table 4.6 shows the effects on project returns of such overinvestment. The financial return would fall to 3.5 per cent from 7.1 per cent. This is because the adverse effects of overdimensioning the terminal, including additional upfront capital investment and additional terminal operating costs, are higher than the favourable effects, which would consist of incremental revenue from extra passengers late into the project life.

The economic return before externalities would fall to 14.4 per cent from 19.6 per cent, as the additional benefits from reducing deterred and diverted traffic far into the future are less than the additional investment and operating costs in the near future. The project generates more value than the smaller project, EUR562 million versus EUR479.9 million respectively (row 36 in both tables). However, since the additional value is less than the extra investment required, the rate of return on investment falls. Externalities would also contribute to increasing the value created by the project, as the additional costs, particularly the additional environmental costs brought about by more generated traffic (as generated traffic is now crowded out by diverted traffic later into the future) are smaller than the environmental benefits of reducing the number of passengers diverted by land transport to alternative airports (rows 46 and 41, respectively). The overall return of the project after externalities, at 17 per cent, is still lower than the 22.2 per cent generated with the smaller airport.

Note that tax revenues increase as a result of the overinvestment, as taxes vary directly with investment costs and operating costs, both of which are higher now. This serves to illustrate two issues. First, whereas higher tax revenues are often cited by project promoters as benefits to society, tax revenues and social returns do not necessarily go hand in hand. A project that produces higher tax revenues is not necessarily a project that produces better returns for society if those revenues come from misallocating resources. The

Table 4.6 Financial and economic returns of terminal expansion with larger capacity but with no price increase

		PV/Year	14	15	16	17	18	25	30	35	42
	FINANCIAL RETURNS										
	Airport passenger capacity										
(1)	with project	(thousand)		1,200	1,200	1,200	1,200	3,600	3,600	3,600	3,600	3,600
(2)	without project	(thousand)		1,200	1,200	1,200	1,200	1,200	1,200	1,200	1,200	1,200
	Passenger throughput										
(3)	with project	(thousand)		1,374	1,443	1,515	1,591	1,671	2,351	3,000	3,829	4,788
(4)	without project	(thousand)		1,374	1,443	1,515	1,591	1,596	1,596	1,596	1,596	1,596
	Operating cashflows (after tax)										
(5)	with project	(EUR m)	433.7	16.6	17.8	19.0	20.2	14.0	24.3	34.6	48.2	64.8
(6)	without project	(EUR m)	303.7	16.6	17.8	19.0	20.2	20.6	20.6	20.6	20.6	20.6
(7) = (5) - (6)	Net benefit	(EUR m)	130.0	0.0	0.0	0.0	0.0	-6.6	3.7	14.0	27.6	44.2
(8)	Capital investment	(EUR m)	177.3	50.0	50.0	50.0	50.0					
(9)	Subsidy	(EUR m)	0.0	0.0	0.0	0.0	0.0					
(10) = (7) - (8) + (9)	Net cash flow to operator	(EUR m)	**-47.3**	-50.0	-50.0	-50.0	-50.0	-6.6	3.7	14.0	27.6	44.2
(11)	Operator FRR		**3.5%**									

(12) = (5) - (8) + (9)	Private value of airport with project	(EUR m)	256.4	-33.4	-32.2	-31.0	-29.8	14.0	24.3	34.6	48.2	64.8
	Government financial flows											
(13)	with project	(EUR m)	212.6	14.2	14.4	14.7	15.1	9.0	12.0	14.8	18.3	22.2
(14)	without project	(EUR m)	139.2	14.2	14.4	14.7	15.1	7.5	7.5	7.5	7.5	7.5
(15) = (13) - (14)	Net revenue	(EUR m)	73.5	0.0	0.0	0.0	0.0	1.5	4.5	7.2	10.7	14.6
(16) = (10) + (15)	Operator + government flows	(EUR m)	**26.2**	-50.0	-50.0	-50.0	-50.0	-5.1	8.2	21.3	38.4	58.8
	Private and Government FRR		**5.7%**									

ECONOMIC RETURNS

	Diverted passengers											
(17)	with project	(thousand)	0.0	0.0	0.0	0.0	0.0	0.0	0.0	0.0	0.0	0.0
(18)	without project	(thousand)	0.0	0.0	0.0	0.0	0.0	0.0	490.6	1,067.1	1,802.9	3,186.6
	Deterred passengers											
(19)	with project	(thousand)	0.0	0.0	0.0	0.0	0.0	0.0	0.0	0.0	0.0	0.0
(20)	without project	(thousand)	600.0	0.0	0.0	0.0	0.0	74.6	264.1	337.1	430.3	605.4
	Cost of diversion											
(21) = (17) × time cost	time cost with project	(EUR m)	0.0	0.0	0.0	0.0	0.0	0.0	0.0	0.0	0.0	0.0

(Continued)

Table 4.6 (Continued)

			PV/Year	14	15	16	17	18	25	30	35	42
(22) = (18) × time cost	time cost without project	(EUR m)	470.3	0.0	0.0	0.0	0.0	0.0	17.9	43.1	80.4	163.2
(23) = ((17) − (18)) × other costs	op & safety costs of diverted pax approapriated by operator and gov.	(EUR m)	191.9	0.0	0.0	0.0	0.0	0.0	8.8	19.2	32.5	57.4
(24)		(EUR m)	170.6	0.0	0.0	0.0	0.0	0.0	7.8	17.1	28.8	51.0
(25) = − (21) + (22) + (23) − (24)	Net benefit	(EUR m)	299.7	0.0	0.0	0.0	0.0	0.0	18.9	45.2	84.0	169.5
Cost of deterrement												
(26) = 0.5 × (19) × time costs	time cost with project	(EUR m)	6.6	0.0	0.0	0.0	0.0	0.0	0.0	0.0	0.0	15.4
(27) = 0.5 × (20) × time costs	time cost without project	(EUR m)	73.1	0.0	0.0	0.0	0.0	1.2	4.8	6.8	9.6	15.5
(28) = 0.5 × ((19) − (20)) × other costs	op. & safety costs of deterred pax	(EUR m)	29.7	0.0	0.0	0.0	0.0	0.7	2.4	3.0	3.9	0.0
(29)	approapriated by operator	(EUR m)	52.8	0.0	0.0	0.0	0.0	1.2	4.2	5.4	6.9	0.1
(30) = − (26) + (27) + (28) − (29)	Net benefit	(EUR m)	66.5	0.0	0.0	0.0	0.0	0.7	3.0	4.4	6.6	0.1
Cost of congestion												
(31)	with project	(EUR m)	89.7	5.2	5.5	5.9	6.3	0.0	0.0	0.0	0.0	0.0
(32)	without project	(EUR m)	111.8	5.2	5.5	5.9	6.3	6.5	7.4	8.2	9.1	10.4
(33) = − (31) + (32)	Net benefit	(EUR m)	22.1	0.0	0.0	0.0	0.0	6.5	7.4	8.2	−12.7	−20.8
(34)	Surplus appropriated from captive traffic	(EUR m)	0.0	0.0	0.0	0.0	0.0	0.0	0.0	0.0	0.0	0.0
(35)	Gross producer surplus airport B	(EUR m)	21.3	0.0	0.0	0.0	0.0	0.0	1.0	2.1	3.6	6.4
(36) = (11) + (25) + (30) + (33) − (34) − (35)	Economic flows (ex externalities)	(EUR m)	562.0	−50.0	−50.0	−50.0	−50.0	2.1	36.6	77.0	112.6	201.2
	ERR without externalities		**14.4%**									

Externalities

From land transport diversion											
(37) = ((18) - (17)) × GHG cost	greenhouse gas	(EUR m)	593.2	0.0	0.0	0.0	0.0	20.5	51.8	101.5	220.6
(38) = ((18) - (17)) × noise cost	noise	(EUR m)	32.0	0.0	0.0	0.0	0.0	1.5	3.2	5.4	9.6
(39) = ((18) - (17)) × air pollution cost	air pollution	(EUR m)	21.3	0.0	0.0	0.0	0.0	1.0	2.1	3.6	6.4
(40) = ((18) - (17)) × safety cost	safety cost	(EUR m)	3.2	0.0	0.0	0.0	0.0	0.1	0.3	0.5	1.0
(41) = (37) + (38) + (39) + (40)	Total	(EUR m)	649.7	0.0	0.0	0.0	0.0	23.1	57.5	111.0	237.4
From generated air transport											
(42) = ((20) - (19)) × GHG cost	greenhouse gas	(EUR m)	160.8	0.0	0.0	0.0	2.5	11.1	16.4	24.2	0.4
(43) = ((20) - (19)) × noise cost	noise	(EUR m)	9.9	0.0	0.0	0.0	0.2	0.8	1.0	1.3	0.0
(44) = ((20) - (19)) × air pollution cost	air pollution	(EUR m)	6.6	0.0	0.0	0.0	0.1	0.5	0.7	0.9	0.0
(45) = ((20) - (19)) × safety cost	safety cost	(EUR m)	1.0	0.0	0.0	0.0	0.0	0.1	0.1	0.1	0.0
(46) = (42) + (43) + (44) + (45)	Total	(EUR m)	178.3	0.0	0.0	0.0	2.9	12.5	18.2	26.5	0.4
(47) = (41) - (46)	Net external effect	(EUR m)	471.3	-50.0	-50.0	-50.0	-2.9	10.7	39.3	84.5	237.0
(48) = (36) + (47)	Project net economic flows	(EUR m)	1,033.3	-50.0	-50.0	-50.0	-0.9	47.3	116.3	197.2	438.3
	Project ERR		17.0%								

second issue is that the government may have a financial incentive to allow overinvestment.

The consequences of allowing overinvestment do not end with the results of Table 4.6. In the example under discussion, government regulation sets a target rate of return for the private sector of 7.1 per cent. For this to occur with the oversized new 2.4 million passenger terminal project, revenue per passenger would have to be increased by 16.3 per cent, relative to that of the 1.2 million passenger terminal project. Since the airport operator has more direct control over aeronautical charges than non-aeronautical revenues, the bulk of the increase would tend to come from increases in charges, with some implications for traffic levels.

Table 4.7 shows the results of the 16.3 per cent charge increase. Whereas the financial return goes up significantly from 3.5 per cent to the targeted 7.1 per cent, the economic return before externalities decreases marginally from 14.4 per cent to 14.3 per cent. The main effects of the price increase are threefold. First, there is a welfare transfer from passengers to both the private operator and, through taxes on revenues, to the government. On the passenger side this is measured by an increase in the appropriation of consumer surplus from diverted traffic from EUR170.6 million to EUR212.3 million (row 24), and from captive, or 'existing,' traffic that would have travelled anyway without the project, and which now must pay a higher charge (row 34). From the recipient side, there is an increase in the present value to the private sector from a negative EUR47.3 million, to a positive EUR71.5 million (row 10), and of tax revenue to the government from EUR25.9 million to EUR163.3 million.

Second, there are changes in resource use, bringing about changes in social welfare, as opposed to just transfers. The higher charges deter some traffic, reducing traffic generated by the project (rows 20 minus 19), although generated traffic remains higher than without overinvestment. On the other hand, less generated traffic reduces congestion costs marginally (row 31). The net effect is a small loss of welfare, consisting of the deadweight loss, identified for the consumer by area cef in Figure 4.1, plus some loss in producer surplus related to deterred traffic. The combination of these losses causes the small fall in economic value generated by the project before externalities from EUR562 million to EUR556.8 million (row 36) and in the economic return, relative to the scenario of overinvestment without the price increase.

Finally, there is a change in external effects. The loss of generated traffic improves the environmental and safety performance of the project (row 47), increasing the economic returns marginally to 17.2 per cent up from the 17 per cent achieved in the overinvestment scenario without the price increase.

Comparing Table 4.7 with Table 4.5, the effects of the overinvestment can be summarised as follows. The promoter sees an increase in present value of the investment from EUR37.7 million to EUR71.5 million (row 10) while returns per euro invested remain constant. The government sees an increase in tax revenue from EUR53.2 million to EUR93 million (row 15). Both the

Table 4.7 Financial and economic returns of terminal expansion with larger capacity and with price increase

		PV/Year	14	15	16	17	18	25	30	35	42
FINANCIAL RETURNS											
Airport passenger capacity											
(1)	with project	(thousand)		1,200	1,200	1,200	1,200	3,600	3,600	3,600	3,600	3,600
(2)	without project	(thousand)		1,200	1,200	1,200	1,200	1,200	1,200	1,200	1,200	1,200
Passenger throughput											
(3)	with project	(thousand)		1,356	1,423	1,494	1,569	1,648	2,318	2,959	3,776	4,788
(4)	without project	(thousand)		1,374	1,443	1,515	1,591	1,596	1,596	1,596	1,596	1,596
Operating cashflows (after tax)											
(5)		(EUR m)	552.5	20.9	22.3	23.7	25.2	19.3	31.7	44.0	60.2	80.7
(6)		(EUR m)	303.7	16.6	17.8	19.0	20.2	20.6	20.6	20.6	20.6	20.6
(7) = (5) − (6)	Net benefit	(EUR m)	248.8	4.3	4.5	4.7	5.0	−1.3	11.1	23.4	39.6	60.1
(8)	Capital investment	(EUR m)	177.3	50.0	50.0	50.0	50.0					
(9)	Subsidy	(EUR m)	0.0	0.0	0.0	0.0	0.0					
(10) = (7) − (8) + (9)	Net cash flow to operator	(EUR m)	**71.5**	−45.7	−45.5	−45.3	−45.0	−1.3	11.1	23.4	39.6	60.1
(11)	Operator FRR		7.1%									

(Continued)

Table 4.7 (Continued)

			PV/Year	14	15	16	17	18	25	30	35	42
(12) = (5)–(8) + (9)	Private value of airport with project	(EUR m)	375.2	-29.1	-27.7	-26.3	-24.8	19.3	31.7	44.0	60.2	80.7
	Government financial flows											
(13)	with project	(EUR m)	232.2	14.9	15.2	15.5	15.9	9.9	13.2	16.3	20.2	25.0
(14)	without project	(EUR m)	139.2	14.2	14.4	14.7	15.1	7.5	7.5	7.5	7.5	7.5
(15) = (13) – (14)	Net revenue	(EUR m)	93.0	0.7	0.7	0.8	0.8	2.3	5.7	8.8	12.7	17.4
(16) = (10) + (15)	Operator + government flows	(EUR m)	**164.5**	-45.0	-44.8	-44.5	-44.2	1.1	16.8	32.2	52.3	77.6
	Private and Government FRR		**9.5%**									
	ECONOMIC RETURNS											
	Diverted passengers											
(17)	with project	(thousand)		0.0	0.0	0.0	0.0	0.0	0.0	0.0	0.0	0.0
(18)	without project	(thousand)		0.0	0.0	0.0	0.0	0.0	490.6	1,067.1	1,802.9	3,186.6
	Deterred passengers											
(19)	with project	(thousand)		18.9	19.9	20.9	21.9	23.0	32.4	41.3	52.7	600.0
(20)	without project	(thousand)		0.0	0.0	0.0	0.0	74.6	264.1	337.1	430.3	605.4
	Cost of diversion											
(21) = (17) × time cost	time cost with project	(EUR m)	0.0	0.0	0.0	0.0	0.0	0.0	0.0	0.0	0.0	0.0

$(22) = (18) \times$ time cost	time cost without project	(EUR m)	470.3	0.0	0.0	0.0	0.0	0.0	17.9	43.1	80.4	163.2
$(23) = ((17) - (18)) \times$ other costs	op & safety costs of diverted pax	(EUR m)	191.9	0.0	0.0	0.0	0.0	0.0	8.8	19.2	32.5	57.4
(24)	approapriated by operator and gov.	(EUR m)	212.3	0.0	0.0	0.0	0.0	0.0	9.8	21.3	35.9	63.5
$(25) = - (21) + (22) + (23)-(24)$	Net benefit	(EUR m)	257.9	0.0	0.0	0.0	0.0	0.0	17.0	41.0	76.9	157.1
	Cost of deterrement											
$(26) = 0.5 \times (19) \times$ time costs	time cost with project	(EUR m)	15.5	0.3	0.3	0.3	0.3	0.4	0.6	0.8	1.2	15.4
$(27) = 0.5 \times (20) \times$ time costs	time cost without project	(EUR m)	73.1	0.0	0.0	0.0	0.0	1.2	4.8	6.8	9.6	15.5
$(28) = 0.5 \times ((19) - (20)) \times$ other costs	op. & safety costs of deterred pax	(EUR m)	25.5	-0.2	-0.2	-0.2	-0.2	0.5	2.1	2.7	3.4	0.0
(29)	appropriated by operator	(EUR m)	56.4	-0.4	-0.4	-0.4	-0.4	1.0	4.6	5.9	7.5	0.1
$(30) = -(26) + (27) + (28) - (29)$	Net benefit	(EUR m)	57.6	-0.1	-0.1	-0.1	-0.1	0.3	1.7	2.7	4.3	0.1
	Cost of congestion											
(31)	with project	(EUR m)	81.6	5.1	5.4	5.8	6.2	0.0	0.0	0.0	21.5	31.3
(32)	without project	(EUR m)	111.8	5.2	5.5	5.9	6.3	6.5	7.4	8.2	9.1	10.4
$(33) = - (31) + (32)$	Net benefit	(EUR m)	30.2	0.1	0.1	0.1	0.1	6.5	7.4	8.2	-12.4	-20.8
(34)	Surplus appropriated from captive traffic	(EUR m)	93.1	5.4	5.7	5.9	6.2	6.3	6.3	6.3	6.3	6.3
(35)	Gross producer surplus airport B	(EUR m)	21.3	0.0	0.0	0.0	0.0	0.0	1.0	2.1	3.6	6.4
$(36) = (11) + (25) + (30) + (33) - (34) - (35)$	Economic flows (ex externalities)	(EUR m)	556.8	-50.4	-50.4	-50.5	-50.5	1.5	35.7	75.8	111.2	201.2
	ERR without externalities		14.3%									

(*Continued*)

Table 4.7 (Continued)

		PV/Year	14	15	16	17	18	25	30	35	42
Externalities											
From land transport diversion											
(37) = ((18) - (17)) × GHG cost	greenhouse gas	(EUR m)	593.2	0.0	0.0	0.0	0.0	0.0	20.5	51.8	101.5	220.6
(38) = ((18) - (17)) × noise cost	noise	(EUR m)	32.0	0.0	0.0	0.0	0.0	0.0	1.5	3.2	5.4	9.6
(39) = ((18) - (17)) × air pollution cost	air pollution	(EUR m)	21.3	0.0	0.0	0.0	0.0	0.0	1.0	2.1	3.6	6.4
(40) = ((18) - (17)) × safety cost	safety cost	(EUR m)	3.2	0.0	0.0	0.0	0.0	0.0	0.1	0.3	0.5	1.0
(41) = (37) + (38) + (39) + (40)	Total	(EUR m)	649.7	0.0	0.0	0.0	0.0	0.0	23.1	57.5	111.0	237.4
From generated air transport											
(42) = ((20) - (19)) × GHG cost	greenhouse gas	(EUR m)	139.8	-0.6	-0.6	-0.7	-0.7	1.8	9.7	14.4	21.2	0.4
(43) = ((20) - (19)) × noise cost	noise	(EUR m)	8.5	-0.1	-0.1	-0.1	-0.1	0.2	0.7	0.9	1.1	0.0
(44) = ((20) - (19)) × air pollution cost	air pollution	(EUR m)	5.7	0.0	0.0	0.0	0.0	0.1	0.5	0.6	0.8	0.0
(45) = ((20) - (19)) × safety cost	safety cost	(EUR m)	0.8	0.0	0.0	0.0	0.0	0.0	0.1	0.1	0.1	0.0
(46) = (42) + (43) + (44) + (45)	Total	(EUR m)	154.8	-0.7	-0.7	-0.8	-0.8	2.0	10.9	15.9	23.2	0.4
(47) = (41) - (46)	Net external effect	(EUR m)	494.8	0.7	0.7	0.8	0.8	-2.0	12.2	41.5	87.8	237.0
(48) = (36) + (47)	Project net economic flows	(EUR m)	1,051.7	-49.7	-49.7	-49.7	-49.6	-0.5	47.9	117.3	199.0	438.3
	Project ERR		17.2%									

private sector and the government have an incentive to overinvest. Meanwhile, consumers see their surplus affected. Those who would anyway have travelled through the airport without the project have to pay an extra EUR93.1 million in present value terms to travel (row 34). Travellers who would have diverted without the project see a small improvement in welfare of EUR20.6 million (EUR257.9 − EUR237.3 in row 25) as the larger capacity eliminates traffic diversion towards the end of the life of the project, a benefit which is not fully captured by the increase in charges. There is more generated traffic as less traffic is deterred towards the end of the life of the project, but the increase in charges tames the associated welfare gain. In terms of external costs, there is a net improvement as the external benefits from avoiding passenger diversion outweigh the external costs of more generated traffic. All in all, however, whereas society sees extra value created (row 48), it is achieved by devoting disproportionately more resources, resulting in a loss of welfare generation per euro invested, as is evidenced by the decline in economic returns from 22.2 per cent to 17.2 per cent. The less efficient capital allocation should result in lower productivity for the overall economy, subject to the existence of both budget constraints and alternative investment opportunities (which is usually the case).

To the extent that the project has low risks and, in particular, to the extent that the promoter can rely on the willingness of the government to allow the necessary tariff adjustments to maintain the 7.1 per cent return over time, the promoter can further increase returns by leveraging the investment with debt. If the cost of debt financing is less than the 7.1 per cent return on investment, the promoter can debt finance the additional EUR100 million investment, so that the difference between the cost of debt and the return on investment becomes additional return on equity to the promoter.

The discussion so far helps illustrate the fact that economic regulation, whether through rate of return regulation or through a price cap (with an implicit rate of return target), may not be sufficient to further the interests of society at large. Oversight of capital investment programmes in order to ensure that new capacity is commensurate with reasonable projections of traffic growth may be required. One problem is that such oversight would tend to be carried out through a government agency and, as is shown above, the government may also have an incentive to overinvest because of the positive effects on tax revenues. Therefore, it would be necessary for the agency in charge of approving the investment programme to be kept independent, free from political pressures.

It is important to highlight that the potential for overinvestment ultimately arises from the un-monetised consumer surplus, combined with pricing power by the airport operator. For such pricing power to exist there must be imperfect competition, requiring government regulation, or a strong competitive advantage. Such conditions arise in cases where an airport provides superior accessibility to substantial parts of its catchment area. If competition among airports is close enough to perfect, such room for overinvestment disappears because more efficient capacity planning by the competitor(s) means that the airport that did the overinvesting would experience inferior profitability and would eventually be driven out of business.

4.6 Enlarging a runway

Runway capacity affects the quality and cost of the air services an airport can offer in two respects. First, runway width and length determine the size of the aircraft the airport can accommodate and whether those aircraft can operate at maximum take-off weight (MTOW). Because larger aircraft have lower operating costs, a larger runway allows airlines to offer services at a lower price per seat or per tonne, or indeed to keep prices unchanged and increase profits, depending on the competitive environment. Also, a longer runway allows airlines to offer longer haul flights, since long-haul routes need heavier take-off weights, if only to carry more fuel. Second, runway capacity determines the maximum number of aircraft movements the airport can accommodate within a given period of time, usually measured as movements per hour. This determines both the range of destinations an airport can offer at a given hour and the departure frequency to those destinations, a key determinant of airline schedule quality. It should be noted that beyond the number and size of runways, the runway capacity of an airport is affected by available taxiways, navigational aids, the landscape of surrounding areas (the presence of physical obstacles), and, in airports with more than one runway, by how independently runways can operate from each other.

A runway only rarely constitutes a binding constraint on the passenger capacity of an airport, because limitations on departure frequency can be overcome through increases in the size of aircraft. Runway capacity would constitute a constraint on the passenger throughput capacity of an airport when the runway operates at maximum aircraft movement capacity *and* airlines operate at the highest take-off weight the runway can accommodate. But runway investment projects do not tend to occur in such conditions of absolute necessity. Instead, the decision is based on the willingness to accommodate larger aircraft or to offer greater departure frequency.

This section of the chapter addresses the appraisal of investments to enlarge a runway and section 4.7, which follows, addresses the case for adding an additional runway. In order to simplify the presentation and help the reader focus attention on air transport issues, the analysis assumes no taxes. The treatment of taxes in economic appraisal is illustrated in the airport terminal case. In addition, in contrast to the greenfield airport and terminal expansion cases, this example will assume that, but for some insulation of nearby houses, which is a typical cost of runway expansion projects, airlines have all their externalities internalised.

The project example consists of the simultaneous widening and lengthening of the existing single runway at an airport. Assume that traffic patterns show that the airport handles an average of 2,000 long-haul passengers a day. The airport does not have a sufficiently large runway to handle International Civil

Aviation Organisation (ICAO) Code-D aircraft.[18] As a consequence, the long-haul passengers have to fly to one of three hub airports located one hour's flight away and connect on to intercontinental flights from there.

An airline approaches the airport with a traffic study suggesting that direct flights to the most popular intercontinental destinations could attract 50 per cent of the 2,000 daily long-haul passenger movements currently connecting through one of the nearby hubs, allowing the airport to convert those passenger movements from short-haul to long-haul traffic. For the other 1,000 passengers per day the viable direct flights would not constitute a viable travel alternative. To accommodate the long-haul passenger movements, it will be necessary to enlarge the runway to accommodate Code-D operations. A presentation to the airport executives convinces them of the traffic potential and they decide to conduct an appraisal of the investment to check whether it makes financial sense.

For the long-haul passengers originating or ending their trip at the airport, avoiding the connection at any of the three closest hubs would save three hours from the average intercontinental trip. At an average value of time of EUR15 per hour, saving those three hours would reduce the average behavioural generalised cost per one-way trip from EUR720 to EUR675. This means that in addition to the 1,000 passengers per day diverted from short-haul connecting flights to long-haul direct flights at a generalised cost elasticity of demand of −1.2, the lower generalised cost could generate a 7.5 per cent increase in traffic, or new trips that would not have taken place without the project.

This generated traffic would account for the main financial gain of the airport. This is because any revenues from the additional charges to the new intercontinental flights would be at the expense of revenues from charges to short-haul connecting flights.[19] On the costs side, the airport would have to invest in lengthening and widening the runway, widening some sections of the existing taxiway (no full parallel taxiway is deemed necessary), and modifying the baggage claim area at the terminal. The capital investment cost at the airport site would be EUR90 million. In addition, the longer runway would mean that aircraft operations would exceed noise limits for nearby residents, requiring the installation of double glazing in many houses. This would add another EUR20 million to the cost, bringing the total investment cost of the project to EUR110 million.

Table 4.8 shows the estimation of project returns, focusing only on the long-haul traffic of the airport that would be affected by the project, initially 1,000 passengers per day, or 365,000 passengers per year. The difference in passenger throughput with and without the project (rows 1 and 2) constitutes traffic generated by the project by reducing the generalised cost of travelling long-haul through the airport. This traffic difference also accounts for the difference between operating cash flows with and without the project (row 5), as the unit costs and unit revenues (or passenger yield) of the airport are the same in both scenarios. The resulting financial return for the airport is strongly negative, with a project NPV of a negative EUR89.4 million.

Table 4.8 Financial and economic returns of a runway enlargement project with no change in aeronautical charges

			PV/Year	1	2	3	4	10	15	20	25	28
FINANCIAL RETURNS												
	Passengers											
(1)	with project	(thousand)		365.0	383.3	402.4	452.7	606.7	774.3	988.2	1,261.2	1,460.0
(2)	without project	(thousand)		365.0	383.3	402.4	422.5	566.2	722.7	922.3	1,177.2	1,362.7
	Operating cashflow											
(3)	with project	(EUR m)	155.3	5.5	5.7	6.0	6.8	9.1	11.6	14.8	18.9	21.9
(4)	without project	(EUR m)	146.0	5.5	5.7	6.0	6.3	8.5	10.8	13.8	17.7	20.4
(5) = (3) - (4)	net benefit	(EUR m)	9.3	0.0	0.0	0.0	0.5	0.6	0.8	1.0	1.3	1.5
(6)	Capital investment	(EUR m)	81.0	20.0	35.0	35.0						
(7)	Intern. of external costs	(EUR m)	17.7	0.0	10.0	10.0						
(8) = (5) - (6)-(7)	Operator financial flows	(EUR m)	-89.4	-20.0	-45.0	-45.0	0.5	0.6	0.8	1.0	1.3	1.5
	Operator FRR		**N/A**									
ECONOMIC RETURNS												
	Time benefits											
(9) = (4) × time costs	to diverted pax	(EUR m)	35.4	0.0	0.0	0.0	1.3	2.0	2.9	4.0	5.7	7.0
(10) = 0.5 × ((3) - (4)) × time costs	to generated pax	(EUR m)	1.3	0.0	0.0	0.0	0.0	0.1	0.1	0.1	0.2	0.2
	Lower ticket prices											
(11)	to diverted pax	(EUR m)	0.0	0.0	0.0	0.0	0.0	0.0	0.0	0.0	0.0	0.0
(12)	to generated pax	(EUR m)	0.0	0.0	0.0	0.0	0.0	0.0	0.0	0.0	0.0	0.0
(13) = (9) + (10) + (11) + (12)	Total gain to passengers	(EUR m)	36.7	0.0	0.0	0.0	1.4	2.1	3.0	4.2	5.9	7.2
(14)	Profit gain to airline	(EUR m)	465.6	0.0	0.0	0.0	22.6	30.3	38.7	49.4	63.1	73.0
(15) = (8) + (13) + (14)	Economic flows	(EUR m)	**412.8**	-20.0	-45.0	-45.0	24.5	33.0	42.5	54.6	70.2	81.7
	Project ERR		**23.5%**									

In addition to airport cash flows, an economic appraisal of the investment would also measure non-monetised benefits to passengers, as well as benefits to the airline(s). At the assumed value of time of EUR15 per hour, project benefits to diverted passengers would have a present value of EUR35.4 million (row 9). Traffic generated by the project would enjoy a consumer surplus of EUR1.3 million (row 10).

These gains in consumer surplus to passengers assume that the airline at hand would offer the same ticket price for direct and connecting long-haul flights. However, the airline will experience substantial savings by operating direct long-haul flights, as it will be saving the costs of flying passengers to the connecting hub. Conversations between the airline and the airport reveal that the airline expects such savings to amount to about EUR50 per passenger. The savings would apply to both diverted and generated traffic and would therefore amount to a very substantial EUR466.6 million (row 14). This signals that the project generates a lot of value that is not being reflected in the aeronautical revenues of the airport. The project has an economic value of EUR412.8 million and an economic return of 23.5 per cent. Again, it is assumed that all externalities are internalised. In the event that they were not, the economic return of the project would be higher, as the main project benefits consist of airline operating costs savings by reducing the need for connecting flights to the hub, and airline externalities are directly related to airline output.

The appraisal shows that the airport does not have an incentive to carry out the project, whereas the airline has a strong interest in the project. Clearly, the airline will have an incentive to contribute some of the expected savings of EUR50 per passenger in order to incentivise the airport to carry out the project. Therefore, the airport suggests to the airline that in order to achieve the 7.1 per cent regulated rate of return on investment, they would need to introduce an increase in landing charges to Code-D aircraft – those benefiting from the project – of EUR12.8 per passenger, leaving savings in operating costs to airlines at EUR37.2 per passenger instead of EUR50.

The implications for project return are shown in Table 4.9. Whereas the increase in charges for Code-D aircraft reduces the benefit to the airline, the project still yields substantial benefits to the airline, amounting to EUR346.4 million in savings (row 14). This increase in charges is not passed on to passengers and does not change resource use, consisting merely of a transfer from the airline to the airport. Hence, whereas the financial value of the project to the airport is now a positive EUR29.8 million (row 8) and the return on investment is 7.1 per cent, the economic value and economic return remain unchanged after the increase in charges at EUR412.8 million and 23.5 per cent, respectively.

Strictly speaking, such a scenario would apply to a context of a monopolistic airline market. However, the airline business is competitive and there will be reactions from other airlines. It is not even necessary to assume that other carriers will enter the direct long-haul route, as the market may be too

Table 4.9 Returns on a runway enlargement project with change in aeronautical charges and limited airline competition

		PV/Year	1	2	3	4	10	15	20	25	28
FINANCIAL RETURNS											
Passengers											
(1) with project	(thousand)		365.0	383.3	402.4	452.7	606.7	774.3	988.2	1,261.2	1,460.0
(2) without project	(thousand)		365.0	383.3	402.4	422.5	566.2	722.7	922.3	1,177.2	1,362.7
Operating cashflow											
(3) with project	(EUR m)	274.5	5.5	5.7	6.0	12.6	16.9	21.5	27.5	35.1	40.6
(4) without project	(EUR m)	146.0	5.5	5.7	6.0	6.3	8.5	10.8	13.8	17.7	20.4
(5) = (3)–(4) net benefit	(EUR m)	128.5	0.0	0.0	0.0	6.2	8.4	10.7	13.6	17.4	20.1
(6) Capital investment	(EUR m)	81.0	20.0	35.0	35.0						
(7) Interm. of external costs	(EUR m)	17.7	0.0	10.0	10.0						
(8) = (5) – (6)–(7) Operator financial flows	(EUR m)	29.8	–20.0	–45.0	–45.0	6.2	8.4	10.7	13.6	17.4	20.1
Operator FRR		**7.1%**									
ECONOMIC RETURNS											
Time benefits											
(9) = (4) × time costs to diverted pax	(EUR m)	35.4	0.0	0.0	0.0	1.3	2.0	2.9	4.0	5.7	7.0
(10) = 0.5 × ((3)–(4)) × time costs to generated pax	(EUR m)	1.3	0.0	0.0	0.0	0.0	0.1	0.1	0.1	0.2	0.2
Lower ticket prices											
(11) to diverted pax	(EUR m)	0.0	0.0	0.0	0.0	0.0	0.0	0.0	0.0	0.0	0.0
(12) to generated pax	(EUR m)	0.0	0.0	0.0	0.0	0.0	0.0	0.0	0.0	0.0	0.0
(13) = (9) + (10) + (11) + (12) Total gain to passengers	(EUR m)	36.7	0.0	0.0	0.0	1.4	2.1	3.0	4.2	5.9	7.2
(14) Profit gain to airline	(EUR m)	346.4	0.0	0.0	0.0	16.8	22.6	28.8	36.8	46.9	54.3
(15) = (8) + (13) + (14) Economic flows	(EUR m)	412.8	–20.0	–45.0	–45.0	24.5	33.0	42.5	54.6	70.2	81.7
Project ERR		**23.5%**									

thin to make room for more than one long-haul operator from the airport. But airlines from other competing hubs would lower their prices in order to minimise the loss of business. The airline that approached the airport may also then be forced to lower the price of its air tickets to retain travellers. But the lower time cost to the passenger enabled by the direct service should still make the airline operating the direct service the preferred choice for many passengers. All in all, a plausible final outcome of the project is shown in Table 4.10. The airline passes, say, EUR20 of its EUR50 savings in unit costs to passengers, corresponding to a EUR40 cut on the average return airline ticket price. This generates further traffic, which in turn allows the airport to reduce its required contribution from the airline via higher aircraft charges from EUR12.8 per passenger to EUR12, while keeping its 7.1 per cent regulated return on investment. The airline ends up with a net gain of EUR172.6 million (row 14), down considerably from the EUR364.4 million that it would have made if the airline industry were not so competitive. Such competition is good for consumers though. Because of the generated traffic from the fare cut, the overall return of the project has increased slightly from 23.5 per cent to 23.8 per cent.

Under an alternative context of political economy, the airline may try to push for the increase in aeronautical charges necessary to finance the project to be spread across all passengers (and airlines) using the airport, irrespective of whether they benefit from the project or not. The airline may claim that the larger runway benefits the local economy by making the region more accessible to the world at large. Lobbyists from the local hotel sector may buy into this argument and support the airline, and politicians may perceive the project as potentially popular. Moreover, the airport operator, rather than limit itself to increasing its regulatory asset base by just EUR90 million, may take advantage of the political momentum in favour of an investment project and propose an even larger runway expansion project, one suitable for Code-E aircraft, larger than the Code-D needed by the airline, and possibly adding a full-length parallel taxiway. The airline may quietly object to the unnecessary higher cost of upgrading capacity to Code-E rather than the sufficient Code-D, but may decide not to antagonise the airport, to profit from the policy momentum, and to accept the higher cost as the price to pay for spreading the charges among all passengers. The final result is that the investment cost will be higher than necessary, the airport operator will make more money by inflating its regulatory asset base (the Averch–Johnson effect, see section 4.6), and the airline will end up paying a slightly higher charge than necessary, although it will not bear the marginal cost of the project, which will be spread across all travellers using the airport. In effect, both the airport and the airline are capturing some of the consumer surplus of all of the passengers using the airport, including those that do not use the long-haul flights prompting the runway extension. As far as society as a whole is concerned, there will be some resource misallocation in the form of a larger runway than would be efficient, as signalled by a fall in the economic return

Table 4.10 Returns on a runway enlargement project with change in aeronautical charges and competitive airline market

		PV/Year	1	2	3	4	10	15	20	25	28
FINANCIAL RETURNS											
	Passengers										
(1)	with project	(thousand)	365.0	383.3	402.4	466.1	624.7	797.2	1,017.5	1,298.6	1,503.3
(2)	without project	(thousand)	365.0	383.3	402.4	422.5	566.2	722.7	922.3	1,177.2	1,362.7
	Operating cashflow										
(3)	with project	(EUR m)	274.5	5.5	5.7	6.0	12.6	16.9	21.5	27.5	35.1	40.6
(4)	without project	(EUR m)	146.0	5.5	5.7	6.0	6.3	8.5	10.8	13.8	17.7	20.4
(5) = (3) - (4)	net benefit	(EUR m)	128.5	0.0	0.0	0.0	6.2	8.4	10.7	13.6	17.4	20.1
(6)	Capital investment	(EUR m)	81.0	20.0	35.0	35.0						
(7)	Intern. of external costs	(EUR m)	17.7	0.0	10.0	10.0						
(8) = (5) - (6) - (7)	Operator financial flows	(EUR m)	29.8	-20.0	-45.0	-45.0	6.2	8.4	10.7	13.6	17.4	20.1
	Operator FRR		**7.1%**									
ECONOMIC RETURNS											
	Time benefits										
(9) = (4) × time costs	to diverted pax	(EUR m)	35.4	0.0	0.0	0.0	1.3	2.0	2.9	4.0	5.7	7.0
(10) = 0.5 × ((3)-(4)) × time costs	to generated pax	(EUR m)	1.8	0.0	0.0	0.0	0.1	0.1	0.1	0.2	0.3	0.4
	Lower ticket prices										
(11)	to diverted pax	(EUR m)	173.8	0.0	0.0	0.0	8.5	11.3	14.5	18.4	23.5	27.3
(12)	to generated pax	(EUR m)	9.0	0.0	0.0	0.0	0.4	0.6	0.7	1.0	1.2	1.4
(13) = (9) + (10)+(11) + (12)	Total gain to passengers	(EUR m)	220.1	0.0	0.0	0.0	10.3	14.0	18.2	23.6	30.7	36.0
(14)	Profit gain to airline	(EUR m)	172.6	0.0	0.0	0.0	8.4	11.2	14.4	18.3	23.4	27.1
(15) = (8) + (13) + (14)	Economic flows	(EUR m)	**422.4**	-20.0	-45.0	-45.0	24.9	33.7	43.2	55.6	71.5	83.2
	Project ERR		**23.8%**									

from the project. Such a scenario could only be prevented by effective regulation, including independent oversight of investment plans.

4.7 Adding a runway

The previous section of this chapter considers an investment to increase the size and take-off weight of aircraft flying from an airport. This section deals with investments aimed at increasing the number of aircraft movements an airport can handle in a given period of time. The aircraft movement capacity of an airport is generally measured in terms of maximum movements at peak hour, rather than number of movements per day. The types of investments may involve improving the capacity of an existing runway by lengthening a parallel taxiway, adding a second parallel taxiway, adding rapid-exit taxiways, or upgrading navigational aids. It can also involve adding a new runway. The analysis below uses as an example the addition of a new runway, but it applies equally to all the investments just mentioned.

Assume there is an airport with a single runway, with a maximum capacity of 50 hourly aircraft movements, 25 takeoffs and 25 landings. The runway sees two peak hours a day, one in the morning and one in the evening, Monday to Friday – that is, an average of 260.7 days a year – when it operates close to capacity. Traffic is growing at 4 per cent per year and peak capacity of 50 movements per hour is expected to be reached in three years. The airport managers are considering whether to invest in a second runway. The investment analysis is presented in Table 4.11.

At the moment, airlines operate at the two peak periods with aircraft averaging 100 passengers per flight. This means that in the year, the peak hours see a throughput of about 2.4 million passengers (rows 1 and 15). If a new runway is built, the peak capacity of the airport doubles to 100 movements per hour. In that case, airlines could expand capacity by increasing the number of aircraft movements without needing to change aircraft size. In the long run, however, as larger aircraft are cheaper to operate and as slot availability involves airports at both ends of the route, airlines naturally tend to increase aircraft size as traffic grows. The airport executives calculate that with the new runway, aircraft size will increase on average by some 1 per cent per year, meaning that by year 27, towards the end of the economic life of the project, the average load per aircraft will be 127 passengers (row 2).[20]

The airport managers assume an elasticity of aircraft unit operating cost relative to aircraft size of −0.5, reflecting that larger aircraft are cheaper to operate on a per seat basis. This means that by year 27, when the average load per aircraft will be 127 passengers, airline cost per passenger will be 13 per cent lower (row 3). The savings in operating costs to the airlines resulting from using larger aircraft relative to the aircraft used at present would have a present value of EUR156.1 million (row 9). Should these cost savings be passed on to passengers, there would be some generated traffic. However, since the analysis addresses peak hours under conditions of congestion, it is most probable that

Table 4.11 Economic returns of adding a new runway

			PV/Year	1	2	3	10	20	25	27
	With project									
(1)	Demand at peak	(thousand)		2,403	2,503	2,607	3,431	5,078	6,179	6,683
(2)	Pax per aircraft movement	(unit)		100	100	100	107	118	124	127
(3) through (2)	Change in aircraft op costs	(%)		0%	0%	0%	-4%	-9%	-12%	-13%
(4) through (2)	Capacity at peak	(thousand)		2,607	2,607	5,214	5,590	6,175	6,490	6,621
(5) through (4)	Traffic not diverted	(thousand)		2,403	2,503	2,607	3,431	5,078	6,179	6,621
(6) = (1) - (5)	Traffic diverted	(thousand)		0	0	0	0	0	0	62
(7) = (6) x avg. hours	Hours diverted	(thousand)		0	0	0	0	0	0	147
	Internal effects									
(8) = (7) × VoT	Cost of diversion	(EUR m)	1.0	0	0	0	0	0	0	4
(9) through (3)	Aircraft cost savings	(EUR m)	156.1	0	0	0	6	23	38	45
(10)=-(8) + (9)	Internal benefit	(EUR m)	155.1	0	0	0	6	23	38	41
	External effects									
(11) through (3)	GHG savings	(EUR m)	111.6	0.0	0.0	0.0	3.3	16.9	31.7	39.7
(12) through (3)	Air pollution savings	(EUR m)	6.2	0.0	0.0	0.0	0.2	0.9	1.5	1.8
(13) = (11) + (12)	External benefit	(EUR m)	117.9	0.0	0.0	0.0	3.6	17.8	33.2	41.5
(14) = (10) + (13)	Net benefit	(EUR m)	272.9	0.0	0.0	0.0	9.8	41.2	71.0	82.4
	Without project									
(15)	Demand at peak	(thousand)		2,403	2,503	2,607	3,431	5,078	6,179	6,683
(16)	Pax per aircraft movement	(unit)			100	100	115	140	155	161
(17) through (16)	Change in aircraft op costs	(%)		0%	0%	0%	-7%	-20%	-27%	-30%
(18) through (16)	Capacity at peak	(thousand)		2,607	2,607	2,607	2,995	3,651	4,031	4,193
(19) through (18)	Traffic not diverted	(thousand)		2,403	2,503	2,607	2,995	3,651	4,031	4,193
(20) = (15) - (19)	Traffic diverted	(thousand)		0	0	0	436	1,428	2,148	2,489

(Continued)

Formula	Item	Unit							
(21) = (20) x avg. hours	Hours diverted	(thousand)	0	0	737	2,940	4,884	5,888	
	Internal effects								
(22) = (21) × VoT	Cost of diversion	(EUR m)	0	0	13	64	118	148	424.6
(23) through (17)	Aircraft cost savings	(EUR m)	0.0	0.0	11.1	36.5	55.0	63.8	247.6
(24) =–(22) + (23)	Internal benefit	(EUR m)	0	0	–2	–28	–63	–84	–177.1
	External effects								
(25) through (17)	GHG savings	(EUR m)	0.0	0.0	6.0	26.4	46.1	56.7	174.7
(26) through (17)	Air pollution savings	(EUR m)	0.0	0.0	0.4	1.5	2.2	2.6	9.9
(27) = (25) + (26)	External benefits	(EUR m)	0.0	0.0	6.4	27.9	48.3	59.2	184.6
(28) = (24) + (27)	Net benefit	(EUR m)	0.0	0.0	4.4	0.1	–14.5	–24.8	7.5
	Net project flows								
	Net benefits								
(29) = (10) – (24)	Internal	(EUR m)	0.0	0.0	8.3	51.1	100.6	125.0	332.1
(30) = (13) – (27)	External	(EUR m)	0.0	0.0	–2.9	–10.0	–15.1	–17.8	–66.7
(31)	Investment cost	(EUR m)	50	50					93.0
(32) = (14)–(28) – (31) = (29) + (30) – (31)	Net economic flows	(EUR m)	–50.0	–50.0	5.4	41.1	85.5	107.2	**172.4**
	Project ERR								**11.0%**

the airlines will have pricing power to appropriate such savings, should the airport not appropriate them through higher peak-hour landing charges. The analysis assumes that cost savings are appropriated by the airlines.

In the example at hand, airlines pay for noise externalities via landing charges, but do not pay for greenhouse gas emissions or for air pollution, which remain external costs. Larger aircraft are more fuel efficient on a per passenger basis, so that carrying a given number of passengers on larger rather than smaller aircraft would produce an external environmental benefit by means of reducing emissions. For the average load of 100 passengers per flight the cost of GHG emissions is EUR20 per passenger. This unit external cost would fall in line with the cost-elasticity of aircraft size of −0.5. In addition, the marginal cost of each tonne of GHG emitted will grow by 3 per cent per year. The combined effect of growing aircraft size through time and increasing marginal cost of GHG emissions produces savings in emissions costs, relative to what would be emitted using current aircraft, with a present value EUR111.6 million (row 11). In addition, air pollution costs, valued at EUR2 per passenger, would also fall according to the −0.5 cost-elasticity of aircraft size. Marginal air pollution costs are not assumed to grow through time. This implies that by using larger aircraft there would be savings in emissions costs worth EUR6.2 million (row 12).

Should the runway not be built, airlines would be further encouraged to increase average aircraft size, as doing so is the only possible way of tapping demand at peak hours. Airport managers assume that, in the absence of the new runway, the airlines would double the rate of increase in average aircraft size from 1 per cent to 2 per cent per year. The average load per aircraft would therefore grow from 100 passengers at present to 161 passengers by year 27 (row 16), rather than to the 127 if the runway was built (row 2). The consequences would be twofold. First, savings in aircraft unit operating costs without the runway would increase to 30 per cent instead of 13 per cent with the new runway. The savings through larger aircraft size would amount to EUR247.6 million (row 23). Second, there would be further savings in external costs through lower GHG emissions, valued at EUR174.7 million (row 25); and lower emissions of air pollutants, valued at EUR9.9 million (row 26).

Those passengers willing to travel during peak hours who could not be accommodated despite the increase in aircraft size would be diverted to alternative departure times. Such traffic diversion can be categorised as frequency delay, in the sense that certain departure times would not be available to (a growing number of) passengers, who will have to travel at less than preferred departure or arrival times.[21] It is assumed that in such cases the frequency delay would be initially one hour as airlines schedule alternative departures at the next best departure/arrival time, namely the hour immediately after or before the peak times. As such demand shoulders become increasingly congested, frequency delay increases. Airport managers estimate that the average delay increases by about 2 per cent per year, half the rate of traffic growth.

Similarly, less departure capacity at peak hours could mean that the number of potential destinations with direct links from/to the airport must be less and, therefore, that a higher proportion of passengers will have to connect through intermediate hub airports. It is estimated that passengers who would be forced to travel through connections at an intermediate hub would incur a loss of two hours relative to a scenario where there are direct links to the airport. The proportion of diverted passengers who travel at alternative times and those diverted to connected routes is dependent on the market conditions of each airport. In this case it is assumed that each constitutes 50 per cent, meaning that initially the average delay for diverted passengers would be 1.5 hours. As the shoulders become more congested, the average delay will grow. The resulting numbers of hours of traffic diversion with and without the projects are included in rows 7 and 21, respectively.

Note that the number of passengers with and without the project is assumed to be the same. Terminal capacity does not constitute a constraint on the project and runways place constraints on aircraft capacity, not necessarily passenger capacity. A runway becomes a constraint on passenger capacity when it is operated at maximum departure frequency *and* at maximum aircraft size. Runway investments are very rarely made when facing such conditions. Rather, they constitute a choice to expand the departure frequency, which has implications for aircraft size, both of which are variables that affect social welfare. Therefore, diverted traffic is assumed to travel from the airport and either travel at alternative times or make connections through hubs.

Differences in traffic diversion and operating costs mean that generalised costs change; hence there is room for generated traffic. Indeed, the analysis could be extended by including generated or deterred traffic. However, unlike the previous examples involving terminals and runways, where the project unambiguously generates traffic, the same cannot be said in the case of an additional runway.[22] This is because when adding a runway, traffic generation occurs both with and without the project. In the 'without project' scenario there will be two factors affecting generated traffic, acting in opposite directions: first, traffic may be diverted by an increasing frequency delay and generalised cost relative to the 'with project' scenario; and second, to the extent that aircraft size increases faster than in the 'with project' scenario, airline ticket prices can be potentially lower, generating traffic. Depending on the strength of these two effects, the 'without project' scenario could result in lower or higher traffic than the 'with project' scenario. Ultimately, whether there is net traffic generation with the project relative to the 'without project' scenario rests on the assumptions made about changes in aircraft size in each of the two scenarios. The outcome is very much specific to each project. For simplicity the issue of generated traffic is side-stepped here, which is broadly equivalent to assuming that traffic deterred through greater frequency delay in the 'without project' scenario relative to the 'with project' scenario is offset by traffic generated through higher aircraft size in the 'without project' scenario relative to the 'with project' scenario.

The economic viability of the project would then be determined by a comparison of the investment cost (row 31) with the net savings – aircraft operating costs minus diversion costs – relative to year 1, with the project (row 14) and without the project (row 28). An alternative but equivalent aggregation would be to compare three flows: first, the investment cost of the project (row 31); second, the benefits foregone by the project in terms of lower operating cost and lower external costs that would result from operating larger aircraft, as would be the case without the new runway (rows 23 and 27 minus rows 9 and 13); and third, the project benefits, consisting of the avoidance of costs resulting from passenger diversion to less preferred departure times or routings, thanks to the higher number of aircraft departures allowed by the new runway (row 22 minus row 8). Yet another way to aggregate flows would be to classify benefits into internal (row 29) and external (row 30), and comparing them against investment cost (row 31).

Any of the three ways of aggregation would result in the net project flows as in row 32. The project has an NPV of EUR172.4 million and an economic rate of return of 11 per cent. Since the assumed opportunity cost of capital is 5 per cent, the project would be viable before any budgeting considerations. Note that the viability of the project rests on internal benefits (row 29), and specifically on benefits to passengers in terms of avoided frequency delay (see rows 8 and 22).[23] However, environmental performance subtracts value from the project (row 30), as the smaller aircraft that would accompany the reduction in frequency delay are more polluting on a per seat basis than the larger aircraft that would operate in the absence of the project.

However, it is worth highlighting the extent to which this result is dependent on the definition of the 'with project' and 'without project' scenarios and, in particular, on the assumed behaviour of airlines in each scenario. The viability of the project rests on two key factors: first, the average size of the aircraft operating in the airport, which determines cost savings through changing the aircraft mix; and second, the diversion cost resulting from fewer frequencies, or frequency delay. Both factors depend on the scheduling practices of airlines. The project analyst must make assumptions about such behaviour and the viability of the project will rely largely on such assumptions.

This is illustrated in Table 4.12, which estimates returns on the same project, assuming that aircraft size in the 'without project' scenario grows somewhat faster, at 2.5 per cent per year instead of 2 per cent per year assumed for Table 4.11. This would mean that by year 27 the average number of passengers per flight on the 'without project' scenario would be 181 passengers (row 16), instead of the 161 assumed previously. The outcome of the 'with project' scenario remains the same (row 14). However, the revised assumption improves the performance in the 'without project' scenario in three ways: first, the faster growth in capacity during peak hours in the 'without project' scenario means that fewer passengers are diverted (row 19), which reduces average frequency delay (row 22); second, the use of larger aircraft increases the savings in operating costs (row 23); and third, the environmental performance improves (row 27). The result is to decrease the NPV of the project decisively, to the point of turning it negative, and to turn the rate of return negative as well.

The key to the outcome of the appraisal rests on the assumption of what airlines would do if there was no additional aircraft movement capacity. Assuming that airlines will not increase aircraft size faster in the 'without project' scenario is not realistic, and would only serve to inflate the estimated returns on investing in a runway.

The revised result may be interpreted as reflecting a situation of strong cost economies, whereby it would make little sense to expand capacity when output is below the minimum efficient scale of capacity already installed. But that does not capture the full nature of the situation. This is because output is not homogeneous, as a second runway improves quality of service by lowering frequency delay. More generally, the viability of an investment on aircraft movement capacity depends on the trade-off between frequency delay and cost savings through aircraft size. This makes both the value of time and aircraft technology central. The higher the value of time, the higher the likelihood that an investment in runway capacity will be economically viable. Therefore, the richer the local economy, the stronger the justification for greater runway capacity for any level of traffic.

This is illustrated in Figure 4.2, which revisits Figure 3.2 and applies it to the case of runways. Schedule C stands for operating costs for a given number of aircraft seats supplied, which varies inversely with aircraft size (AS), and 'FD' stands for frequency delay, the cost caused by not having a departure available at the preferred time. Increasing income increases the value of time, which shifts the frequency delay curve from FD' to FD''. This shifts the equilibrium level of frequency from f to f'. Frequency level f is lower than the maximum capacity of a single runway, but frequency level f' would require a second runway. Therefore, the higher income and accompanying higher value of time makes the case for a second runway even at the expense of higher operating costs resulting from operating smaller aircraft. Note that the total number of passengers does not need to change. The case for a third runway would necessitate much higher increases in income.

Figure 4.2 also illustrates the effect of technology. Whereas in the short- to medium-term, technology – hence the shape of the C curve – can be taken as a given, over the longer run technology that improves aircraft cost efficiency will shift down schedule C. Other things being equal, this would help the case for more runways for any given level of income and traffic. On the other hand, for any level of technology an increase in the cost of fuel or GHG emissions would shift the C schedule upwards, calling for fewer runways for a given level of income and traffic. Advances in aircraft technology tend to be geared towards improvements in fuel efficiency. Therefore, looking to the future, rising incomes and advances in technology can be expected to improve the case for

Table 4.12 Economic returns of adding a new runway with faster growth in aircraft size without the project

			PV/Year	1	2	3	10	20	25	27
With project										
(1)	Demand at peak	(thousand)		2,403	2,503	2,607	3,431	5,078	6,179	6,683
(2)	Pax per aircraft movement	(unit)		100	100	100	107	118	124	127
(3) through (2)	Change in aircraft op costs	(%)		0%	0%	0%	-4%	-9%	-12%	-13%
(4) through (2)	Capacity at peak	(thousand)		2,607	2,607	5,214	5,590	6,175	6,490	6,621
(5) through (4)	Traffic not diverted	(thousand)		2,403	2,503	2,607	3,431	5,078	6,179	6,621
(6) = (1) - (5)	Traffic diverted	(thousand)		0	0	0	0	0	0	62
(7) = (6) x avg. hours	Hours diverted	(thousand)		0	0	0	0	0	0	147
	Internal effects									
(8) = (7) × VoT	Cost of diversion	(EUR m)	1.0	0	0	0	0	0	0	4
(9) through (3)	Aircraft cost savings	(EUR m)	156.1	0	0	0	6	23	38	45
(10) = - (8) + (9)	Internal benefit	(EUR m)	155.1	0	0	0	6	23	38	41
	External effects									
(11) through (3)	GHG savings	(EUR m)	111.6	0.0	0.0	0.0	3.3	16.9	31.7	39.7
(12) through (3)	Air pollution savings	(EUR m)	6.2	0.0	0.0	0.0	0.2	0.9	1.5	1.8
(13) = (11) + (12)	External benefit	(EUR m)	117.9	0.0	0.0	0.0	3.6	17.8	33.2	41.5
(14) = (10) + (13)	Net benefit	(EUR m)	272.9	0.0	0.0	0.0	9.8	41.2	71.0	82.4
Without project										
(15)	Demand at peak	(thousand)		2,403	2,503	2,607	3,431	5,078	6,179	6,683
(16)	Pax per aircraft movement	(unit)		100	100	100	119	152	172	181
(17) through (16)	Change in aircraft op costs	(%)		0%	0%	0%	-9%	-26%	-36%	-40%
(18) through (16)	Capacity at peak	(thousand)		2,607	2,607	2,607	3,099	3,967	4,488	4,716
(19) through (18)	Traffic not diverted	(thousand)		2,403	2,503	2,607	3,099	3,967	4,488	4,716
(20) = (15) - (19)	Traffic diverted	(thousand)		0	0	0	332	1,111	1,690	1,967

Formula		Units								
(21) = (20) × avg. hours	Hours diverted	(thousand)		0	0	0	560	2,289	3,843	4,653
	Internal effects									
(22) = (21)xVoT	Cost of diversion	(EUR m)	330.5	0	0	0	10	50	93	117
(23) through (17)	Aircraft cost savings	(EUR m)	347.6	0.0	0.0	0.0	14.6	51.7	81.0	95.3
(24) = - (22) + (23)	Internal benefit	(EUR m)	17.1	0	0	0	5	2	-12	-21
	External effects									
(25) through (17)	GHG savings	(EUR m)	247.1	0.0	0.0	0.0	7.9	37.4	67.8	84.7
(26) through (17)	Air pollution savings	(EUR m)	13.9	0.0	0.0	0.0	0.6	2.1	3.2	3.8
(27) = (25) + (26)	External benefits	(EUR m)	261.0	0.0	0.0	0.0	8.4	39.4	71.0	88.5
(28) = (24) + (27)	Net benefit	(EUR m)	278.1	0.0	0.0	0.0	13.0	41.2	59.3	67.1
	Net project flows									
	Net benefits									
(29) = (10)-(24)	Internal	(EUR m)	137.9	0.0	0.0	0.0	1.6	21.7	49.6	62.4
(30) = (13)-(27)	External	(EUR m)	-143.1	0.0	0.0	0.0	-4.9	-21.6	-37.9	-47.1
(31)	Investment cost	(EUR m)	93.0	50	50	0.0	0.0	0.0	0.0	0.0
(32) = (14) - (28) - (31) = (29) + (30) - (31)	Net economic flows	(EUR m)	-98.2	-50.0	-50.0	0.0	-3.3	0.1	11.7	15.3
	Project ERR		N/A							

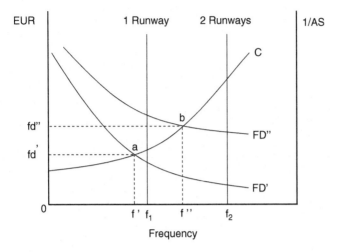

Figure 4.2 Effect of an increase in income on the investment case for a new runway.

more runways, whereas higher costs of energy and GHG emissions would work against new runways.

4.8 Involving the private sector (3): regulatory versus competitive outcome

The above analysis of the investment case for adding a runway does not mention changes in producer surplus, or profitability of the airport operator. Whereas the analysis could have included it, given that the project was assumed not to result in a change in passenger numbers, any change in producer surplus would have reflected largely the structure of airport charges. If the structure of aeronautical charges at the airport were such that the resulting revenue per passenger was constant regardless of the size of aircraft, airport operating revenues would be the same with and without the project.

Any change in airport operating costs would be very case-specific. Airport unit operating costs with the project would increase slightly by operating an extra runway. On the other hand, such costs would be at least in part offset in the 'without project' scenario by the costs of handling larger aircraft, which may require civil works in the terminal, apron, and taxiways.

Therefore, given that the project does not necessarily affect passenger throughput, it is quite likely that the financial incentives to the airport for supplying an additional runway would be weak. Moreover, should the airport market be competitive, with no regime of economic regulation by the government, because of the pervasiveness of economies of density in transport, a private airport operator may prefer to 'sweat the asset' and squeeze as much traffic as possible through the existing infrastructure. This would call for the airport to show a bias for delaying as long as is possible the building of a new runway.

However, if the airport enjoys some monopoly power and is subject to rate of return regulation, the outcome may differ, for two reasons. First, to the extent that 'sweating the asset' generated super-normal profits, these would be short-lived, as the regulator would subsequently adjust downwards the price cap associated with the regulated rate of return in order to eliminate such super-normal profits. Second, runways are expensive capital assets with a weaker link to traffic than terminals. Since the airport will be remunerated by a predetermined rate of return on regulated assets, the airport would have an incentive to overinvest in airside infrastructure, including runways, for any level of traffic, following the Averch–Johnson effect discussed above in section 4.6. The implication is that rate of return regulation can create private incentives to show a bias in favour of new runways, even in situations where airport production functions would call for increasing traffic density and operating the existing installed capacity more intensively.

4.9 Relocating an airport

4.9.1 Background

Airport relocation consists of moving an entire airport from one location to another. Normally this involves moving farther away from an urban area and is made to coincide with a capacity expansion. By moving away from an urban area the relocation has implications for patterns of land transport flows. This could involve differences in airport access and egress conditions between the new and old locations, affecting also land transport users that are neither accessing nor leaving the airport. Airports also occupy large tracts of land. A relocation would also significantly affect land use patterns, quite likely involving substantial opportunities for land redevelopment and redistribution of the external costs of transport among different locations, reflected in land prices.

While relocations do not have to coincide with capacity expansions, they are normally timed to coincide with them. The cases for relocation and for capacity expansion may therefore be put forward as inseparable, when in fact they can be separated. Project analysts have to judge whether the current location could accommodate the capacity expansion. If the answer is negative, then the case for relocation gains strength. If the answer is positive, then the case of relocation tends to strive on the implications that relocation will have on the variables described in the preceding paragraph.[24] But the analyst has to be mindful that what is in fact a poor case for relocation could come across as a sound case by mixing the benefits of capacity expansion with those of relocation.

Let us retake the terminal capacity expansion example of section 4.3 above. We are now in year 22. Recall that back in year 10, the decision makers of the airport in town A, facing faster throughput growth than originally anticipated, began to plan for a capacity expansion. The project at the time consisted of expanding capacity by year 18 to 2.4 million passengers per year (the 'with project' scenario), relative to leaving it at the 1.2 million passenger capacity existing at the time (the 'without project' scenario). As detailed in Table 4.5, such project was expected to produce an economic return of 22.2 per cent.

Recall that section 4.5 of this chapter considered an alternative turn of events, where lobbyists had succeeded in pushing for a tripling of capacity to 3.6 by year 18 (the 'with project' scenario). Table 4.7 showed that this alternative project, when compared to the alternative of leaving capacity constant at 1.2 million passengers (the 'without project' scenario), yielded an economic return of 17.2 per cent. This is an inferior outcome to the 22.2 per cent achieved instead by doubling capacity to 2.4 million, depicted in Table 4.5.

We re-take the line of events from the 2.4 million project in Table 4.5. Decision makers in town A eventually decided to implement this project. Things turned out as expected. Construction of the terminal expansion was finished in year 17 and the added capacity became operative in year 18.

Today is year 22 and traffic is well on its way to reach design capacity by year 26. Congestion is expected to reach unacceptable levels somewhere between 2030 and 2035. New terminal capacity would need to be available by then.

In parallel, planners had been making exploratory analysis regarding increasing runway capacity. Conversations with airlines had suggested that there may be a case in the coming years for enlarging the existing runway, along the lines explored in Table 4.10 in section 4.6 above. Building a second runway would eventually also be needed, but further into the future, and it is deemed that there may be a case for reserving land for such a project. However, this would involve relocating the airport since the current airport site is physically constrained. The possibility of expropriating enough land adjacent to the existing site for a second runway was simply assumed to be far too expensive and politically intractable.

Long-term demand expectations are still for traffic to continue growing at about 5 per cent per year. At that rate it is considered necessary to double terminal capacity from the existing (in year 22) 2.4 million passengers per year to 4.8 million passengers by year 30. Planners expect such terminal capacity expansion would cost about EUR200m.

While prospecting the real estate market in order to acquire land for the capacity expansion to 4.8 million, it became evident that land prices had been increasing significantly. After all, fast traffic growth at the airport was a consequence of the sound performance of the local economy, which in turn meant higher land prices, including those of land in the vicinity of the airport.

A group of property developers had recently approached both the city council and the airport governing bodies suggesting that the airport site would be a sound place for development of residential and commercial real estate. Some local planners had also been suggesting that the current airport site includes a section which overlaps with the optimal routing of a ring road that was being built in phases. Accommodating the optimal routing would not physically require for the airport to move – the ring road could be done underground. But the option of making it underground would increase the costs of the road project substantially, to the point where it would only make sense to route the road through the current airport site if the airport was removed. Should the airport remain in its current site, the ring road would follow an alternative routing, involving longer travelling times to road users.

Airport planners also acknowledged that if the town continued to grow at current rates, land prices would continue to increase and expansion of the airport in the future would be increasingly constrained and expensive. They sensed that there would eventually be a case to move the airport. The question was when.

The planners decided to perform a preliminary economic appraisal to explore the case for relocating the airport. They reasoned that, rather than expanding the terminal now while simultaneously booking land elsewhere for a future relocation, it may well make more economic sense to go for a more ambitious project now and move the airport altogether.

4.9.2 Framing the appraisal

The calculation of the case for relocating the airport makes use of the results of the example of airport capacity expansion project presented so far in this chapter – including Table 4.3 and Table 4.5 in sections 4.1 and 4.3 above, respectively. This makes the presentation shorter and simpler. It also embeds the decision to relocate with that of expanding capacity, helping illustrate the potential error that may arise by mixing the two.

Recall that the estimation in Table 4.3 (as well as that in Table 4.4), conducted earlier, at year 0, consisted of comparing the construction of a greenfield airport in town A (the 'with project' scenario) with continuing to use the airport in town B (the 'without project' scenario). The subsequent estimation in Table 4.5, conducted in year 10, consisted of comparing the expansion of the (by the time already existing) airport in town A from a capacity for 1.2 million passengers per year to a capacity for 2.4 million passengers (the 'with project' scenario), with leaving capacity in the airport in town A constant at 1.2 million passengers (the 'without project' scenario). Such 'without project' scenario would involve traffic diversion and deterrence.

Today, in year 22, the case for moving the airport is carried out by comparing two alternative capacity expansion projects. First, what we may label the 'Expansion at A' project. This consists of comparing expanding capacity from 2.4 million to 5 million at the existing site in town A (the 'with A project' scenario) with not expanding capacity, leaving capacity at 2.4 million in town A (the 'without project' scenario). As usual, the 'without project' scenario would involve some mixture of (i) traffic diverting to town B, (ii) flying from A at less convenient, off peak times, or (iii) not travelling at all.

Second, what we may call the 'Expansion at New A' project. This consists of comparing expanding capacity in town A by shutting down the existing site in town A and creating a 5m passenger greenfield airport 15 minutes drive further away from the city centre (the 'with New A project' scenario), with not creating the new airport, leaving existing 2.4m capacity at the current site in town A (the 'without project' scenario). The 'without project' scenario is therefore exactly the same for these two alternative projects.

The appraisal would then proceed with the following three-step logic, each appraisal step included in a separate row:

'Expansion at A' : *'with A project'* vs *'without project'*

'Expansion at New A' : *'with New A project'* vs *'without project'*

Value of relocation : *'Expansion at New A'* vs *'Expansion at A'*

The reason for taking this extended approach to estimating and displaying project returns is to address the risk of the value of relocation being confused with the value of expanding capacity. So, a positive value of the 'Expansion at New A' project may be taken as proving a case for relocating the airport, when in fact most of the benefits in such estimation may come from capacity expansion rather than the relocation as such. Unless for some reason it is impossible to expand at the existing site, the economic case for relocation should be made net of capacity expansion. As already mentioned, it is not strictly necessary to make coincide a project to relocate an airport with an expansion in airport capacity, although in practice the two tend to coincide.[25]

The analysis also compares whether it is worthwhile to initiate the relocation today or postpone it by 20 years. Figure 4.3 summarises the timings involved in the appraisal exercise. Appraisal is carried out today, in year 22. The first consideration is whether to relocate today. Whichever of the two alternative projects is finally chosen – whether to expand at the existing airport A or to relocate to New A – it would enter operations in year 31, and then go on to have an economic life of 25 years, until the end of year 55, by when new major capital expenditure would be needed. The second consideration – whether to postpone relocation to the following round of capacity expansion versus to leave the airport at the current site and expand capacity further there – would involve expanding capacity to 5m passengers today, commencing the operations phase of such expansion in year 31, and then considering whether to relocate or to expand at the existing site to 10 million passengers in about year 40, for operations to begin in year 51. Again, the economic life of the project would be 25 years, extending this time to year 75.

The reason to perform this timing exercise is to focus attention on the role that the land value of the airport site to be vacated plays in the appraisal. This can be a determining reason for the rationale and viability of the project. There are relatively few problems with estimating the current value of the

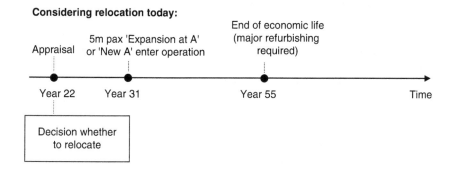

Considering relocation today:

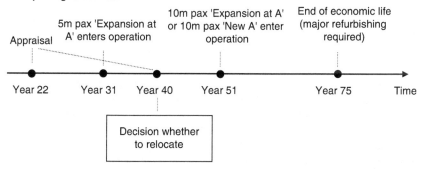

Postponing relocation:

Figure 4.3 Timings involved in the appraisals of (i) relocating airport A today and of (ii) postponing relocation.

land. When thinking about a future relocation, the view to take on the land value of the site can again give rise to confusion.

To simplify, it is assumed that both total traffic and its split into the existing, diverted, and generated categories in the 'Expansion at A' and 'Expansion at New A' projects are exactly the same. This involves an error in that the user generalised cost in accessing and egressing airports New A and A differ. Then there may be a slight difference in total traffic and its split among the categories in the two alternative projects. Since the difference in access and egress conditions, at 15 minutes, is relatively small compared to overall behavioral generalised cost of travel, the error is deemed small.[26] It is a small error deemed worth making as it simplifies the presentation substantially. It eases the comparison between the alternatives and helps identify the sources of project value.

4.9.3 Appraisal results

Table 4.13 summarises the calculation of economic value for both the 'Expansion at A' and 'Expansion at New A' projects. Column a includes the estimation of economic value of initiating relocation today. Columns b and c consider postponing relocation by about 20 years, to the following round of capacity expansion. The value of the postponed project is estimated for a prospective future appraisal exercise performed in year 40 (column b). The resulting values in column b are then discounted to their value today, the beginning of year 22 (column c), applying a discount rate of 5 per cent over the 19-year period. Columns b and c exclude the value of operating the airport from years 31 to 50; that is, they are net of the project to expand from 2.4m to 5m passengers. Finally, column d includes the percentage difference of column c relative to column a.

Expanding the existing site by 2.4m passengers (to 5 million passengers) would involve a capital investment of EUR200m (row 1), double the EUR100 capital expenditure that was needed to expand by 1.2m passengers to the existing 2.4 million passengers (see row 8 in Table 4.5). Likewise, the economic value of expanding to 5 million passengers is approximated pro rata as twice the EUR896.9m (row 48, Table 4.5) value of the of the 1.2m expansion, that is, EUR1.8bn (=896.9m × 2), displayed in row 2. By delaying relocation 20 years − opening in year 51 rather than 31 − the associated expansion (from 5 million to 10 million passengers) would be about twice as large as the expansion involved in relocating today (from 2.4 million to 5 million). The investment and net value of the project are similarly approximated as double the size of the 2.6m expansion today. The capital investment would then be EUR400m (= 200 × 2; cell 1b) and the economic value would be EUR3.6bn (= 1.8 × 2; cell 2b). Expanding capacity at the existing site today to 5 million passengers and again in 20 years time to 10 million passengers both generate substantial economic value, at EUR1.8bn and EUR3.6bn, respectively.

Next we estimate what would be the value of the project if such capacity expansions were instead carried out by relocating the airport, both commencing today or alternatively postponing it by 20 years. The expected capital expenditure involved in relocating the airport is approximated by replicating the cumulative expenditure carried out in the existing site A, involving three magnitudes. Firstly, the EUR400m of the original greenfield airport in A (row 3 in Table 4.13 and row 7 in Table 4.3) with a capacity for 1.2m passengers. Secondly, the EUR100m of the first capacity expansion by 1.2m to the existing 2.4m (row 4 in Table 4.13 and row 8 in Table 4.5). And thirdly, the same EUR200m (row 5) figure incurred in expanding the existing site by 2.6m passengers to 5m passengers per year (row 1). This brings the total investment cost of the combined relocation and expansion project to EUR700m (cell 7a), in sharp contrast to the EUR200m (cell 1a) of expanding at the existing site.

For completeness, it may be worth mentioning that the capital expenditure magnitudes involved in either expanding or expanding and relocating an airport would not necessarily imply replicating or pro-rating past capital expenditures, even adjusting for inflation. Possible causes for divergences in real construction

Table 4.13 Calculation of the economic value of relocating an airport (in EUR m, if not otherwise identified as %)

	Considering relocating today (today: 1 January Year 22)	Postponing relocation by 20 years		Difference in present value
	Current round of capacity expansion: from 2.4 m to 5m pax per year	Next round of capacity expansion consists of expanding capacity from 5m to 10m pax per year		
	Value today (Year 22)	Value in Year 40	Value today (Year 22)	
	(a)	*(b)*	*(c)=(b)/(1+0.05)^{19}*	*(d)=((c)/(a))−1*
Value of expanding existing site ('Expansion at A')	(New 2.6m pax terminal opens in Year 30)	(New 5m pax terminal opens in year 50)		
(1) Capital investment of expanding existing site	200	400	158	−21%
(2) Value of project	**1,794**	3,588	**1,420**	−21%
Value of expanding at new site ('Expansion at New A')	(New A airport opens in Year 31)	(New A airport opens in Year 51)		
Adjustments to airport capex:				
(3) Greenfield to 1.2m pax (T.4.3)	400			
(4) Extra 1.2m pax (T.4.5)	100			

(*Continued*)

Table 4.13 (Continued)

		Considering relocating today (today: 1 January Year 22)	Postponing relocation by 20 years		Difference in present value
		Current round of capacity expansion: from 2.4 m to 5m pax per year	Next round of capacity expansion consists of expanding capacity from 5m to 10m pax per year		
		Value today (Year 22)	Value in Year 40	Value today (Year 22)	
		(a)	(b)	(c)=(b)/(1+0.05)^{19}	(d)=((c)/(a))−1
(5)	Extra capacity for 2.6m pax to reach 5m	200			
(6)	Extra capacity for 5m pax to reach 10m		400	158	−38%
(7)=(3)+(4)+(5)+(6)	Total	700	1,100	435	−45%
(8a)=(3)+(4)×0.2	Saved refurbishing of the existing site	100	140	55	−45%
(8b)=(7a)×0.2					
(9) = −(1)+(7)−(8)	Net additional capex	400	560	222	−45%
	Road transport (private) costs of relocating:				
	Non-users of airport:				
(10)	cost savings to non users	202	374	148	−27%
(11)	Capex savings urban	60	90	36	−41%
	Longer access and egress trips by users and workers:				
(12)	Additional opex and time costs	638	2,157	853	34%
(13)	Additional capex	100	150	59	−41%
(14) = (12) + (13)	Sub-total:	738	2,307	913	24%
(15) = −(10)−(11)+(14)	Net additional cost by relocating	476	1,842	729	53%
	Adjustments to external environmental costs				
(16)	Passengers: GHG	22	101	40	81%
(17)	Air pollution	−63	−160	−63	0%
(18)	Noise	−91	−229	−91	0%
(19)	Subtotal	−132	−289	−114	−13%

		Considering relocating today (today: 1 January Year 22) Current round of capacity expansion: from 2.4 m to 5m pax per year	Postponing relocation by 20 years Next round of capacity expansion consists of expanding capacity from 5m to 10m pax per year		Difference in present value
		Value today (Year 22)	Value in Year 40	Value today (Year 22)	
		(a)	(b)	(c)=(b)/(1+0.05)^{19}	(d)=((c)/(a))-1
(20)	Associated: GHG	22	101	40	81%
(21)	Air pollution	9	23	9	0%
(22)	Noise	6	15	6	0%
(23)	Subtotal	37	139	55	48%
(24)	Non-users: GHG	-7	-25	-10	41%
(25)	Air pollution	0	0	0	
(26)	Noise	0	0	0	
(27)	Subtotal	-7	-25	-10	41%
(28) = (19) + (23) + (27)	Net adjustment to environmental costs	-197	-325	-129	-35%
(29)	Value of current airport site	300	758	300	0%
(30) = (2) - (9) - (15) -(28) + (29)	Value of expansion at New A	1,415	2,268	898	-37%
(31) = (30) - (2)	Value of moving airport	-379	-1,319	-522	38%

costs are many and varied. Construction technology may be different, accessibility to the sites my differ, the type of terrain may make construction more or less costly, income changes may cause differences in the cost of construction, different stages in the economic cycle may affect the relative price of construction, etc. The illustration here adopts a replication of past investment expenditures both as a 'back of an envelope' approximation and to highlight that a relocation involves replicating capacity that is already installed (by some EUR500m in the current case – the difference between EUR700m and EUR200m), which constitutes an important determinant of the economic case for relocating an airport, as we are about to see.

As an additional adjustment relative to the result in row 2, when relocating to New A, replicating the 2.4m passenger capacity already installed in A has the benefit of reducing the need for refurbishing such 2.4m capacity in A. The cost saved is estimated as 20 per cent of the value of accumulated past capital expenditure (row 8). The saved refurbishment costs are higher when relocation is postponed (EUR140m rather than EUR100m) because the capacity replicated is higher. The resulting net additional capital expenditure by relocating amounts to EUR400m when initiating the relocation today and EUR560m when postponing relocation by 20 years (row 9).

The next round of adjustments concerns the private road transport costs caused by the relocation. Firstly, recall that the relocated airport would allow a more efficient routing of a ring road in town A. This would involve a saving of 3 minutes of travel time to users of the ring road, on trips unrelated to air travel, to be valued with a value of time of EUR12 per hour, growing by 2 per cent per year in real terms. It would also cause a reduction in vehicle operating costs of EUR 0.5 per user of the ring road. The initial usage of the ring road is estimated at 30,000 travelers per day, growing also at 2 per cent per year, in line with broader road traffic growth in town A. The combined time savings and lower operating costs over the life of the project result in a benefit valued at EUR202m (cell 10a) when initiating relocation today. The benefits would increase to EUR374m (cell 10b) when postponing relocation. The higher value of the latter reflects simply that the amount of road traffic in the future is higher.

The shorter ring road would also involve lower total investment costs relative to the longer ring road that would be necessary if the airport was not relocated. That saving in capex would be EUR60m if initiating relocation today or EUR90m if relocation is postponed (row 11), when the real relative cost of the ring road project would increase due to future higher population density. For simplicity of presentation, these costs are deemed private in the current analysis by assuming that users would ultimately pay for infrastructure, whether directly or indirectly.

For airport users, relocation involves access and egress trips to and from the airport that are longer by 15 minutes compared to the access and egress trips with the existing airport location. Additionally, each passenger processed at the airport is associated with two land trips to or from the airport, including 'meeters and greeters' and airport workers. The value of time for such users is also valued at EUR 12 per hour, growing in real terms at 2 per cent per year. In addition, there is on average an increase in the land-transport operating cost of accessing to and returning from the airport of EUR 2 per trip. Also, note that airport access and egress traffic grows in line with airport throughput, at an average of 5 per cent per year, rather than the 2 per cent per year of road traffic in general in the city. The resulting additional cost of longer airport access and egress trips amounts to EUR 638 million (cell 12 a) if relocating today and to EUR 2.2 billion (cell 12b) by postponing relocating by 20 years.

Additionally, the capital expenditure involved in upgrading the airport access road to accommodate the heavier road traffic would be EUR 100 million today, and EUR 150 million in real terms if relocation is postponed (row 13). Again, for simplicity it is assumed that such additional capex would constitute a private cost for users of the airport access infrastructure. Also for simplicity we disregard that relocation may prompt the upgrading of access infrastructure to involve alternative land transport modes, such as a tram or a light rail, and assume instead that all access and egress to the airport takes place by road.

The total additional cost related to airport access and egress by airport users (passengers and 'meeters and greeters') and airport workers would be EUR 738m by initiating relocation today, or EUR 2.3bn by postponing relocation (row 14). The net effect of airport relocation on private road transport costs would be the net of the additional costs to airport users and workers minus the savings to airport non-users, included in row 15.

The next adjustment concerns environmental costs, including additional emissions of GHG, air pollutants, and noise associated to airport relocation. We can split the implications of the relocation project for these emissions into three groups of emitters. First would be aircraft emissions, associated to passengers. Recall that it is being assumed for simplicity that the split between existing, diverted, and generated traffic is the same whether the expansion takes place in A or in New A. Relocation would not cause additional aircraft emissions relative to expanding capacity at A. However, whereas the costs associated to GHG are independent of where the emissions takes place, the cost associated with a given amount of emissions of noise and air pollutants varies with the location of those emissions. The closer those emissions take place to populated areas, and the greater the population in those areas, the higher the cost of such emissions. Relocation would therefore involve lower noise and air pollution costs associated to aircraft (and hence to passengers), as the aircraft would operate further away from town A.

The second group would be emissions associated to the longer airport access and egress trips of airport users (including passengers and 'meeters and greeters') and workers for New A, compared to A. Such longer access and egress trips would involve higher GHG emissions from land transport. They would also involve higher air pollution and noise emissions although, on the other hand, with relocation air pollution and noise associated to access and egress may be emitted further away from populated areas; therefore the societal cost associated with the same emissions would differ.

The third emitting group concerns airport non-users, in the current case including users of the ring road. The shorter road trips due to the shorter ring road with relocation would reduce GHG emissions. Regarding noise and air pollution there are two effects acting in opposite direction. On the one hand, the shorter ring road would reduce the amount of air pollution and noise emissions, just as with GHG emissions. On the other hand, the shorter ring road would be deeper within the urban area, closer to populated areas, thereby increasing the cost of any given amount of pollution. It is assumed, for simplicity, that the two effects cancel out, resulting in the net social cost of this third group of emitters being zero.

The classification of emitters displayed in Table 4.13 includes the net emissions per emitter, aggregating their participation on each of the three groups just described. So, the entries under 'passengers' (rows 16 to 19) include emissions associated to aircraft (first grouping) and to airport access and egress (second group) from air transport passengers. The category 'associated' (rows 20 to 23) includes both 'meeters and greeters' and airport workers and consists of emissions associated to airport access and egress (second group). Finally the category 'non-users' (rows 24 to 27) includes emissions associated to the ring-road (third group).

Appendix A4.1 includes the detailed calculation of the emission implications for passengers. The calculation is segregated by the three passenger categories – existing, diverted, and generated. The appendix shows that the resulting incremental effect on each of the three emissions – GHG, air pollutants, and noise – by relocating is the same for each of the three passenger categories. The entries in Table 4.13 from row 16 to row 27 are the results of the calculations included in the appendix. The figures are costs, so a positive number constitutes a cost and a negative number a saving or benefit. In addition, recall that it has been assumed that total traffic and its split among its three categories (existing, diverted, and generated) is the same whether the expansion takes place in A or in New A. Therefore, the entries in rows 16 to 27 constitute adjustments necessary to calculate the value of the 'Expansion at New A' project, but also constitute net differences between the two alternative projects ('Expansion at New A' versus 'Expansion at A'). By relocating there would be an increase in the GHG costs due to the longer airport access and egress trips, totaling EUR22m if relocating now (cell 16a). Postponing relocation would increase such costs to EUR101m, or EUR40m discounted to year 22 (row 16). The higher value resulting from delaying reflects largely the higher amounts of traffic and the compounded growth in the social cost of GHG emissions, at 3 per cent per year.

The net cost from air pollution consists of a saving of EUR63m (cell 17a) if relocating now and 160m (cell 17b) if doing it in 20 years. The present value in year 22 of the EUR160m savings, at EUR63m (cell 17c), coincides with the savings if relocating today (cell 17a) because the rate of growth in air traffic and the social discount rate are coincidentally the same at 5 per cent, implying a difference of 0 per cent in column d. This does not occur with GHG emissions because of the additional 3 per cent annual growth in the social cost of GHG, leading to an increase in present value (cell 16d). Air pollution cost plays therefore a neutral role in the decision of when to relocate, while the costs associated with climate change play a growing role as time passes.

For noise the situation is similar as for air pollution. Whereas the amount of noise from aircraft remains the same whether there is relocation or not, and while the noise from access and egress trips grows with relocation, relocation yields a saving in the costs associated to noise (row 18), as a greater amount of that noise is emitted more distantly from populated areas.

Overall, relocating the airport contributes to lower the external environmental costs inflicted by air travelers (row 19). While there are higher GHG emissions due to the longer access and egress trips to the more distant local airport, the costs to humans of air pollution and noise decrease.

The second category of emitters concerns 'associated' traffic, including 'meeters and greeters' and airport workers. Here the effect of the project is to increase emissions due to longer access and egress trips, resulting in higher costs for all three emission types (rows 20 to 23).

The third category are 'non-users' of the airport, consisting in this project of users of the ring road that becomes shorter with the relocation of the airport. The savings in costs associated to GHG emissions (row 24) are between a third and a fourth of the increase in costs associated to the GHG emissions incurred through longer access and egress trips by 'associated' traffic (row 20). The same happens when compared to the access and egress trips from passengers (row 16). The reason is twofold. First, the length of the ring road saved is shorter than the length of the extra access needed for the airport. Second, non-user traffic grows at 2 per cent per year while air travel grows at 5 per cent. To the extent that aviation traffic grows faster than land-based traffic, the land-based transport costs and benefits associated to air travel would tend to grow in importance over time (depending on starting magnitudes) relative to other land-based transport costs and benefits, not directly associated with air travel, that the airport relocation may bring about. As we will see further down, this effect plays a significant role when appraising the timing of any relocation.

Row 28 includes the resulting net adjustment to environmental costs associated to relocating. Despite the longer access and egress trips, relocating the airport would generate a substantial saving in environmental costs. Most of these savings arise from lower costs associated to air pollution and noise. This type of benefit is likely to be reflected in an increase in the value of property located in areas where noise levels and air pollution decreases as a result of the relocation of the airport, most likely in property surrounding existing airport A. Care should be taken not to take any such change in property prices as an additional benefit of the project over and above environmental benefits. The portion of any change in property prices that is equal to changes in environmental externalities constitute rather a capitalisation (by the property market) of such environmental costs and benefits.

This takes us to the next benefit of relocating the airport – the economic value of the airport site in A being vacated. The land of the A airport site may be valued today, in year 22, at EUR300m (cell 29a), based on the value of surrounding property. This is a benefit, where the land price measures the value the site contributes to its alternative use. As a starting point, this value could in principle be assumed to grow over time in line with the discount rate, which over the long run should be in line with the rate of growth of the economy. If so, the real price in year 40 would be EUR758m (cell 29b). This line of reasoning is revisited further down.

We have now concluded all of the necessary adjustments. The value of expanding at New A would then be the value of expanding at A (row 2) plus all of the adjustments. Running from the top of the Table 4.13 downwards, the first adjustment is to subtract the additional airport capex required by the relocation project (row 9). Next down are the additional costs arising from changes in land transport. First we include the private costs, shown in row 15. Then we subtract the (adjustments to) environmental costs from air passengers as well as from other land-use related stakeholders. As we saw, relocation yields a net saving in all environmental externalities (row 28). Finally we add the economic value of the site of the existing airport at A (row 29). The result in this case is that the relocated airport would produce a societal value of EUR1,415m (cell 30a) if stating the relocation process today, in year 22.

Note that it would be erroneous to interpret this result as making the economic case for relocating the airport. It would be tempting to present a capex of EUR700m (cell 7a) as yielding a net value to society of EUR1.4bn (cell 30a). However, relocating is not the option that yields the highest value to society, which is rather the EUR1.8bn of expanding at A (row 2). The case for relocation is made by comparing the value of expanding at New A with the value of expanding at the existing site, as displayed in row 31. The result is that expanding capacity through relocating the airport, while yielding value to society, is inferior to expanding at the existing site. Relocation would bring about a loss of value to society, estimated at EUR379m (cell 31a).

Postponing the relocation by 20 years is expected to cause an even larger loss. The main driver of such higher loss is the additional costs associated to the longer access and egress trips to the relocated airport. Among the bundle of rows that constitute the necessary adjustments (rows 9, 15, 28, and 29), access and egress costs (row 15) are the largest cost item in absolute terms (see cell 15c, compared to cells 9c, 28c, and 29c) and the largest in relative terms (see cell 15d, compared to cells 9d, 28d, and 29d). As noted above, when air travel grows faster than general land-based traffic, the land-based traffic associated to air travel grows faster than general land-based traffic. Therefore the land-based traffic costs and benefits associated to a relocation gain in relative importance over time, to the point, in the current case, of being determinant to the appraisal outcome. The additional private road transport cost related to the relocated airport (row 15) are greater than the loss of value of relocating (row 31), meaning that these land transport costs are sufficient to determine whether the project adds value to society or not.

A key variable in considering the case for relocating the airport consists of the economic value of the vacated airport site. Airport relocating projects tend to consist of moving airports away from within the conurbation of cities. Existing airports considered for relocation nowadays owe their current location to decisions made early in the development of air transport in the first half of the 20th century, and tend to be located adjacent to urban areas that have since sprawled. The value of the vacated land would tend to be idiosyncratic to each project, thereby requiring at least one land valuation study.

The example at hand has assumed that the value of the land of the existing airport site in A would increase in line with that of the economy at large and that the current value in year 22 correctly discounts future increases in prices. So, the estimated market value of the site in year 40 (cell 29b), when discounted to the present (cell 29c), equals the estimated price today, in year 22 (cell 29a). Growing congestion is likely to increase the relative value of central location. But expectations of such increase should be reflected in current land prices. It is therefore hard to make a case today for a future relocation purely on projections of future land values. The analyst would have to argue that current prices do not reflect the true value of the site. The case for future relocation, if it turns out to exist, would rather be made retrospectively in the future once land values have exceeded current expectations.

Other than that, the case for moving an airport would tend to rest on the current value of land. While that should be sufficient to justify immediate relocation, in practice the case to relocate is most readily apparent when the existing site is physically constrained, impeding a capacity expansion of the airport in the current site, or requiring land expropriations that would turn out to be too expensive. That is, in turn, just a reflection of the argument for relocating on the grounds of current land value, since such expensive expropriations would indicate that the value of the existing site is already sufficiently high to justify relocating today.

Appendix A4.1: Net environmental costs of airport users in airport relocation project

The relocation project is appraised by comparing an expansion on the existing site ('Expansion at A') versus an expansion through relocating the airport ('Expansion at New A'), as discussed in section 4.9.2. This appendix addresses the differences in environmental externalities between the two. The resulting environmental external cost or benefit therefore consist of the resulting net environmental externalities of relocation as such ('Expansion at New A' vs 'Expansion at A'), not of the total externalities of the new airport ('with New A project'). Since, for simplicity, both the airline passenger traffic and the airport operating characteristics at A and New A are taken to be identical, the resulting net environmental externalities from this appendix, when added to the 'with A project' scenario, results in the 'with New A project' scenario as far as airport users is concerned. The appraisal would also need to include stakeholders that are not users of the airport.

Table A4.1 includes the calculation segregated between the three traffic types. The table starts with the 'existing' traffic category. Recall that this is traffic that without the capacity expansion project (i) continues to travel from town A – that is, it is not diverted to the airport at B – and (ii) is not diverted to less convenient times because of insufficient capacity in A. The pollution in the with and without project scenarios is the same for this traffic category. Rows 1 and 2 concern pollution from air travel. Since the air pollution is the same, the incremental cost of the project is zero (row 3). We assume that because of the vicinity of the airport to the city centre, pollution when accessing and eggressing would not differ from the normal day to day pollution of the passenger and therefore neither access nor egress pose any incremental cost. Even if this was not the case – that is if pollution was higher or lower than normal day to day activities – existing traffic travels both with and without the project, so the net effect is zero anyway.

If instead the expansion is made through New A, then two things change relative to the without project scenario of not expanding A at the existing location. First, there is additional pollution associated to the longer access and egress trips (row 4).[27] Second, the air trip phase of the journey involves the same GHG emissions, but lower air pollution and noise costs (row 5), than in the without project scenario (row 7). Recall that the emission of air pollutants and noise are the same in the two locations, but the costs associated to those in New A are lower than in A because New A is located further away from high population areas than the existing location of airport A. Relocation involves an extra 15 minutes (0.25 hours) of access and egress by land. The environmental costs of such extra 15 minutes are 1/8th of the costs involved in the two hour diversion to B (rows 4 and 12). The net result of New A is more GHG emissions and associated costs, but savings in the cost associated to air pollution and noise (row 8). The results are the same when comparing expanding New A versus expanding at A (row 9).

Turning now to 'diverted' passengers, recall that this category involves traffic that travels by air both with and without the project, but that in the absence of the project incurs two alternative forms of costly diversion. First, those that are diverted to travelling at less convenient times than they would have preferred to travel – what we refer to as 'diversion in time'. Second, those that divert to an alternative airport, incurring longer access and egress trips to the alternative airport – referred to as 'diversion in mode'. The project benefits diverted passengers by allowing them to travel from the project airport without incurring such costs of diversion.

When expanding at the existing site in A, the air travel part of the trip involves the same environmental costs whether the traveler flies without incurring diversion (row 10), whether it is diverted in time (row 11), or whether is diverted to an alternative airport (row 13). But when diverting to B, it causes an incremental external cost due to the longer access and egress trips to and from B

Table A4.1 Environmental costs across scenarios in the appraisal of the airport relocation project (in EUR)

		GHG	Air pollution	Noise
	Per 'existing' passenger			
	'Expansion at A'			
(1)	With project (...when flying from A)	20	2	3
(2)	Without project (...when flying from A)	20	2	3
(3) = (1) - (2)	Incremental cost	0	0	0
	'Expansion at New A'			
	With project			
(4) = (12)/8	...added access/egress costs	0.125	0.1875	0.125
(5)	...when flying from New A	20	0.5	1
(6) = (4) + (5)	total	20.125	0.6875	1.125
(7)	Without project (...when flying from A)	20	2	3
(8) = (6) - (7)	Incremental cost	0.125	-1.3125	-1.875
(9) = (8) - (3)	Incremental cost New A vs A	**0.125**	**-1.3125**	**-1.875**
	Per 'diverted' passenger			
	'Expansion at A'			
(10)	With project (...when flying from A)	20	2	3
	Without project			
(11)	Traffic diverted in time (...when flying from A)	20	2	3
	Traffic diverted in mode:			
(12)	...when diverting to B	1	1.5	1
(13)	...and then flying from B	20	2	3
	Incremental cost			
(14) = (10) - (11)	Traffic diverted in time	0	0	0
(15) = (10) - (12)-(13)	Traffic diverted in mode:	-1	-1.5	-1
	'Expansion at New A'			
	With project			
(16) = (4)	...added access/egress costs	0.125	0.1875	0.125
(17) = (5)	...when flying from New A	20	0.5	1
	Without project			
(18)	Traffic diverted in time (...when flying from A)	20	2	3
	Traffic diverted in mode:			
(19) = (12)	...when diverting to B	1	1.5	1
(20) = (13)	...and then flying from B	20	2	3
	Incremental cost			
(21) = (16) + (17) - (18)	Traffic diverted in time	0.125	-1.3125	-1.875
(22) = (16) + (17)-(19) - (20)	Traffic diverted in mode:	-0.875	-2.8125	-2.875
	Incremental cost New A vs A			
(23) = (21) - (14)	Traffic diverted in time	**0.125**	**-1.3125**	**-1.875**

(Continued)

Table A4.1 (Continued)

		GHG	Air pollution	Noise
(24) = (22) - (15)	Traffic diverted in mode:	**0.125**	**-1.3125**	**-1.875**
	Per 'generated' passenger			
(25) = (1) = (10)	'Expansion at A' (...when flying from A)	20	2	3
	'Expansion at New A'			
(26) = (4) = (16)	...added access/egress costs	0.125	0.1875	0.125
(27) = (5) = (17)	...when flying from New A	20	0.5	1
(28) = (26) + (27)	total	20.125	0.6875	1.125
(29) = (28) - (25)	Incremental cost New A vs A	**0.125**	**-1.3125**	**-1.875**

(row 12). The result is that, when appraising whether to add capacity to A or leaving capacity constant, traffic diverted in time does not suppose any net increase in environmental cost (row 14), but diversion in mode does (row 15).

When expanding capacity by relocating the airport, the expansion involves the costs of the longer access and egress trips (row 16), already identified in row 4. On the other hand, when travelling through New A, the air pollution and noise costs (row 17) would be lower than in the without project scenario, whether this involves flying at a less convenient time from A or diverting to B (row 20). In the latter case there is on top the associated additional access and egress costs of diverting to B (row 19). The incremental costs of traffic diversion to B are relatively hefty in environmental terms (row 22), when compared to those of diverting in time (row 21).

Note that these savings to diverted traffic do not necessarily correspond to the benefits of relocating. They combine the benefits of expanding capacity with those of relocating. Those of relocating are distilled by comparing expansion at New A with expansion at A. The result for diverted traffic are in rows 23 and 24, and are the same whether traffic diverts in time or in mode.

Finally, traffic generated by expanding airport capacity at the existing airport A would cause the same external costs as any other passenger that accesses or egresses the airport. Recall that airport A is very close to the city centre and therefore access and egress pollution is assumed to be the same as the pollution that the traveler would perform in the normal day to day activities in the absence of travelling by air, meaning no incremental emissions. The incremental emissions related to generated traffic are therefore those of flying only (row 25). Similarly, if capacity is expanded by relocating to New A, each generated passenger trip will cause the same external cost by accessing or eggressing (row 26) and flying (row 27) as existing and diverted passenger trips. The incremental environmental external costs of relocating to New A are the same for this traffic category as for the other two.

Note that for each of the three pollutant categories (GHG, air pollution, and noise), the net environmental cost of relocating, relative to expanding at A, are the same for each type of traffic. There is an incremental cost of 12.5 euro cents in terms of GHG emissions per passenger, due to the longer access and egress trips by road. And there are savings worth EUR1.31 in air pollution and EUR 1.88 in noise per passenger, as the longer access and egress trips are dwarfed by the reduction in costs by moving aircraft operations further away from densely populated areas.

Notes

1 'Propensity to travel' means the trip generation capability of town A, whether as origin or destination; that is, the magnitude includes both trips carried out by town A residents and trips attracted to town A from non-residents, which depend equally on the population size and income of town A. Tourism destinations and hub airports require additional considerations that are not dealt with here.
2 The EUR1 result would come by simplifying the calculation by focusing on the cost of fatalities only and not of minor or serious injuries. If the chances of dying on a commercial flight were 1 in 2 million, and the value of statistical life in the country at hand was EUR2 million, by multiplying both figures, the value of the risk of travelling by air would work out at EUR1 per passenger.
3 At this stage, the only safety cost included is the value of safety or the value of statistical life, which is determined by user willingness to pay and, hence, affects traveller decision-making. Additional, external accident marginal costs such as medical costs incurred by the rest of society are excluded at this stage. See European Commission 2019 and HEATCO 2006.
4 Note that the estimate of generalised cost could also include a measure of frequency delay. This would increase the data requirements and would necessitate making strong assumptions about flight schedules in the future airport. In addition, if it is assumed that departure frequency conditions would be similar in both airports – at least for the most preferred destinations for citizens in A – frequency delay would cancel out. It would still affect the relative difference between generalised costs and the estimate of generated traffic. In the present example, assuming an average 1.5-hour frequency delay in both airports would mean that generated traffic would be 17.7 per cent of observed traffic, rather than 19 per cent. In practice, since the difference it makes to relative generalised costs is unlikely to be large, and is based on strong assumptions, it may be simpler to ignore frequency delay altogether in terminal capacity projects, unless the nature of the project demands otherwise. As has already been mentioned, and as is illustrated below in section 4.8 and in Chapter 5, section 5.1, frequency delay plays a critical role in airside (i.e. aircraft movement capacity) projects.
5 This could be taken to consist of capacity supplied with an IATA-ACI 'optimum' level of service (see IATA-ACI 2019), approximately equivalent to the former IATA level of service C (see IATA 2004 and de Neufville and Odini 2013).
6 For simplicity, land is treated just like any other capital asset or input into the project. However, the analyst should be aware that land raises a number of issues in economic analysis related to restrictive licensing policies, price controls, expropriation policies, forced resettlement, etc., which affect the relationship between the price paid by the project promoter and the opportunity cost of land. Since these issues are not specific to aviation, they are not dealt with further here.
7 As is mentioned in Chapter 2, note 2, the assumption about value of time growth must correspond with the assumption made for growth in both labour costs and productivity. For simplicity it is assumed here that labour cost increases are fully compensated by productivity gains.
8 As mentioned in note 3 in section 3.1 of Chapter 3, delays caused by congestion may bring about knock on costs to users elsewhere on the air transport network. The US

FAA has calculated an average delay propagation multiplier for aircraft of 1.57 for major US airports in 2008 (see FAA 2010). Taking the delay to aircraft as a lower boundary for the delay to passengers, and assuming that it reflects the schedule relationship between the current airport and the rest of the air transport network, the multiplier could be applied to the costs in rows 26 and 28. The effect on this particular project would be small but significant, adding EUR24.5 million to costs, reducing the NPV by just below 7 per cent to EUR341.7 million. In this particular example the impact is negative, which is counter-intuitive since it could be expected that a project would alleviate congestion. The reason for the negative result is that in this particular case the alternative airport is assumed to be free of congestion and that it could accommodate all traffic diverted from the project airport. Here the assumption that without the project the rest of agents in the economy adjust capacity in accordance to the situation they face in such scenario, plays a defining role. This was referred to in Chapter 3, section 3.3.4, discussing counterfactual capacity, as the 'life continues' assumption.

9　It is assumed that airport B displays constant returns to scale. Otherwise, a subtraction of passengers may result in higher marginal costs for users of airport B, resulting in a welfare loss, following the analysis in Chapter 2, section 2.7.3.

10　It is assumed for simplicity that all distortions in the price of inputs concern government taxes.

11　The noise costs are additional to the EUR20 million already included in the investment cost as the cost of installing double glazing in nearby properties.

12　This risk cost imposed on the rest of society is additional to the EUR1 cost incurred by the user, included in the estimate of user generalised cost, as shown in Table 4.2 above

13　The EUR1 of safety cost is additional to the EUR3 included in the estimate of private generalised cost of transport in Table 4.2 above.

14　The higher the generalised cost of travelling through the alternative airport, the more likely would passengers be to choose to travel through the project airport at less preferred times. Therefore, in cases where the alternative airport constitutes a costly alternative in terms of additional generalised costs, because of being too distant, say, for example, five hours away, or because significant sea crossings were involved, it would be critical to perform a survey of traveller behaviour since more of the otherwise diverted traffic would travel from the airport at less preferred times.

15　It is not the remit of this book to evaluate alternative models of private sector involvement, only to illustrate how investment appraisal plays a role in determining the value of the infrastructure. For a review of models of private sector participation in airports see Winston and de Rus 2008.

16　The case considered here would not, strictly speaking, be one of economic regulation of monopoly, since there is an alternative airport two hours away. Taking proximity to customer as a service attribute, the market would, rather, be described as one of monopolistic competition. However, economic regulation may still apply on two grounds: first, the infrastructure is operated by the private sector; and second, the market is poorly contestable because of the presence of strong barriers to entry and exit, including sunk costs.

17　The seminal paper, 'Behaviour of the firm under regulatory constraints' by H. Averch and L.L. Johnson 1962, models the incentives faced by firms with an abstract production function including labour and capital. The effect is well known in economics and is widely discussed in utility regulation textbooks. Whereas attempts have been made to de-incentivise such behaviour by firms through the use of price-cap regulation, all price-cap regulation must over the long run pursue attainable rates of return targets in order to incentivise the private sector to invest at all. Therefore, in practice, the Averch–Johnson effect tends to apply to price-cap regulation as well. The topic of regulation and incentives is complex. For treatment specific to airports see Adler et al. 2015, Niemeier 2009 and Winston and de Rus 2008.

18 Aircraft codes as designated by ICAO are driven mostly by wingspan. Each additional code entails incremental design requirements for airports. Code-D aircraft are the smaller of the mid- to long- haul aircraft, such as the B-757 and B-767. Its closest replacement, the B-787, is a Code-E, although Boeing is reportedly working on a B-797 that would be closer to the B-757 and B-767. Airbus's Code-D was the A-310, no longer in production. Currently projects like the one being discussed would target Code-E aircraft. On the other hand, variants of the latest generation of Code-C aircraft, such as the A-321 XLR, are now capable of long-range, inter-continental services. In an airport that can handle Code-C aircraft, accommodating this type of long haul aircraft may involve lengthening the runway, without widening either the runway or taxiways, reducing the capital expenditure needed. The upgrade from Code-C to D used here underscores the notional nature of the illustrative project. The mechanics of calculation, of what constitutes a benefit and what a cost, do not change with the extent of the upgrade.

19 It is assumed that passenger charges are the same for all passengers and that average aircraft landing charge per passenger also works out the same for all aircraft sizes. In reality, aircraft landing charges may be structured in a way that renders the average landing charge per passenger lower for larger aircraft, worsening the financial case for the project.

20 During the first few years after opening a runway the average aircraft size may well drop as airlines schedule more flights in order to secure slots, as long-term investment. The 1 per cent rate of growth of aircraft size would be a long-term assumption.

21 Traffic diversion of this type may also be categorised as stochastic delay in the sense that there is no capacity available at the desired flight because of very high load factors. In the case at hand it is just a question of semantics though. The key aspect is that passengers will suffer diversion due to unavailability of flights.

22 It is worth insisting that we are generally referring to adding new runways to an airport where the existing runway(s) could still accommodate larger aircraft. Where the runway is completely saturated in terms of being unable to accommodate new passengers through larger aircraft, particularly at peak times, a new runway would unambiguously generate traffic.

23 Even if operating costs were passed on to passengers, passengers would be willing to trade time savings for higher operating costs, as they value the additional frequency delay (EUR424.6 million − EUR1 million = EUR423.6 million) more than the additional savings in operating costs (EUR247.6 million − EUR156.1 million = EUR91.5 million).

24 The focus here is purely on the economic case. The development of airport capacity close to urban areas involves a wider range of issues. See Niemeier 2013 for a review with practical cases in Germany.

25 One could think of an airport project that would not include a capacity expansion, driven purely by land transport or land use considerations. However, in practice, relocations are considered in tandem with capacity expansions. Capacity expansions tend to exacerbate land scarcity at the existing site, while requiring a commitment to put up with such scarcity for a long period. The time required to plan and execute a capacity expansion is normally at least 5 years − although this varies from country to country. Following the completion of works, economic and financial viability normally require the expanded capacity to be operated for about 20–30 years. This means that deciding to carry out a capacity expansion project commits the airport operator to the existing site for about 25–35 years. Meanwhile, a relocation project would normally need at least 10 years for planning and execution. Therefore, if a relocation is in the cards, making the case for a capacity expansion naturally brings the case for relocation into the discussion since the decision to expand at the existing site implies shelving considerations of relocation for 15–25 years.

26 Take the calculation of generated traffic in Table 4.2 above, using the initial situation in year 0, when considering the greenfield investment in A as an example. Diverting from A to B would deter 19 per cent of traffic in A or, in other words, 19 per cent of traffic in A would consist of generated traffic (row 20). To simulate an increase in access or egress time to A by 15 minutes (the conditions offered by New A, compared to A) would involve two considerations. First, diversion from town A to the alternative airport in town B would still take 2 hours and 15 minutes, so row 4 remains unchanged at 2.25 hours. But now if we do not divert we are only deducting 1 hour and 45 minutes (i.e. 1.75 hours) from diversion, rather than 2 hours. So the entry in row 12 becomes 1.75 instead of 2. This implies lower relative time, operating, and safety costs when diverting from New A to B than when diverting from A to B, rendering New A comparatively less attractive. That change results in generated traffic of 16.6 per cent, down from 19 per cent. This is within the margin of error of any such calculation.

27 See section 4.1 above. These costs are reflected in rows 31 to 33 in Table 4.3.

5   Air traffic management

Introduction

There are two broad types of Air Traffic Management (ATM) infrastructure investments. The first type comprises those aimed at increasing system capacity to handle aircraft movements in a given time period. In terms of investment appraisal, such ATM projects can be approached similarly to an airport investment aimed at increasing the aircraft movement capacity of its runway(s). They would therefore need to incorporate the tradeoff between aircraft movement capacity and aircraft size, as airspace capacity constraints can also be partly circumvented by increasing the size of aircraft. Section 5.1 below includes an illustration of one such project. The second type of project involves those aimed at improving the efficiency of flight procedures. This project type also has similarities with airport investments, namely those aimed at improving aircraft operations on the ground.[1] This type of projects is illustrated in section 5.4.

ATM can be an important source of foreign exchange. There are two distinctive characteristics in this respect. Firstly, among the various sub-sectors in aviation, ATM is the one which most closely matches conditions of natural monopoly, conveying substantial pricing power. Secondly, ATM projects can derive revenues from en route passengers, for whom the consumption of ATM services is a very small proportion of the generalised cost of their trip, whom may not even be aware of the country they are buying ATM services from and whom, in any case, may often be non-resident (nor voters) of the country. There is a clear opportunity to exert market power. Section 5.3 deals with the appraisal of foreign exchange generating capacity of an ATM project. It does so for circumstances where the country hosting the project is subject to trade distortions, which mean that the generation of foreign exchange by the project may not be reflected fully in project cashflows.

5.1 Greater movement capacity

The treatment of investments aimed at increasing aircraft movement capacity is essentially the same for ATM as for airport runways, facing a trade-off between frequency delay and airport operating costs, as illustrated by

Figure 3.2 in Chapter 3. However, there are distinctions to be made depending on the type of airspace sector concerned, whether ground, tower, approach/terminal, or en route. Ground control is essentially a component of airport airside operations, aimed at improving capacity before the runway for a given weather condition. Investment in such ATM infrastructure is treated essentially as an investment in taxiways. Tower control infrastructure concerns runway operations and its treatment is the same as a runway project aimed at increasing aircraft movement capacity. Approach/terminal airspace, involving aircraft in and out of airports, to and from their en route sectors, can also be treated as runway investments aimed at increasing aircraft movement capacity.

For en route airspace sectors, an airline is slightly less constrained than when flying in and out of an airport. In the case of insufficient en route airspace capacity, the airline has a choice between diverting to an alternative departure time (similar to the constraints posed by runway capacity), delay on the ground (also similar to the constraints posed by runways), or diversion to alternative en route sectors (different from the constraints posed by runway capacity). If the airline chooses to change route, it will generally involve a longer, and hence more costly, routing than the preferred choice. The costs involved include higher aircraft operating costs for the airline, longer travel time for passengers, and greater greenhouse gas (GHG) emissions externalities if these are not internalised.

Airlines may also react as they respond to constraints posed by runways, by increasing aircraft size. So lack of airspace capacity may also generate benefits – as is the case with runways – by forcing airlines to operate larger aircraft, thereby lowering operating costs per seat and reducing societal costs associated to any non-internalised GHG emissions per passenger-kilometre. The impact of air pollutants and noise on en route sectors is debatable. Therefore the treatment of environmental impact in this chapter focuses on GHG emissions, which are assumed to be non-internalised.

To summarise, ATM investments aimed at increasing aircraft movement capacity are essentially the same as runway investments with the same aim. The exception would be en route sectors where the airline faces the additional option of altering the route, diverting to alternative sectors.

Another difference between airport and ATM infrastructure investments is that in the latter a greater element of the costs consists of operating costs, instead of capital investment costs, because air traffic controllers can constitute a significant share of the costs of supplying capacity. Since capital investment costs are incurred upfront and operating costs are spread over the operating life of the asset, economic (and hence potential financial) returns on investment will tend to be higher, other things being equal.

Table 5.1 illustrates the estimation of economic returns of a proposed project consisting of upgrading the capacity of an en route sector from 20 to 25 movements per hour, involving investment in IT equipment and employing additional controllers.[2] This capacity limit is reached on working days, three times per day, meaning just over 260 days per year. At an average of 120

Table 5.1 Economic returns on an ATM project aimed at increasing aircraft movement capacity

Ref			PV	Year 1	2	3	5	10	15	20	25	27
With project												
(1)	Demand at peak	(thousand)		1,935	2,016	2,100	2,271	2,763	3,362	4,091	4,977	5,383
(2)	Pax per aircraft movement	(unit)		120	122	124	127	137	148	159	172	177
(3) through (2)	Change in aircraft op costs	(%)		0%	-1%	-2%	-3%	-7%	-12%	-16%	-21%	-24%
(4) through (2)	Capacity at peak	(thousand)		1,877	1,877	2,346	2,417	2,604	2,805	3,022	3,256	3,354
(5) through (4)	Traffic not diverted	(thousand)		1,877	1,877	2,100	2,271	2,604	2,805	3,022	3,256	3,354
(6) = (1) - (5)	Traffic diverted	(thousand)		58	139	0	0	159	557	1,068	1,721	2,029
(7) = (6) × avg. hours	Hours diverted	(thousand)		18	44	0	0	60	231	488	869	1,065
	Internal effects											
(8) = (7) × VoT	Time cost of diversion	(EUR m)	65.6	0.0	0.0	0.0	0.0	1.1	4.6	10.7	21.0	26.7
(9) through (6)	Op cost of diversion	(EUR m)	54.4	0.5	1.2	0.0	0.0	1.3	4.6	8.9	14.3	16.9
(10) through (3)	Aircraft cost savings	(EUR m)	70.5	0.0	0.3	0.8	1.6	4.1	6.6	9.3	12.2	13.5
(11) = -(8) - (9) + (10)	Internal benefits	(EUR m)	-49.5	-0.5	-0.8	0.8	1.6	1.7	-2.6	-10.3	-23.1	-30.2
	External effects											
(12)	GHG cost through diversion	(EUR m)	25.1	0.2	0.5	0.0	0.0	0.6	2.1	4.1	6.6	7.8
(13)	GHG savings through aircraft size	(EUR m)	32.4	0.0	0.0	0.4	0.8	1.9	3.0	4.3	5.6	6.2
(14) = -(12) + (13)	External benefit	(EUR m)	7.3	-0.2	-0.5	0.4	0.8	1.3	0.9	0.2	-1.0	-1.6
(15) = (11) + (12)	Net benefit	(EUR m)	-42.3	-0.7	-1.3	1.1	2.4	3.0	-1.7	-10.1	-24.0	-31.8
Without project												
(16)	Demand at peak	(thousand)		1,935	2,016	2,100	2,271	2,763	3,362	4,091	4,977	5,383
(17)	Pax per aircraft movement	(unit)		120	122	125	130	143	158	175	193	201
(18) through (17)	Change in aircraft op costs	(%)		0%	-1%	-2%	-4%	-10%	-16%	-23%	-30%	-34%
(19) through (17)	Capacity at peak	(thousand)		1,877	1,877	1,877	1,953	2,156	2,381	2,628	2,902	3,019

(Continued)

Table 5.1 (Continued)

			PV/Year	1	2	3	5	10	15	20	25	27
(20) through (19)	Traffic not diverted	(thousand)		1,877	1,877	1,877	1,953	2,156	2,381	2,628	2,902	3,019
(21) = (16) - (20)	Traffic diverted	(thousand)		58	139	223	318	607	981	1,462	2,075	2,364
(22) = (21) × avg. hours	Hours diverted	(thousand)		18	44	73	108	228	406	668	1,047	1,241
Internal effects												
(23) = (22) × VoT	Time cost of diversion	(EUR m)	104.7	0.3	0.7	1.1	1.8	4.1	8.0	14.6	25.3	31.2
(24) through (21)	Op cost of diversion	(EUR m)	95.3	0.5	1.2	1.9	2.7	5.1	8.2	12.2	17.3	19.7
(25) through (18)	Aircraft cost savings	(EUR m)	77.8	0.0	0.5	0.9	1.9	4.4	7.2	10.3	13.7	15.2
(26) = -(23) - (24) + (25)	Internal benefits	(EUR m)	-122.2	-0.8	-1.4	-2.1	-2.5	-4.7	-9.0	-16.5	-28.8	-35.6
External effects												
(27)	GHG cost through diversion	(EUR m)	44.0	0.2	0.5	0.9	1.2	2.3	3.8	5.6	8.0	9.1
(28)	GHG savings through aircraft size	(EUR m)	36.0	0.0	0.2	0.4	0.9	2.0	3.3	4.8	6.3	7.0
(29) = -(27) + (28)	External benefit	(EUR m)	-8.1	-0.2	-0.3	-0.4	-0.4	-0.3	-0.4	-0.9	-1.6	-2.1
(30) = (26) + (29)	Net benefit	(EUR m)	-130.3	-1.0	-1.7	-2.5	-2.9	-5.0	-9.5	-17.3	-30.5	-37.7
Net project flows												
(31) = -(8) + (23)	Avoided time costs of diversion	(EUR m)	39.2	0.3	0.7	1.1	1.8	3.0	3.5	3.9	4.3	4.4
(32) = -(9) + (10) + (24) - (25)	Net aircraft cost savings	(EUR m)	33.5	0.0	-0.1	1.7	2.4	3.4	2.9	2.3	1.5	1.1
(33) = (14) - (29)	GHG savings	(EUR m)	15.3	0.0	-0.2	0.8	1.1	1.6	1.4	1.1	0.7	0.5
(34) = (31) + (32) + (33) = (15) - (30)	Differential net benefits	(EUR m)	88.0	0.3	0.4	3.6	5.3	8.0	7.8	7.3	6.4	6.0
(35)	Increase ATC op cost	(EUR m)	3.8	0.0	0.0	0.3	0.3	0.3	0.3	0.3	0.3	0.3
(36)	Investment cost	(EUR m)	13.9	7.5	7.5							
(37) = (34) - (35) - (36)	Net economic flows	(EUR m)	70.3	-7.2	-7.1	3.3	5.0	7.7	7.5	7.0	6.1	5.7
	Project ERR		**32%**									

passengers per aircraft movement, the capacity of the sector at peak hours would increase from 1.88 million to 2.35 million passengers per year (rows 4 and 19). However, growing traffic means that aircraft size increases with time, increasing the passenger (but not aircraft movement) capacity of the sector through time. As demand is expected to grow faster than aircraft size, planners wish to find out whether it pays to expand movement capacity to 25 movements per hour or whether it is better to signal to airlines that capacity will not be increased in that sector for years, encouraging airlines to increase aircraft size faster.

Analysts estimate that aircraft operating costs are EUR3,000 per block hour and assume that with the project, aircraft size will increase at 1.5 per cent per year, resulting in an equivalent increase in the average load per flight (row 2). This results in aircraft operating cost savings per seat, governed by an elasticity of unit operating costs relative to aircraft size of −0.5. The analysis assumes that cost savings are not passed on to passengers. The increase in capacity means that traffic diversion will be postponed (row 6), as will the diversion costs incurred by passengers – calculated with a value of time of EUR15 per hour, growing at 2 per cent per year – (row 8) and the associated additional operating costs to airlines (row 9).

The use of larger aircraft will reduce GHG emissions per passenger. At 120 passengers per flight, GHG costs are estimated at EUR1,386 per block hour.[3] Emissions are assumed to vary proportionally with aircraft operating costs. Aircraft emissions costs savings per passenger through the use of larger aircraft relative to the situation in year 1 are included in row 13. The project also postpones GHG emissions costs associated with diverted traffic (row 12).

Without the project, analysts assume that airlines will increase aircraft size faster, at 2 per cent per year, rather than 1.5 per cent with the project. Whereas this mitigates the capacity shortage, more traffic is diverted without the project (row 21) than with the project (row 6). The larger aircraft also produce cost efficiency gains relative to the project scenario (rows 25 and 10). However, since more traffic is now diverted, higher operating costs (row 24), time costs (row 23) and GHG emissions costs (row 27) are borne without the project.

The net benefits of the project will depend on the extent to which the lower diversion costs and lower aircraft operating and emissions costs through more direct routing with the project are offset by the use of larger aircraft without the project. On balance the project improves the performance of air transport on all relevant counts. It produces net savings in diversion costs to passengers of EUR39.2 million (row 31). The shorter routing with the project outweighs the operating cost penalty of lower aircraft size, resulting in net aircraft operating cost savings of EUR33.5 million (row 32). Lower aircraft operating costs also translates in emissions savings worth EUR15.3 million (row 33).

The project costs to the air navigation service provider (ANSP) consist of capital investment in equipment with a present value of EUR13.9 million (row 36), and an increase in operating costs by EUR300,000 per year, mostly by requiring more controller hours. The net flows of the project are included in row 37. The project does produce a net benefit worth EUR70.3 million, constituting a very strong return on capital investment of 32 per cent.

Note, however, that towards the end of the project life benefits decrease with time, as the cumulative effect of increasing aircraft size over time begins to yield significant differences in operating costs. Indeed, a lot depends on the assumed scenarios regarding aircraft size increases with and without the project. Should the analyst assume that aircraft size with the project will increase at 1 per cent per year, instead of the assumed 1.5 per cent, the returns from the project would decrease from 32 per cent to 6 per cent. If, in addition, the analyst assumes that aircraft size without the project will increase at 2.5 per cent instead of 1 per cent, then the project will generate negative returns. As in the case of runways, the benefits of investments in increasing ATM capacity rely substantially on assumptions about the ability of airlines to accommodate traffic growth through larger aircraft. The same cannot be said about ATM investments aimed at enabling more efficient operation of aircraft, as can be seen in the project example in section 5.4 below.

Note that so far, and as was the case with the runway project, the analysis does not include producer surplus. In effect, the analysis assumes that ANSP revenues are exactly the same with and without the project and therefore cancel out. This involves two assumptions. First, it is assumed that with and without the project the same number of passengers is served. This is not necessarily a controversial assumption, as the direction of any generated traffic is not obvious. It would result from the balance between the cost of diversion to alternative sectors and the benefits of lower operating costs through larger aircraft (should such costs be eventually passed on to passengers). On the other hand, and regarding the financial analysis, it may well be that traffic is diverted to a sector managed by a separate ANSP, in which case there would be a loss of revenue to the promoter. The next section of this chapter, dealing with private sector involvement, addresses this issue.

The second assumption is that the air navigation charge per passenger is the same with and without the project. This may well be the case – as when air navigation is paid as a levy on ticket price – but it is generally not so in practice. The implications are discussed in the next section.

5.2 Involving the private sector (4): pricing policy

ANSPs are mostly operated by the public sector, even if they are 'corporatised', and when they are privatised they are operated as regulated monopolies. Beyond any rate of return regulation, which, as seen in Chapter 4, section 4.5, incentivises overinvestment, the pricing structure may itself affect incentives to invest for a private sector ANSP.

ANSPs usually follow International Civil Aviation Organisation (ICAO) guidelines regarding air navigation charges, structuring them according to both route length and aircraft size. The precise implementation of such guidelines varies across ANSPs, though. Some apply formulas, whereas others determine price lists organised by ranges of flight distance and aircraft weight. Other ANSPs are remunerated through a levy set as a percentage of air ticket price or per flight. Where formulas are used, an example may be the following, used by Eurocontrol:

$$charge = UnitRate \times \frac{Distance}{100} \times \left(\frac{MTOW}{50}\right)^n$$

where the unit rate is a constant, measured in the applicable currency; route length is measured as the great-circle distance in kilometres between the two extremes of the airspace section where the ANSP controls the flight; the weight is measured by the aircraft's maximum take-off weight (MTOW); and n manages the proportionality between aircraft weight and the charge. The air navigation charge increases with distance and with aircraft weight, meeting ICAO recommendations.

Assuming a unit rate of EUR50, an MTOW of 75 tonnes for a Code-C aircraft, and n = 1 (not necessarily the factor used by Eurocontrol), the charge applicable to the average flight in the ATM project example in section 5.1 above would be:

$$charge = 50 \times \frac{1,000}{100} \times \left(\frac{75}{50}\right)^1 = EUR750.00$$

The EUR750 charge would be paid by the airline irrespective of the number of passengers on board. However, setting an average charge per passenger is useful for the discussion at hand. Following the assumption in the project example that the flight carries on average 120 passengers in year 1, the ATM charge per passenger would be EUR6.25.

The price formula is such that an increase in the aircraft size, carrying on average more passengers, would result in a higher charge overall for the flight, but a lower charge per passenger. For example, if the aircraft can carry an extra 25 passengers at the same load factor and has an MTOW higher by 5 tonnes, the resulting total charge would be EUR800 and the charge per passenger EUR5.52.

Table 5.2 uses the example in Table 5.1 to simulate the effect on ANSP revenues of applying a formula of this type. To simplify, it is assumed that aircraft technology and the n exponential factor applicable are such that as aircraft size increases, the resulting air navigation charge per passenger decreases by half the percentage saving in aircraft unit operating costs.[4] The table measures the increases in revenues relative to revenues in year 1 with and without the project. The difference between the increase in revenues with and without the project would then measure net revenue increase, which is determined only by the changes in the charge applicable to traffic, since the total amount of traffic does not change.

Table 5.2 Financial returns for an ANSP of investing in greater aircraft movement capacity

			PV\Year	1	2	3	5	10	15	20	25	27
DIVERTED TRAFFIC STAYS WITH THE SAME ANSP												
With Project												
(1)	Incr. revs. from traffic not diverted	(EUR m)	59.7	0.0	0.0	1.4	2.4	4.4	5.5	6.6	7.7	8.1
(2)	Incr. revs. from diverted traffic	(EUR m)	35.5	0.0	0.5	-0.4	-0.4	0.6	3.1	6.3	10.4	12.3
(3) = (1) + (2)	Total incremental revenues	(EUR m)	95.2	0.0	0.5	1.0	2.1	5.0	8.6	12.9	18.1	20.5
Without project												
(4)	Incr. revs. from traffic not diverted	(EUR m)	29.5	0.0	0.0	0.0	0.5	1.7	2.9	4.2	5.4	5.9
(5)	Incr. revs. from diverted traffic	(EUR m)	66.2	0.0	0.5	1.0	1.6	3.4	5.8	8.8	12.6	14.4
(6) = (4) + (5)	Total incremental revenues	(EUR m)	95.8	0.0	0.5	1.0	2.1	5.1	8.7	12.9	18.0	20.3
Net project flows												
(7) = (3) - (6)	Net revenue gain	(EUR m)	-0.6	0.0	0.0	0.0	0.0	-0.1	-0.1	0.0	0.0	0.1
(8)	Increase ATC op cost	(EUR m)	3.8	0.0	0.0	0.3	0.3	0.3	0.3	0.3	0.3	0.3
(9)	Investment cost	(EUR m)	13.9	7.5	7.5							
(10) = (7) - (8) - (9)	Financial flows	(EUR m)	-18.3	-7.5	-7.5	-0.3	-0.3	-0.4	-0.4	-0.3	-0.3	-0.2
	FRR		**N/A**									
DIVERTED TRAFFIC FLIES THROUGH AN ALTERNATIVE ANSP												
(11) = (1) - (4)	Rev. gain from non diverted traffic	(EUR m)	30.1	0.0	0.0	1.4	2.0	2.7	2.6	2.4	2.3	2.2
(12) = (11) - (8) - (9)	Financial flows	(EUR m)	12.4	-7.5	-7.5	1.1	1.7	2.4	2.3	2.1	2.0	1.9
	FRR		**11.7%**									

The resulting financial return of the project, measured against what would have happened in the 'without project' scenario, is negative. The operator does not have an incentive to invest, even though – it is important to recall – the project has a strong economic return of 32 per cent (see Table 5.1). Note that any gain or loss in revenue would come from a change in price and would constitute a transfer between the ANSP and the airline or the passenger and, therefore, does not represent a net change in welfare to be added to the calculation of economic return.[5]

The lower part of Table 5.2 calculates the same scenario, but assuming that diverted traffic flies instead through a sector managed by an alternative ANSP. Now, obviously, not carrying out the project would result in 'lost customers' and therefore the financial return of the project increases and in the current case becomes a positive 11.7 per cent. As far as the economic appraisal is concerned, the producer surplus of the alternative ANSP is treated equally to that of the promoter at hand, and therefore can again be ignored.

Therefore, other than when traffic would divert to an alternative ANSP, the ANSP does not have an incentive to invest, even when the project produces strong economic returns. This outcome is the product largely of the pricing policy. Economic efficiency would call for prices to be set at marginal cost which, on a long-term perspective, can be taken to mean average cost. The cost that a controlled flight causes to the ANSP depends on the amount of time it needs to be controlled and, therefore, on distance and speed. Jet passenger aircraft of different sizes travel at similar speeds and require the same amount of workload and resources from the ANSP. Therefore economic efficiency would call for jet aircraft to be charged the same amount regardless of their size. Instead, by applying common pricing policy whereby charges increase with aircraft weight, passengers in larger aircraft may end up paying less for air navigation services than passengers in smaller aircraft, although they are still cross-subsidising them.

The distortion is more acute with smaller propeller aircraft. They tend to be slower and hence require more controller workload per distance travelled; they can also occupy a given section of airspace for longer than a jet aircraft. Economic efficiency would require slower propeller aircraft to be charged more than jet aircraft. Instead they are usually charged less.

Putting aside the issue of propellers and remaining with jets, if prices were set efficiently, by speed and distance rather than weight and distance, the 'without project' scenario in the example in Table 5.2 would have seen a substantial fall in revenues, because the ANSP would not be able to price-discriminate against passengers on larger aircraft. The result would be to improve the financial performance of the project, encouraging the ANSP to invest in more capacity.

By enabling ANSPs to price-discriminate against larger aircraft, ICAO may be adding an element of solidarity into paying for aircraft services. But it is also reducing the incentive to expand capacity by allowing ANSPs to profit from passengers switching to larger aircraft. It may be disincentivising investment even in cases where, as the example above suggests, the investment would produce strong economic returns.

In practice, however, ANSPs operated by the private sector would have their price caps tied to rate of return regulation, which in turn is tied to the asset base of the operator. As is seen in Chapter 4, section 4.5, rate of return regulation incentivises investment, and indeed overinvestment, in capacity. In the case of ATM, increases in flight movement capacity generally go hand in hand with a larger asset base. Therefore, rate of return regulation would incentivise investment that the current pricing policy disincentivises. On the other hand, not all asset base increases involve increases in capacity. They may also improve safety, the quality of communications, reduce controller or pilot workload, and so on.

To conclude, a private ANSP operating under rate of return regulation and with economically efficient prices would have strong incentives to invest in added capacity. The current pricing policy of discriminating against passengers in larger aircraft somewhat diminishes that incentive, even in cases where capacity expansion is justified. Rate of return regulation would tend to ensure that investment is always forthcoming. On the other hand, the incentive to invest would not necessarily be in increasing capacity but rather on upgrading technology.

5.3 ATM as a source of hard currency

5.3.1 Introduction

The purpose of this section is to illustrate the implications of trade barriers and foreign exchange scarcity for project appraisal, using an ATM project as an example. The provision of ATM services can be an important source of hard currency revenues. Often, most equipment is generally imported and must be paid in hard currency as well. But ATM tends to be a profitable sector and where foreign exchange inflows tend to be larger than foreign exchange outflows. For small and low income countries, in particular, the net inflow of revenues can make a meaningful difference to the national balance of payments.

But the business plan, profit and loss account, or cash flow statement of an ATM operator, even if they single out transactions in hard currency, may not be accurate indicators of the net gains of hard currency provided by the sector. Many countries are subject to trade distortions. Most commonly these consist of tariffs on imports, although they can also include subsidies, mostly to exports, and non-tariff barriers, such as quotas. This means that the market prices observed in the ANSP business plan and accounts are distorted, diminishing their accuracy when gauging the ability of ANSP investment projects to generate hard currency.

When performing a financial appraisal, the market prices that the ANSP receives for producing ATM services or for making data available to other

ANSPs and the prices it pays for inputs, determine ANSP cash flows and constitute the basis on which to make the investment decision from a business or financial point of view. From the point of view of the domestic economy it would be different. The project analyst may be tempted to adjust prices by identifying any tariffs paid on the import of equipment and reducing equipment costs accordingly. That is certainly part of the necessary adjustment (or, in CBA language, 'shadow pricing'), but is not sufficient. It overlooks that inputs that are not traded internationally also have an opportunity cost in terms of hard currency. For example, IT personnel and controllers employed by the project are normally skilled labour that could be deployed to other uses in the local economy that could also generate hard currency. Their salaries, even if paid in hard currency, do not necessarily reflect the opportunity cost of labour in terms of its ability to generate foreign exchange. Similarly, construction of buildings and other civil works required by the project, which are not traded internationally either, may come at the expense of, say, expanding the local port or hotel capacity, which are also generators of hard currency. Without trade distortions, market prices in such non-tradable sectors would reflect the opportunity cost of the sector in terms of foregone value in other sectors, including in terms of hard currency. But not when there are trade distortions.

Such considerations may seem trivial from the vantage point of developed countries or countries with negligible trade distortions or with otherwise ample access to hard currency. But in poorer countries, particularly relatively small ones, where hard currency is scarce, or in countries with otherwise significant balance of payments problems, such considerations are important. Indeed, the techniques used to appraise projects under such circumstances were developed on the second half of the 20th century, and popularised by the World Bank (see Ward 2019), in a world operating with controlled exchange rates, and therefore where such situations were pervasive. Since the 1970s , when the US abandoned the peg of the US dollar to gold, leading to a system of fiat money, balance of payment constraints became less stringent because of the ability of countries with currencies widely accepted internationally to print money. But balance of payment constraints still exist – they are the main area of activity of the International Monetary Fund – as do trade distortions.

In the context of ATM, think of a small developing country controlling substantial en route traffic that wishes to expand ATM capacity. The country would need to undergo a hard currency outflow now in order to generate further hard currency in the future. The hard currency outflow would come at the expense of alternative uses in activities that would also generate or save hard currency. These would include items such as importing machinery, software, and other equipment for other export or import substitute sectors such as, say, textile manufacturing or food processing. Likewise, the civil works in the ATM project comes at the expense of civil works in other tradable sectors such as a seaport upgrade.

The next section offers a summary of the adjustments necessary in an appraisal to measure generation and use of foreign exchange in the presence of trade distortions, introducing the concept of numeraire. A full treatment of the rationale and the adjustments here described is beyond the scope of this book. The reader is referred to, for example, Curry and Weiss (2000), Boardman et al. (2018) or, referring back to original World Bank use, Squire and van der Tak (1975). This is followed by a project illustration in sections 5.3.3 and 5.3.4, each section using an alternative numeraire.

5.3.2 Trade distortions and economic value

This section makes a schematic presentation of the adjustments necessary for the prices used in project appraisal to reflect the opportunity cost of foreign exchange (or hard currency). The adjustments consist of applying corrective, or conversion, factors to the observed market prices of inputs and outputs in order to come up with economic prices, normally referred to in CBA literature as 'shadow' prices. The corrective factors are determined by the type and magnitude of trade distorting measures applied by the host country. The resulting economic prices reflect, or approximate, actual hard currency consumption and generation of the priced item. This correction can be done following two alternative approaches. Firstly, converting all prices to international (or border) prices – thereby the appraisal adopting what is referred to as an international price *numeraire*. Or, secondly, converting all prices to domestic prices – whereby the appraisal would follow the domestic price numeraire. The two approaches are alternative but, as will be seen, produce equivalent appraisal results albeit with different magnitudes.[6] It is also worth pointing out that 'numeraire' is also referred to sometimes as 'price structure'.

The adjustments are applied by first making an overarching classification of all goods and services, whether inputs or outputs, into two categories: *tradable* and *non-tradable*. Tradable produce, whether goods or services, are those that can be sold across the border, that is, exported or imported internationally. They do not need to be actually *traded* across the border. Being tradable is sufficient. If they are sold to the domestic market they assume the role of an import substitute. Non-tradables are products such as housing and infrastructure that provide services that can only be consumed domestically.

Any output, whether tradable or non-tradable, is normally produced by a combination of tradable and non-tradable inputs. So, a tradable output, such as a car, is produced with tradable inputs, such as parts and energy, and non-tradable inputs, such as real estate – the assembly plant – and labour. Likewise, say, housing, a non-tradable output, is produced by tradable inputs, such as building materials and energy, and non-tradable inputs, such as labour, land, and the services provided by infrastructure around the construction site.

What follows now is a summary of the adjustments made to perform the appraisal with, in turn, the world and the domestic price numeraires. For each of the two numeraires a distinction is made between the four possible combinations of produce: tradable inputs; tradable outputs; non-tradable inputs; and non-tradable outputs.

Starting with the international, or world, price numeraire, the adjustment for tradable inputs and outputs is relatively simple. The adopted price is the 'border price'. If it is a good, it is either the CIF (cost, insurance and freight) price when imported, or the FOB (free on board) price when exported. If it is a service, it is the price at which that service is traded internationally before adding any domestic import duties and after deducting any domestic export subsidies.

If it is a non-tradable input, the theory would suggest repeating the following four-step process a number of times. Firstly, decomposing that (tier one) input into all the (tier two) inputs used to produce it. Secondly, grouping those (tier two) inputs into tradable and non-tradable. Thirdly, applying the border price to tradable (tier two) inputs. And fourthly, for non-tradable (tier two) inputs, repeating the first three steps in the process, decomposing them into their own tradable and non-tradable (tier three) inputs. The process is repeated in succession until eventually the analyst ends up with land and labour as the ultimate non-tradable inputs. The result is a *full-fledged* account of distortions where every tradable produce in the economy involved in producing the project is priced at its border price.

The process behind the full-fledged method can be tedious and expensive in terms of analyst time. It is therefore rarely applied to derive economic prices for the appraisal of any one single project. The process would instead normally be applied in the production of a manual or vade mecum for guidance purposes, to yield economic prices to be used for a number of projects. Most commonly, individual appraisals follow a shortcut in the form of a standard conversion factor (SCF), as follows:

$$SCF = \frac{M + X}{(M + T_m - S_m) + (X - T_x + S_x)}$$

where M and X are total imports and exports in the economy, respectively, at border prices. T_m are taxes (or tariffs) on imports and T_x are taxes on exports. S_m are subsidies to imports and S_x subsidies to exports.

The result of the formula is an average measure of the tax and subsidy distortions in the domestic economy. It is applied to all non-tradables. The analyst can also combine the full-fledged method and the shortcut SCF formula, applying the former to a certain number of tiers – usually up to about two – and then applying the SCF on the remainder.

A key problem with the shortcut measure is that it leaves out non-tariff barriers (NTBs) such as quotas. The full-fledged approach does not have this problem since it can compare prices of individual items with border prices. To the knowledge of the author there is no proposed method in the literature to deal with this drawback in the shortcut approach. A method suggested by the author to attempt to gauge the extent of such NTBs is briefly presented in Appendix A5.1.

For non-tradable outputs, the method calls for a consumption conversion factor (CCF) based on expenditure patterns in the domestic economy (Squire and van der Tak 1975). But practice normally relies on the same SCF as for inputs.

Intuitively, the SCF amounts then to how many units of foreign exchange are foregone (gained) by producing (giving up) one unit of domestic income. Note that the appraisal with the domestic price numeraire can be expressed both in a foreign (typically hard) currency or in domestic currency.[7]

Switching now to the alternative numeraire – the domestic price numeraire – the adjustment process is reversed relative to that using the world price structure that has just been introduced. When following the domestic price numeraire the price of tradables are converted into their domestic equivalent. The logic is to include into tradables the same degree of trade distortion that non-tradables reflect. So non-tradables are valued at observed domestic prices (after allowing for any non-trade related distortions) and tradables, at border prices, are applied a shadow exchange rate (SER), which is simply the inverse of the SCF, as follows:

$$SER = \frac{1}{SCF} = \frac{(M + T_m - S_m) + (X - T_x + S_x)}{M + X}$$

Intuitively, the SER is the income foregone in acquiring one unit of foreign exchange (Ward et al. 1991). In extended form: it is the benefit (as money income or otherwise) in terms of produce in domestic prices given up in order to acquire one unit of foreign exchange. As with the world price numeraire, the appraisal with the domestic price numeraire can be conducted both in foreign or in local currency.[8]

Appraisals using the world price numeraire (i.e. using SCF) and the domestic price numeraire (i.e. using the SER) yield the same project value conclusions albeit with different magnitudes. The next two sections illustrate this by applying in section 5.3.3 the world price numeraire, followed by section 5.3.4 with an application of the domestic price numeraire for the same project.

5.3.3 ATM project appraised with the world price numeraire

The illustration proceeds with the example of sections 5.1 and 5.2, taking as a starting point the situation depicted in Table 5.2. The project promoting ANSP ignores time savings to passengers and cost savings to airlines. This would reflect an extreme example of a project that has implications only for en route traffic within its airspace and where the country hosting the project appraises projects focusing only on benefits and costs to nationals. Since none of the en route traffic is national, the benefits and costs to this traffic segment does not count in the economic appraisal. In economic appraisal terms en route passengers would be referred to as having 'no standing' in the economic appraisal.

The exercise makes now the additional modification relative to Table 5.2 that the host country is subject to substantial trade distortions. These include export subsidies, import tariffs, and other non-tariff barriers (NTB), such as quotas, licensing, lengthy administrative procedures, etc. Regarding the outputs and inputs of the project at hand, we assume that revenues are not subject to any taxes or tariffs, but that some of the inputs to the project, including mostly imported ATC equipment and software, are subject to an import tariff of 25 per cent. Still, the fact that the domestic economy is subject to substantial trade distortions means that the project may have wider, indirect foreign exchange implications via the effects of the project on secondary markets. That is, the project may have implications for the generation and use of foreign exchange in the host economy that may not be reflected in the financial flows of the project converted at the official exchange rate (OER).

We assume no capital controls with a fully convertible currency and therefore the OER would also correspond to the market or prevailing exchange rate. The local currency is referred to as LCU (local currency unit) and has a market exchange rate of EUR–LCU = 2, so that 1 euro buys 2 LCUs.

The analyst proceeds to estimate a standard conversion factor as specified in section 5.3.2. The host country exports X = EUR10bn and imports M = EUR5bn every year. On average, the country applies a tariff of 50 per cent to all imports – implying import tariff revenues T_m = EUR5bn and subsidises exports by 50 per cent, implying a subsidy bill of S_x = EUR2.5bn. It applies no subsidies to imports nor taxes exports, therefore S_m and T_x, respectively, are both 0. The SCF is therefore:

$$SCF = \frac{M + X}{(M + T_m - S_m) + (X - T_x + S_x)}$$
$$= \frac{10 + 5}{(10 + 5 - 0) + (5 - 0 + 2.5)} = 0.6667$$

The analyst knows that the local economy also uses many NTBs, but is unsure of the extent to which the wedge that on aggregate they create between domestic and border prices. The analyst therefore follows the rationale set out in the Appendix A5.1 and performs a second check to see how the real effective exchange rate compares to what would be expected given the per capita GDP of the host economy. A shortcut to this is offered by the Big Mac index published by The Economist newspaper (see the Appendix A5.1).

The price of a Big Mac burger in the closest McDonald's restaurant to the offices of the analyst is LCU10, or EUR5 at the OER. Yet, following The Economist newspaper, the income level (GDP per capita) of the country would suggest that the price of the Big Mac at the local restaurant should be EUR3.5, or LCU7 at the OER.

According to the logic explained in the appendix, the ratio of expected to actual Big Mac prices suggests a SCF of 7/10 = 0.7. This SCF = 0.7 value is very close to the SCF = 0.6667 estimate using tariffs and subsidies alone.

Moreover, the analyst knows that the SCF = 0.7 ratio has been quite stable over the last three or four years, suggesting that the real exchange rate is unlikely to be in the process of adjustment to any macro-economic shock. The analyst concludes that NTBs in aggregate do not contribute in net terms to differences in price levels between the domestic and border prices. Hence NTBs do not seem to account for any significant additional net rent or transfer relative to those accounted for by tariffs and trade subsidies. The analyst therefore decides to continue the calculations of project value with the SCF = 0.6667 as calculated with tariffs and subsidies only.

Table 5.3 displays the result of the appraisal. Columns a and b include the calculation process using the world price numeraire, expressed either in foreign exchange EUR (column a) or in local currency LCU (column b). Columns c and d display the calculation process using the domestic price numeraire, discussed in the next section.

As in Table 5.2, the calculation proceeds with two alternative assumptions. First, that diverted traffic stays with the promoter ANSP, displayed in rows 1 to 15 in Table 5.3. Second, that diverted traffic would fly through an alternative ANSP, requiring further adjustments, displayed in rows 16 to 19.

Following the world price numeraire involves pricing all tradable inputs and outputs at border prices, while applying standard conversion factor (SCF) to all non-tradable inputs and outputs. As mentioned in section 5.3.2, the application of the SCF is a shortcut.

The project output is measured by comparing incremental revenues with and without the project, included in rows 1 and 3, respectively, in Table 5.3. These correspond to rows 3 and 6 in Table 5.2, respectively. The output of the project, air traffic management, is a tradable service. Indeed the current example assumes that all traffic flows benefiting from the project are en route flows, meaning that 100 per cent are exports. It is worth underlining though that the important element here is that the output is tradable rather than an actual export. If the en route flows consisted instead of domestic airlines, so that revenues were not an export, the treatment would be exactly the same as for foreign airlines. Also, no taxes or subsidies are applied to the output of the project; therefore the revenues require no further adjustment, whether expressed in EUR (column a) or in LCU (column b).

The increase in operating costs resulting from the project are included in row 5, corresponding to row 8 in Table 5.2. These operating costs consist mostly of labour and property-related costs, which are deemed non-tradable. The operating costs would then be applied the standard conversion factor SCF = 0.67, resulting in an economic cost of EUR2.6m (row 6).

For the capital investment cost, half of the items are tradable (row 8), namely the equipment and software, and the other half are non tradable (row 11), including civil works, installation, etc. For the share that is tradable, there is an import tariff of 25 per cent, half the rate of the average applied by the country across all imports. By removing the 25 per cent tariff we are left with

Table 5.3 Appraisal results of ATM project hosted by a country with barriers to trade

		World (EURm) (a)	World (LCUm) (b = a × OER)	Domestic (EURm) (c)	Domestic (LCUm) (d = c × OER)
		Price numeriare			
DIVERTED TRAFFIC STAYS WITH THE SAME ANSP					
(1)	With project, incremental revenues	95.2	190.4	95.2	190.4
(2) = (1) × SER	With project, incremental revenues, at SER			142.8	285.6
(3)	Without project, incremental revenues	95.8	191.5	95.8	191.5
(4) = (3) × SER	Without project, incremental revenues, at SER			143.6	287.3
Adjustments to project costs					
(5)	Increase in operating cost	3.8	7.7	3.8	7.7
(6) = (5) x SCF	Increase in operating cost, adjusted with SCF	2.6	5.1		
(7)	Investment cost	13.9	27.9	13.9	27.9
(8) = (7)/2	Tradable	7.0	13.9	7.0	13.9
(9) = (8)/(1 + 0.25)	Tradable, at CIF prices	5.6	11.2	5.6	11.2
(10) = (9) × SER	Tradable, at CIF prices, at SER			8.4	16.7
(11) = (7)/2	Non-tradable	7.0	13.9	7.0	13.9
(12) = (11) × SCF	Non-tradable, with SCF	4.6	9.3		
(13a) = (9a) + (12a)	Investment cost at economic prices	10.2	20.5	15.3	30.7
(13c) = (10c) + (11c)					
Net project flows					
(14) = (1) − (3) − (5) − (7)	Unadjusted financial flows	-18.3	-36.7	-18.3	-36.7
(15a) = (1a) − (3a) − (6a) − (13a)	(Financial) flows at economic prices	**-13.3**	**-26.7**	**-20.0**	**-40.0**
(15c) = (2c) − (4c) − (5c) − (13c)					
DIVERTED TRAFFIC FLIES THROUGH AN ALTERNATIVE ANSP					
(16)	Rev gain from traffic not diverted	30.1	60.3	30.1	60.3
(17) = (16) × SER	Rev gain from traffic not diverted, at SER			45.2	90.4
(18) = (16) − (5) − (7)	Unadjusted financial flows	12.4	24.7	12.4	24.7
(19a) = (16a) − (6a) − (13a)	(Financial) flows at economic prices	**17.4**	**34.7**	**26.0**	**52.1**
(19c) = (17c) − (5c) − (13c)					

the price of the equipment and software at border, CIF prices, amounting to an investment of EUR5.6 million (row 9). The non-tradable half of the investment cost is adjusted by the SCF, just as was the case for operating costs in row 6, resulting in an investment in non-tradables at economic prices of EUR4.6m (row 12). To come up with the full investment cost at economic prices we add the tradable elements at border CIF prices and the non-tradable items adjusted by the SCF, resulting in a total capital investment cost at economic prices of EUR10.2m (cell 13a).

Note the difference with the investment cost at financial prices of EUR13.9m (cell 7a). This means that what may appear as an investment cost of EUR13.9m, actually involves a cost to the domestic economy of EUR10.2m after accounting for import tariffs to tradable inputs and, critically, to non-tradable inputs. Such non-tradable inputs either use themselves tradables in their construction or manufacturing or have an opportunity cost in terms of alternative uses as inputs for tradables.

To estimate the economic value of the project we follow the same procedure as for the financial value but operating with the adjusted (or 'shadow') prices, where applicable. So the value of the project in economic prices would be the difference in incremental revenues (row 1 minus row 3), minus both adjusted (or, in CBA terms, shadow-priced) operating (row 6) and investment costs (cell 13a, or cell 13b if the calculation proceeds in LCU).

Note the difference in the economic value of the project of −EUR13.3m (cell 15a) at economic prices, compared to the −EUR18.3m (cell 14a) at financial prices. The figures expressed in local currency are −LCU26.7 (cell 15b) and −LCU36.7 (cell14b), respectively.

The analysis reveals that the financial value loss of EUR18.3m from the project, masks a smaller loss to the economy of EUR13.3m. The reason for this difference is twofold. Firstly, some of the tradable inputs include a tariff, hence the adjustment of removing the tariff from row 8 to row 9. This is equivalent to a standard adjustment in economic appraisals of removing taxes from input costs. If we were to calculate the gains and losses to the economy from the project by simply looking at the financial business plan of the project, this adjustment would be a fairly obvious one to make. What would be less apparent is the second reason for the difference in the size of the loss, namely, an adjustment also needs to be made to estimate the foreign exchange opportunity cost of non-tradable inputs, for both for operating costs (row 5, adjusted in row 6) and investment cost (row 11, adjusted in row 12). Those inputs, while non-tradable, come at the expense of tradables.

Let us dwell somewhat more on the intuition behind the result. An intuitive take on the adjustment to non-tradable inputs could be made in two ways, taking operating costs as an example. Firstly, we know that the SCF measures the extent of the average distortion to foreign trade in the economy. We could assume that the non-tradable inputs of the project are themselves made of components that are representative of the average use of foreign exchange in the economy. Then the actual amount of tariffs we expect to be embedded in the price of the non-tradable input is measured by the SCF. In the perhaps less readily intuitive case of the salaries of air traffic controllers, such items could include, for example, training abroad that is taxed domestically (to, say, protect domestic trainers), or a policy of including in the compensation package an imported company car, subject to a tariff.

Secondly, in a freely trading, undistorted market economy, inputs of non-tradables worth EUR3.8m should be exchangeable in the domestic market for EUR3.8m of tradable inputs. If we were then to exchange the tradable inputs at the border, they would generate, at the prevailing exchange rate, EUR2.6m of foreign exchange. Therefore consuming EUR3.8m of non-tradable inputs comes at the expense of generating EUR2.6m of foreign exchange. But when there are trade distortions, as in the current example, consisting in this case of tariffs in the price of inputs, whether directly because they are tradable, or indirectly when they are not tradable, the actual consumption of foreign exchange is not as high as suggested by market prices. The EUR13.3m loss measures the value of the project if all inputs and outputs were free of distortions, at world (border) prices. This can be expressed in either foreign exchange (column a) or in local currency (column b), by simply converting at the market exchange rate.

Assuming alternatively that there is a competing ANSP, in rows 16 to 19, the project becomes profitable, as was seen in Table 5.2. When allowing for trade barriers, the value of the project to the national economy is higher than apparent from financial flows. A positive value of EUR12.4m (cell 18a in Table 5.3 and row 12 in Table 5.2) becomes a value of EUR17.4m (cell 19a).

5.3.4 ATM project appraised with the domestic price numeraire

In order to avoid duplicating explanations about the illustrative example, this section is meant to be read in sequence with the preceding section 5.3.3. The section focuses on comparing the calculation process when following the domestic price numeraire with the calculation process of following the world price numeraire, discussed in the preceding section. It concludes with a short discussion of the merits of each numeraire.

The calculation process when following the domestic price numeraire is inverse to that when following the world price numeraire. The adjustment takes place on tradables, while non-tradables are left at the observed price, after adjusting for any non-trade related distortion. Adjustments take place with the SER, which as seen in section 5.3.2 is simply the inverse of the SCF. Section 5.3.3 illustrated the calculation of the SCF for the example at hand. Here we then simply take the inverse, namely:

$$SER = \frac{1}{SCF} = \frac{1}{0.6667} = 1.5$$

The process of calculating project value is illustrated in columns c and d in Table 5.3, expressed in euro as foreign exchange and the local currency unit, respectively. The output of the project, air traffic management services, is a tradable product and is therefore converted at the SER, in rows 2 and 4 in Table 5.3. In the case at hand, 100 per cent of the operating costs (largely property and labour) are non-tradable and are therefore left at domestic prices. This is a simplification since some inputs necessary for running ATM operations, such as energy, tend to be tradable (except, perhaps, in islands or in nations unconnected to an international grid).

For investment cost, the SER is applied to the 50 per cent of inputs that are tradable (such as IT and communications equipment), as shown in row 10. Non-tradable components of investment cost, included in row 11, are left at observed, market prices. Note that when adding up the various components to estimate investment cost at economic prices, the underlying logic (i.e. adding up only economic prices) remains the same as with the world price numeraire, even if the formulae in row 13 uses different rows for each numeraire.

Similarly, the formulae for aggregating project flows in row 15 differs slightly between cells 15a and 15c, but the logic of using only economic prices remains the same. The results show that using the domestic price numeraire yields a higher economic loss that, at EUR20m (cell 15c), is higher than the EUR18.3 (cell 14c) loss when using unadjusted financial prices. This is a relative difference of +9 per cent (= $(-20.0/-18.3) -1$). This is in contrast with the results when following the world price numeraire. There the economic loss, at EUR13.3m (cell 15a), was lower than the EUR18.3 (cell 14a) loss using financial prices, yielding a difference between financial and economic prices of −27 per cent (= $(-13.3/-18.3) -1$).

The difference between the resulting financial and economic values under each numeraire (the +9 per cent and −27 per cent just estimated) are therefore of a different order of magnitude and of the opposite sign when using the alternative numeraires. The magnitude of the relative difference depends on the balance of tradable and non-tradable items in the project at hand. As for the sign of the relative difference, the higher loss in domestic prices implies that the price level in the domestic economy is higher than in the world economy, due to the presence of tariffs in the domestic economy.

The results under the two numeraires, though, are mutually consistent. Note that if we take the EUR20 (cell 15c) loss estimated when using the domestic price numeraire and apply to it the SCF in order to convert it to world prices, it would yield EUR −13.3 (= -20×0.67), the same result as the estimation of project value at world prices in cell 15a.

The same principles apply to the calculation of project value in rows 16 to 19. It may be worth recalling that the figures in row 16 correspond to row 11 in Table 5.2. This time the SER needs to be applied to the (tradable) incremental output (i.e. controlled traffic) of the project.

The question then arises about which of the two numeraires to use. Analysts should a priori be indifferent as to whether conducting project appraisals with the world or the domestic price numeraire. Both methods convey a valid measure of project value that incorporates the opportunity cost of foreign exchange, so long as they are compared with other projects valued with the same numeraire. The case for each numeraire is then one of convenience.

Expressing project value at world prices is convenient when comparing projects across different countries. Remember that this is not the same as saying that the results of the different projects are to be expressed in the same currency. Rather it says that the results are expressed at the price level and structure that the different countries can find at their respective borders. This does not need to be exactly the same price level and structure across every country, since transport costs to reach the border of each country may differ across countries. That in itself is relevant for international resource allocation, at least from the perspective of absolute cost advantage. Also, the difference in prices across countries may well be lower when using the world price numeraire than when using the domestic numeraire, which is more idiosyncratic to each country. It is therefore understandable why the World Bank chose to follow the world price numeraire, enabling easier comparison of projects across very different, and very distant, countries.

In turn, the domestic price numeraire should be easier to interpret by decision makers comparing projects within the same country. If the decision makers happen to be from or based in the country at hand, they may perhaps relate more intuitively to the domestic price level and structure, whether expressed in LCU or in hard currency.

5.4 Flight efficiency

This section addresses projects that are aimed not at increasing capacity but at making existing flights more efficient, generally by making more direct flights (horizontal efficiency), and more smooth, uninterrupted climbs and descends (vertical efficiency). Efficiency and capacity are not independent from each other. Routes that are more direct can also increase capacity by minimising the use of airspace and controller input. Also, during busy periods, attempting to improve efficiency of individual flights can penalise system capacity by imposing constraints on other flights.

For clarity, this section of the chapter addresses a project aimed exclusively at improving flight efficiency, with no implications for capacity. An ATM project aimed at improving flight efficiency but with a knock-on impact on capacity would also need to incorporate the appraisal approach discussed in section 5.1 above. It should be noted that the method presented here could also be applied to projects aimed at improving aircraft operations at airports, such as new taxiways that diminish taxying distance and time.

The project consists of the installation of ground navigational aids and IT equipment to enable an airport and the associated approach ANSP to offer airlines continuous climb departures (CCD) and continuous descent approaches (CDA) – the latter are also known as optimised profile descent (OPD) in the US. Both procedures improve the vertical efficiency of aircraft operations, minimising the need for level segments at altitudes lower than cruising, where flying is more expensive in terms of fuel burn. For the airport at hand, the CCD is estimated to reduce fuel burn by 10 per cent, and the CDA by 40 per cent in the climb and descent segments, respectively. The optimised procedures are expected to apply to 15 per cent of flights, occurring at off-peak hours, or about 10 departures and 10 arrivals a day.

Fuel is assumed to cost EUR600 per tonne, including EUR105 as the cost of GHG emissions, which are fully internalised through airline ticket prices.[9] Before the project the average departure is assumed to consume 2 tonnes of fuel and the average arrival 250kg. The benefits in terms of lower operating costs would accrue to the airlines and, if markets are sufficiently competitive, would eventually be passed on to the passengers. The greater number of efficient procedures would also reduce noise impact and improve air quality in the vicinity of the airport, externalities that are not internalised, unlike GHG emissions. The impact of noise is currently estimated to average EUR100 per aircraft movement, and the improved procedures to reduce the incidence by 20 per cent. The cost in terms of local air quality is estimated at EUR125 per aircraft movement and the project would reduce the incidence by 15 per cent. The benefits from reducing these externalities accrue to residents in the airport's vicinity.

In projects aimed at increasing ATM capacity discussed in section 5.1 above, the analyst has to make assumptions about airline behaviour in the 'with project' and, perhaps more critically, in the 'without project' scenarios. If a project is not carried out airlines may chose alternative routings or larger aircraft sizes and passengers may decide on alternative routings or departure times. These assumptions that the analyst must make about airline behaviour are not self-evident, yet they can be decisive for the estimated returns of the project. In the case of projects aimed only at improving flight efficiency there is no need to make assumptions about passenger or airline behaviour in a 'without project' scenario. The 'without project' scenario is simply the current situation.[10]

Table 5.4 presents the key input variables and the result. The benefits consist of fuel saved by the airlines (row 5) and lower air pollution and noise to residents in the vicinity of the airport (rows 6 and 7, respectively). The costs consist of the capital investment (row 9). No significant operating cost differences are expected and the operating life of the equipment installed is expected to be 20 years. The investment is clearly viable, with a strong economic return of 19 per cent.

Note that there are no changes in revenues to the ANSP. Departures and approaches are generally paid according to great circle distances between the aircraft's points of entry and exit in the area within which it is controlled, instead of to actual distance travelled or time under control. Therefore the ANSP has no incentive to carry out the investment, other than by increasing the asset base used for regulatory purposes.[11] Moreover, if ATM was remunerated through a share of airline ticket prices, and the airline markets in question were competitive, the investment may actually reduce ANSP revenues, as airlines pass fuel savings to passengers via lower air ticket prices. On the other hand, cash benefits to the airlines are sufficient to justify the investment. If the regulatory setting allowed it, the ANSP could negotiate with the airlines an increase in the air navigation charge to fund the project, leaving both airlines and ANSP better off.

This is a similar situation to that identified in the runway enlargement project example discussed in Chapter 4, section 4.6. The financial analysis concludes that the infrastructure operator does not have a financial incentive to carry out the infrastructure improvement (other than through inflating the regulatory asset base, should the operator be subject to economic regulation, as discussed in Chapter 4, section 4.5). But the economic analysis, by identifying who benefits from the project and by how much, enables the infrastructure operator and the main economic beneficiaries to negotiate sharing the benefits from, and the financing of, the project, in order to generate the incentive to carry out the investment. Note that the beneficiaries that would have an incentive to help finance the project include not only the airlines, which would save fuel with the project, but also residents in the vicinity of the airport, who would benefit from lower noise and air pollution. The latter group could be approached directly, through the airport or through their political representatives. However, normally the most economically efficient way to tackle the externality would be to internalise it. This could be done with a tax on the air ticket or on the landing charge that reflected the costs from noise and air pollution. That would devolve the issue of incentives to carry out the project back to the airlines and the ANSP. It would reinforce the incentive of the airlines to encourage the ANSP to carry out the project (should the ANSP not have it already in the form of an incentive to expand the regulatory asset base). The most economically efficient way would be (subject to second-best considerations) by means of proposing an increase in the approach and departure charge.

Table 5.4 Economic returns on an ATM investment project aimed at improving flight efficiency

		PV\Year	1	2	3	4	5	10	15	20	21
(1)	Approaches	(unit)	3,650	3,796	3,948	4,106	4,270	5,195	6,321	7,690	7,998
(2)	Departures	(unit)	3,650	3,796	3,948	4,106	4,270	5,195	6,321	7,690	7,998
(4) through (2)	Fuel saved in departures	(tons)	0	759	790	821	854	1,039	1,264	1,538	1,600
	Internal benefits										
(5) through (3) and (4)	Value of fuel saved	(EUR k)	11,335	0	683	711	739	769	935	1,138	1,384	1,440
	External benefits										
(6) through (1) and (2)	Air pollution benefits	(EUR k)	2,362	0	142	148	154	160	195	237	288	300
(7) through (1) and (2)	Noise benefits	(EUR k)	2,519	0	152	158	164	171	208	253	308	320
(8) = (5) + (6) + (7)	Total benefits	(EUR k)	16,216	0	977	1,017	1,057	1,100	1,338	1,628	1,980	2,059
(9)	Investment costs	(EUR k)	5,714	6,000								
(10) = (8) -(9)	Net economic flows	(EUR k)	10,501	-6,000	977	1,017	1,057	1,100	1,338	1,628	1,980	2,059
	Project ERR		19%									

Appendix A5.1: SER based on a productivity-adjusted real exchange rate

A5.1.1 The shortcoming in the SER formula

This appendix describes a procedure to estimate a shadow exchange rate (SER) that includes the combined effects of both tariff and non-tariff barriers, discusses its limitations, and suggests procedures to circumvent them. While the appendix refers only to the SER, it also concerns the SCF, which is simply the inverse of the SER (SCF = 1/SER).

The traditional formula to calculate the SER includes only tariff distortions and their inverse, namely subsidies to exports and imports. Data on tariffs at national level are normally readily available. Data on subsidies to exports and imports less so and, indeed, there may be incentives to hide evidence of such subsidies. For this reason the traditional, tariff-based SER formula is often simplified further by including tariffs only, excluding subsidies.

What the traditional SER formula always excludes is non-tariff barriers (NTBs) and related effects such as market power in exporting and importing sectors. While the main example of NTBs is quotas, NTBs also include a wide number of measures, ranging from the legal at one end – such as health regulations; the procedural – such as customs bureaucracy; and the illegal at the other end – such as corruption (see Donnelly and Manifold, 2005 for an overview and, for a more detailed treatment, Deardorff and Stern 1998). All of them normally have the effect of artificially increasing the price of imports, thereby encouraging the production and (at times super-normal) profitability of import substitutes.

More generally, market power in the domestic economy, whether in tradable or non-tradable sectors, increases the domestic price level. The super-normal profits of an importer would have the same effect as an import tariff, but one where the wedge between the world price and the domestic price accrues to the importer, rather than to the government, and is thereby not registered by tariff statistics. Similarly, a monopoly exporter pricing monopolistically would have the same effects as a tax on exports, but one that is not reflected on trade statistics. If the production of an export depends on a distorted, non-tradable input, such as land subject to an artificial constraint on supply, then super-normal profitability would accrue to landowners as well.

The effect of tariff barriers, NTBs and otherwise imperfect competition is the same: altering the price level in the domestic economy relative to border, world prices. Domestic prices then include an element of rent that does not reflect opportunity costs (assuming, for the small project, elastic supply). However the traditional SER formula captures only price level differences caused by tariffs and subsidies, and not differences that may be caused by NTBs and imperfect domestic competition. The SER therefore may not offer a sufficient adjustment to prices to reflect the opportunity costs incurred when trading internationally.

A way used by the author to correct for this shortcoming consists of computing an income-adjusted real exchange rate and then comparing it to the actual price level. The difference between the two would measure the full extent of trade barriers, whether tariff or otherwise, in the absence of other distortions. The next section in this appendix presents how this would be done.

A5.1.2 The framework

In a distortion-free world, the price level would be the same across all countries – what is known in international economics as the law of one price (LOP), whereby:

$$P_i = P_j \times PER(j{:}i)$$

where P_i and P_j are the price levels in countries i and j, respectively, and PER $(j{:}i)$ is the prevailing (or market, or observed, or official) exchange rate, defined as the price of the number of local currency units (LCU) of country i per LCU of country j.[12] This describes a condition whereby the price of products across countries, when converted at the PER, is the same. This outcome, in turn implies that the real exchange rate (RER) is always 1, as follows:

$$RER(j{:}i) = PER(j{:}i) \times \frac{P_j}{P_i} = 1$$

The RER is the units of LCU of country i necessary to buy the same basket of goods as with one unit of LCU of country j in country j. The RER is most commonly found in the calculation of (normally, per capita) income adjusted by the purchasing power parity (PPP), as follows:

$$Y_{ij}^{ppp} = \frac{Y_{ij}^{n}}{\left(\dfrac{P_i}{P_j}\right)}$$

where Y_{ij}^{ppp}, the income per capita at PPP of country i expressed in the currency of the reference country j, is equal to the nominal income per capita Y_{ij}^{n} estimated at the nominal exchange rate, or PER, between the currencies of the two countries, divided by the ratio of the price levels of the two countries. The denominator at the right hand side of the equation consists of the RER, in this case referred to as the PPP conversion factor (PCF).

Let us abstract from nominal differences arising from idiosyncratic currency denomination by assuming that PER = 1 for the currencies of two countries. Then, at one extreme, when the price levels of the two countries differ due only to tariff barriers, the traditional SER, as estimated only with tariffs and subsidies, introduced in section 5.3.2, would be equal to the RER (i.e. SER = RER).[13] While at the opposite extreme, assuming that the difference in the price level between the two countries is due entirely to NTBs, the traditional SER formula would yield a SER = 1, and differ from the RER (i.e. SER ≠ RER).

Of these two extreme cases, in the latter case the traditional SER formula fails to deliver the correct adjustment to prices for CBA to measure the opportunity costs of foreign exchange, while the RER yields the correct adjustment in both cases, since it reflects both tariff barriers and NTBs.

A solution would then be to simply use the RER, or the PCF, as the shadow exchange rate. However, price levels differ also from factors other than trade barriers, whether tariff or non-tariff. While an often cited such factor would be transportation costs, the share of international transport costs on the price level of the whole economy tends to be minuscule.

A more important factor would be differences in income levels, whereby more productive countries would have higher price levels than less productive countries. This is known as the Harrod-Balassa-Samuelson (HBS) effect, of which there is ample empirical evidence (Tica and Druzic 2006, Taylor 2010). In its simplest, early formulation, the HBS effect is explained through differences in productivity between the tradable and non-tradable sectors of an economy (although such simple formulation has since evolved, see Rogoff 1996). Countries with competitive tradable sectors would see the salaries in those sectors increase. Non-tradables tend to be mostly services, and arguably less subject to competition and hence less productive. Non-tradables compete with tradables for labour in the domestic economy, so that salaries of the less competitive, non-tradable sector rise in tandem with those in the more competitive, tradable sector, thereby increasing the price level of the country.

The HBS effect implies that, in the absence of any trade barrier, whether tariff or non-tariff, the RER of countries would differ due to productivity differences between countries. This means that for a SER based on the RER to seek to reflect price level differences due only to trade barriers, it would have to allow for the effects of the HBS effect on the RER.

The HBS effect could, at its simplest, be estimated as follows:

$$\frac{RER_i}{PER_{ij}} = P_i = \alpha + \beta Y_i + \mu_i$$

where j is normally the USD, and where μ_i is the estimated error factor for country *i*.

The proposed SER method would then consist on interpreting the term μ_i as due only to trade barriers, whether tariff or non-tariff. The SER would then be:

$$SER_i = \frac{P_i^E + \mu_i}{P_i^E} = \frac{P_i^A}{P_i^E}$$

where the superscript E stands for expected, or estimated, using the HBS equation, and the superscript A stands for actual, or observed. In words, the SER would be the relative difference between (i) the estimated price level of country i plus the error factor observed in country i, and (ii) the estimated price level. In short, it is the ratio between the observed price level and the price level expected after allowing for the HBS effect. For appraisals following the international price numeraire, the SCF would be the inverse of the SER, namely the ratio between the price level expected after allowing for the HBS effect and the observed price level.

A5.1.3 Limitations, other objections, and practice

This section briefly addresses four objections that could be raised against the proposed productivity adjusted SER and suggests possible solutions where the objection has merit. The four objections are: the method assumes that the RER is always in equilibrium; the method requires laborious calculations; there may be remaining distortions in border prices; and the method not allowing for product quality differences across countries. These objections are addressed in turn.

The main shortcoming of the proposed method is that it assumes that the RER is always in equilibrium. In practice, the RER can be altered through macroeconomic shocks, which would mean that μ_i would incorporate the effects of shocks in addition to trade barriers. The difficulty is that such shocks are not always apparent. Moreover, the RER may be subject to more than one shock simultaneously. Such shocks may reinforce each other or act in opposite directions.

Other than complex macro-economic modeling, a way out may be offered by allowing for shock signals in the RER. Empirical evidence (see Taylor 2010) suggests that about 50 per cent of the effect of macroeconomic shocks are dissipated from the RER in about 1–2 years. In practice then, if a RER is seen to be stable for about 2–3 years, it could be deemed approximately shock-free. If instead, the RER is seen to be volatile over a number of years, the analyst may attempt to average out the effect by taking the average RER over the last, say, ten years.

A second objection to the productivity adjusted RER is that the calculation process can be laborious. While this is correct, it also tends to be the case for many other shadow prices used in economic appraisal. It simply reflects that the world economy is subject to many distortions. In trying to allow for these distortions, the analyst unavoidably faces a trade-off between complexity and approximation.

To calculate the SER with this technique in the most exhaustive way the analyst would need to start by regressing the price level of as many countries around the world as possible against income per capita. The International Comparison Programme (ICP) calculates indexed price levels for all world countries.[14] The index can be regressed against the nominal income per capita at market exchange rates, also supplied by ICP. A much quicker, proxy alternative, would be to use the Big Mac Index computed by The Economist newspaper.[15] Fortunately, The Economist publishes a version of the index adjusted to income per capita. The SER would then simply be the ratio of the actual price of the Big Mac hamburger at market exchange rates to the estimated or expected price of the Big Mac hamburger given the GDP per person of the country.

A third potential possible objection is that the productivity adjusted SER takes average world price as the border price and that such price could itself be distorted. But this criticism, sometimes raised even in CBA circles, is based on the mistaken belief that the world or border price is meant to be a distortion-free price. The SER and SCF adjustments do not seek to remove all distortions present in the price of a traded good, but rather to account for domestic distortions to trade that mask opportunity costs. As the traditional SER formula makes clear, distortions beyond the border are ignored, for a reason.

The border price is the price at which a product is made available at the border of a country. It determines the terms at which the country can trade internationally and hence generate or use foreign exchange. Say that country A, hosting our project, trades with countries B, C, and D. If countries B, C, and D subsidise their exports to A, that subsidised price constitutes the terms at which A can import such produce. Why would A not seek to benefit from the generosity of foreigners? The exception would perhaps be if the subsidy is intended to be a temporary dumping measure to harm domestic producers in A, in a sector that A considers ultimately desirable to host. But other than that exception, as far as an appraisal in A is concerned, the subsidy paid for by B, C, and D does not require any further adjustment in appraisals in A. The same applies to any other distortion that B, C, and D may want to apply to the products traded with A.

The following quote summarises well the nature of the border prices:

> World prices reflect conditions in a range of international markets some of which will be manifestly uncompetitive, dominated by small producer groups or cartels. They are used not because they are seen as competitive prices but because they represent the terms on which a country can participate in world trade and are therefore the opportunity costs of using or producing traded goods.
>
> Curry and Weiss (2000), p.104.

The productivity adjusted RER approach to the SER presented here takes the border price to be the average price of products after removing price differences (a priori, mostly on non-tradable products) that are explained by differences in income levels across countries. It is worth recalling that all SER (and SCF), however calculated, are meant to be averages. They constitute a short-cut tool to the alternative, full-fledge method of accounting for every actual or foregone foreign exchange flow embedded in every good and service in the full input chain of the project under appraisal. The average world price would then be the price at which the world, on average, would make the average tradable produce available for international trade.

A fourth objection concerns differences in the quality of products across countries. This is indeed a problem, shared with any PPP estimation. A way to circumvent the shortcoming would be to use RER estimated with price comparisons controlling for quality differences. The Big Mac index by The Economist is one such attempt. Measures including a broader set of products could also be used.

Notes

1 In the case of airports this tends not to be a frequent stand-alone investment and is not discussed in Chapter 4, on airports. The treatment for airports would be equivalent to the treatment of flight efficiency in section 5.4 of this chapter.

2 For simplicity, the analysis does not include taxes. For an illustration of the treatment of taxes in economic appraisals see the airport terminal cases studied in Chapter 4, sections 4.1 to 4.5.

3 The analysis assumes a flat real cost of GHG emissions of EUR35 per tonne of emissions throughout the project life. This is an alternative approach to the airport runway case, where a cost of EUR20 per tonne in year 1 is assumed, growing at 3 per cent per year throughout the life of the project.

4 Since it is assumed in turn that the elasticity of aircraft unit operating costs with respect to aircraft size is −0.5, the parameters of the price formula are such that, say, a 10 per cent increase in aircraft size, resulting in a 5 per cent fall in aircraft unit operating cost, would cause a 2.5 per cent fall in the applicable air navigation charge per passenger.

5 Only a price change resulting in generated traffic would generate a change in welfare to be added to the economic returns. The resulting relative price changes to airline tickets, however, tend to be small, so that any generated or deterred traffic can also be expected to be small.

6 The approach based on the world or international price numeraire was developed formally by Little and Mirrlees 1968, 1974 for the OECD and adopted by the World Bank (Squire and van der Tack 1973). The alternative method based on the domestic price numeraire was developed by Dasgupta et al. 1972 for the United Nations Industrial Development Organisation (UNIDO). Both approaches are interchangeable and produce the same conclusions about projects, albeit with different magnitudes. See Little and Mirrlees (1974, ch.18) for a comparison of the two methods.

7 When using the world price numeraire, the adjustment, via the SCF, is applied to non-tradables. A non-tradable product has an opportunity cost in terms of a tradable product in three possible ways: an export, an import, and an import substitute. As illustration, assume that trade distortions in a country consist exclusively of ad valorem tariffs of 25 per cent on all traded products, so that SCF = 0.8. Assume also an official exchange rate OER of LCU-EUR = 2. Six scenarios can then be envisaged for interpreting the SCF when relating non-tradables to tradables:

1 EUR1 (LCU2) of non-tradable produce produced and consumed comes at the expense of producing an export that would generate EUR0.8 (LCU1.6) worth of foreign exchange.

2 EUR1 (LCU2) of non-tradable produce produced and consumed comes at the expense of importing a tradable worth EUR0.8 (LCU1.6) of foreign exchange.

3 EUR1 (LCU2) of non-tradable produced and consumed comes at the expense of producing an import substitute that would save EUR0.8 (LCU1.6) worth of foreign exchange.

4 EUR 1 (LCU2) of non-tradable produce given up allows producing an export yielding 0.8 (LCU1.6) worth of foreign exchange.

5 EUR1 (LCU2) of non tradable produce given up allows importing a good worth EUR0.8 (LCU1.6) at the border.

6 EUR1 (LCU2) of non-tradable produce given up allows producing an import substitute worth 0.8 (LCU1.6) at the border.

One could also think of comparing non-tradables, since non-tradables have opportunity costs in terms of other non-tradables that ultimately come at the expense of a tradable.

Another, perhaps more abstract, way of interpreting the SCF would be as follows: how many foreign exchange units would (EUR 1 worth of) a domestic non-tradable product be worth in international markets if it was made tradable. All in all, in the specific example at hand, something that is priced at EUR0.8 at the border, by it being made available at EUR1 in the domestic market, implies that local consumers are getting poor value for money, due to tariffs.

8 We continue with the same numerical example as in the preceding footnote. That is, assuming, firstly, that trade distortions in a country consist exclusively of ad valorem tariffs of 25 per cent on all traded products so that SER = 1.25 and, secondly, an OER of LCU−EUR = 2. The SER is applied to tradables, relating their opportunity cost to non-tradable produce in six different ways, mirroring those in the preceding footnote. That is:

1 Generating EUR1 (LCU2) worth of foreign exchange by producing export produce comes at the expense of foregoing EUR1.25 (LCU2.50) worth of producing and consuming a non-tradable.

2 Spending EUR1 (LCU2) worth of foreign exchange on imports comes at the expense of foregoing EUR1.25 (LCU2.5) worth of production and consumption of a non-tradable.

3 Saving EUR1 (LCU2) worth of foreign exchange by producing an import substitute, comes at the expense of foregoing producing and consuming EUR1.25 (LCU2.5) worth of non-tradable produce.

4 Giving up the production of an export that would generate EUR1 (LCU2) worth of hard currency will enable the production and consumption of EUR1.25 worth of non-tradables.

5 Saving EUR1 (LCU2) worth of foreign exchange by producing and consuming an import substitute − worth EUR1 (LCU2) at the border and EUR1.25 (LCU2.5) domestically − comes at the expense of foregoing EUR1.25 (LCU2.5) worth of production and consumption of non-tradables.

6 Saving EUR1 (LCU2) worth of foreign exchange by not importing produce worth EUR1.25 (LCU2.5) domestically allows the production of EUR1.25 (LCU2.5) worth of non-tradables.

One can think also of combinations between tradables, such as producing (foregoing) an export, to forego (produce) an import substitute. Another, more abstract interpretation of the SER is that a tradable worth EUR1 at the border, if it was made non-tradable, would be worth 1.25 domestically.

9   GHG emissions are assumed to be 3 tonnes of GHG per tonne of fuel and are priced at EUR35 per tonne in real terms throughout the life of the project. Neither of the two assumptions – price and internalisation – hold at the time of writing. They are used in order to illustrate the treatment of alternative regulatory circumstances in project appraisal. See previous project examples for the treatment of alternative market and regulatory contexts.

10 If the airline market were competitive and the cost savings were passed on to passengers, the project might generate traffic. In that case, traffic volumes with and without the project would differ. However, for this type of project the effects can be expected to be small, and omitting generated traffic would only make a small difference to the estimated returns.

11 See section 5.2 above for a discussion of pricing policy and investment incentives in ATM; and Chapter 4, section 4.5, for a discussion of the incentives to investment under economic regulation of charges.

12 The trade and exchange rate literature tends to refer to the market or prevailing exchange rate (PER), while the CBA literature has tended to use the term observed, or official, rate (OER). Here the terms are used interchangeably.

13 See Ward et al. 1991 for a discussion of the relationships among PPP, RER, SER and OER (or PER) in the context of forecasting exchange rates for project appraisal in the presence of inflation, tariff barriers, and structural adjustment programs.

14 See, https://www.worldbank.org/en/programs/icp#5 (last accessed September 2020).

15 See, https://www.economist.com/node/21569171?page=10 (last accessed September 2020).

6 Airlines

Introduction

When acquiring new aircraft, airlines alter their fleet along two dimensions: expansion and renewal. Airlines expand their fleets to address the growth in the demand for air travel and, if the airline is commercially successful, to capture market share from competitors. Fleet expansion can take place by buying more and/or bigger aircraft. Today airlines operate in highly competitive environments, reflected in thin profit margins and high operator turnover (namely entry and exit activity). This means that fleet expansion plans should be based more on the airline having a clear competitive advantage, enabling it to operate profitably, than merely on expected traffic growth, since a loss-making airline that grows its fleet can only expect to grow its losses, negating the investment case for a fleet expansion.

Likewise, the fleet replacement decision tends to be determined by commercial decisions under competitive conditions. Properly maintained, aircraft can fly for many decades. Some aircraft dating from the 1930s and 1940s are still airworthy today and still operate commercially, including, notably, the Douglas DC-3. And yet, airlines tend to replace their aircraft after around 20 years of operation, with some airlines doing so much earlier. The justification for this is twofold: first, new aircraft tend to offer significant operating efficiency improvements; and second, passengers may appreciate newer aircraft. Therefore competition incentivises airlines to renew their fleet despite the aircraft in their current fleet having many airworthy years ahead of them.

The decision-making process as to what aircraft to buy and when is purely a commercial one and follows the standard financial business plan. Airlines model their current and planned route network to see how different aircraft would perform in the various routes. They then set the operational suitability of different aircraft types against the price, delivery and after-sale service offered by the various manufacturers, reaching a decision on purely commercial grounds.[1]

Given that the decision to invest is a commercial one and that it is frequently made under competitive markets, economic appraisal, distinct from financial appraisal, has a limited role in the aircraft investment decision.

Its main use would be in shedding light on effects on investment returns of changes in government policies in situations where there are market distortions, such as taxes, subsidies, entry barriers, or environmental externalities. A financial analysis would capture the impact of the environmental measures proposed by authorities, and only that. Gauging the full extent of the distortion caused by environmental externalities and, hence, the possible impact of potential additional future policy changes, would require an economic appraisal.

GHG emissions are an interesting example in this respect. For airlines, MBMs are so far the policy instrument of choice to internalise this externality. As discussed in Chapter 2, with such a mechanism in place, so long as the resulting emission price is above zero, the emission price correctly reflects the societal opportunity cost of the project, even if the emission price differs from the SCC. Since the MBM price makes it into the financial analysis, no further adjustments are necessary in this respect. Yet, in the case of the EU ETS, a continued discrepancy between estimates of the SCC and the market price of emission allowances has raised calls for the introduction of taxes on aviation fuel, supplementing MBMs. Economic appraisal could use the SCC as a guide to the eventual full carbon emissions bill, reached either through increases in the price of allowances or through supplemental taxation.

Another example of the use of economic appraisal would be to evaluate air services that enjoy government subsidies, whether paid directly to airlines or indirectly to, say, the airports. Economic analysis would unveil the potential return of the air service should the government change its policy on subsidies to air transport in the future.

More generally, economic appraisal is useful when estimating the economic returns of air services to society, which is useful to airlines when attempting to influence the government policymaking process. The value of air transport to society is often claimed to be measured by the contribution of the air transport industry to gross domestic product (GDP). Since airlines tend to pay for all capital costs, including infrastructure, it would follow that the value of air transport to society could be measured by the contribution of airline services to GDP, minus non-internalised environmental costs. In reality, such measures greatly underestimate the economic contribution of aviation to society, which has more to do with its poor substitutability, a condition that is poorly captured by GDP metrics, as will be shown in this chapter.

It should be noted that in addition to the traditional role of economic appraisal – or cost-benefit analysis – in informing about capital allocation in investment appraisal, the techniques used also play a role in the investment process indirectly by helping forecast demand. The concepts of value of time, generalised cost of travel, and schedule delay allow the airline to forecast demand for a new route. The case of expanding a runway in Chapter 4, section 4.6 shows how introducing a direct service produces time savings, which are valuable to passengers, giving an indication of the demand generation potential of the service.[2] However, since such analysis falls more closely into the realm of demand forecasting than of measuring investment returns, it is not pursued further here.

This chapter has two main objectives. First, it looks at estimating the returns of aircraft fleet investments in the presence of market distortions. One key distortion is external costs via environmental pollution. The chapter addresses noise, air pollution, and carbon externalities, but places emphasis on the last of these three. The presentation illustrates project appraisal when the externality is left unaddressed, when dealt with through carbon taxation, and when addressed through an MBM. It also addresses the situation when either taxes or MBMs differ from the social cost of carbon and the consequences of attempting to remedy such discrepancy by combining an MBM and a tax. The chapter starts by looking at fleet replacement and follows with fleet expansion, including the valuation of options on aircraft.

The second objective of the chapter is to contrast correct and incorrect ways of estimating the socio-economic benefits of aviation to society. In so doing, the chapter also illustrates investment appraisal when the alternative to the project is another transport mode, or when scenario-building focuses on inter-modal competition.

6.1 Fleet replacement

6.1.1 Appraisal with a tax on emissions

An airline has a short- to medium-range fleet of 50 Code-C aircraft ('Old C'), with a seating density of 150 seats. This fleet is approaching 20 years of age and the airline is considering replacing it with newer aircraft of the same category ('New C'). The New C aircraft would cost EUR45 million each and would be delivered over three years. As deliveries are made, the Old C aircraft would be sold at EUR5 million each. At the average sector length of 1,000 kilometres and load factor of 70 per cent, which characterise the network and operations of the airline, New C will be 15 per cent more cost-efficient than Old C, reducing unit costs from 6 cents per available seat-kilometre (ASK) to 5.1 cents per ASK. At these sector length and load factor, New C would also reduce GHG emissions by 17 per cent, or from 0.33 kg/RPK to 0.274 kg/RPK, where RPK stands for revenue passenger-kilometre.

Each aircraft in the fleet operates an average of 229.95 million RPK each year, and the competitive position of the airline is such that financially each aircraft produces an operating margin before depreciation and airline overheads of 25 per cent on sales. The operating margin of the airline as a whole would be lower after including costs for administration, marketing, etc. Since such overheads are assumed to be the same with and without the aircraft replacement, they cancel out.

The management of the airline is fairly certain that the company can maintain its competitive position over the medium to long term, so it will be able to sustain the current degree of pricing power in the future. The main benefit of the project will therefore consist of increased operating profits through cost savings. That is, the operating cost savings would leave the airline ticket price the same as without the project. The load factor would also remain the same. For illustrative purposes, an exception is made for policy measures to internalise externalities. Any change in the airline cost base to pay for environmental taxes or to buy emission allowances or offsets would be passed on to passengers through higher ticket prices. This would work through traffic volumes by affecting the load factor.[3]

Assume initially that there is no economic policy instrument – whether tax or MBM – to internalise GHG emissions and that there is uncertainty about possible future taxes for carbon emissions. There has been talk of them being introduced, and although the authorities are not expected to reach a decision before the airline needs to decide on the project, even if they decide against their introduction, the possibility of new policy initiatives for such taxes would remain through the operating life of the new aircraft. Current projections are that the marginal cost of carbon and, hence, the possible extent of such a tax, would average EUR40 per tonne over the long term. The presentation will also assume the effect of a higher social cost of carbon.

For simplicity, other taxes on revenues or costs are excluded from the analysis. In any case, since revenues with and without the project would be the same, the effect of taxes on revenue can be ignored in the economic calculation. The effects of including taxes on costs would depend on the nature of the taxes. Assuming that they are proportional to costs, the effect would be equivalent to the effect of a tax on GHG emissions, illustrated below. Finally, it is assumed that the newly acquired aircraft would have the same residual value after 20 years of operation as the Old C aircraft would command during project implementation.

Table 6.1 shows the results of the investment appraisal, assuming that GHG emissions are not taxed. The calculation of financial returns consists simply of comparing the operating profits (cash generated from operations) that the airline will generate with the New C aircraft (row 6) against those that it would generate with the current Old C fleet (row 14), subtracting the investment cost (row 18) and adding the proceeds from the sale of the current fleet (row 19). The resulting net financial flows (row 20) add to a net present value of EUR71 million, equivalent to a financial return of 5.5 per cent. The estimate is conservative as it does not include difficult to quantify factors such as some passengers being warded off by old-looking aircraft. Still, the return is not large and is close to the cost of capital of 5 per cent.

An economic appraisal of the investment would consist of adding the external costs with and without the project (rows 7 and 14, respectively) to the flows used for the financial appraisal. The result (row 19) shows that the economic return of the project, at 7.7 per cent, is higher than the financial return as the newer aircraft produce fewer emissions than the older aircraft. This higher return tells management that under conditions of efficient pricing, that is, under conditions where externalities are internalised, the project would be more profitable than with prices resulting from current government policy.

This result implies that a higher social cost of carbon would increase the ERR of the project. So, assuming that the average cost of carbon throughout the life of the project is EUR80 per tonne rather than EUR40 per tonne, the ERR of the project would increase from 7.7 per cent to 10 per cent (the simulation is not shown). The FRR would remain unchanged at 5.5 per cent.

Table 6.2 includes the same calculation assuming that GHG emissions are fully internalised through a tax on fuel. The response of all competing airlines would be to pass on the cost of the tax to users by increasing airline ticket prices. This is reflected in higher revenues (rows 4 and 12) and costs (rows 5 and 13). In turn, the external costs disappear (rows 7 and 15).

Note that the introduction of a tax lowers overall traffic, both with and without the project. This can be seen in the differences in RPKs in Table 6.2 relative to those in Table 6.1, both with the project (comparing rows 2 on each table: 11,038 m vs 11,498 m) and without the project (comparing rows 10 of each table: 10,969 m vs 11,498 m). However, with a tax on fuel, traffic increases slightly relative to without the project (rows 1 versus 9 in Table 6.2), by some 0.6 per cent (=(11,038/10,969) −1), as the more efficient aircraft lowers the emission tax per passenger, a saving which is passed on to passengers through a lower ticket price, stimulating traffic. The overall effect of the project on emissions is a decrease though, as the 0.6 per cent increase in traffic compares to a reduction of 17 per cent in emissions per passenger. The result is that with the internalising of external GHG emissions costs, the financial return of the project would be higher, at 8 per cent instead of the 5.5 per cent achieved in the scenario with externalities. The tax penalises the airline for continuing to operate the more polluting fleet.

Note that internalising externalities means that, other things remaining constant, the financial return and the economic return are equal. It is worth noting two implications of this. Firstly, the tax as set in this example, equal to SCC, is consistent with allocative efficiency. The tax alters the financial incentives facing an airline when considering an investment in a way that aligns private financial value with societal economic value. Secondly, the result highlights the role that the economic return measure assumes in the case with no internalisation of externalities (Table 6.1), namely that of signalling to the airline management the underlying desirability of the investment by revealing the consequences of likely future policy action.

6.1.2 Comparing emission taxes and MBMs

Assume that instead of a tax, the policy tool of choice is an MBM and, initially, that the market price of emissions resulting from the MBM is equal to the social cost of carbon at EUR40 per tonne. This would imply, if the MBM was a cap and trade system, that the cap would be efficiently set in terms of allocative efficiency. If instead the MBM was an offset system, then the condition that the market price equates the social cost of carbon would imply that the world would be mitigating carbon to the extent that it would be efficient

Table 6.1 Financial and economic returns on a fleet replacement project with external emissions costs

		PV\Year	1	2	3	4	5	10	15	20	21	22
With project												
(1)	ASK	(million)	16,425	16,425	16,425	16,425	16,425	16,425	16,425	16,425	16,425	16,425
(2)	RPK	(million)	11,498	11,498	11,498	11,498	11,498	11,498	11,498	11,498	11,498	11,498
(3)	Passengers	(million)	11.5	11.5	11.5	11.5	11.5	11.5	11.5	11.5	11.5	11.5
(4)	Revenues	(EUR m)	14,702	1,117	1,117	1,117	1,117	1,117	1,117	1,117	1,117	1,117	1,117
(5)	Operating costs	(EUR m)	11,193	956	897	838	838	838	838	838	838	838	838
(6) = (4) − (5)	Profits	(EUR m)	3,509	161	220	279	279	279	279	279	279	279	279
(7)	GHG externality	(EUR m)	1,658	126	126	126	126	126	126	126	126	126	126
(8)	Redistributive taxation	(EUR m)	0	0	0	0	0	0	0	0	0	0	0
Without project												
(9)	ASK	(million)		16,425	16,425	16,425	16,425	16,425	16,425	16,425	16,425	16,425	16,425
(10)	RPK	(million)		11,498	11,498	11,498	11,498	11,498	11,498	11,498	11,498	11,498	11,498
(11)	Passengers	(million)		11.5	11.5	11.5	11.5	11.5	11.5	11.5	11.5	11.5	11.5
(12)	Revenues	(EUR m)	14,702	1,117	1,117	1,117	1,117	1,117	1,117	1,117	1,117	1,117	1,117
(13)	Operating costs	(EUR m)	12,972	986	986	986	986	986	986	986	986	986	986
(14) = (12) − (13)	Profits	(EUR m)	1,730	131	131	131	131	131	131	131	131	131	131
(15)	GHG externality	(EUR m)	1,998	152	152	152	152	152	152	152	152	152	152
(16)	Redistributive taxation	(EUR m)	0	0	0	0	0	0	0	0	0	0	0

(Continued)

Table 6.1 (Continued)

Net project flows

		PV\Year	1	2	3	4	5	10	15	20	21	22
(17)	Aircraft deliveries	(units)	10	20	20							
(18)	Investment cost	(EUR m)	2,022	450	900	900						
(19)	Sale of old aircraft	(EUR m)	419	50	100	100				50	100	100
(20) = (6) – (14) – (18) + (19)	Financial flows	(EUR m)	71	–370	–711	–652	148	148	148	148	198	248	248
	FRR		5.5%										
(21) = (20) – (7) + (8) + (15) – (16)	Economic flows	(EUR m)	410	–345	–686	–626	174	174	174	174	224	274	274
	ERR		7.7%										

Table 6.2 Financial and economic returns on a fleet replacement project with emisions costs internalised

		PV\Year	1	2	3	4	5	10	15	20	21	22
With project												
(1)	ASK	(million)	16,425	16,425	16,425	16,425	16,425	16,425	16,425	16,425	16,425	16,425
(2)	RPK	(million)	11,038	11,038	11,038	11,038	11,038	11,038	11,038	11,038	11,038	11,038
(3)	Passengers	(million)	11.0	11.0	11.0	11.0	11.0	11.0	11.0	11.0	11.0	11.0
(4)	Revenues	(EUR m)	16,294	1,238	1,238	1,238	1,238	1,238	1,238	1,238	1,238	1,238	1,238
(5)	Operating costs	(EUR m)	12,811	1,096	1,027	959	959	959	959	959	959	959	959
(6) = (4) – (5)	Profits	(EUR m)	3,482	142	211	279	279	279	279	279	279	279	279
(7)	GHG externality	(EUR m)	0	0	0	0	0	0	0	0	0	0	0
(8)	Redistributive taxation	(EUR m)	0	0	0	0	0	0	0	0	0	0	0
Without project												
(9)	ASK	(million)	16,425	16,425	16,425	16,425	16,425	16,425	16,425	16,425	16,425	16,425
(10)	RPK	(million)	10,969	10,969	10,969	10,969	10,969	10,969	10,969	10,969	10,969	10,969
(11)	Passengers	(million)	11.0	11.0	11.0	11.0	11.0	11.0	11.0	11.0	11.0	11.0
(12)	Revenues	(EUR m)	16,192	1,230	1,230	1,230	1,230	1,230	1,230	1,230	1,230	1,230	1,230
(13)	Operating costs	(EUR m)	14,878	1,130	1,130	1,130	1,130	1,130	1,130	1,130	1,130	1,130	1,130
(14) = (12) – (13)	Profits	(EUR m)	1,314	100	100	100	100	100	100	100	100	100	100
(15)	GHG externality	(EUR m)	0	0	0	0	0	0	0	0	0	0	0
(16)	Redistributive taxation	(EUR m)	0	0	0	0	0	0	0	0	0	0	0

(*Continued*)

Table 6.2 (Continued)

Net project flows

		PV \ Year	1	2	3	4	5	10	15	20	21	22
(17)	Aircraft deliveries	(units)	10	20	20							
(18)	Investment cost	(EUR m)	450	900	900							
		2,022										
(19)	Sale of old aircraft	(EUR m)	50	100	100					50	100	100
		419										
(20) = (6) − (14) − (18) + (19)	Financial flows	(EUR m)	−358	−689	−621	179	179	179	179	229	279	279
		460										
	FRR	**8.0%**										
(21) = (20) − (7) + (8) + (15) − (16)	Economic flows	(EUR m)	−358	−689	−621	179	179	179	179	229	279	279
		460										
	ERR	**8.0%**										

(in allocative terms) to do so, as the cost of abatement would equal the marginal damage cost of carbon emissions. Whichever of the two MBM schemes the project would be dealing with, the results of including airlines in an MBM would be as depicted in Table 6.2, the same as an efficient tax on carbon.

The only difference between the two alternative tools (taxes and MBMs) would be on the effect of the project on total societal emissions. As mentioned in the preceding section, the project causes a 17 per cent fall in emissions per passenger while, by resulting on lower ticket prices, increasing passenger traffic by 0.6 per cent. This means that the project would result in a reduction in emissions by the airline of 16.4 per cent (= 0.6% − 17%). Given the arguments in Chapter 2, in the case of a tax, this 16.4 per cent decrease in emissions by the airline would also constitute a decrease in societal emissions. Meanwhile, in the case of a cap and trade MBM, the project would mean a reduction of 16.4 per cent in the amount of emission permits required by the airline, but these permits would then be taken up by some other emitter, leaving societal emissions unchanged. Finally, in the case of an offset MBM, the project would cause a reduction in the demand of offsets by the airline of 16.4 per cent, reducing also the production of offsets in the economy by the corresponding absolute amount, leaving net societal emissions unchanged.

6.1.3 MBM too loose or tax too low

Let us assume now that the SCC remains at EUR40 per tonne but the private cost of emitting is now EUR20 per tonne rather than EUR40 per tonne. In the case of a cap and trade MBM, it would imply that the cap is too loose. In the case of an offset MBM it would imply that the world is in the relatively fortunate position of being able to mitigate carbon at a lower cost than the marginal damage cost from carbon emissions.

Either way, the implications for the economic appraisal are the same, as seen in Chapter 2. The correct economic price to use in the economic appraisal of the project is the price of the MBM so long as this is above EUR0. The MBM price measures the opportunity cost of offsetting a tonne of GHG. The fact that the social cost of carbon is above (or below) the market price of emissions does not alter the economic calculation. The SCC measures the cost of a net increase in emissions. With an MBM there is no net increase in emissions because the extra tonne of emissions is either used instead by another emitter or offset. The correct economic price is then the opportunity cost of such offsetting.

Table 6.3 includes the calculation results for this scenario with MBMs. The mechanics of calculation are exactly the same as in Table 6.2. The lower price of internalising the externality means that traffic is higher both with and without the project than the corresponding traffic for a market price of EUR40 (compare rows 2 and 9 between Tables 6.2 and 6.3). The FRR and the ERR are both lower than in Table 6.2, implying that there is a lesser

Table 6.3 Financial and economic returns on a fleet replacement project with emissions costs internalised through an MBM where the permit price is lower than the SCC

		PV\Year	1	2	3	4	5	10	15	20	21	22
With project												
(1)	ASK	(million)	16,425	16,425	16,425	16,425	16,425	16,425	16,425	16,425	16,425	16,425
(2)	RPK	(million)	11,268	11,268	11,268	11,268	11,268	11,268	11,268	11,268	11,268	11,268
(3)	Passengers	(million)	11.3	11.3	11.3	11.3	11.3	11.3	11.3	11.3	11.3	11.3
(4)	Revenues	(EUR m)	15,514	1,179	1,179	1,179	1,179	1,179	1,179	1,179	1,179	1,179	1,179
(5)	Operating costs	(EUR m)	12,019	1,028	963	899	899	899	899	899	899	899	899
(6) = (4) – (5)	Profits	(EUR m)	3,495	151	215	279	279	279	279	279	279	279	279
(7)	GHG externality	(EUR m)	0	0	0	0	0	0	0	0	0	0	0
(8)	Redistributive taxation	(EUR m)	0	0	0	0	0	0	0	0	0	0	0
Without project												
(9)	ASK	(million)	16,425	16,425	16,425	16,425	16,425	16,425	16,425	16,425	16,425	16,425
(10)	RPK	(million)	11,233	11,233	11,233	11,233	11,233	11,233	11,233	11,233	11,233	11,233
(11)	Passengers	(million)	11.2	11.2	11.2	11.2	11.2	11.2	11.2	11.2	11.2	11.2
(12)	Revenues	(EUR m)	15,467	1,175	1,175	1,175	1,175	1,175	1,175	1,175	1,175	1,175	1,175
(13)	Operating costs	(EUR m)	13,948	1,060	1,060	1,060	1,060	1,060	1,060	1,060	1,060	1,060	1,060
(14) = (12) – (13)	Profits	(EUR m)	1,519	115	115	115	115	115	115	115	115	115	115
(15)	GHG externality	(EUR m)	0	0	0	0	0	0	0	0	0	0	0
(16)	Redistributive taxation	(EUR m)	0	0	0	0	0	0	0	0	0	0	0

(Continued)

Table 6.3 (Continued)

Net project flows

		PV\Year	1	2	3	4	5	10	15	20	21	22
(17)	Aircraft deliveries (units)		10	20	20							
(18)	Investment cost (EUR m)	2,022	450	900	900							
(19)	Sale of old aircraft (EUR m)	419	50	100	100							
(20) = (6) − (14) − (18) + (19)	Financial flows (EUR m)	268	−364	−700	−636	164	164	164	164	214	264	264
FRR		6.8%										
(21) = (20) − (7) + (8) + (15) − (16)	Economic flows (EUR m)	268	−364	−700	−636	164	164	164	164	214	264	264
ERR		6.8%										

incentive to renew the fleet because the cost of saved emissions is lower. But the key result is that, other things being equal, the FRR equals the ERR, despite the discrepancy between the MBM prevailing market price and the SCC.

Let us assume now that the instrument to internalise emissions is instead a tax. The SCC is at EUR40 per tonne, while the tax on GHG emissions is EUR20 per tonne. The results are displayed in Table 6.4. The traffic figures are exactly the same as those in Table 6.3, with a too loose MBM. Passengers end up paying the same EUR20 per tonne emitted. But this time, the emission is not offset. Therefore there is a cost imposed on society of EUR40. Of these EUR40, EUR20 are already internalised through the tax. The remaining EUR20 per tonne consists of a residual externality, included in rows 7 and 15.

This time, with a tax, in contrast to with an MBM, there is a divergence between the FRR and the ERR. The former, at FRR = 6.8 per cent, is lower than the ERR = 7.8 per cent because it registers only a portion (half in this case) of the benefit of reducing emissions with the more fuel efficient aircraft. The ERR being higher than the FRR implies that there are additional societal benefits to the project than those apparent from cash flows.

6.1.4 Combining emissions taxes and MBMs

Consider now an MBM supplemented by an emissions tax. The price of polluting as determined by the MBM is at EUR20 per tonne, while the social cost of carbon is EUR40 per tonne. The authorities therefore introduce a tax of EUR20 per tonne in order to close the gap left by the MBM. The tax would affect the quantity demanded of air travel, just as a higher MBM price would. But since the tax operates in addition to an MBM, it would also affect the demand for emission permits (cap and trade MBM) or offsets (offset MBM) by airlines. The discussion here focuses in the case of a cap and trade system. The implications for an offset system are equivalent, following the presentation in Chapter 2.

The situation is depicted in Figure 6.1. The graph builds from that in Appendix A2.1 in chapter 2. Solid lines consist of functions observed in the market: actual demand and supply schedules. Dash–dotted lines are introduced further on in the discussion. The left hand graph (a) represents the airline air travel market while the right hand side graph (b) the market for emissions permits under a cap and trade MBM. Note that the chart magnifies the effects of the project at hand. The size of aircraft acquisition projects would normally be small relative to the total size of the carbon allowances market, so that the effect on allowance prices would be small.

S_{axp} is the airline supply function excluding environmental taxes and permits. Recall the assumption that operating cost savings other than those related to environmental taxes or permits are pocketed by the airline, generating a rent, while operating cost changes related to environmental taxes and permits are passed on to passengers. Therefore S_{axp} remains the same with and without

Table 6.4 Financial and economic returns on a fleet replacement project with emission costs internalised through a tax that is lower than the SCC

	PV\Year	1	2	3	4	5	10	15	20	21	22
With project											
(1) ASK (million)		16,425	16,425	16,425	16,425	16,425	16,425	16,425	16,425	16,425	16,425
(2) RPK (million)		11,268	11,268	11,268	11,268	11,268	11,268	11,268	11,268	11,268	11,268
(3) Passengers (million)		11.3	11.3	11.3	11.3	11.3	11.3	11.3	11.3	11.3	11.3
(4) Revenues (EUR m)	15,514	1,179	1,179	1,179	1,179	1,179	1,179	1,179	1,179	1,179	1,179
(5) Operating costs (EUR m)	12,019	1,028	963	899	899	899	899	899	899	899	899
(6) = (4) – (5) Profits (EUR m)	3,495	151	215	279	279	279	279	279	279	279	279
(7) GHG externality (EUR m)	812	62	62	62	62	62	62	62	62	62	62
(8) Redistributive taxation (EUR m)	0	0	0	0	0	0	0	0	0	0	0
Without project											
(9) ASK (million)		16,425	16,425	16,425	16,425	16,425	16,425	16,425	16,425	16,425	16,425
(10) RPK (million)		11,233	11,233	11,233	11,233	11,233	11,233	11,233	11,233	11,233	11,233
(11) Passengers (million)		11.2	11.2	11.2	11.2	11.2	11.2	11.2	11.2	11.2	11.2
(12) Revenues (EUR m)	15,467	1,175	1,175	1,175	1,175	1,175	1,175	1,175	1,175	1,175	1,175
(13) Operating costs (EUR m)	13,948	1,060	1,060	1,060	1,060	1,060	1,060	1,060	1,060	1,060	1,060
(14) = (12) – (13) Profits (EUR m)	1,519	115	115	115	115	115	115	115	115	115	115
(15) GHG externality (EUR m)	976	74	74	74	74	74	74	74	74	74	74
(16) Redistributive taxation (EUR m)	0	0	0	0	0	0	0	0	0	0	0

(*Continued*)

Table 6.4 (Continued)

		PV/Year	1	2	3	4	5	10	15	20	21	22
Net project flows												
(17)	Aircraft deliveries	(units)		10	20	20							
(18)	Investment cost	(EUR m)	2,022	450	900	900							
(19)	Sale of old aircraft	(EUR m)	419	50	100	100					50	100	100
(20) = (6) – (14) – (18) + (19)	Financial flows	(EUR m)	**268**	–364	–700	–636	164	164	164	164	214	264	264
	FRR		**6.8%**										
(21) = (20) – (7) + (8) + (15) – (16)	Economic flows	(EUR m)	**431**	–352	–688	–624	176	176	176	176	226	276	276
	ERR		**7.8%**										

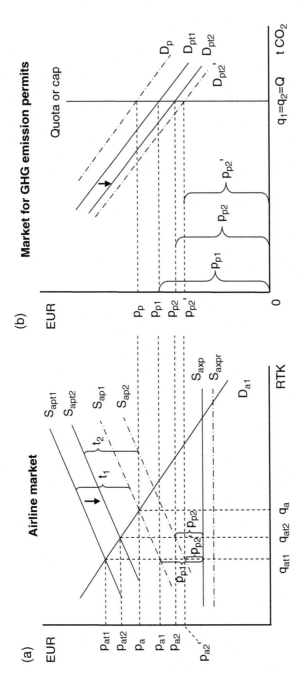

Figure 6.1 An aircraft fleet replacement project for an airline operating within an emissions cap and trade system supplemented with an emissions tax.

the project. The long-dashed line S_{axpr} would represent the supply curve if all cost savings non-related to environmental taxes and permits were passed on to passengers. The term r standing for (monopolistic) rent, S_{axpr} would then be the supply curve excluding both environmental permits and rents.

S_{ap1} is the airline supply function including permits (that is, S_{axp} plus permits), before the project. The function becomes upward sloping as a greater quantity of RTKs supplied implies, other things being equal, a greater amount of emission permits which come at an increasing price. With this policy setting, the price of airline tickets would be p_a along the vertical axis of the left hand side graph. This would correspond to a price p_p in the permits market, on graph (b), given a total demand for permits represented by schedule D_p.

The introduction of a supplementary tax on carbon shifts the airline supply curve upwards to the continuous line S_{apt1}. Relative to the policy setting in which carbon emissions are priced only through the cap and trade MBM, the effect of the tax is to increase the price of airline tickets from p_a to p_{at1} and reduce the quantity of air travel from q_a to q_{at1}. This lower quantity demanded of air travel reduces the demand for emission permits from D_p to D_{pt1} on graph (b), which implies also a fall in the price of permits from p_p to p_{p1} on graph (b), corresponding with a fall in the airline ticket price net of the supplementary emissions tax from p_a to p_{a1}.

Note that while with the introduction of the tax airlines use fewer emission permits, total emissions in the economy do not fall relative to the situation without the tax, staying at Q. The effect of the tax is to substitute pollution away from the airline to other participants in the cap and trade system such as, say, manufacturing.

Let us now consider the effects of the project at hand. The greater fuel efficiency of the new aircraft relative to that of those being substituted would shift the airline supply curve downwards from S_{apt1} to S_{apt2}, including the supplementary tax, and from S_{ap1} to S_{ap2}, net of the supplementary tax. The resulting outcome of the project in the airline market is both to lower the airline ticket price from p_{at1} to p_{at2} and to increase the quantity demanded of air travel from q_{at1} to q_{at2}. The airline ticket price net of the supplementary tax would be p_{a2}.

On the permits market in graph (b) the project causes a fall in the demand for permits from D_{pt1} to D_{pt2}. It is illustrative to categorise this shift in the demand curve of permits into two simultaneous effects, each acting in opposite directions. First, traffic becomes more emissions efficient in that emissions per passenger go down, which lowers the demand for permits. This effect would be described by a shift in the demand for permits from D_{pt1} to $D_{pt2'}$, whereby the price of permits would fall from p_{p1} to $p_{p2'}$ in graph (b). The corresponding move in the net of tax airline ticket price would be from p_{a1} to $p_{a2'}$ in graph (a). Second, the reduction in the final (i.e. inclusive of tax) price of airline tickets from p_{at1} to p_{at2} increases traffic beyond q_{at1}, to q_{at2}, increasing the demand for permits, pushing the schedule above $D_{pt2'}$ to D_{pt2} on graph (b). The net result of these two effects in the permits market is a fall in the

Table 6.5 Financial and economic returns on a fleet replacement project with emission costs internalised through an MBM supplemented with a tax, which combined equal the SCC

		PV\Year	1	2	3	4	5	10	15	20	21	22
With project												
(1)	ASK	(million)		16,425	16,425	16,425	16,425	16,425	16,425	16,425	16,425	16,425	16,425
(2)	RPK	(million)		11,038	11,038	11,038	11,038	11,038	11,038	11,038	11,038	11,038	11,038
(3)	Passengers	(million)		11.0	11.0	11.0	11.0	11.0	11.0	11.0	11.0	11.0	11.0
(4)	Revenues	(EUR m)	16,294	1,238	1,238	1,238	1,238	1,238	1,238	1,238	1,238	1,238	1,238
(5)	Operating costs	(EUR m)	12,811	1,096	1,027	959	959	959	959	959	959	959	959
(6) = (4) – (5)	Profits	(EUR m)	3,482	142	211	279	279	279	279	279	279	279	279
(7)	GHG externality	(EUR m)	0	0	0	0	0	0	0	0	0	0	0
(8)	Redistributive taxation	(EUR m)	796	60	60	60	60	60	60	60	60	60	60
Without project												
(9)	ASK	(million)		16,425	16,425	16,425	16,425	16,425	16,425	16,425	16,425	16,425	16,425
(10)	RPK	(million)		10,969	10,969	10,969	10,969	10,969	10,969	10,969	10,969	10,969	10,969
(11)	Passengers	(million)		11.0	11.0	11.0	11.0	11.0	11.0	11.0	11.0	11.0	11.0
(12)	Revenues	(EUR m)	16,192	1,230	1,230	1,230	1,230	1,230	1,230	1,230	1,230	1,230	1,230
(13)	Operating costs	(EUR m)	14,878	1,130	1,130	1,130	1,130	1,130	1,130	1,130	1,130	1,130	1,130
(14) = (12) – (13)	Profits	(EUR m)	1,314	100	100	100	100	100	100	100	100	100	100
(15)	GHG externality	(EUR m)	0	0	0	0	0	0	0	0	0	0	0
(16)	Redistributive taxation	(EUR m)	953	72	72	72	72	72	72	72	72	72	72

(*Continued*)

Table 6.5 (Continued)

Net project flows

		PV\Year	1	2	3	4	5	10	15	20	21	22
(17) Aircraft deliveries	(units)		10	20	20							
(18) Investment cost	(EUR m)	2,022	450	900	900							
(19) Sale of old aircraft	(EUR m)	419	50	100	100							
(20) = (6) − (14) − (18) + (19) Financial flows	(EUR m)	**460**	−358	−689	−621	179	179	179	179	229	279	279
FRR		**8.0%**										
(21) = (20) − (7) + (8) + (15) − (16) Economic flows	(EUR m)	303	−370	−701	−633	167	167	167	167	217	267	267
ERR		**7.0%**										

demand for emission permits (from D_{pt1} to D_{pt2}), implying that the net effect of the project is to lower airline emissions.[4] As before, though, total emissions in the economy remain the same at Q.

Let us now see the implications for the calculation of project return, included in Table 6.5. As already seen, the supplementary tax applied on a sector within an MBM does not change net societal emissions. Therefore, while levied on pollution, the tax does not have any effect on the external emission costs of the project (rows 7 and 15). Instead, the tax assumes a redistributive role (rows 8 and 16). The effect of the supplementary tax on the performance of the investment project is, as all redistributive taxes and subsidies, to increase the wedge between FRR and ERR.

Let us dwell somewhat more on this result. The tax, by penalising GHG emissions, increases the financial incentive to the airline to switch to technologies that reduce the consumption of fossil fuel. However, because the airline already operates within an emissions cap and trade system, the reduction in fossil fuel use by the airline does not lead to a reduction in total emissions in the economy at large. The FRR of 8 per cent reflects an increase in profits with a present value of EUR2,169 m (=3,482 − 1,314; rows 6–14). The calculation of these profits includes in the operating costs of the airline the tax bill resulting from the supplementary emissions taxation. But the tax does not reflect any incremental societal cost: it simply switches who emits. Yes, it is levied on GHG emissions and therefore appears to follow the 'polluter pays' principle. But by operating within a cap and trade system, the tax simultaneously lowers the price of emission permits and allows another producer, who would not have polluted in the absence of the tax, to pollute.

Since the tax is redistributive, it is paid by the airline and, like all taxes, must be deducted from operating costs and added back to the value of supplying air transport, as done in rows 8 and 16. Note that the extent of redistributive taxation is higher without the project than with the project. This is simply because the older aircraft emit more and therefore bear a higher tax bill. Adding back those taxes to the social value of the project therefore lowers the gain in social value from the project relative to the without project scenario, resulting in an ERR of 7 per cent, lower than the FRR.

The fact that the ERR is lower than the FRR indicates that the project is adding less value to society than may appear from cash flows. The tax inflates the incentives to invest in clean technology, but does so in an inefficient way. Allocative efficiency concerns allocating resources in a way that maximises societal value. The incentives for a private investor are deemed to be aligned with allocative efficiency when the financial return of the investment project to the investor is equal to the economic return to society (i.e. when FRR = ERR). When ERR < FRR, the private investor is investing too much. At least part, if not all, of the resources invested may generate greater societal value in some other use.

Contrast this situation of Table 6.5 with that in Table 6.2. The project outcome would be more efficient, leading to a higher ERR, if instead of combining taxes and MBM permits (at EUR20 per tonne each to total EUR40 per tonne), policy consisted instead either of an EUR40 per tonne tax outside an MBM, or an MBM with a price of around EUR40 per tonne. The price increase in the MBM would be carried out, in a cap and trade system, by tightening the cap.

6.2 Fleet expansion

The aircraft acquisition programmes of airlines generally include fleet renewal and expansion simultaneously. The investment appraisal of the fleet renewal and fleet expansion components differ in two respects. The first is that, in competitive conditions, the analysis of a fleet expansion project does not require an ad hoc 'without project' scenario to be devised. Should the airline not expand its fleet, the traffic is simply absorbed by competing airlines. That is, under competitive conditions the 'without project' scenario is simply the opportunity cost of the project inputs. The financial evaluation of the investment follows a standard commercial business plan, where the airline sets expected revenues against investment and operating costs, instead of the differential cash flow approach applied for fleet replacement. The economic returns will coincide with the financial return, other than for the usual corrections for taxes and externalities.

If the airline market is not competitive, a counterfactual or 'without project' scenario is necessary, in order to conceive what passengers would do in the absence of additional air transport capacity. In the financial analysis, the airline, facing growing demand, will be capable of increasing prices and will exert monopoly profits. The economic analysis will register the inefficiencies of doing this. Incidentally, measuring the economic returns of airline fleet expansions in conditions of monopoly is illustrative of the economic value of air transport, which is explored in the next section.

The second difference between the analysis of fleet replacement and expansion is that, generally, an expansion involves a greater degree of risk, in two respects, including the amount of future demand growth and the extent of future competition. Whereas demand for air travel tends to grow over the long term, the degree of growth depends on general economic growth, which is less certain. Moreover, economic growth and demand are cyclical, and aircraft deliveries may coincide with traffic downturns. As for the degree of competition, when expanding its fleet the airline will be generally venturing into new, lesser-known markets. This may involve entering into competition with airlines with which the project airline was hitherto not competing and which managers of the project airline may know less well. The result is that airlines will tend to have less visibility of future competitive conditions and may therefore wish to have greater flexibility to decide on the extent of the capacity expansion. For these reasons, airline fleet expansion programmes generally combine firm aircraft orders with options.

6.2.1 Firm orders and options

An option to buy an aircraft is a right, but not an obligation, to buy an aircraft in the future. Given that options may cost money, or at least will be

Table 6.6 Traffic and investment return scenarios for an airline considering an expansion of its fleet

		PV\Year	1	2	3	4	5	10	15	20	24
(1)	RPK	(million)		11,038	11,369	11,710	12,061	12,423	14,402	16,695	19,354	21,784
(2)	Diff RPK	(million)			331	672	1,023	1,385	3,364	5,658	8,317	10,746
(3)	Required fleet	(units)			2	3	5	6	15	26	38	49
(4)	Aircraft options exercised	(units)					6					
(6)	Expanded RPK	(million)					1,023	1,316	1,316	1,316	1,316	1,316
(7)	Investment	(EUR m)	257				270					
	Optimistic scenario											
(8)	Operating cash-flow	(EUR m)	372	0	0	0	26	33	33	33	33	63
(9) = (8) – (7)	Net flows	(EUR m)	**150**	0	0	0	–244	33	33	33	33	63
	FRR		**12.5%**									
	Base scenario											
(10)	Operating cash-flow	(EUR m)	227	0	0	0	16	20	20	20	20	50
(11) = (10) – (7)	Net flows	(EUR m)	**5**	0	0	0	–254	20	20	20	20	50
	FRR		**5.3%**									
	Pessimistic scenario											
(12)	Operating cash-flow	(EUR m)	82	0	0	0	5	7	7	7	7	37
(13) = (12) – (7)	Net flows	(EUR m)	**–140**	0	0	0	–265	7	7	7	7	37
	FRR		**N/A**									

contingent upon placing firm orders, the question then becomes: How much are those options worth to the airline and, therefore, how much should it be willing to pay for investing in them?

The value of buying options instead of firm orders depends on the potential future payoffs and the degree of uncertainty surrounding those payoffs. Let us continue with the airline example in the previous section, taking the conditions of year 1 in Table 6.2 as starting point. This means that all externalities are internalised, whether through an efficient tax or, alternatively, through an MBM. Let us assume that airline management is fairly certain about future growth prospects. Traffic is expected to grow at 3 per cent per year and infrastructure constraints combined with sound economic growth means that they can expect the expansion to take place without affecting real yields (that is, yields net of inflation).

Row 1 in Table 6.6 describes the total RPKs that would result from growing existing traffic by 3 per cent per year. Row 2 includes the increase in RPKs relative to the starting year, and row 3 the number of additional New C aircraft that would be required to accommodate such traffic levels. The additional RPKs in row 2 would require buying additional emission permits or paying additional emission taxes, whichever tool has been chosen to internalise emissions. But since it has been assumed that these are included in the airline ticket, no additional adjustment is required. As discussed in section 6.1 above as well as in Chapter 2, in the case of MBMs the project would imply higher and growing emissions by the airline but no net increase in societal emissions. In the case of taxes the growing emissions by the airline would also constitute growing societal emissions.

Assume that assemblage capacity constraints mean that in the first three years of the project the aircraft manufacturer can only deliver the 50 firm orders already placed for fleet replacement. The airline will therefore have to meet that growing demand by delaying the phasing out of Old C aircraft. But in year 4 the manufacturer has free slots to deliver six aircraft. Taking delivery of six additional aircraft in year 4 would generate 1,023 million RPKs in year 4 and 1,316 million thereafter (row 6). The question management faces is whether it is worth ordering those six new aircraft.

Suppose that the optimistic scenario reflects the conditions expected by management. In this scenario, the present value of the operating cash flow generated from the operation of the six aircraft will be EUR372 million (row 8). At an aircraft price of EUR45 million per unit, the investment has a present value of EUR257 million (row 7), which at a discount rate of 5 per cent means that the investment will be worth EUR150 million (row 9), or generate a return of 12.5 per cent. The airline deems such a return adequate and will place that firm order for aircraft. Indeed, if the airline is quite certain about future prospects, the airline will go beyond those six orders, as similar analysis of further deliveries in the future will show also positive returns. Following the demand projections in row 2, by year 15, for example, it will require 26 new aircraft.

But let us assume instead that future prospects are far less certain and positive. In particular, airline management is divided about future competition prospects. Pessimists argue that the airline market will turn increasingly competitive, particularly because of the growth of low-cost carriers, forcing the airline to decrease real yields by as much as 20 per cent. The outcome of such a fall in yields would be as depicted by the pessimistic scenario in Table 6.6. Buying the six aircraft will only generate EUR82 million of operating profits (row 12) which, when set against the cost of investing in the six aircraft, will mean a negative value of the investment of EUR140 million (row 13), and a negative return on investment.

Management agreed that the optimistic and pessimistic scenarios are within the realm of the possible, and took them as extreme cases. Other managers saw less extreme scenarios and, taking together the opinion of all managers, they built an additional scenario referred to as the 'Base case', whereby real yields would fall by 10 per cent. Under this scenario, the investment in six aircraft would produce operating profits with a present value of EUR227 million (row 10). However, when setting this against the investment cost, the project would have a present value of only EUR5 million, or a return of 5.3 per cent, deemed borderline by management and probably not worth the risk.

Such a result, however, is independent of the dispersion of possible positive and negative outcomes. The net present value (NPV) of the investment is equally a gain of EUR6 million, whether management considers that this base scenario constitutes a certain outcome, whether the base case can only be given a probability of 50 per cent and the two extreme scenarios of 25 per cent each, or indeed any other probabilities resulting from different probability distribution of outcomes.[5] And yet it is clear that the greater the dispersion of possible results, the greater the likelihood that the optimistic scenario will materialise. If managers decided not to invest and in the following years the market were to evolve in a way that vindicated the view of the optimists, the airline would have foregone a profitable investment opportunity. Options enable the airline to delay taking a decision on whether to acquire the aircraft until future market trends become clearer, reducing the risks involved in placing the order while enabling them to profit from the investment opportunity should markets evolve favourably. In fact, options are most useful in circumstances when the present value of the project is not satisfactory (after all, if it was satisfactory the airline would simply place firm orders) but there is a reasonable chance that circumstances might evolve in the future in such a way that the project would offer a satisfactory return.

Such an option must obviously be valuable to the airline. The question then becomes how much the options are worth to the airline and, therefore, what would be the maximum price that the airline should be willing to pay for them.

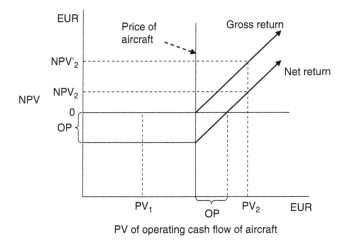

Figure 6.2 Option price and value at expiration and investment returns.

6.2.2 The value of options on aircraft

The relationship between option value, option price and project profitability is illustrated in Figure 6.2, which summarises the situation the airline faces when exercising the option a few years into the future.[6] The vertical axis of Figure 6.2 represents the NPV of the project per aircraft, calculated by comparing the cash flow from operating the aircraft estimated at the time of exercising the option, the price of the aircraft (the exercise price, or strike price, of the option), and the price at which the option was bought. The horizontal axis measures the present value (PV) of operating the aircraft, estimated at the time of exercising the option.

OP is the option price, or price paid by the airline for the option at the time it was bought, inflated by the cost of capital and inflation. PV_1 could represent either the pessimistic or base scenarios materialising. In any of those two cases, the airline will not exercise the option, which will expire and lose its value. The investment in the options would have resulted in a loss to the airline equal to the present value of the money paid for the option, measured by OP on the vertical axis.

However, if at the time of exercising the option it turns out that trends in the airline market look favourable and management views shift to those projected in more optimistic scenarios, so that a discounted cash flow (DCF) calculation produces a positive NPV, the option would be exercised. The 'Gross return' line measures the NPV calculated from the aircraft purchase cost (which constitutes the exercise price of the option) and the expected cash flows from operating the aircraft, ignoring the present value of the option price – that is, taking bygones as bygones. The 'Net return' is the gross return minus the present value of the price paid for the option. Assuming that at the time of exercising the option the estimated operating profit from operating the aircraft is PV_2, then buying the aircraft would produce a return of NPV'_2. That will also be the value of the option at the time. The option would clearly be exercised. Even after subtracting the present value of the money paid for the option, an investment decision to first buy options and then exercise them would still have made sense, with a positive return of NPV_2 on the vertical axis.

An interesting case would be one where the estimated PV of the future cash flows of operating the aircraft was positive but less than the present value of the price paid for the options, that is, if the PV on the horizontal axis fell somewhere within the OP bracket on the horizontal axis. In such a case, the net return of the project, including the price paid for the option in the past, would be negative. However, in investment decisions what matters is the return expected at the point when the decision is made – bygones are bygones. At that point, looking forward, the airline can expect to make a positive return – above the cost of capital – by exercising the option, as determined by the gross return schedule, and should therefore exercise the option, even though the value of the option is less than the present value of the price paid for it.

The illustration has focused on what the airline should do at the time of making the decision of whether exercising the option or not given the price and value of the option. However, this is a situation the airline will face a few years into the future. The question that the airline has to address is what the value of each option is when deciding whether to buy the options, a few years ahead of deciding whether to exercise them.

The standard method of calculating option value is the Black–Scholes formula, suitable for financial options with a predetermined exercise date (called 'European options').[7] The expression is as follows:[8]

$$C = N(d_1)S - N(d_2)Ke^{-rT}$$

where C is the option value, S is the value of the underlying asset, or the DCF of operating the aircraft, K is the strike price of the option, or the cost of the firm aircraft orders, r is the risk-free rate of return and T is the time to maturity of the option. N is the standard normal distribution and d_1 and d_2 are option parameters as follows:

$$d_1 = \frac{\ln\left(\frac{S}{K}\right) + \left(r + \frac{\sigma^2}{2}\right)T}{\sigma\sqrt{T}}$$

$$d_2 = d_1 - \sigma\sqrt{T}$$

where σ is the volatility of the cash flows of the underlying asset, that is, of operating the aircraft, which can be estimated as follows:[9]

$$\sigma = \frac{\ln\left(\frac{S_{opt}}{S_{pes}}\right)}{4\sqrt{t}}$$

where S_{opt} is the underlying asset value under the optimistic scenario, S_{pes} is the underlying asset value under the pessimistic scenario, and t is the project lifetime.

The calculation process therefore starts with an estimate of the volatility of returns which, in our example at hand, as detailed in Table 6.6, would be estimated as follows:

$$\sigma = \frac{\ln\left(\frac{372}{82}\right)}{4\sqrt{20}} = 8.46 \; per \; cent$$

Given the maximum (optimistic) return of EUR372 million, and a minimum (pessimistic) return of EUR82 million, estimated over a project life of 20 years, the volatility of the underlying asset class, that is of the cash flows of operating the aircraft, is 8.5 per cent. With this the option parameter d_1 can be estimated as follows:

$$d_1 = \frac{\ln\left(\frac{227}{270}\right) + \left(0.05 + \frac{0.846^2}{2}\right)4}{0.846\sqrt{4}} = 0.2392$$

And with the value of d_1 the parameter d_2 is calculated as follows:

$$d_2 = 0.2392 - 0.846\sqrt{4} = 0.0699$$

The formula of the value of the option would then be:

$$C = N(0.2392)\,227 - N(0.0699)\,270e^{-0.05 \times 4}$$

The $N(d_1)$ and $N(d_2)$ functions are standard normal distributions, which normally come as default functions in spreadsheets. The resulting figures are:

$$N(0.2392) = 0.5945$$
$$N(0.0699) = 0.5279$$

The resulting value of the options is therefore:

$$C = (0.5945 \times 227) - (0.5279 \times 270)\,e^{-0.05 \times 4} = 18.2179$$

The value of the options for the six aircraft included in our example adds up to EUR18.2 million, which works out to an option value of almost EUR3.04 million per aircraft. Therefore, even though under the base case the net present value of the operating cash flows for the six aircraft is very low, at EUR5 million (row 11), it still pays the airline to buy options for the six aircraft, so long as those options cost less than EUR3 million each.

The calculation of the option value in this section of the chapter has consisted purely of a financial value, on the grounds that all possible externalities of the investment project are internalised. When there are external costs (or benefits) altternative calculations would have to be carried out for the financial and the economic values of options. This is illustrated in Chapter 7, section 7.2.2, where investments in the aeronautical sector are discussed.

6.3 The value of air transport

Air transport pays for itself, both in the passenger and the freight sectors. Aviation is one of the few modes of transport that covers all operating and infrastructure costs. The one exception at the time of writing is emissions costs, although this shortcoming is gradually being addressed, in the case of GHG emissions through MBMs. But air transport could pay for all its emissions costs and remain viable, and strongly so. Instead, passenger rail transport tends to rely on subsidies, whereas rail freight has a greater ability to pay for itself. Road transport rarely pays for the cost of infrastructure, although it is generally accepted that it is a transport mode that could pay for itself. Maritime transport, particularly maritime freight, also tends to pay for all costs except emissions, a situation similar to air transport. Maritime passenger transport is viable only on a relatively small number of routes.

The financial and economic viability of air transport arises from a substantial competitive advantage relative to other modes, based on the ability to provide fast and safe transportation along longer distances at an affordable cost. The economic viability of air transport also reflects the value of air transport to society. This section deals with how to measure such value.

6.3.1 Invalid approaches to measuring value

It is at times implied that the value of air transport to society is measured by an estimation of airline profitability, assuming that airlines pay for all its environmental costs. This approach is mistaken for three main reasons. First and most importantly, it does not take into account additional value to consumers in the form of consumer surplus. Second, it ignores the producer surplus of infrastructure providers. Whereas the opportunity cost of capital invested in infrastructure should be reflected in airline operating costs and, in principle, should not require any additional treatment, most other passenger transport modes do not pay for their infrastructure costs; hence it is incorrect to treat infrastructure

Table 6.7 Contribution to GDP and generalised cost of a hypothetical passenger trip across various route lengths

Route length	(km)	500			1,000			2,000		
		Air	HS Rail	Road	Air	HS Rail	Road	Air	HS Rail	Road
CONTRIBUTION TO GDP										
(1) Salaries	(EUR)	30			50			60		
(2) Airline profit	(EUR)	7.5			12.5			15		
(3) Profit of service providers	(EUR)	15			25			30		
(4) Taxes	(EUR)	22.5			37.5			45		
(5) = (1) + (2) + (3) + (4)	(EUR)	**75**			**125**			**150**		
GENERALISED COST										
Time cost										
(6) Access time	(hours)	1.5	0.5	0	1.5	0.5	0	1.5	0.5	0
(7) Egress time	(hours)	1.5	0.5	0	1.5	0.5	0	1.5	0.5	0
(8) In-vehicle time	(hours)	0.75	2	4.5	1	4	9	2	9	18
(9) = (6) + (7) + (8) Total travel time	(hours)	3.75	3	4.5	4	5	9	5	10	18
(10) Value of time per hour	(EUR)	30	30	30	30	30	30	30	30	30
(11) = (9) × (10) Time costs	(EUR)	112.5	90	135	120	150	270	150	300	540
Money cost										
(12) Ticket price	(EUR)	150	100	0	250	200	0	300	300	0
(13) Other operating costs	(EUR)	0	0	50	0	0	100	0	0	250
(14) Other infrastructure costs	(EUR)	0	50	15	0	100	25	0	200	60
(15) = (12) + (13) + (14) Money cost of operation	(EUR)	150	150	65	250	300	125	300	500	310

(*Continued*)

Table 6.7 (Continued)

Route length	(km)		500			1,000			2,000	
		Air	HS Rail	Road	Air	HS Rail	Road	Air	HS Rail	Road
External costs										
(16) GHG emissions	(EUR)	10	0	2	15	0	4	25	0	8
(17) Air pollution	(EUR)	2	0	0.5	3	0	1	5	0	2
(18) Noise	(EUR)	5	3	3	5	5	5	5	10	10
(19) = (16) + (17) + (18) Total external cost	(EUR)	17	3	5.5	23	5	10	35	10	20
Generalised cost										
(20) = (11) + (12) + (13) User	(EUR)	262.5	190	185	370	350	370	450	600	790
(21) = (20) + (14) + (19) .... = (11) + (15) + (19) Total	(EUR)	279.5	243	205.5	393	455	405	485	810	870
Value of aviation										
(22) = (20) − (20) User	(EUR)	−77.5			−20			150		
(23) = (21) − (21) Total	(EUR)	−74			12			385		
(24) = (5) + (23) Hybrid measure	(EUR)	1			137			535		

Note: lowest GC circled and best alternative to air transport underlined.

costs for aviation and for other modes of transport equally. Third, it does not take into account subsidies to operators of alternative modes of transport.

Another attempt to measure the value of aviation to society would be by measuring the contribution of aviation to Gross Domestic Product (GDP). To recap, GDP consists of any of three equivalent measures, namely, the monetary value of output produced, the total income received by the owners of the factors of production, or the net expenditure on the sector.[10] However, GDP does not include any measure of consumer surplus. Moreover it does not consider the opportunity cost of resources and, therefore, whether the output should be produced at all. After all, an unviable business may still generate GDP.[11] So long as the salaries paid by a company are higher than the financial losses of the company in absolute terms, the company will make a positive contribution to GDP. Finally, GDP does not measure environmental externalities.[12]

To illustrate this it is worth first pinning down the differences in gauging air transport operations in terms of contribution to GDP and in terms of generalised costs. These are illustrated in Table 6.7, which includes for a hypothetical passenger comparisons of contribution to GDP of a trip by air, and the generalised cost of the same trip, across different route lengths. The figures are indicative since the purpose of the exercise is to illustrate the measuring processes rather than to arrive at any empirical finding.

Rows 1 to 4 include the contribution of the trip to GDP, measured through income, including income to workers in the air transport sector via salaries, income to the owners of capital via profit to the airline and other service providers, and income to the government via taxes. For a route of 500 kilometres the contribution of the trip to GDP would be EUR75, for a trip of 1,000 kilometres it would be EUR125, and for a trip of 2,000 kilometres it would be EUR150 (row 5).

The generalised cost of travel is calculated for three transport modes: air, high-speed rail (HSR), and road via private car. It is assumed that in the case of air transport the trip involves 1.5 hours of access and egress time, both including passenger processing time at the terminal. This is lower for rail, as train stations tend to be closer to city centres than airports and involve shorter passenger processing time. In-vehicle time varies with route length. The summation of these three time components constitutes total (door to door) travel time. Air travel performs better in terms of travel time relative to other transport modes as route distance increases. It is assumed that the value of time to the passenger is EUR30 per hour. Since the comparison is for the same passenger, the value of time is taken to be the same for all transport modes. The product of total travel time and value of time yields the time cost component of the generalised cost (row 11).

The money cost of travel includes all expenditures by society to operate the service (rows 12 to 15). In the case of air, all costs are included in the ticket price. In the case of HSR the ticket price includes only operating cost, but no infrastructure cost, which is included as an additional cost, borne by the taxpayer. For road, all operating costs are paid directly by the user, except for infrastructure costs. Finally, the generalised cost includes all external costs to members of society other than the transport user and the producer of transport services, including emissions of GHG, air pollutants, and noise (rows 16 to 19). It is assumed that HSR is powered fully by renewable energy, yielding no GHG or pollutant emissions. For simplicity, the calculation ignores safety issues. Including them would favour air transport, particularly against road transport.

The generalised cost consists of the summation of the time, money, and external costs. A difference is made between generalised cost for the user – or behavioural generalised cost, and for society at large – or total generalised cost. The former includes only costs borne by the user (row 20), whereas the latter includes those borne by the user and by other members of society (row 21). For each route length, the lowest generalised cost among the various modes (i.e. the best option) is circled, and the best alternative to air transport is underlined. The value created by aviation is calculated by comparing the generalised cost of aviation to that of the best alternative transport mode. Again, a different value is calculated for the user (row 22) and for society at large (row 23). The results show that aviation creates value in longer distances. This does not mean that it cannot create value in shorter distances, but it would tend to do so only on routes where for reasons of say, geography or low traffic density, there is poor provision of alternative modes of transport. Also, the example of 1,000 kilometres, where the best alternative to the user differs from the best alternative to society, illustrates how inefficient pricing or subsidies (in the current case largely the latter) could shift traffic to less socially efficient modes.

Comparing the contribution to GDP (row 5) and the generalised cost (row 21) reveals how GDP misses out on signalling whether production is worthwhile. For shorter distances, whereas aviation may make a contribution to GDP, it may well be that society may be better off investing in alternative modes of transport. For longer distances, contribution to GDP grossly underestimates the value of aviation since it excludes non-monetised benefits. All in all, the fault of contribution to GDP as a guide to investment decisions lies in the fact that it does not correct for price distortions and ignores opportunity costs.

One may be tempted to construct a measure of the full value to society of the output produced by aviation by adding its contribution to income plus the savings in generalised cost – the latter effectively being the consumer surplus attributable to aviation net of other resources invested by third parties. The resulting 'hybrid' measure (row 24) would bring the GDP figure closer to opportunity cost. So in the illustration of travel on a 500-kilometre route, the value of the output of aviation would fall from EUR75 per passenger to EUR1, reflecting the fact that other activities would produce higher income. At the other extreme, the value figure would increase from EUR150, as measured by GDP, to EUR535 after taking into account all of the consumer surplus and other resources used.

However, such a hybrid measure of value can only be considered a curiosity of no valid practical use. It does not measure income as it takes into account non-money flows, particularly time savings. Likewise, it cannot guide investment decisions because it does not measure correctly resource costs (most importantly, GDP computes labour costs as a benefit) and incorrectly double-counts tax revenues as a benefit.

6.3.2 Valid approach to measuring value

Instead, the viability of air transport should be measured using the same tools as are used in the economic appraisal of aviation investments presented so far, based on comparing generalised costs to society of alternative transport modes. This is because such an approach measures total welfare created to society, namely net willingness to pay for the output produced, regardless of whether it is actually paid or not, while valuing resources used in production at opportunity cost.

The estimation of the full value of aviation is illustrated by measuring the benefits generated to society by investment in an aircraft. It is important to emphasise that, while the input numbers are realistic, they do not refer to an actually existing route, and that the exercise consists of an illustration of the method of measurement, rather than producing an empirical finding. The illustration takes the same aircraft operation as used so far in Chapter 6 on airlines: a New C code aircraft flying back and forth along a route of 1,000 kilometres at 70 per cent load factor. The aircraft will fly almost 230 million RPKs each year. Average GHG per passenger will be EUR14, based on an average cost of carbon of EUR40 per tonne. It is assumed that the airports involved in the route are close to urban areas, yielding a re-latively high noise impact of EUR10 per passenger.[13] Likewise, the impact of air pollution will be relatively high at EUR5 per passenger. It is assumed that neither the emissions of GHG, air pollutants, or noise are internalised. Also, it is assumed that the door-to-door trip by air would take four hours.

The alternative mode is HSR and it is assumed that 100 per cent of the electricity consumed is renewable or nuclear, so there are no emissions of GHG or air pollutants. It is also assumed that the train follows a thinly po-pulated route, so the noise impact is half that of aircraft. As is common with existing HSR services, at similar ticket prices to those offered by air, the rail service would require subsidies to cover costs. It is estimated conservatively that the proportion of costs not covered through operating revenues represents 25 per cent of total costs, including infrastructure costs. It is also assumed that the rail service is already operational, so that no investment is needed. Therefore, the exercise formally addresses the question of whether it pays to invest in an aircraft to cover the route, given that there is an HSR service already in operation.[14]

The door-to-door rail trip would take five hours, so that by travelling by air over the 1,000 kilometres, air travellers would save one hour. Assuming that the prices of the air and rail ticket are the same at EUR150 per one-way trip, di-version to air would take place in order to save one hour of travel. The value of time is assumed to be EUR30 per hour, growing in real terms at 1.5 per cent per

Table 6.8 Returns on investing in an air service

	Air		PV/Year	0	1	2	10	20
(1)	RPK	(million)		0.0	230.0	230.0	230.0	230.0
(2)	Revenues	(EURm)	429.9	0.0	34.5	34.5	34.5	34.5
(3)	Revs after tax	(EURm)	390.8	0.0	31.4	31.4	31.4	31.4
(4)	Op costs	(EURm)	312.6	0.0	25.1	25.1	25.1	25.1
(5)	Op costs before tax	(EURm)	284.2	0.0	22.8	22.8	22.8	22.8
(6) = (2) − (5)	Gross producer surplus	(EURm)	145.7	0.0	11.7	11.7	11.7	11.7
(7) = (3) − (4)	Net producer surplus	(EURm)	78.2	0.0	6.3	6.3	6.3	6.3
(8) through (1)	GHG	(EURm)	40.1	0.0	3.2	3.2	3.2	3.2
(9) through (1)	Air pollution	(EURm)	14.3	0.0	1.1	1.1	1.1	1.1
(10) (through (1)	Noise	(EURm)	28.7	0.0	2.3	2.3	2.3	2.3
(11) = (8) + (9) + (10)	Total external cost	(EURm)	83.1	0.0	6.7	6.7	6.7	6.7
(12)	Investment	(EURm)	50.0	50.0				
(13)	Taxes	(EURm)	4.5	4.5				
(14) = (12) − (13)	Investment net of tax	(EURm)	45.5	45.5				
	Alternative mode (HSR)							
(15)	RPK	(million)		0.0	205.3	205.3	205.3	205.3
(16)	Revenues	(EURm)	383.8	0.0	30.8	30.8	30.8	30.8
(17)	Subsidies	(EURm)	102.3	0.0	8.2	8.2	8.2	8.2
(18)	GHG	(EURm)	0.0	0.0	0.0	0.0	0.0	0.0
(19)	Air pollution	(EURm)	0.0	0.0	0.0	0.0	0.0	0.0
(20) through (15)	Noise	(EURm)	12.8	0.0	1.0	1.0	1.0	1.0

(*Continued*)

Table 6.8 (Continued)

	Air		PV/Year	0	1	2	10	20
(21) = (18) + (19) + (20)	Total external cost	(EURm)	12.8	0.0	1.0	1.0	1.0	1.0
	Pax consumer surplus							
(22) through (1) × VoT	Diverted traffic	(EURm)	86.7	0.0	6.2	6.3	7.0	8.2
(23) through (1) × VoT	Generated traffic	(EURm)	5.2	0.0	0.4	0.4	0.4	0.5
(24)	Access & egress op cost	(EURm)	20.5	0.0	1.6	1.6	1.6	1.6
(25) = (22) + (23) − (24)	Net consumer surplus	(EURm)	71.4	0.0	4.9	5.0	5.8	7.0
	Financial returns							
(26) = (7) − (12)	Airline net cashflows	(EURm)	28.2	−50.0	6.3	6.3	6.3	6.3
	Airline FRR		11.0%					
(27) = (6) − (14)	Airline flows gross of tax	(EURm)	100.2	−45.5	11.7	11.7	11.7	11.7
	Airline gross FRR		25.4%					
(28) = (17) + (27)	Differential flows	(EURm)	202.5	−45.5	19.9	19.9	19.9	19.9
	Differential FRR		43.7%					
	Economic returns							
(29) = (6) − (14) + (17) + (25)	Without externalities ERR	(EURm)	273.9	−45.5	24.8	24.9	25.7	26.9
			54.9%					
(30) = (29) − (11) + (21)	Net economic flows ERR	(EURm)	203.6	−45.5	19.1	19.2	20.1	21.3
			42.6%					

year. In addition, it is assumed that the airline passenger would incur an additional EUR8 in access and egress vehicle operating costs to and from the airports. Working through the total private generalised cost in a way similar to previous cases (see Chapter 4, section 4.1, for example), it would mean that about 12 per cent of the travellers by air would be generated and the rest diverted.

Table 6.8 displays the results of the calculation. This time the calculation assumes that the investment is made at the beginning of the first year, when the aircraft is delivered. To avoid discounting the investment, the calculation includes a year 0. Also, the economic appraisal excludes taxes from prices in order to compute opportunity costs.

The airline would generate EUR34.5 million per year (row 2), higher than the EUR30.8 million of HSR (row 16), due to traffic generation by the airline. Airline revenues and costs are taxed (rows 2 to 5 and 13), unlike HSR, which, in addition, is subsidised (row 17). For HSR, revenues are assumed to cover both operating and infrastructure costs except for the subsidy requirement. The infrastructure costs of the air service are included in the airline ticket price.

The air service produces an operating profit before depreciation (producer surplus) both gross and net of taxes (rows 6 and 7). Comparing this surplus with the investment cost gross of taxes yields the value of the service to the airline (row 26) discounted at the cost of capital of 5 per cent, which is equivalent to a financial return of 11 per cent. The total financial return of the air service would be gross of taxes (row 27), which would constitute the total return to the government should the airline be owned by the government.

Continuing with the assumption that the airline is owned by the government, should the government be able to scale back the HSR service after introducing the air service, the financial return to the government would be higher. This is because the HSR service constitutes a net financial liability to the government, equal to the total annual subsidy. The flows to the government, assuming that each airline passenger is accompanied by a proportional decrease in the subsidy to the railway, are included in row 28, and show that the financial return to the government would be a very high 43.7 per cent.

The economic profitability of the investment includes measures of consumer surplus and externalities resulting from the project. Consumer surplus results from both travel time savings to passengers who divert from HSR to the airline and the willingness to pay for the air services by generated passengers. Without any other economic distortion or any cost economies in secondary markets resulting from the project (see Chapter 2, section 2.7.3), the consumer surplus incorporates the benefits to the wider economy in terms of productivity gains and, more widely, welfare gains that can be attributed to the air service. The resulting net economic value of the project is EUR273.9 million (row 29), a large return for an investment of EUR45.5 million worth of resources, as indicated by an economic IRR of 54.9 per cent.

To arrive at the final return of the project, externalities need to be accounted for. Note that externalities are not just disturbances. They may also register loss of productivity to the bearer. Once externalities are included, the economic value falls to EUR203.6 million and economic return to 42.6 per cent. The value and returns generated by the project are very large. In NPV terms, the air service generates a net return to society that is over four times the resources invested as capital expenditure. This is value over and above that which would have been generated if passengers had been forced to travel by HSR.

Whereas the objective of the exercise was not to produce empirical results, the orders of magnitude employed were realistic, which means that such high returns perhaps merit some comment. The value of aviation arises from two main factors. Firstly, cost-effective high speed at cruising altitude, which allows substantial time savings beyond a minimum distance of about 500–700 kilometres. Behind the willingness to pay for such time savings lie elements such as personal, commercial, and cultural relationships which are better maintained as a result of the investment due to improved access. In addition, generated traffic means that new relationships are established because of the presence of air transport links. The second source of value of aviation arises from the fewer infrastructure requirements of air transport relative to land transport modes, increasing the cost-effectiveness of aviation. Both factors combine to strengthen the advantage of aviation over longer routes, as distance enhances both the speed advantage of aviation and the infrastructure requirements of its land-based competitors.

Notes

1 See Clark 2017 for a guide to the issues involved.
2 In the past, when airline capacity was subject to government regulation, general transport planning concepts like traffic diversion and generation would have been useful in the process of requesting new routings. Indeed the concept of frequency delay and other concepts, such as stochastic delay (passenger diversion through high load factors), were developed by airline analysts at the time. Today, the freedom to establish new routes, combined with the high mobility of aircraft, mean that formal demand modelling is less critical. Many airlines use proprietary information on demand flows and test route potential with some form of gravity model (see Doganis 2010 and Vasigh et al. 2008). Some airlines, though, are readier to simply test out potential through trial services. Airlines tentatively deploy aircraft on a new route and, depending on results, decide whether to keep, grow or withdraw a service.
3 The simulation relates prices to traffic through the load factor. It assumes that a given percentage increase in the airline ticket price will translate into a change in percentage points (not a percentage change) of the load factor of a tenth of the increase in price. So, say, a 30 per cent increase in prices would cause a drop in the load factor by 3 (= 30% × 0.1) percentage points, from 70 per cent to 67 per cent. Given the prices assumed in the simulation, the implied price elasticity of demand ranges from about −1 to about −1.5. In the without project scenario, the factor relating prices to load factor is higher, assumed to be 1.15, by the same 15 per cent proportion as the difference in operating costs between the with and without project scenarios before environmental costs. This is an ad hoc adjustment intended to approximate market conditions whereby the higher ticket price resulting from higher pollution in the without project scenario implies a somewhat higher price elasticity of demand. The resulting demand figures are therefore approximations, resulting from basing calculations on the load factor rather than on an exogenously determined price elasticity of demand. But this approximation is deemed

of secondary importance given the purpose of the exercise, which is to illustrate the CBA treatment of an investment project. Such treatment is unaffected by the assumptions used in modelling demand. An analyst seeking accuracy in traffic figures would need to address a wide range of assumptions, including the pricing and load factor strategies followed by the yield management system of the airline.

4 Projects that consist exclusively of fleet replacement by more fuel efficient aircraft, with no accompanying fleet expansion, will always result in a reduction of emissions and hence in a fall in permit prices. That is, the effect of lowering emissions per passenger by the use of more efficient aircraft will outweigh the opposite effect of increased emissions due to an increase in traffic caused by the resulting lower price of the airline ticket. Notionally, with a horizontal, infinitely elastic, airline demand curve, the two opposite effects would each have the same implications for emissions albeit with opposite signs, cancelling each other and resulting in no reduction in emissions. For fleet expansion projects the net effect tends to be an increase in demand for and price of permits.

5 This exercise will be solved calculating the option value through the Black–Scholes method; therefore the underlying probability distribution of outcomes is assumed to be lognormal. Other methods of calculating option value can relax this assumption. An example of such an alternative method, the binomial method, is illustrated in Chapter 7, section 7.2, regarding the option value of research and development in the aeronautics industry.

6 The introduction to option valuation here is schematic, as such material is broadly available in the literature. Accessible sources include Kodukula and Papudesu 2006 and Brealey et al. 2008.

7 Alternatively, American options can be exercised at any time before the expiry date. Whereas airlines are normally free to convert options into fixed orders at any time (the formal exercise of the option), the actual exercise date of the option (the delivery of the aircraft) is constrained by assembly line schedules, effectively removing exercise date flexibility from a standard American option. Therefore in practice aircraft options tend to have elements of European rather than American options. Should the aircraft manufacturer offer sufficient flexibility regarding delivery dates, the options could then be considered American. The modelling of the actual option facing an airline must be tailored to the circumstances applying to each case. The important thing here is to illustrate the use of real option analysis to help make investment decisions. Chapter 7, section 7.2.1, includes an example of valuing a real option using the binomial method, which is better suited to American options.

8 An exposition of the theory of real options or the theoretical justification behind the Black–Scholes method is beyond the scope of this book; the reader should consult the many available references. For a formal exposition of the case for real option analysis see Dixit and Pyndick 1994. For a more accessible guide to real option applications see Kodukula and Papudesu 2006. Koller et al. 2010 also include accessible applications using alternative procedures.

9 This is just one method of calculating volatility, based on management assumptions about future scenarios. Other methods of estimating volatility rely either on extensive historical data or on assumptions by the analyst. Alternatively, volatility can be borrowed from projects or securities that could be expected to have similar cash flow profiles and are subject to similar degrees of uncertainty as the project being appraised. See Kodukula and Papudesu 2006 for accessible discussion of volatility estimation, and Koller et al. 2010 for a worked example using a traded security as a proxy.

10 For accessible presentations of the components of GDP see Moss 2014 or Johnson and Briscoe 1995.

11 Imagine a company that makes no profit – and that never will because there are better technologies around – and pays EUR1 million in salaries a year. It will contribute to GDP by EUR1 million, by means of income to labour. However, once it is recognised that

labour and capital have an opportunity cost, that is, viable alternative uses, then salaries are not a benefit, but a cost, and the capital invested will have to be charged an opportunity cost of capital – the rate of discount on an investment appraisal. In those circumstances, even though the company still makes a contribution to GDP, the negative return indicates that its resources would be better deployed on some other activity.

12 As argued in Chapter 2, section 2.7.1, in perfectly competitive markets the observed financial profitability of a project can be taken as the economic profitability. Varian 1992 shows how under such perfect conditions, income and economic viability coincide. However, it should be borne in mind that income in that context does not correspond to the GDP measure, which does not allow for the opportunity cost of factors of production.

13 As a comparison, the European Commisison (2019) recommends a marginal cost per pasenger (landing and take-off cycle, or LTO) ranging from EUR0.6 to EUR1.2, and an average cost of EUR2.1 per passenger per flight (LTO).

14 The simplification of not including HSR investment cost is made because an investment in a new railway line is not comparable to an investment in an aircraft. A train normally has a much higher capacity than aircraft serving comparable routes. In addition, the investment in infrastructure on a railway line is route-specific, whereas for aviation, airports are not specific to a given route. Making a direct comparison always involves strong assumptions regarding infrastructure expenditure, including the use of average costs, whereas investment appraisals should be made with marginal costs.

7 Aeronautics

Introduction

This chapter addresses investment appraisal in a subset of the aeronautics sector, including the manufacturing of civilian aeroplanes and helicopters.[1] It excludes vehicles more frequently associated with aerospace such as rocketry, as well as lighter-than-air craft such as airships. Whereas the underlying economic principles in those sectors are the same as for aeroplanes and helicopters, the former differ in two respects. Firstly, they are more geared to freight transport, where operating cost, rather than travel time, may play a more significant role. Secondly, and more importantly, development programmes and production rates are generally more closely tailored to specific customers than is the case in aeroplane and helicopter manufacturing, requiring alternative considerations in the investment appraisal process.

Aeronautics is a high-tech manufacturing sector, as opposed to the other sectors reviewed in this book, which are all services. This involves two considerations. First, traditionally, a distinction in investment appraisal between manufacturing and service sectors involves the presence of inventories of finished products. However, this does not really apply to aircraft manufacturing since aircraft are built to order. Second, manufacturing generally involves a greater scope for research, development, and innovation (RDI), which clearly applies to aeronautics. This elevates the role that uncertainty, irreversibility, and sunk costs play in the sector and with them the case for phasing investment projects and waiting for uncertainty to resolve, increasing the role for real option analysis (ROA).[2]

But launching new aircraft does not necessarily involve risks or uncertainty tied to technological innovation. New aircraft can also consist of differentiated products that target untapped market segments with technology that is conventional or at least relatively well tested. Examples include the A-380, to a lesser extent the C-Series – seeking to tap a middle ground between regional and Code-C aircraft – the reintroduction of supersonic commercial aircraft or, in the freight sector, the reintroduction of airships. Aircraft manufacturers develop such products in an attempt to develop monopolistically competitive outcomes that grant them pricing power.

Considerations of primary and secondary markets are also important in aeronautical projects. As mentioned in Chapter 2, section 2.7.3, appraisals should consider secondary markets when these are distorted. The valuation of innovative aircraft that improve environmental performance over alternatives would need to consider whether airlines operate in markets where externalities are internalised or not.

This chapter is organised into three themes. The first concerns relatively low risk projects facing little uncertainty, involving the development of a new aircraft model to replace an older aircraft on a tried and tested segment of the aircraft market. The presentation explores the implications of alternative policy and competitive settings. Second is the development of a highly innovative component, the market prospects for which are surrounded by a high degree of uncertainty, illustrating the application of ROA. Third is the case for reintroducing supersonic commercial aircraft, more a situation of risk than uncertainty, where understanding user willingness to pay is essential for gauging both market prospects and societal benefits.

7.1 Low uncertainty

7.1.1 Standard product in (almost) perfectly competitive or oligopolistic markets

An aircraft manufacturer is planning to launch a new aircraft model to replace an existing very successful model (or platform) that is now deemed too old a design and has exhausted upgrade potential. The manufacturer is a well-established brand, with sound after-sales support, trusted by airlines. Indeed airlines have encouraged the manufacturer to launch the new model and a few are willing to help in the design process, as well as to participate as launch customers. The final assembler can therefore be quite confident that it can generate sufficient orders to make the project at least reasonably successful.

The market is supplied by a small number of aircraft manufacturers, all producing comparable aircraft at a comparable price. The price is set either in an oligopolistic manner, through market signals, custom, price leadership, etc., or competitively.[3] The implication as far as project appraisal is concerned is the same either way; the investing promoter does not have any distinctive pricing power from that of its competitors and will be immediately followed should it deviate from existing prices. The project appraisal therefore takes the sale price as given. In the current case, the aircraft will be sold at EUR50 million per unit, plus 10 per cent of sales tax.

Total development cost will be EUR6 billion over six years and it will experience average recurring costs of EUR20 million per aircraft produced, including test aircraft. The final assembler will be building a production line with capacity for producing 5 aircraft per month or 60 a year, a delivery rate it expects to achieve into the third year of production. It assumes that the aircraft will sell for 15 years before a new version, requiring a new investment programme in product upgrade, is necessary. The analysis ignores residual value after those 15 years because of the uncertainty of the state of the industry in the future and, therefore, of the likely required investments for an upgraded version. The government will assist the development through EUR300 million of grants for certain qualifying RDI activities.

The calculation and results are displayed under scenario 1 in Table 7.1. A simple financial analysis shows that the net present value of the project is EUR7.4 billion (row 8), and that the rate of return for the promoter is 15.4 per cent. The economic return would build upon the financial calculation by making the necessary adjustments for transfers or distortions. In the current case, this consists of adding back to costs the development costs financed through the government subsidy and adding to project benefits the money transferred to the government as taxes.[4] The resulting economic net present value (NPV) is EUR9.2 billion (row 9); and the economic rate of return is 16.5 per cent, slightly higher than the private financial return.

It is worth mentioning in passing that given the combination of low risk assumed to be carried by this investment and the accompanying relatively high financial return would signal an oligopolistic outcome. A perfectly competitive outcome would mean that the financial return would be equal to the opportunity cost of capital, in this case a rate of return of 5 per cent. As far as the economic appraisal is concerned, oligopolistic and perfectly competitive outcomes are treated equally, in that the project does not bring about any price changes in either primary or secondary markets.

The analysis does not incorporate any effect for the externalities caused by the operation of the aircraft. The price paid for the aircraft represents the value of the marginal product of capital (in this case, the aircraft) to the airlines. That is, it reflects the extent to which the output of the manufacturer contributes to the net financial benefit generated by the airline, including both revenues and costs. In the event that externalities are internalised, these will affect both the operating costs of the aircraft and the demand for air travel and such flows will be reflected in the airline's willingness to pay for the aircraft. Where the external costs are not internalised, insofar as the aircraft market is competitive and there are no significant differences in the environmental performance of the different competing aircraft, the airline market is a secondary market where prices and quantities faced by the airlines will not be affected by the project. The amount of pollution with and without the project is therefore the same and has no effect on the economic returns of the project.

Still, in cases where externalities are not internalised, it is always worthwhile to test what would be the impact on the project should the airlines be forced to internalise them. This is done in Scenario 2 in Table 7.1. Should government impose taxes on carbon, aircraft noise, and air quality, the airlines will pass on these costs to passengers by increasing the price of air tickets, resulting in a decrease in traffic and hence in demand for aircraft. Assuming that the combined environmental taxes would increase average air ticket prices by 20 per cent, and that the price elasticity of demand for air travel is -1.25, the

Table 7.1 Returns on investment in the aeronautical sector under alternative scenarios regarding competition and external costs

			PV\Year	1	2	3	4	5	6	7	8	9	21
SCENARIO 1: Competitive outcome means project does not alter aircraft numbers on (secondary) airline market													
(1)	Aircraft deliveries	(units)								15	30	60	60
(2)	Cummulative deliveries	(units)								15	45	105	825
(3)	Revenues after tax	(EUR m)	27,636							750	1,500	3,000	3,000
(4)	Taxes	(EUR m)	2,764							75	150	300	300
(5)	Recurring costs	(EUR m)	9,739				50	30	30	310	610	1,210	1,210
(6)	Non-recurring costs	(EUR m)	5,076	1,000	1,000	1,000	1,000	1,000	1,000				
(7)	Subsidies	(EUR m)	272	100	100	100							
(8) = (3) – (5) – (6) + (7)	Net financial flows	(EUR m)	7,405	–900	–900	–900	–1,050	–1,030	–1,030	440	890	1,790	1,790
	FRR		**15.4%**										
(9) = (8) + (4) – (7)	Net economic flows	(EUR m)	9,195	–1,000	–1,000	–1,000	–1,050	–1,030	–1,030	515	1,040	2,090	2,090
	ERR		**16.5%**										
SCENARIO 2: Assumes externalities on (secondary) airline market are (unexpectedly) taxed													
(10)	Aircrat deliveries	(units)								11	23	45	45
(11) = ((1) – (10)) × price	Reduced after tax revenues	(EUR m)	6,898							200	350	750	750
(12) = ((1) – (10)) × tax	Reduction in taxes	(EUR m)	690							20	35	75	75
(13) = ((1) – (10)) × unit cost	Reduction in recurring costs	(EUR m)	2,759							80	140	300	300

(Continued)

Table 7.1 (*Continued*)

			PV\Year	1	2	3	4	5	6	7	8	9	21
(14) = (8) – (11) + (13)	Net financial flows	(EUR m)	4,317	–900	–900	–900	–1,050	–1,030	–1,030	320	680	1,340	1,340
	FRR		11.9%										
(15) = (9) – (11) – (12) + (13)	Net economic flows	(EUR m)	5,592	–1,000	–1,000	–1,000	–1,050	–1,030	–1,030	375	795	1,565	1,565
	ERR		13.0%										

SCENARIO 3: Adjusts Scenario 1 to assume that project increases competition in the (primary) aircraft market. Externalities are either ignored or assumed to be internalised.

(16) = 10 × ((1) × 19%)	Fall in deadweight loss	(EUR m)	793	0	0	0	0	0	0	29	58	115	115
(17) = (9) + (16)	Net economic flows	(EUR m)	9,988	–1,000	–1,000	–1,000	–1,050	–1,030	–1,030	544	1,098	2,205	2,205
	ERR		17.2%										

SCENARIO 4: Adjusts Scenario 3 to assume that externalities are not internalised.

(18) = (2) × 4 × 0.19 × 2	External costs	(EUR m)	4,213	0	0	0	0	0	0	23	69	162	1,269
(19) = (17) – (18)	Net economic flows	(EUR m)	5,775	–1,000	–1,000	–1,000	–1,050	–1,030	–1,030	521	1,028	2,044	936
	ERR		14.0%										

(*Continued*)

Table 7.1 (*Continued*)

		PV \ Year	1	2	3	4	5	6	7	8	9	21
SCENARIO 5: Adjusts Scenario 1 to assume that aircraft is better performing than competitors. Environmental costs are not internalised												
(20) = (2) × 0.5	Gain in noise efficiency	(EUR m)	1,369	0	0	0	0	0	8	23	53	413
(21) = (9) + (20)	Net economic flows	(EUR m)	10,565	−1,000	−1,000	−1,050	−1,030	−1,030	523	1,063	2,143	2,503
	ERR		17.4%									
SCENARIO 6: Adjusts scenario 4 to assume that the aircraft is better performing that competitors. The project increases competition and externalities are not internalised.												
(22) = (19) + (20)	Net economic flows	(EUR m)	7,144	−1,000	−1,000	−1,050	−1,030	−1,030	528	1,051	2,096	1,349
	ERR		15.2%									

taxes would result in a fall in demand of 25 per cent. This would result in a fall in demand for aircraft, resulting in lower sales (row 10 versus row 1), reduced revenues (row 11) and taxes (row 12), but also lower recurring costs (row 13).[5] The result is that the financial return of the project to the promoter falls from 15.4 per cent to 11.9 per cent and the economic return would fall from 16.5 per cent to 13 per cent. This indicates that, despite no immediate prospect of the externalities in the secondary market being internalised, should they be internalised, the project would still make financial and economic sense.[6]

7.1.2 Entering a monopolistic competitive market

The analysis has assumed so far that the project does not alter the total number of aircraft in the market. Should the project not be produced, other well-established aircraft manufacturers would produce aircraft of similar quality at a similar price. An alternative scenario would be that the new aircraft supplied by the project would alter the structure of the aircraft market, affecting the price of aircraft offered to airlines. This could be the case of a project consisting of entering an aircraft segment until then supplied by a monopolist on conditions of monopolistic competition. Normally, in such conditions the monopolist would be enjoying monopoly rents by charging a higher price than the competitive price. The project promoter would intend to bring prices down to a competitive level, forcing the monopolist to follow suit.[7]

The situation is illustrated in Figure 7.1. The upper diagram, 7.1 (a), corresponds to the aircraft market and the lower diagram, 7.1 (b), to the (secondary) airline market that makes use of the aircraft. In Figure 7.1 (a) the incumbent monopolist aircraft manufacturer generates super-normal profits by setting the aircraft sale price where marginal revenues (MR) equal long-run marginal cost (LRMC), resulting in the monopoly outcome of price per aircraft p_m and quantity of aircraft supplied q_m. As the project promoter enters the market segment, competition between the two manufacturers brings the price down to the competitive price p_c equal to LRMC, which is consistent with normal profits for the manufacturers, the competitive outcome. The result can be split into two effects. First, there is a transfer of welfare (in the form of income via lower prices) from the manufacturer to the airlines equal to the area $p_m aep_c$. Total welfare to society remains unchanged by this effect. Second, there is a reduction in the deadweight loss that resulted from monopoly pricing. As the lower price of aircraft encourages airlines to place more aircraft orders, there is a net gain in welfare equal to the area of triangle ade, plus the increase in (normal) profits in the aeronautical sector resulting from the expanded output.

The impact on the airline market, depicted in Figure 7.1(b), is to decrease the airlines' long-run marginal cost (ALRMC) curve from $ALRMC_1$ to $ALRMC_2$. The airline market is competitive and therefore the airlines transfer the welfare gain received from the manufacturers to passengers by lowering fares from f_m to f_c, causing an increase in traffic from t_m to t_c. This results in a

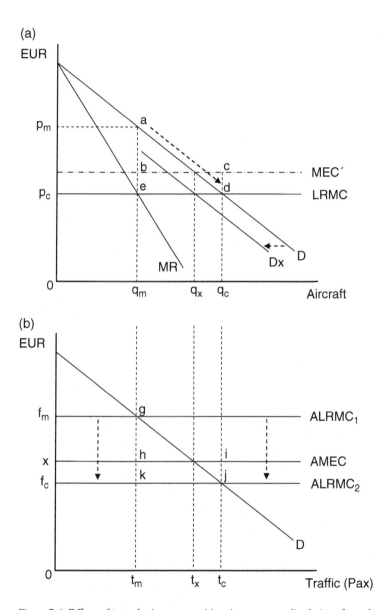

Figure 7.1 Effect of introducing competition in a monopolised aircraft market.

final transfer of welfare from the airlines to its passengers of area $f_m gkf_c$ and a net gain in welfare measured by the area gjk, plus the growth in the (normal) profits of the airlines, resulting from the growth in output from t_m to t_c.

The implications for the calculation of project return are illustrated in scenario 3 in Table 7.1. Scenario 3 assumes that the outcome of the project to the promoter is as described in scenario 1 – that is, private profitability remains as described in row 8 – and goes on to make the necessary adjustments to the economic returns to incorporate the alternative competitive scenario. Also, it is assumed that airline external costs are internalised or, alternatively, the illustration disregards externalities. The final price of aircraft with the project remains the same as in scenario 1, at EUR55 million, but it is assumed that the price charged by the monopolist incumbent before the project was EUR65 million, a fall of EUR10 million per aircraft, or a reduction in price by 15 per cent. With a price elasticity of demand for aircraft of −1.25, the fall in prices would cause an increase in the quantity of aircraft demanded, so that about 19 per cent of the aircraft sold by the project would consist of a net increase in sales in the market segment.[8] The reduction in deadweight loss results from multiplying the change in quantity demanded (19 per cent of aircraft delivered) from the change in prices in absolute terms (EUR10 million). There is no need to divide by two, as would be necessary following the rule of a half, as Table 7.1 reflects the changes for the promoter, not the entire market.[9]

The gain by eliminating the deadweight welfare loss is added to the economic benefits of the project. The transfer of welfare from the incumbent (and the government that appropriated 10 per cent of the revenues of the incumbent via a sales tax) to the airlines (area $p_m aep_c$ in Figure 7.1(a)) and on to the passengers (area $f_m gkf_c$ in Figure 7.1(b)) is ignored because, as a transfer, it does not change total welfare. The result is then an additional gain in welfare of EUR793 million (row 16), increasing the net present value of the project to almost EUR10 billion (row 17) from the EUR9.2 billion in the scenario where prices do not change (row 9). This would correspond to an increase in the economic returns of the project from 16.5 per cent to 17.2 per cent. The additional welfare gain corresponds to area ade in Figure 7.1(a). It ultimately corresponds to area gjk in Figure 7.1(b), as the final beneficiaries of the increased competition in the aircraft market are the airline passengers. However, the benefits of the project through reducing deadweight loss are either (preferably) area ade, or (as a surrogate measure) area gjk. Adding up the two areas would constitute double-counting.

In scenario 3 the project results in a change in the total number of aircraft in the market by virtue of having forced a fall in the price of aircraft. Clearly, and unlike in scenario 1, where the total number of aircraft did not change with the project, the question of whether externalities in the (secondary) airline market are internalised or not becomes important for the estimate of economic profitability, since any change in external costs in the secondary market as a result of the greater number of flights enabled by the project can be attributed to the project. Scenario 4 builds upon scenario 3, but assumes that externalities in the airline market are not internalised. That is, scenario 4 assumes that the outcome of the project as far as the promoter is concerned is as described in scenario 1, implying that the net present value of private financial flows to the promoter is as described in row 8, but makes the necessary adjustments to the calculation of economic profitability to incorporate the new assumption about externalities. The airline marginal environmental cost (AMEC) caused by the aircraft is depicted by the AMEC schedule in Figure 7.1(b). As seen when discussing scenario 3 above, the project has brought about an increase in the total demand for aircraft from airlines from q_m to $q_{c'}$, in tandem with an increase in traffic from t_m to t_c and a reduction in airline fares from f_m to f_c. However, the extra passengers ($t_c - t_m$) are not paying the full cost of their air travel, as they are causing an environmental externality ($x - f_c$) per trip, resulting in a total external cost equal to area hijk. This is a direct consequence of the project and therefore needs to be taken into account when measuring economic returns.

Alternatively, the external environmental cost of the project could be measured through the aircraft market as the area of rectangle bcde in Figure 7.1(a). MEC stands for marginal environmental cost per aircraft, and the MEC line is dotted and an apostrophe added to underscore that this is an alternative, parallel approach, basing the calculation on emissions per aircraft rather than emissions per passenger. Adding areas bcde in Figure 7.1(a) and hijk in Figure 7.1(b) as costs in the analysis would result in double-counting the environmental costs of the project.

The total annual environmental cost of operating an aircraft is estimated at EUR4 million per year, including emissions of greenhouse gases (GHG), air pollutants, and noise, all of which are assumed not to be internalised, remaining as an external cost. Area hijk in Figure 7.1(b) would correspond to the EUR4 million cost per aircraft, multiplied by the total number of aircraft in operation in the market segment that can be attributed solely to the project and that would not have existed had the project not taken place. This latter figure would be 19 per cent of the cumulative deliveries, where 19 per cent is the estimated traffic generated by the project. The figure must account for all aircraft in the segment, meaning that it must include those of the other competitor, which is assumed to retain a 50 per cent market share. The external environmental cost each year is therefore twice 19 per cent of the total cumulative aircraft deliveries, times EUR4 million (row 18). Note that, as demand for air transport grows, the demand curves in Figure 7.1(a) and (b) would shift rightwards every year, implying that area hijk in Figure 7.1(b) would grow every year.

The estimate of economic profitability of the project (row 19) now combines the gain in avoided deadweight loss estimated in row 16, brought about by the increase in aircraft in operation in the market segment as a direct result of the project, with the environmental cost that such additional aircraft bring about in the secondary market (row 18). The economic value of the project falls considerably, by EUR4.2 billion, to EUR5.8 billion (row 19), and the economic return from 17.2 per cent to 14 per cent. Note that the net financial value of the project to the promoter would still be EUR7.4 billion (row 8) and the financial rate of return 14.4 per cent, both higher than the economic return. The difference is explained by the environmental externalities, the business gained from the incumbent and the government subsidies.

If, once the investment had been carried out, the government suddenly introduced taxes internalising all of the external costs of aviation, the adjustment to the estimation process would be akin to that in scenario 2. The taxes would mean that airline fares would rise from f_c to x in Figure 7.1(b), and the LRMC schedule of airlines would effectively become the AMEC schedule. The resulting quantity demanded of air travel would be t_x. The impact on the aeronautics market of such an increase in airline costs and fares would be that the aeronautics industry would face a fall in demand, represented by the move from schedules D to D_x in Figure 7.1(a). For an aircraft price of $p_{c'}$ the quantity demanded of aircraft would be q_x. The estimates of financial and economic return would have to be adjusted to incorporate the lower number of aircraft deliveries and the external cost would disappear as a separate item from the estimate of economic profitability.

7.1.3 Entering a market with an improved product

Finally, let us consider the case of producing an aircraft that yields improvements in operating performance relative to older models. Let us assume that the performance is environmental in terms of emissions of GHG, air particles, or noise. Following the discussion above, if the regulatory framework of the airline industry is such that external costs are internalised, when calculating the economic returns there is no need to make any consideration different from those made for estimating the financial return. The improved environmental and economic performance will be reflected in the demand for the aircraft. If all competing manufacturers produce aircraft with the same improved performance, the economic return will be equal to the financial return and will be equal for investments across all manufacturers. This would correspond to the lower left quadrant in Figure 7.2, which sets out the relationship between

	Internalised environmental costs	External environmental costs
Distinctive product	FRR = ERR ...and different from those of competitors over the short run.	**FRR ≠ ERR** ...and sustainable over the long run.
Standard product	FRR = ERR ...and equal across competitors.	FRR = ERR ...since the amount of pollution in the secondary (airline) market is unaffected by the project.

Figure 7.2 Treatment of environmental costs in the economic appraisal of investments in competitive aircraft manufacturing markets.

financial and economic returns in competitive markets, as determined by whether environmental costs are internalised or not, and by whether the promoter differentiates its output from the competition through a distinctive product.

It may well be that the project manufacturer has a distinctive capability that enables its product to be uniquely high-performing environmentally relative to those of its competitors. Continuing with the scenario that all external costs are internalised, the financial and economic returns of the project would continue to be equal. But the returns would be higher than those of competitors, as the competitive advantage would be reflected by means of a higher market share or the aircraft commanding a higher price. This situation corresponds to the upper left quadrant in Figure 7.2. The fact that the product is based on a distinctive capability means that other competitors will not be able to replicate the performance for the foreseeable future. In competitive markets such a situation is not sustainable over the long run. If a manufacturer is permanently superior it will end up capturing the entire market. Competitors will tend to exploit their own distinctive capabilities to provide value to the airlines, equating investing performance over the long run, or being driven out of the market.

The outcomes would change if externalities were not internalised in the airline industry. Then there may be differences between the financial and the economic return. Again, let us consider two possible scenarios regarding differentiation in product performance relative to those of competing manufacturers. Firstly, if other aircraft manufacturers produce models with the same improvements in performance, no improvements in environmental performance can be attributed to the project. In the absence of the project, the environmental performance of the airline industry would be the same as with the project, due to the improved aircraft produced by the competition. In terms of the mechanics of estimation, as far as the (secondary) airline market is concerned, the 'without project' scenario enjoys the same environmental performance as the 'with project' scenario. As far as environmental factors are concerned, the financial and economic return of the project would be the same. This would correspond to the lower right quadrant in Figure 7.2. The implication of this conclusion is that in an investment appraisal exercise under competitive conditions and where externalities are present in a secondary market, regardless of how much better the environmental performance of the product is relative to preceding generations, no environmental benefit should be assigned to the investment, since the product does not make a difference to the secondary market. The two key assumptions here are that the primary market is competitive and that the output of different participants in the primary market are perfect substitutes; that is, the participants offer the same performance at the same price.

The second possibility while externalities are not internalised is that the project differentiates itself from competitors by having a better environmental performance. This would correspond to the upper right quadrant in Figure 7.2.

As the improved performance concerns an environmental cost that is not in-ternalised, airlines may not be willing to pay for it and competitors may not even seek to match the environmental performance of the product. Other things being equal, the aircraft with the better environmental performance would only command the market price and the same market share as any other competing aircraft. In such situations, the financial return will be the same for all competing aircraft manufacturers. However, the economic appraisal of the project would require special consideration, especially since, unlike the situation in the upper left quadrant, the current situation is sustainable over the long run.

Scenario 5 in Table 7.1 illustrates the situation of the upper right quadrant in Figure 7.2. Assume that the environmental performance concerned is noise and that the aircraft is slightly quieter than those of competitors, reducing external costs by an estimated EUR0.5 million per year per aircraft. In a competitive market (either perfectly competitive or an oligopoly) such ex-ternal benefits would accrue to all aircraft sold by the promoter. The welfare gain resulting in reducing the noise externality amounts to EUR1.4 billion (row 20). This constitutes an improvement in the economic value of the project that would now total EUR10.6 billion (row 21), up from the EUR9.2 billion of scenario 1 (row 9). The financial return to the promoter remains as in scenario 1.

Likewise, in the context of an aircraft that ends the monopoly of the in-cumbent manufacturer in a particular market segment (that is, a market characterised by monopolistic competition before the project), the benefit would also apply to all aircraft sold by the entrant manufacturer. In terms of Figure 7.1 the introduction of the new aircraft would constitute a downward shift in the AMEC curve, producing an area equal to EUR0.5 million along the vertical axis times t_c (or q_c) on the horizontal axis. Since the project produces a distinctive product that would not be replicated in the 'without project' scenario, the gain in environmental performance from the project applies to all aircraft sold by the project, whether substitutes from the in-cumbent, or generated through lower prices ($q_c - q_m$ in Figure 7.1(a)). The situation is illustrated in scenario 6 in Table 7.1. The result is that the eco-nomic value of the project improves relative to that of scenario 4, bringing net economic value to EUR7.1 billion (row 22) and improving the returns of the project from 14 per cent to 15.2 per cent. The financial value of the project to the promoter remains unchanged and as estimated in row 8.

7.2 High uncertainty

7.2.1 An innovative project contingent on external developments

A manufacturer of aircraft engines is considering investing in the development of a new engine that will yield a substantial performance leap in terms of life-cycle costs in general and fuel consumption in particular. The commercial prospects, however, depend on two critical factors. First, the new engines would require significant changes in the way aircraft are designed, involving heavy investment on the side of final aircraft assemblers, which cannot be taken for granted. This would in turn be influenced by the second factor, which is future government regulation on aircraft operating and emissions standards. The outlook regarding these two interrelated factors is highly uncertain, but management expect these issues to be resolved within the next five years.

Developing the engine will require substantial research and development (R&D) investments over a prolonged period of time including, in present value terms, EUR1.5 billion in research and an extra EUR500 million to adapt existing manufacturing facilities, bringing total project investment to a present value of EUR2 billion. Should the project fail, or be abandoned, practically all of the R&D investment will be lost with no obvious alternative use for the promoter. The promoter can only be sure of selling some of the facilities for a present value of about EUR15 million. The investment is therefore to be treated as a non-recoverable or sunk cost. An adverse scenario whereby the promoter would spend EUR2 billion and receive only EUR15 million in return could potentially bring the engine manufacturer to bankruptcy and would certainly prompt a replacement of top management. On the other hand, should developments in the regulatory and airframe assembler sides evolve favourably and no competitor develop similar engines, the competitive advantage of the manufacturer would be virtually impossible to match for a number of years, until competitors developed comparable engines. This would give the promoter a first-mover advantage that could prove extraordinarily lucrative. The project could easily generate free cash flow with a present value of EUR10 billion.

The management of the engine manufacturer carried out a discounted cash flow (DCF) analysis of the investment, including a very wide range of scenarios, reflecting the uncertainty surrounding the project. There was a wide variety of opinion and the median scenario was finally chosen, including a relatively modest sales projection by assuming that competitors may develop engines that could potentially tame the prospects of the project. Because of the high risk, the cash flows were discounted at 25 per cent, including a substantial risk premium, compared to the firm's standard target return on investment of 15 per cent and the risk-free rate of 5 per cent. The result of that median scenario was a present value of free cash flow before investment of EUR1.2 billion. As the present value of launching the project now is EUR2 billion, the project would have a financial net present value of a negative EUR800 million, so that management was bound to reject the project.

However, those in the management team who feel most strongly for the project objected that, given the substantial uncertainty and the wide range of possible outcomes, relying on the median forecast alone offers too narrow a guide to the range of opportunities that lie ahead.[10] They argued that whereas standard DCF analysis shows that the project is not worth undertaking as things stand, it may still be worthwhile to keep open the option of launching the project and delay taking the decision until there is less uncertainty about future prospects.

They therefore proposed to complement the DCF analysis with an estimate of the option value of the project at the current moment. The objective would be to find out whether it is worthwhile to spend money today to start up the initial phases of the project – thereby keeping the option open – and, if so, how much.

Management decided to estimate the option value in a way that made more visible their ability to exercise it before the expected expiry date of the option in five years' time, opting for the binomial method.[11] Whereas this method allows them to model changes in input variables such as volatility and investment costs (the latter being the strike price of the option) throughout the life of the option, they decided to carry out the simplest possible estimation.[12]

The first step consists of estimating of the implied volatility resulting from the scenarios put forward by management which, following the same method illustrated in Chapter 6, section 6.2.2, regarding options on aircraft, would be estimated as follows:

$$\sigma = \frac{\ln\left(\dfrac{S_{opt}}{S_{pes}}\right)}{4\sqrt{t}} = \frac{\ln\left(\dfrac{10{,}000}{15}\right)}{4\sqrt{20}} = 36.35 \; percent$$

where σ is the volatility of the cash flows of the project, that is, the sale of engines (or the full service programme if applicable), S_{opt} is the underlying asset value under the optimistic scenario, or EUR10 billion as mentioned above, S_{pes} is the underlying asset value under the pessimistic scenario (EUR15 million), and t is the period over which volatility is estimated, or project lifetime (20 years). The resulting volatility of 36.35 per cent underlines the high degree of uncertainty surrounding the project.

With the estimate of volatility, the up and down factors and the risk-neutral probability can be estimated, which will enable the building of the binomial tree. The calculation of the three items proceeds in turn, as follows:

$$u = e^{\sigma\sqrt{\delta t}} = e^{0.3635\sqrt{1}} = 1.4383$$

where u is the up factor and δt the time associated to each step in the tree, in this case 1 year;

$$d = \frac{1}{u} = \frac{1}{1.4383} = 0.6952$$

where d is the down factor; and:

$$p = \frac{e^{r\delta t} - d}{u - d} = \frac{e^{0.05 \times 1} - 0.6952}{1.4383 - 0.6952} = 0.4791$$

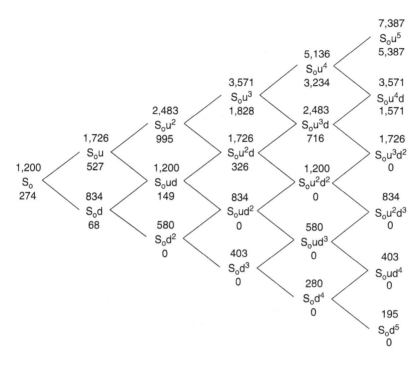

Figure 7.3 Binomial tree for the financial real option value of an aircraft engine project.

where p is the risk-neutral probability and r the risk-free interest rate, in this case 5 per cent.

Figure 7.3 presents the binomial tree or lattice for the project. Each column represents a year, starting from column 0 at the left, representing the present, and ending with column 5 at the right, representing the maximum life of the option, namely 5 years. Each cell within each column represents a possible outcome. The calculation of the binomial lattice begins with the estimated present value of future cash flows (before investment cost) that management takes as its central case scenario, namely EUR1.2 billion. This is the current asset value S_o, in the far left cell, in column 0. Subsequent cells are named with up (u) and down (d) identifiers, with the exponential representing the cumulative number of moves up or down followed to arrive at that cell.

Starting from cell S_o the asset values in successive years are estimated using the up and down factors (u and d, respectively) estimated above. So for the first year, the up and down asset values in thousands of euros are:

$$S_o u = 1,200 \times 1.4383 = 1,726$$

$$S_o d = 1,200 \times 0.6952 = 834$$

The same method is followed to estimate the asset values for successive cells of the binomial tree.

The real option value (ROV) for each cell is calculated once the asset values (the upper figure in each cell) are calculated for all cells, and is included at the bottom of each cell. The calculation of option values starts from the right end of the binomial tree, that is, the last column – column 5 in the current example – following a process known as backward induction. The calculation procedure for the final column differs slightly from that for all the other columns preceding it.

At the final column – including what are known as the terminal nodes or terminal cells – the uncertainty surrounding the future revenues of the project is expected to be resolved. By then, the government will have reached a decision regarding the regulation of emissions standards and airframe manufacturers could therefore be expected to have reached a decision as to whether to develop new aircraft that would accommodate the new engine technology being contemplated by the project promoter. At that point the decision to make the investment in the new engine must be taken. Given the way the project has been defined, whereby no further delay is possible, waiting has no value. The value of the option is simply the value of the project (after investing).[13] The investment will be made if the value of the expected cash flows exceeds the EUR2 billion investment cost (where the latter is also the strike price of the option). At S_ou^5, for example, the cash flow is worth EUR7.4 billion which, after an investment of EUR2 billion, would render a net present value for the project of EUR5.4 billion, which is the value of having the option to invest at that moment. In cell s_oud^4 the present value of cash flows is EUR403 million. An investment of EUR2 billion would have a negative NPV of EUR1.6 billion; therefore the investment will not be made and the option to invest at that moment is worth zero.

In effect, the value of the option at the bottom of each cell represents the value-maximising decision at that stage. The possible decisions include (i) investing, (ii) keeping the option alive, or (iii) abandoning both the option and the project. Each of these possible decisions is discussed in turn. First, if the value of carrying out the investment at that point (that is, the NPV, or the asset value minus the investment cost) is higher than the value of the option (the value of waiting) at that point, the investment will be made and therefore the value of waiting is 0. The option value becomes the value of the project and therefore the lower figure in the cell includes the NPV of the project. Note that making this decision of investing in the project or not is inescapable in column 5, the final column, since by then the option expires – it cannot be kept alive any longer. In that column the lower figure in each cell either includes the NPV of the project if it is carried out, which is the value of the option at that point in time conditional on being exercised then, or 0, which is the value of the option if the project NPV is negative and hence not worth carrying out.

Second, if the value of the option is higher than the NPV of the investment, it will be rational to wait, that is, to keep the option alive, and the cell includes the option value. For example, in cell $S_o u^3$, at the top of column 3, the present value of the project cash flows is EUR3.6 billion which, after the EUR2 billion investment cost would result in a project NPV of EUR1.6 billion. The option value is higher, at EUR1.8 billion, or, in other words, it is better to wait; therefore the option is not exercised and is kept alive. The cell incorporates the option value, rather than either the NPV of the project or 0. Finally, if the NPV of the investment is negative in that cell and the option is worthless, the option value inserted in the cell is 0. It is worth abandoning, or killing, the option (unless it is free of charge) as well as the project.

As has been seen above, in the last column – column 5, when the option expires – the value of the real option is either the project NPV or 0. For all preceding columns – columns 0 to 4 – the value of the real option at each cell corresponds to the weighted average of all possible future real option values, estimated from the real option values in the subsequent up and down cells. As an example, the option value at cell $S_o u^4$, at the top of column 4, would be as follows:

$$ROV_{S_o u^4} = \left[p \left(ROV_{S_0 u^5} \right) + (1 - p) \left(ROV_{S_0 u^4 d} \right) \right] \cdot e^{-r\delta t}$$

resulting in the following value:

$$ROV_{S_o u^4} = [0.4791 \, (5, \, 387) + (1 - 0.4791) \, (1,571)] \cdot e^{-0.05 \cdot 1} = 3,234$$

The binomial tree is completed backwards (leftwards) by applying the above formulas to each preceding cell. Column 0, in the far left of the binomial tree, includes the current value of the real option, which is EUR274 million.[14] The value of the option is positive and higher than the NPV of the project at this point (which is negative: EUR1.2 billion – EUR2 billion = –EUR0.8 billion), therefore it is worth keeping the option alive.

Using the traditional DCF analysis, the engine manufacturer would not carry out the project as the NPV is negative. However, the uncertainty embedded in the DCF analysis masks a wide array of possible results, including very profitable outcomes dependent on events that will happen in the future and which could make the project very profitable. Based on the analysis of future possible returns, at this stage, it is worthwhile to pay up to EUR274 million today to keep open the possibility of carrying out the project within the next five years. The investments carried out in keeping the option alive could consist of starting the early development phases, including hiring specialist personnel, developing initial design concepts, etc. Such investments to keep the option alive would be developed further, or abandoned, depending on how events evolve as time progresses. The option value at each point in time indicates the maximum amount that it is worth spending in order to keep the option alive.

Three observations can be made at this point. First, looking at the binomial lattice, it seems rather unlikely that the project will be carried out. By year 5, only in two out of six future scenarios is the project worth undertaking. Those who object to the project may use such results to claim that it may be better not to waste money in keeping the option alive. Still, the rational thing to do today is to keep the option alive. The option gains its value from the potentially very large returns should circumstances over the next five years evolve in a way that would favour the project.

Second, even if events develop in such a way that a DCF analysis makes the project viable at some point in the future, it may still be worth waiting rather than proceeding with the project. This is the case depicted in cell S_ou^2 in column 2, for example. The estimated asset value in that situation would be EUR2.48 billion. At the strike price of EUR2 billion, this means that the project is expected to have a positive NPV of EUR483 million. Still, the option is worth EUR995 million. This signals that, whereas the DCF analysis signals that, on a risk-weighted basis, the project is already worth investing in, the degree of uncertainty about the future is such that being able to wait until the future reveals more about the likely outcome of the project is worth more than the expected NPV of the project. Therefore it is still worth waiting rather than investing. In fact, the binomial tree shows that it will be worth waiting to make the investment decision until the option expires in year 5.

Finally, the third observation consists of an extreme version of the preceding observation, depicted in cell S_ou^4 in year 4 in Figure 7.3. The project managers may conclude that since the option value (EUR3.2 billion) − or in other words, the amount that would be worth spending to keep the option alive − is higher than the total investment cost (EUR2 billion), it may be worth carrying out the project at that point anyway. However, the value of carrying out the project at that stage (EUR5.1 billion − EUR2 billion = EUR3.1 billion) is still less than the option value. This reveals that, if waiting involves a sufficiently low opportunity cost, it is better to wait. After all, one thing is how much one should be willing to pay and another thing is when to pay it. If little is gained by bringing the decision forward, one may as well wait and make the decision under a greater degree of certainty.

7.2.2 Financial versus economic real option value

The analysis in the preceding section focused exclusively on returns to the aircraft engines manufacturer. It did not address socio-economic value. Let us suppose that the government wishes to carry out an economic appraisal of the proposed investment project, which they plan to do by building upon the financial appraisal performed by the private promoter. The private financial analysis carried out by the manufacturer of aircraft engines would require three adjustments.

First, the economic analysis would need to add back sales taxes on inputs and outputs paid by the promoter to project benefits. Let us assume that taxes are such that the value of the project before investments would increase from EUR1.2 billion to EUR1.4 billion. The effect of increasing the pay-off would be to increase the value of the real option. At the same time, the capital investment cost would decrease when converted to economic terms by deducting taxes. Let us say that the economic cost of the capital investment would be EUR1.9 billion instead of the EUR2 billion in the financial evaluation.

Second, like most RDI investments, the project is likely to generate spillover effects through knowledge creation which could have applications either in aeronautics or in other sectors. By definition such benefits are a (positive) externality and not taken into account in the financial return calculations of the promoter, as any internal benefit would be. In the aeronautical industry, however, knowledge spillovers are not large – most knowledge tends to be retained within the value chain (Niosi and Zhegu 2005). Assume that such benefits would amount to an extra EUR100 million, bringing the present value of the project before investment from EUR1.4 billion to EUR1.5 billion. That spillover knowledge would be available whether the project succeeds or not, which would mean that the worst-case scenario would consist of a higher benefit. This could be used to argue for a lower volatility of returns, depressing the real option value. However, it could equally be argued in turn that should the project succeed, the positive payoff could also be higher, keeping volatility constant. The answer to this issue is obviously project-specific. In the current case, for simplicity it is assumed that volatility stays constant.

Third, there are several reasons why the government may use a lower rate of discount to evaluate investments than the private sector.[15] One reason is that if the project is sufficiently small relative to the size of the economy, the government (and society) would have a greater ability than the private sector to bear the non-diversifiable risks inherent in the project, as the risk would be small relative to the size of the economy. Another reason is that capital markets may be subject to distortions such as taxes, which may discriminate between the public and private sectors. Also, the product market where the project takes place may be imperfectly competitive and individual firms may demand higher rates of return than would be the case in more competitive markets. Another is that the government may wish to address inter-generational externalities or other ethical considerations by lowering the discount rate for benefits and costs in the distant future. Whichever discount rate is applied by the government, particularly when acting on a tight budget constraint, a good reason should be given for it to be deemed lower than the long-term real rate of interest of public debt, as this rate reflects the marginal cost of funds to the government and society. In practice, social discount rates applied by the government or, if estimates are not available, long-term government borrowing rates, tend to be lower than discount rates applied by private firms. The effect of using a lower discount rate to value the stream of future flows of benefits (before investment) is to increase their value.

Let us assume that in the current project, the lower discount rate applied by the government would result in the value of the benefit flows increasing from EUR1.5 billion to EUR2 billion. The value of the project would be EUR2 billion and of the investment, as mentioned above, EUR1.9 billion. The project would have an economic net present value of EUR100 million which, by virtue of being a positive economic value combined with a negative financial value (the EUR800 million loss identified in section 7.2.1 above), would render the project as a candidate for government support. Whether it would actually merit financing would depend on the government budget constraint and the socioeconomic profitability of alternative projects. Such a low economic return (EUR100 million for an investment of EUR1.9 billion) would likely make it a borderline project. However, the government recognises, just as the private promoter did, that there is a large degree of uncertainty surrounding the benefit stream. The returns of the project may be much larger than the mean or expected return and therefore a real option analysis may reveal more value in the project.

Figure 7.4 includes the binomial tree calculated using the economic flows rather than the private financial flows, including the three adjustments mentioned above. To recap, the adjustments had the result of increasing the present value of the asset to EUR2 billion from the EUR1.2 billion of the private sector financial analysis; and of decreasing the total investment cost (the strike price of the option) from the EUR2 billion borne by the private sector in the financial analysis to an economic investment cost of EUR1.9 billion. The result shows that the economic real option value of the project, at EUR865 million, is substantially higher than the private financial option value of EUR274 million (Figure 7.3). If for, say, budgeting reasons or indivisibilities in required investment effort, the EUR274 million private real option value were not enough for the private sector to keep the option of carrying out the project alive, there may be a strong case for the government to help finance the option.

Moreover, there may be an economic case for the government to help finance real options to the private sector even when the option value to the private sector is 0. This is signalled by the circled lower figures in cells S_od^2, S_oud^2, and $S_ou^2d^2$ in Figure 7.4, which display positive economic real option values on the project, in situations where the private real option is worthless (same cells in Figure 7.3).[16] Such a result would help justify the case for the government to support the financing of research programmes with commercial prospects too uncertain to be of any value to the private sector, but which may generate such a value in the future depending on the development of events.

In the current example, real option analysis strengthens the case for a project with an economic NPV that was positive but borderline. It is worth pointing out that the situation described in section 7.2.1 of this chapter in the context of private financial value, where real option analysis was applied to a project with a negative NPV, would also apply in the context of socio-economic value. That is, there can be valid cases for public-funding research programmes that

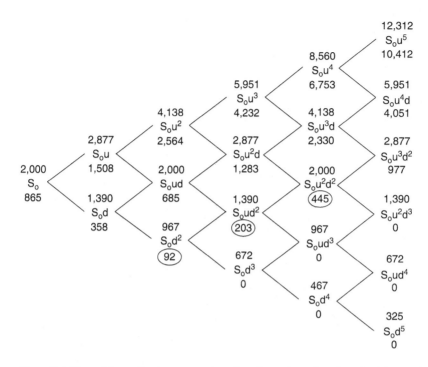

Figure 7.4 Binomial tree for the economic real option value of an aircraft engine project.

keep options alive on projects for which standard socio-economic appraisal finds the prospects too uncertain to justify carrying them out at the time of the appraisal, but which have positive economic real option values. This would be the situation depicted in Figure 7.3, assuming that the values used for the private sector example represented economic values.

Finally, note that the case described has implicitly assumed that the governmental body in charge of reaching the decision on whether to support the option is independent of the governmental body deciding on the regulation of future emissions standards. In effect, it has been assumed that the private sector and the government both face the same degree of uncertainty. This may not be so in practice. In fact, an alternative for the government to providing research grants to help keep options open would be to provide more regulatory certainty.

7.3 Supersonic flight

7.3.1 Introduction

Writing in 2020, the last two decades have been unusual in the history of commercial civil aviation. Since its beginnings in the early 20th century, the industry had been characterised by a trend of increasing aircraft speed. The introduction into commercial service of the Tupolev Tu-144 and of Concorde in the 1970s, cruising at speeds of just above Mach 1.5 and Mach 2, respectively, brought supersonic flight to the industry. The Tu-144 had a poor safety record and a very short life of commercial operation, while Concorde operated commercially for about two and a half decades until service was discontinued in 2003. There was no replacement for Concorde and so the year 2003 marked not only the breach of the trend for greater speed, but a one-off step back, with commercial jet services since all being sub-sonic, at speeds of slightly over Mach 0.8.

Concorde was from inception a highly political project, with serious doubts about its economic case (Woolley 1972, Edwards and Woolley 1973).[17] The organisation of the aviation industry at the time was markedly different from today. There was heavy state involvement in the aircraft manufacturing sector, as part of a more general interventionist approach to industrial policy at the time, including the development of 'national champions'. The world was immersed in the Cold War, during which displays of technological prowess was but one of the various battlegrounds. The development of supersonic transport (SST), as it was known at the time, was initially a three-way race. The USSR developed the Tu-144 largely in tandem to Concorde, while the US, which had been pursuing its own supersonic aircraft, saw its project rejected by the US Congress on economic grounds (Lawrence 1971).

Meanwhile the airlines, many of which were also state owned, operated in regulated markets with limited scope for competition. Most domestic markets were subject to regulation. International airline markets were governed by bi-lateral agreements (often referred to as 'bilaterals') between country pairs (Dobson 2017, Doganis 2019). These bilaterals specified the destinations from each country that could be served with international routes and the capacity, departure frequencies, and prices of those services, which were normally operated by one designated 'flag carrier' (sometimes two) from each country. In such an environment, many governments could dictate what aircraft airlines bought.

The message is that, as evidenced by the objections voiced at the time about the economics of the project, the case for developing and launching SST at the time was political, or geo-political. Both Concorde and the Tu-144 happened because competition on showcasing state-led technological prowess usually primed over economics.

Yet the commercial failure of the first projects has not led to abandoning the quest for speed. Since Concorde, new concepts have been and are being explored, including not only resuming services at about Mach 2, but also re-taking the original trend and proposing speeds of Mach 5 or 6, currently labelled as 'hypersonic flight'. Technology for Mach 2 has existed for many decades now. It seems to be only a question of time until concept technology for Mach 5–6 is deemed technically feasible.

The push for speed follows from the nature of demand for transport. As discussed in Chapter 2, transport is an intermediate service, demanded for some ulterior motive, namely work or leisure at the destination. Transport users want to minimise the resources consumed by transport, as measured by the generalised cost of travel, which crucially includes travel time (the door-to door time spent by transport users).

Think of the total time (person-hours) spent in a plane by people around the world as both a private and a societal cost that users and governments seek to minimise. Two long term socio-economic developments work in favour of developing technology to minimise such in-vehicle travel time. First is globalisation, which implies growing demand for long distance trips and with that an ever growing amount of person-hours spent in a plane at any one period of time (say, per year). Second, growing international productivity as measured by raising incomes, which result in a greater willingness to pay by businesses and individuals to save travel time. Combining these two factors implies that, by sticking to sub-sonic flight, the private and societal cost to the world economy of time spent on long distance travel would continue to grow over time for decades to come. At some point in time, the economic case for resuming supersonic commercial aviation is bound to become evident and, soon afterwards, overwhelming.

The question would then seem to be not whether, but when and how, supersonic speed is re-introduced in commercial aviation. The challenge of technological development is, as in all fields, one of technical and economic viability in tandem, addressing the question of what would be the economic value of different bundles of aircraft operating characteristics.

Following the line of argument throughout the book, the economic viability can in turn be viewed at two levels. Firstly, and more broadly, what is the value to society – that is, to all stakeholders, whether travellers or all those indirectly affected by air travel – of a given bundle of supersonic aircraft operating characteristics? This would determine whether the investment to develop such an aircraft should go ahead at all or not on economic grounds. The vantage point for governments here would be delivering a socially desirable transportation service (enhancing accessibility). Secondly, and more narrowly, what would be the commercial value of the project? The vantage point for governments in this case would be one of industrial policy: whether it would be economically desirable for the country to produce such an aircraft. This second vantage point was the one followed by Woolley (1972) analysing Concorde.

If the answers to both questions are positive, the private sector could be expected to develop the aircraft. More likely, the first question would be positive before the second one is, meaning that there may be at least a case for public support for the project on transportation (or accessibility) grounds. At the same time, the expectation that growing world incomes and demand for air travel will eventually make the second question positive also, may prompt an intervention case for governments seeking a technological first-mover advantage on industrial policy grounds.

The focus in this book is on the first question: societal benefits and costs *over and above* revenues and money costs, provided by the transportation service. The key societal benefit (above revenues) is societal willingness to pay for faster air travel. The key societal cost (beyond money costs) would be those associated to environmental externalities.

At the time of writing, externalities of air travel related to climate change are on course to being internalised, mainly through MBMs. This turns the climate change performance of supersonic travel into part of the calculation of commercial viability. The other critical environmental cost concerns noise, including also the 'sonic boom' specific to supersonic travel. These were already important constraints faced by Concorde. At the time they were addressed mostly through regulation, including constraining the sonic boom to take place only over sea water. This limited Concorde services to destinations close to the shore. Indeed, much of the ongoing research effort on supersonic aircraft concerns technologies related to noise and sonic boom performance.

The implication would then be that any future supersonic aircraft project that is sufficiently solid to be considered a sound candidate for development would need to be commercially viable after paying for its costs related to climate change and after addressing the noise-related constraints of supersonic travel. For the calculation of economic viability, environmental costs could therefore be assumed to be internalised into the ticket price, either through MBMs, taxes, or regulation. The economic case for public support would then rely on the benefits to society of faster air travel over and above the benefits measured by airline revenues. The next section sketches a simplified version of such an economic appraisal.

7.3.2 Appraisal of developing a supersonic passenger aircraft

The economic appraisal measures the benefits to the full value chain of international air transport and with it the world economy at large. It does not narrow the appraisal to the benefits to the national economy (or economies) developing the aircraft, thereby focusing on the manufacturing element, which was the approach followed by Woolley (1972) for the appraisal of Concorde. Such a national appraisal would pay particular attention to the value of foreign exchange, as illustrated in Chapter 5. It is also assumed that there will be few spill-over effects in that much of the knowledge generated in the R&D phase would be retained within the industrial value chain of the promoters of the project, including final assembler and suppliers.

The project consists of developing a supersonic aircraft, which we will label Supersonic Transport 2 (shortened to S2). It would fly at speeds of about Mach 2, with a seating capacity of 120 seats, a similar type of aircraft as Concorde and the Tu-144. The project would still require heavy R&D investment as S2 would incorporate technological advances since the 1960s and 1970s and knowledge generated during the operating phases of those two earlier aircraft. Much R&D capital expenditure would go into improving the noise and sonic boom performance of the aircraft. As mentioned in the preceding section 7.3.1, being able to perform the sonic boom over land would greatly improve the commercial (and economic) prospects of the aircraft. The appraisal assumes that any remaining noise externality is internalised through taxes or other means and reflected in the price of the airline ticket. The same consideration applies to other environmental externalities.

For simplicity, the project is expected to last about 20 years, with all investments in year zero and 20 years of operating life thereafter. This is obviously a substantial simplification, made for illustrative purposes. The emphasis here is placed on categorising what is a cost and what a benefit and on the aggregation process to come up with a measure of economic value. Detailed modelling of each variable would require a far more complex exercise.

Table 7.2 displays the economic appraisal calculation process. Two scenarios are assumed, one for sales of 100 S2 aircraft, in column b, and the other for sales of 200 aircraft in column c. Column a includes the comparative performance of existing sub-sonic aircraft, focused on the most immediately relevant variables for the calculation of the generalised cost of travel and the resulting gain in consumer surplus from the project. The aircraft would operate at an average load factor of 70 per cent (row 2) and average four flight stages (or landing and takeoff cycles, LTO) a day (row 3) in 320 days per year (row 4). This would imply some 107,520 passengers per aircraft per year (row 5).

Upfront, non-recurring capital expenditure would be EUR10bn, independent of the number of S2 aircraft eventually sold. The private sector promoting the aircraft would launch the project only if it yields a return of 15 per cent on invested capital over a 20 year economic life of the project. There needs to be an estimate of what this return implies for aircraft price for different amounts of aircraft sold. A detailed calculation would need to simulate the timing of such sales. Here a simplified 'back of an envelope' calculation is followed. It converts the EUR10bn capital investment into a 20 year annuity yielding 15 per cent, implying an annual annuity payment of around EUR1.6bn. Total revenues to the aircraft producers over the 20-year life of the project would then need to be EUR32bn (=EUR1.6bnx × 20), to cover the non-recurring capital expenditure alone. This is included in row 7 as capital cost.

In addition, each aircraft produced would involve a recurring cost of EUR50m for the manufacturer (row 8), which would need to be covered with revenues from the sale of aircraft as they take place. The implication of these non-recurring and recurring costs for aircraft price under each of the two scenarios is included in row 10. The price of EUR370m per aircraft if 100 aircraft are sold and of EUR210m per aircraft if 200 units are sold would constitute actual revenues to the manufacturer per aircraft sold. Industry marketing practice means that the aircraft list price could easily be double those estimates.

The total revenues raised by the manufacturer over the life of the project

Table 7.2 Calculation of economic value of project to develop a supersonic aircraft

			Without project	With project Aircraft sold:	
			(a)	100 (b)	200 (c)
Operating characteristic of project aircraft:					
Seating capacity per ac	(1)	(units)		120	120
Load factor	(2)	(average)		70%	70%
Flights/ac/day	(3)	(units)		4	4
Operating days/ac/year	(4)	(units)		320	320
Pax/ac/year	(5) = (1) × (2) × (3) × (4)	(units)		107,520	107,520
Aircraft production costs, sales and price:					
Non-recurring capex	(6)	(EUR bn)		10	10
Cost of capital	(7) = Σannuity payments for IRR(6) = 15%	(EUR bn)		32	32
Recurring costs per ac.	(8)	(EURm)		50	50
Total aircraft sold	(9)	(units)		100	200
Price per ac.	(10) = ((7) × 1,000)/(9)) + (8)	(EUR m)		370	210
Total revenues	(11) = (7) + ((8) × (9)/1,000)	(EUR bn)		37	42
Implied pax/year	(12) = (5) × (9)/1,000,000	(m)		10.8	21.5
Total pax lifetime	(13) = (12) × 20	(m)		215.0	430.1
Cost per pax	(14) = (11) × 1,000/(13)	(EUR)		172.1	97.7
Passenger generalised cost (GC) and traffic generation:					
Average flight length	(15)	(hours/trip)	10	4	4
Access/egress	(16)	(hours/trip)	2	2	2
Total time	(17) = (15) + (16)	(hours/trip)	12	6	6
Time cost	(18) = (17) × VoT	(EUR/pax)	2,400	1,200	1,200

(*Continued*)

Table 7.2 (*Continued*)

| | | Without project | With project Aircraft sold: | |
| | | | 100 | 200 |
		(a)	(b)	(c)
Average ticket price	(EUR/pax)	2,000	3,074	3,000
GC	(EUR/pax)	4,400	4,274	4,200
Difference in GC vs current			−2.9%	−4.5%
Pax per year (100 aircraft)	(m)	10.4	10.8	
Pax per year (200 aircraft)	(m)	20.5		21.5
Traffic generation			2.9%	4.5%
Changes in consumer surplus:				
Per year	(EUR bn)		1.3	4.2
Over project lifetime	(EUR bn)		26.6	84.1
Present value	(EUR bn)		**17.4**	**54.9**
Distant destinations:				
Share of total traffic:	(average)		25%	25%
Benefit disparity through distance	(average)		30%	30%
Share of local residents in traffic	(average)		50%	50%
Resulting consumer surplus:				
Per year	(EUR bn)		0.22	0.68
Present value	(EUR bn)		**2.8**	**8.9**

$(19a) = 2,000$; $(19c) = 3,000$
$(19b) = 3,000 + (14b) − (14c)$
$(20) = (18) + (19)$
$(21) = ((20) − (20a))/(20a)$
$(22b) = (12)$; $(22a) = (22b) \times (1 + (\varepsilon \times (21)))$
$(23c) = (12)$; $(23a) = (23c) \times (1 + (\varepsilon \times (21)))$
$(24b) = ((22) − (22a))/(22a)$
$(24c) = ((23) − (23a))/(23a)$

$(25b) = ((20a) − (20)) \times (((22) − (22a))/2)/1,000$
$(25c) = ((20a) − (20)) \times (((23) − (23a))/2)/1,000$
$(26) = (25) \times 20$
$(27) = \text{NPV}((25)$ at SDR$)$

(28)
(29)
(30)

$(31) = (25) \times (28) \times (1 + (29)) + (30)$
$(32) = (27) \times (28) \times (1 + (29)) + (30)$

would be in the EUR37bn to EUR42bn range (row 11), depending on the actual number of aircraft sold. Dividing this by the total number of passengers flying the aircraft over the 20 year life of the project (row 13), yields the cost borne by each passenger in paying for the production of the aircraft (row 14), which varies from EUR172 and EUR98, depending on the number of aircraft sold. To simplify we ignore additional revenues to the manufacturer from servicing and supplying spare parts through the life of the aircraft, or simply assume that these the included in the cost of capital calculation in row 7.

The final airline ticket price paid by passengers needs to incorporate also all of the other costs associated to operating the aircraft beyond those related to the aircraft manufacturer. These include the operating and capital costs of the airlines and their inputs including, among others, infrastructure providers and associated services. Say that the project would target a demand segment that, without the project, pays in sub-sonic aircraft an average airline ticket of EUR2,000 per segment on routes that would be served by S2 (cell 19a). This is very high yield traffic with a high value of time, corresponding mainly to passengers currently flying with unrestricted business and first class tickets, as well as many of those flying on private jets. Under a central case scenario of 200 S2 aircraft sold, the ticket price for these passengers would be EUR3,000 per flight stage, or trip (cell 19c). Should S2 sales total 100 aircraft instead of 200, the resulting airline ticket price would be EUR3,074 per trip (cell 19b).

Relative to sub-sonic aircraft, S2 would cut the average flight time on the routes it would target from 10 to 4 hours (row 15). Adding two hours of average access and egress time (row 16) would mean that the average door-to-door travel time would fall from 12 hours to 6 hours (row 17). Valuing such difference in door-to-door travel time with a value of time per passenger of EUR200 per hour would mean that the project would reduce time cost per passenger from EUR2,400 per trip to EUR1,200 (row 18).

Adding the difference in ticket price to these time costs would yield a measure of the behavioural generalised cost of travel. The generalised cost without the project is then EUR4,400 per trip (row 20). With the project it would fall to between EUR4,274 and EUR 4,200 per trip, depending on the number of S2 aircraft sold. The saving in generalised cost produced by the project then ranges, rounding, from 3 per cent to 5 per cent (row 21).

With these figures it is possible to calculate traffic generation with the project. The calculation is simplified here in two respects. First, it takes total number of passengers flown per S2 aircraft per year (row 5) as the binding constraint. Second, it adopts an end-point, rather than a starting-point, demand elasticity, which means that the number of passengers without the project in the scenario with 200 S2 aircraft sold, at 20.5m passengers (cell 23a), is not double the number of passengers without the project in the scenario with sales of 100 S2 aircraft, at 10.4m passengers (cell 22a).[18] Taking the elasticity of demand for air travel with respect to generalised cost of travel to be −1, the project would then generate traffic by the same percentage reduction in generalised cost, namely between 3 per cent and 5 per cent, depending on the number of S2 aircraft sold (row 24). Again, traffic generation is calculated relative to the end point.

Having the four key data points, namely, prices and quantities both with and without the project, we can proceed to calculate the gain in consumer surplus produced by the project. This gain in consumer surplus measures societal willingness to pay for the gain in speed from S2 over and above what aircraft users actually pay, thereby measuring the additional economic value of the project to society over and above that registered in financial flows. This 'societal' willingness to pay refers to the subset of stakeholders that actually pay for airline tickets, including tourists and businesses in the various sectors of the economy paying the travel of their employees. Businesses would be willing to pay for such tickets to the extent that the faster service adds value to their own customers. So if, say, a lawyer consumes with S2 one day to fly to and from a meeting, instead of two days with conventional, sub-sonic aircraft, so long as the additional cost of the ticket is less than the daily fees (and hotel night) of the lawyer, the, say, pharmaceutical company employing the lawyer would be happy to pay for S2. The savings to the pharmaceutical company by paying for S2 travel would then be reflected in higher profits and/or lower prices to consumers, depending on how competitive is the market where the pharmaceutical company operates. The value added to customers is reflected in the original willingness to pay for S2, even though the final beneficiary is the shareholder of the pharmaceutical producer or a consumer of medicines. The important message is that willingness to pay measures societal value – a value that is not necessarily pocketed by the airline passenger.

This measure of societal value that relies on willingness to pay for travel includes also the implied taxes that are associated to the trip, as described in Appendix A2.1 to Chapter 2. As mentioned in that appendix, a more accurate appraisal would measure user (passenger) behaviour with net of tax value and societal value with gross of tax value. In practice, for simplicity, appraisals often use a common measure of value of time for estimating both passenger behaviour and societal value.

For illustrative purposes, borrowing Figure 7.1 (b) as an approximation to the project at hand, assuming that it represents the market segment for high yield traffic, the gain in consumer surplus from the project would correspond to the area of trapezoid $f_m g j f_c$.

The measure of consumer surplus would be EUR1.3bn per year if the project ends up producing 100 S2 aircraft and EUR4.2bn per year if 200 aircraft are produced (row 25). These gains would add up to EUR26.1bn and EUR84.1bn over the life of the project (row 26). On a present value basis discounted at the social discount rate of 4 per cent, it would yield a value of EUR17.4bn and EUR54.9bn, respectively. These would be estimates of the value of the project to the world economy, over and above any value registered through financial flows. The appraisal has assumed that the full value chain is competitive and undistorted; therefore there is no additional societal value to be extracted in project revenues. That is, revenues reflect opportunity costs.

While it is perhaps not necessary to emphasise the importance of traveller value of time for a project aimed at increasing speed, let us make a very brief aside to illustrate this. Assuming a time value of EUR250 per hour instead of EUR200, would (more than) double the savings in generalised cost relative to sub-sonic flight to a range of −8.5 per cent to −10 per cent for the two scenarios, up from the −2.9 per cent to −4.5 per cent range (row 21). The same magnitudes, albeit of the opposite sign, would apply to traffic generation (row 24). As a result, the societal value of the project would increase to a range of EUR57.3bn to EUR133.5bn, up from EUR17.4bn to EUR54.9bn (row 27). An increase in the value of time of 25 per cent, doubles or triples the societal value of the project.

7.3.3 'Standing' and other considerations

The estimation of socio-economic value of the project could have been done more narrowly to include only benefits and costs to the countries producing the aircraft, in line with the appraisal by Woolley (1972) for Concorde. Such an estimate would require separating stakeholders between national and foreign, consider all benefits and costs to nationals, ignore all benefits and costs to foreigners, and treat all transfers from nationals to foreigners as costs and all transfers from foreigners to nationals as benefits. In the language of economic appraisal it would be an appraisal where nationals would have *standing* in the appraisal and foreigners would not, an issue briefly touched on in Chapter 3, section 3.3.1.

Such an appraisal would focus on three elements. Firstly, the industrial element, consisting of the business case for producing the aircraft. If the opportunity cost of capital reflects the cost of foregone investment opportunities then the profits of industrial production would not constitute an additional benefit over and above what has been considered here, yielding a net value of EUR0. There may be some (national) industrial spillover effects, but in the aeronautical industry these tend not to be substantial as most benefits are retained within the aircraft manufacturing value chain (Niosi and Zhegu 2005).

The second element would be international trade and the associated flows of foreign exchange, in line with the considerations in Chapter 5. However, any additional value in gains from hard currency would not be substantial if the producing country has few trade distortions, as is broadly the case for advanced industrial countries at the time of writing.

And thirdly, the analysis would include changes in consumer surplus, driven mostly by the balance between travel time savings and changes in airline ticket prices, as identified in row 27 of Table 7.2. This element was excluded in Woolley (1972), who conducted the study at the time when cost-benefit analysis was less advanced than today. Crucially, economists were still developing the analytical framework to incorporate time into the microeconomic theory of consumption, whereby time would assume the role of a commodity and a resource (Jara-Díaz 2007). Today, the value of time is central to the economic analysis of transportation, as has been made evident throughout the book. An economic appraisal in which only the countries producing the aircraft are given standing would only value the change in consumer surplus of nationals.

Let us dwell somewhat more on this last element. The countries that could be expected to benefit disproportionately from the transport service offered by the project are those that meet two conditions: firstly, they are located most distantly from the globe's main centres of traffic generation; and secondly, they are relatively high income countries and therefore generate sufficient high yield traffic themselves.[19] The calculations in Table 7.2 are for the average flight operated by S2, representing an average gain in door-to-door travel time of six hours. For high income countries that are relatively distant that gain would be larger than the average.

Let us make a quick calculation of project benefits where only nationals of those distant countries have standing. The actual manufacturing of the aircraft would take place on a third country, so that the manufacturing industry would have no standing in the appraisal. Say that a set of particularly remote destinations account for about 25 per cent of S2 traffic (row 28). Because of the longer flights, the consumer surplus gains associated with such traffic would be, say, 30 per cent larger than the average (row 29). Also, say that nationals of those remote countries would account for 50 per cent of the S2 traffic to those countries (row 30). Then the benefit of the project to the domestic economies of these countries would amount to between EUR200 and EUR700 million per year (row 31). The benefits over the life of the project would have a present value of between EUR3bn and EUR9bn (row 32). Circumstances could be conceived whereby these countries would put together an incentive scheme to prompt aircraft developers in third countries to launch S2. The EUR3bn to EUR9bn would constitute the maximum amount that these countries should be willing to fund, absent other benefits such as manufacturers from those remote countries benefitting from the project.

In such an appraisal, where only nationals from the set of distant countries have standing, the funding from distant countries to the manufacturers would constitute a cost. This is in contrast to an appraisal with universal standing, where such funding would be a transfer from the distant countries to the manufacturing country.

Normally, though, such projects would be offered support from the national governments hosting the development of the aircraft. As already mentioned, if the production of supersonic aircraft was deemed a high tech, high value added sector, viable in the long term, governments may want to develop first-mover advantages in hosting it. Remote countries could vie for a share of the value chain.

Notes

1 The term 'original equipment manufacturer', or OEM, is not used in the book since the use of the term is somewhat ambiguous. Whereas it seems to have referred originally to manufacturers of components or final products – as its name suggests – it is now also

frequently used to refer to final assemblers or value-added resellers. This book uses instead the terms component manufacturer and final assembler.

2 Whereas air traffic management (ATM) is also a high-tech sector, it is subject to much weaker competitive pressures than aircraft manufacturing. Similarly, investments in ATM technology, particularly the most innovative elements, tend to be more closely coordinated with technology users, usually involving the public sector.

3 For an accessible discussion of market coordination outcomes in conditions of less-than-perfect competition and without communication among players, see Kay 1995. For a formal exposition of alternative models of competition see any textbook on industrial organisation, for example Belleflamme and Peitz 2015 or Martin 2010.

4 Other typical adjustments for this type of project may be removing the cost of taxes on inputs and any shadow price of labour should any of the R&D or manufacturing activities be located in areas of high unemployment. However, these are general economic appraisal issues (see, for example, de Rus 2010 and Campbell and Brown 2016) not specific to aviation and we ignore them for simplicity. For a broader discussion of shadow prices see Londero 2003.

5 Note that the effect on the primary market (i.e. the aircraft manufacturing market) is a fall in demand (a shift in the demand curve) rather than a fall in the quantity demanded (resulting from an increase in price), since the increase in price occurs in the secondary (i.e. the airline) market. The difference is important because price changes in the primary market have additional welfare implications for the project, as is illustrated in the next section of this chapter.

6 Note that it is assumed that the introduction of the environmental tax occurs after the aircraft manufacturer has either carried out or at least committed to the installation of sufficient capacity for a delivery rate of 60 aircraft per year. Otherwise, if the manufacturer expected an environmental tax, it would revise downwards its delivery rate and install less assembly capacity. Such a move would help improve the returns of the project somewhat. Still, the returns would be lower than in the scenario of no environmental taxes, since the fall in investment cost would not be proportionate to the fall in production capacity, as project R&D costs would be unaffected.

7 Note that a key difference in the underlying assumption between this situation and the oligopoly or competitive outcome reviewed in section 7.1.1 of this chapter is that in the current case, in the absence of the project the status quo would have remained, whereas in the competitive or oligopolistic case, in the absence of the project competitors would have taken up the capacity otherwise supplied by the project promoter. The market structure and competitive conditions play a crucial role in investment appraisals in sectors where competition is possible, which means that building the 'with project' and 'without project' scenarios must be grounded on industrial organisation models. For further reading on models of competition see Belleflamme and Peitz 2015 or Martin 2010.

8 The increase in the number of aircraft with the project is approximate, in two respects. First, for simplicity of presentation the total number of aircraft delivered in scenario 3 is assumed to be the same as in scenario 1. For ease of computation and reference, the effect of the EUR10 million price difference on changes in quantity demanded through the price elasticity of demand is calculated as a price increase from the final number of aircraft, rather than as a price fall from the original market size without the project. Second, aircraft cannot be delivered in fractions, so that final demand figures must necessarily be rounded.

9 It is assumed that the former monopolist is left with a 50 per cent share of the market segment. That is, following the entry of the competitor the incumbent does not see its sales fall by 50 per cent, but rather by 50 per cent minus the 19 per cent generation in sales resulting from the fall in prices. Therefore the same reduction in deadweight loss is attributable to the monopolist sales. By not accounting for the welfare gain resulting

from the reduction in the deadweight loss attributable to the sales made by the competitor by lowering prices, the calculation effectively incorporates the rule of a half.

10 In addition they may argue that by not doing the project, they run the risk of another competitor taking a lead with the same or similar technology, curtailing the promoter's future position to one of follower. The boundaries of the investment question can be widened, therefore, to simulate potential outcomes for the firm as a whole. The line of reasoning would be similar but the scenarios modelled differently.

11 The binomial method is an approximation to the Black–Scholes formula used in Chapter 6, section 6.2.2, on airline fleet expansion. The binomial method is more transparent, more flexible about the construction of scenarios, and better suited to American options (those that can be exercised at any time before expiry). The Black–Scholes formula addresses European options that can only be exercised at a pre-specified date. See Kodukula and Papudesu 2006.

12 Modelling the precise conditions of the options embedded in a project can potentially become a computationally burdensome exercise. As in any other project appraisal exercise, it is up to the analyst to decide how much detail is worth going into and whether relatively simplified estimates can give useful insights. The objective here is to illustrate the use of the real option analysis method. For more complex modelling the reader should consult the specialist literature. For modelling investments under imperfect competition, a topic particularly relevant to the aeronautical sector, see Smit and Trigeorgis 2004.

13 That is, if the option to invest could be traded, it would be traded at the NPV of the project. It is useful to think of the value of the option at this stage as akin to the value of a notional licence to carry out the project.

14 The value of the real option calculated with the Black-Scholes method is EUR266 million. It is normal for such small differences to occur, as the binomial method is an approximation to the Black-Scholes result, while adding more transparency and flexibility in the definition of project scenarios.

15 Social discount rates and their relationship to private or market discount rates are standard topics in any book on cost benefit analysis. Accessible discussions on this topic are included in Boardman et al. 2018, de Rus 2010 and Campbell and Brown 2016. For a discussion on a developing country context see Brent 1998.

16 Note that the lower figure in cell $S_0u^3d^2$ in the fifth column of Figure 7.4 is not circled because it consists of an expected project net present value, or the value of the option at expiration, where delaying the project further is not possible. See section 7.2.1 of this chapter.

17 Woolley 1972 conducted a cost-benefit analysis of the Concorde project from the perspective of industrial policy of the countries producing the aircraft. The appraisal exclude benefits to passengers over and above those reflected in airline revenues. The next section discusses this point further.

18 Adopting a mid-point demand elasticity, generally considered the least biased approach, would also imply that the number of passengers without the project would not differ by a factor of 2 for the two project scenarios. Again, the reason is the assumption taken of using the number of passengers flown annually by each S2 aircraft (row 5) as a binding constraint.

19 A non-exhaustive sample of such countries at the time of writing could include countries such as, in alphabetical order, Australia, Chile, New Zealand, and the somewhat less remote South Africa.

8   Concluding remarks

The presentations of appraisal methods in this book have focused on identifying costs and benefits, measuring them, and avoiding double-counting or neglect. Inevitably, all appraisals are based on models, and models are simplifications of reality. Models can always be made more detailed in an attempt to reflect a more accurate representation of actual conditions. In addition to the simplifications listed in Chapter 1, section 4, four possible dimensions along which to add detail to the models include benefits, costs, timing, and strategic interaction.

First, regarding project benefits, perhaps the most fruitful area for refinement concerns delay to users, including both measuring the actual delay caused to users and the cost of such delay. In the case of airports, more accurate delay functions can be constructed with data and simulations performed in the process of project planning and facility design. Relevant items that may be addressed include facility utilisation and capacity constraints in the terminal, user access and egress travel profiles, travel conditions on alternative airports and modes of travel, and airline behaviour in the presence of capacity constraints.

Models of airline behaviour become particularly relevant for air traffic management (ATM) projects. These go hand in hand with estimations of airspace capacity and likely delay profiles. Generally, the data to perform such simulations are likely to be available only from the air navigation service provider (ANSP).

For airline appraisals, established airlines generally have databases with substantial evidence on passenger behaviour across various fare categories. These can be used for estimating the traffic effects of network changes that may result from the introduction of new aircraft.

Reliable estimates of user willingness to pay to reduce trip duration are important for aircraft manufacturers in estimating the underlying demand potential for new products, particularly when they are innovative. The money value of time is central to inform decisions about: (i) whether to produce smaller aircraft aimed at direct services between secondary airports, or larger aircraft serving hub networks; (ii) whether to go for faster, more comfortable but more expensive regional jets versus turboprops; (iii) the extent to which engine technology should prioritise fuel-saving over speed; or (iv), and more innovatively, whether to invest in more expensive aircraft that fly closer to, or beyond, the sound barrier. The analyst may wish to enhance estimates of values of time readily available from governmental agencies with further analysis on the variance of recommended average estimates, particularly how values of time may change with income levels of different traffic segments. For example, the analysis of variance in values of time would be helpful when justifying investments in private aviation or in exploring the prospects for reintroducing supersonic commercial air travel.

Second, regarding the cost estimates in the appraisal models, the underlying conditions assumed should reflect the applicable cost economies, on which there is plenty of evidence in the academic literature. Aviation, like any transport infra-structure or vehicle operation, enjoys economies of scale (lower unit costs through larger capacity), density (lower unit costs by using existing capacity more in-tensively), and scope (lower unit costs by sharing existing capacity to produce different products). Such economies will affect the unit costs resulting from pro-jects that change physical capacity, and the resulting impact on costs may at times be important in determining project viability. The failure to recognise scope and density economies tends to lie behind the often flawed – yet frequent – proposals for tourist-dedicated airports, freight-dedicated airports, or dedicated business-class airlines. Similarly, any scale economies resulting from larger facilities should be set against the time cost to users caused by the accompanying longer throughput processing time. Such an exercise would require sound estimates of facility oper-ating costs, passenger processing time, and the value of time for affected passengers.

Third, project timing and phasing are important drivers of investment performance and, more generally, the efficient allocation of resources. Real option analysis can help maximise value by guiding project design and phasing. Modelling the precise array of options available on any investment can be a computationally complex task. This topic, however, is general to investment appraisal across most sectors of the economy, with no particular remarks to make about aviation. Suffice it to say that the valuation of timing and phasing is very much project-specific, and the evaluation should be tailored to reflect project circumstances. The use of real option analysis on a level beyond a simple, first, rough estimate, almost inevitably requires detailed work on the timing aspects specific to the project being appraised.

And fourth, strategic interaction between competitors can also play an important role in project appraisal. This would consist of the project promoter building al-ternative scenarios about how competitors may be expected to react to alternative investment strategies. The investment decision therefore becomes contingent on expected competitor reactions. This is important in particular for the aeronautical industry and for airports, both sectors operating in competitive markets char-acterised by product differentiation and sunk costs. Where there is more limited scope for product differentiation and sunk costs are few, as in many airline market segments, the role for strategic interaction models is more limited. This is because the investor can be expected to face competition from a virtually endless series of competitors, all essentially behaving similarly. For ATM, where there is little scope for competition, the role that strategic interaction plays in the investment decision is naturally marginal. Competitive interaction calls for managers to appraise a wider range of scenarios, each depending on competitor response. In that sense, rather than adding detail to the models, the investment appraisal exercise is enriched to explore a wider array of circumstances. Ideally, such analysis would make use of insights offered by both industrial organisation and game theory into the incentive profiles of the various competitors, and their likely responses.

There are, no doubt, other elements where additional detail could be added beyond those mentioned in the four areas just discussed. And yet, in investment appraisal, as in many other activities, diminishing returns eventually set in. It is up to the analyst to judge whether the extra effort required in adding complexity to the analysis pays off in terms of new insights or enhanced estimate reliability. That is, whether it is likely to make a difference to the investment decision making. It would be ironic if in carrying out an economic appraisal aimed at attaining an efficient allocation of resources, the analyst were to end up inefficiently allocating too many resources to the appraisal. When making such a judgement, the analyst should bear in mind that the investment appraisal involves making assumptions about future conditions, assumptions that become stronger as the projections reach further into the project life. There is little point in devoting many resources to adding detail about conditions observable in year 1, when the following 19 years of the estimated project life (itself often an expectation or a convention) are increasingly uncertain, so that each detail added must then rely on new suppositions. The intended message is that economic appraisals need not be cumbersome or expensive exercises. Often, a small number of key variables will prove sufficient to build a fairly reliable picture about the merits of an investment project.

Appraisal resources could then perhaps be more productively deployed to assist the project conception decision making process. There, relatively simple analyses, focusing on key benefits and costs, where alternative project conceptions and designs can be modified at little analysis cost, can pay a critical role in informing an evolving project conception and planning discourse. This suggestion points towards the underlying rationale for conducting economic appraisals. Aviation uses large amounts of resources, and whereas it generates much value, it is not free from waste or from large potential losses. Managers, regulators and planners need to make informed choices regarding the conception of the project, including whether to carry out the project at all. When making such choices, viewing the project from a societal, economic perspective helps in identifying areas of risk and opportunity that escape a financial analysis. More generally, conducting an economic appraisal gives as comprehensive a view as can be gathered about the value of an investment, both to society and to the investor, whether from the public or private sector.

References

Adler, N., Forsyth, P. Mueller, J. and Niemeier, H.-M. 2015. An economic assessment of airport incentive regulation. *Transport Policy*, 41 (July), 5–15.

Airports Commission. 2015a. *Economy: Transport Economic Efficiency Impacts*. London: Airports Commission. [Online]. Available at: https://assets.publishing.service.gov.uk/government/uploads/system/uploads/attachment_data/file/439169/economy-updated-transport-economic-efficiency-impacts.pdf (accessed: 4 May 2020).

Airports Commission. 2015b. *Economy: Wider Economic Impacts Assessment*. London: Airports Commission. [Online]. Available at: https://assets.publishing.service.gov.uk/government/uploads/system/uploads/attachment_data/file/439681/economy-wider-economic-impacts-assessment.pdf (accessed: 4 May 2020).

Airports Commission. 2015c. *Airports Commission: Final Report*. London: Airports Commission. [Online]. Available at: https://assets.publishing.service.gov.uk/government/uploads/system/uploads/attachment_data/file/440316/airports-commission-final-report.pdf (accessed 4 May 2020).

Averch, H. and Johnson, L.L. 1962. Behaviour of the firm under regulatory constraint. *American Economic Review*, 52(5), 1052–69.

Banister, D. and Berechman, J. 2001. *Transport Investment and Economic Development*. London: UCL Press.

Belleflamme, P. and Peitz, M. 2015. *Industrial Organization: Markets and Strategies*. 2nd Edition. Cambridge, UK: Cambridge University Press.

Boardman, A., Greenberg, D., Vining, A. and Weimer, D. 2018. *Cost-Benefit Analysis: Concepts and Practice*. 5th Edition. Cambridge, UK: Cambridge University Press.

Brealey, R.A., Myers, S.C. and Allen, F. 2017. *Principles of Corporate Finance*. 12th Edition. New York: McGraw-Hill.

Brent, R.J. 1998. *Cost-Benefit Analysis for Developing Countries*. Cheltenham, UK: Edward Elgar.

Bruninx, K., Ovaere, M. and Delarue, E. 2019. *The long term impact of the Market Stability Reserve of the EU Emission Trading System*. TME Working Paper EN2019-07. KU Leuven Energy Institute. [Online]. Available at: https://www.mech.kuleuven.be/en/tme/research/energy-systems-integration-modeling/pdf-publications/wp-en2019-07 (accessed: 25 April 2020).

Campbell, C. and Brown, R. 2016. *Benefit-Cost Analysis: Financial and Economic Appraisal Using Spreadsheets*. 2nd Edition. Abingdon, UK: Routledge.

Clark, P. 2017. *Buying the Big Jets: Fleet Planning for Airlines*. 3rd Edition. Abingdon, UK: Routledge.

Coldren, G.M., Koppelman, F.S., Kasturirangan, K. and Mukherjee, A. 2003. *Air Travel Itinerary Share Prediction: Logit Model Development at a Major U.S. Airline*. Conference Proceedings of the Transportation Research Board 82nd Annual Meeting. Washington DC: Transportation Research Board.

Curry, S. and Weiss, J. 2000. *Project Analysis in Developing Countries*. 2nd Edition. Houndmills, UK: Palgrave Macmillan.

Crompton, J.L. 2006. Economic impact studies: instruments for political shenanigans? *Journal of Travel Research*, 45 (August), 67–82.

Daley, B. 2010. *Air Transport and the Environment*. Farnham, UK: Ashgate.

Dasgupta, P., Marglin, S. and Sen, A. 1972. *Guidelines for Project Evaluation*. New York: United Nations.

Deardorff, A.V. and Stern, R.M. 1998. *Measurement of Nontariff Barriers*. Ann Arbor: The University of Michigan Press.

de Jong, G. 2007. Value of freight travel-time savings, in Hensher, D. and Button, K. (Ed.) *Handbook of Transport Modelling* (Vol. 1) 2nd Edition. Bingley, UK: Emerald.

de Jong, G.C. Kouwenhoven, M. Bates, J. Koster, P. Verhoef, E. Tavasszy, L. and Warffemius, P. 2014. New SP-values of time and reliability for freight transport in the Netherlands. *Transportation Research Part E: Logistics and Transportation Review*, 64, 71–87.

de Neufville, r. and Odini, A. 2013. *Airport Systems: Planning, Design, and Management*. 2nd Edition. New York: McGraw-Hill.

de Rus, g. 2010. *Introduction to Cost Benefit Analysis: Looking for Reasonable Shortcuts*. Cheltenham, UK: Edward Elgar.

Dixit, R.K. and Pindyck, R.S. 1994. *Investment Under Uncertainty*. Newark, NJ: Princeton University Press.

Dobson, A. 2017. *A History of International Civil Aviation: From its Origin through Transformative Evolution*. Abingdon, UK: Routledge.

Doganis, R. 2019. *Flying Off Course: Airline Economics and Marketing*. 5th Edition. Abingdon, UK: Routledge.

Dolnicar, S. Grabler, K. Grün, B. and Kulnig, A. 2011. Key drivers of airline loyalty. *Tourism Management*, 32, 1020–26.

Donnelly, W. A. and Manifold, D. 2005. *A compilation of reported non-tariff measures: description of the information. Office of Economics Working Paper no. 2005-05-A*. Washington D.C.: U.S. International Trade Commission. [Online]. Available at: https://www.usitc.gov/publications/332/EC200505A.pdf (accessed 27 October 2019).

Douglas, G.W. and Miller III, J.C. 1974. Quality competition, industry equilibrium, and efficiency in the price-constrained airline market. *American Economic Review*, 64, 657–69.

Edwards, C.B. and Woolley, P.K. 1973. A cost-benefit analysis of the Concorde project (comment and rejoinder). *Journal of Transport Economics and Policy*, 7(3), 300–2.

Ernst and Young. 2012a. *Aviation capacity cost benefit economic assessment*. Joint Study on Aviation Capacity in the Sydney Region. Technical Paper C13, Volume 5. Canberra: Australian Government, Department of Infrastructure, Transport, Regional Development and Communications. [Online]. Available at: https://www.westernsydneyairport.gov.au/sydney_av_cap (accessed 3 May 2020).

Ernst & Young. 2012b. *Economic impact of not proceeding with additional aviation capacity in the Sydney region*. Joint Study on Aviation Capacity in the Sydney Region. Technical Paper B7, Volume 2. Canberra: Australian Government, Department of Infrastructure, Transport, Regional Development and Communications. [Online]. Available at: https://www.westernsydneyairport.gov.au/sydney_av_cap (accessed 3 May 2020).

Eurocontrol 2018. *Standard Inputs for Eurocontrol Cost Benefit Analyses*. Edition 8.0, January. [Online]. Available at: https://www.eurocontrol.int/publication/standard-inputs-eurocontrol-cost-benefit-analyses-edition-8 (accessed: 22 May 2020).

European Commission 2014. *Guide to Cost-Benefit Analysis of Investment Projects*. Brussels: Directorate General Regional Policy. [Online]. Available at: https://ec.europa.eu/regional_policy/sources/docgener/studies/pdf/cba_guide.pdf. (accessed: 11 April 2019).

European Commission. 2019. *Handbook on the External Costs of Transport*. Brussels: European Commission, Directorate-General for Mobility and Transport. [Online]. Available at: https://ec.europa.eu/transport/sites/transport/files/studies/internalisation-handbook-isbn-978-92-79-96917-1.pdf (accessed: 13 April 2020).

European Union, 2018. *Directive (EU) 2018/410 of the European Parliament and the Council of 14 March 2018 amending Directive 2003/87/EC to enhance cost-effective emission reductions and low-carbon investments, and Decision (EU) 2015/1814. Official Journal of the European Union L76*, 3–27. [Online]. Available at: https://eur-lex.europa.eu/legal-content/EN/TXT/PDF/?uri=CELEX:32018L0410&from=EN (accessed 23 September 2020).

Federal Aviation Administration 1999. *FAA Airport Benefit-Cost Analysis Guidance*. FAA Office of Aviation Policy and Plans, Washington DC: United States Department of Transport. [Online]. Available at: http://www.faa.gov/regulations_policies/policy_guidance/benefit_cost/ (Accessed 1 May 2020).

Federal Aviation Administration 2010. *Addendum to FAA Airport Benefit-Cost Analysis Guidance*. FAA Office of Policy and Plans, Washington DC: United States Department of Transport. [Online]. Available at: http://www.faa.gov/regulations_policies/policy_guidance/benefit_cost/ (accessed: 1 May 2020).

Florio, M. 2014. *Applied Welfare Economics: Cost-Benefit Analysis of Projects and Policies*. London: Routledge.

France Stratégie. 2013. *Cost Benefit Assessment of Public Investment*. Final Report. Summary and Recommendations. Paris: Commissariat Général à la Stratégie et à la Prospective. [Online]. Available at: https://www.strategie.gouv.fr/sites/strategie.gouv.fr/files/atoms/files/cgsp-calcul_socioeconomique_english4.pdf (accessed 12 April 2020).

Fishwick, F. 1993. *Making Sense of Competition Policy*. London: Kogan Page.

Forsyth, P. 2006. *Estimating the costs and benefits of regional airport subsidies: a computable general equilibrium approach*. German Aviation Research Society Workshop, Netherlands, June-July. [Online]. Available at: https://www.researchgate.net/publication/228384851_Estimating_the_Costs_and_Benefits_of_Regional_Airport_Subsidies_A_Computable_General_Equilibrium_Approach (accessed: 3 May 2020).

Garrow, L.A. 2010. *Discrete Choice Modelling and Air Travel Demand: Theory and Applications*. Burlington, VT: Ashgate.

Ghobrial, A. 1993. A model to estimate the demand between U.S. and foreign gateways. *International Journal of Transport Economics*, 20(3), 271–83.

HEATCO 2006. *Developing Harmonised European Approaches for Transport Costing and Project Assessment*. Deliverable 5: Proposal for Harmonised Guidelines. Report by the Transport Research & Innovation Portal (TRIP), funded by the European Commission 6th Framework Programme for Research and Technological Development.

Hess, S., Adler, T. and Polak, J.W. 2007. Modelling airport and airline choice behaviour with the use of stated preference survey data. *Transportation Research, Part E*, 43(3), 221–33.

Hummels, D. and Schaur, G. 2013. Time as a Trade Barrier. *American Economic Review*, 103(7), 2935–59.

Hummels, D. and Nathan Associates Inc. 2007. *Calculating Tariff Equivalents for Time and Trade*. Washington DC: United States Agency for International Development (USAID). [Online]. Available at: http://www.krannert.purdue.edu/faculty/hummelsd/research/tariff_equivalents.pdf (accessed: 30 May 2020).

IATA. 2004. *Airport Development Reference Manual*. 9th Edition. Geneva: International Air Transport Association.

IATA-ACI. 2014. *Airport Development Reference Manual*. 10th Edition. Geneva: International Air Transport Association.

IATA-ACI. 2019. *Airport Development Reference Manual*. 11th Edition. Geneva: International Air Transport Association.

Jara-Díaz, S. 2007. *Transport Economic Theory*. Bingley, UK: Emerald.

Jiang, H. and Zhang, Y. 2016. An investigation of service quality, customer satisfaction and loyalty in China's airline market. *Journal of Air Transport Management*, 57, 80–88.

Johansson, P.-O. 2015. *Tradable Permits in Cost-Benefit Analysis*. CERE Working Paper 2015, 11, and SSE Working Paper in Economics No 2015:3. [Online]. Available at: http://www.cere.se/en/research/publications/694-tradable-permits-in-cost-benefit-analysis.html (accessed: 20 February 2019).

Johansson, P.-O. 2016. *On the Treatment of Emissions Trading and Green and White Certificates in Cost-Benefit Analysis*. SEE Working Paper in Economics No 2016:2. [Online]. Available at: https://papers.ssrn.com/sol3/papers.cfm?abstract_id=2824983 (accessed 20 February 2019).

Johansson, P.-O. 2020. The 2018 Reform of EU ETS: Consequences for Project Appraisal. *Journal of Environmental Economics and Policy*. (https://www.tandfonline.com/doi/full/10.1080/21606544.2020.1835738) (accessed: 7 November 2020).

Johansson, P.-O. and Kriström, B. 2015. *Cost-Benefit Analysis for Project Appraisal*. Cambridge: Cambridge University Press.

Johansson, P.-O. and de Rus, G. 2019. On the treatment of foreigners and foreign-owned firms in the cost-benefit analysis of transport projects. *Journal of Transport Economics and Policy*, 53(3), 285–287.

Johnson, C. and Briscoe, S. 1995. *Measuring the Economy: A Guide to Understanding Official Statistics. New Edition*. London: Penguin.

Jorge, J.D. and de Rus, G. 2004. Cost-benefit analysis of investments in airport infrastructure: a practical approach. *Journal of Air Transport Management*, 10, 311–26.

Jorge-Calderón, D. 2013. Airport valuation: using passenger generalised cost to measure competitive advantage and pricing power. *Journal of Airport Management*, 7(3), 255–64.

Jorge-Calderón, D. and Johansson, P.-O. 2017. Emissions trading and taxes: an application to airport investment appraisals. *Journal of Transport Economics and Policy*, 51(4), 1–14.

Just, R.E., Hueth, D.L. and Schmitz, A. 2004. *The Welfare Economics of Public Policy: A Practical Approach to Project and Policy Evaluation*. Cheltenham: Edward Elgar.

Kay, J. 1995. *Foundations of Corporate Success*. Oxford: Oxford University Press.

Kodukula, P. and Papudesu, C. 2006. *Project Valuation Using Real Options: A Practitioner's Guide*. Fort Lauderdale, FL: J Rosh.

Koller, T., Goedhart, M. and Wessels, D. 2010. *Valuation: Measuring and Managing the Value of Companies*. 5th Edition. Hoboken, NJ: Wiley.

Lambin, J.J. and Schuiling, I. 2012. *Market-Driven Management: Strategic and Operational Marketing*. 3rd Edition. New York: Palgrave Macmillan.

Lawrence, D. S. 1971. The initial decision to build the Supersonic Transport. *The American Journal of Economics and Sociology*, 30(4), 403–12.

Ling, F.-I., Lin, K. and Lu, J.-L. 2005. Difference in service quality of cross-strait airlines and its effect on passengers' preferences. *Journal of the Eastern Asia Society for Transportation Studies*, 6, 798–813.

Little, I.M.D. and Mirrlees, J.A. 1968. *Manual of industrial project analysis. Vol. 2. Development Centre Studies*. Paris: Organisation for Economic Co-operation and Development.

Little, I.M.D. and Mirrlees, J.A. 1974. *Project Appraisal and Planning for Developing Countries*. London: Heinemann Educational Books.

Londero, E.H. 2003. *Shadow Prices for Project Appraisal: Theory and Practice*. Cheltenham, UK: Edward Edgar.

Lu, J.L. and Tsai, L.N. 2004. Modelling the effect of enlarged seating room on passenger preferences of domestic airlines in Taiwan. *Journal of Air Transportation*, 9(2), 83–96.

Mackie, P. and Pearce, B. 2015. *A note from expert advisors, Prof. Peter Mackie and Mr. Brian Pierce, on key issues considering the Airports Commission economic case*. Airports Commission. [Online]. Available at: https://assets.publishing.service.gov.uk/government/uploads/system/uploads/attachment_data/file/438981/economy-expert-panelist-wider-economic-impacts-review.pdf (accessed: 4 May 2020).

Martin, s. 2010. *Industrial Organization in Context*. Oxford: Oxford University Press.

Moss, D.A. 2014. *A Concise Guide to Macroeconomics: What Managers, Executives, and Students Need to Know*. 2nd Edition. Boston, MA: Harvard Business School Press.

Motta, M. 2004. *Competition Policy: Theory and Practice*. Cambridge, UK: Cambridge University Press.

Niemeier, H.-M. 2009. *Regulation of large airports: status quo and options for reform*. International Transport Forum Discussion Paper 2009–10. Paris: Organisation for Economic Cooperation and Development. [Online]. Available at: https://www.itf-oecd.org/sites/default/files/docs/dp200910.pdf (accessed: 30 May 2020).

Niemeier, H.-M. 2013. *Expanding airport capacity under constraints in large urban areas: the German experience*. International Transport Forum Discussion Paper 2013–4. Paris: Organisation for Economic Cooperation and Development. [Online]. Available at: https://www.oecd-ilibrary.org/transport/expanding-airport-capacity-under-constraints-in-large-urban-areas_5k46n45fgtvc-en (accessed: 29 May 2020).

Niosi, J. and Zhegu, M. 2005. Aerospace clusters: local or global knowledge spillovers? *Industry and Innovation*, 12(1), 1–25.

Nordas, H.K. 2006. Time as a trade barrier: implications for low-income countries. *OECD Economic Studies*, 42(1), 137–67. [Online]. Available at: https://www.oecd-ilibrary.org/economics/time-as-a-trade-barrier-implications-for-low-income-countries_eco_studies-v2006-art4-en (accessed: 30 May 2020).

Perino, G. 2018. New ETS Phase 4 rules temporarily puncture waterbed. *Nature Climate Change*. 8 (April), 262–4. [Online]. Available at: https://www.nature.com/articles/s41558-018-0120-2 (Accessed: 25 April 2020).

Perino, G. 2019. Reply: EU ETS and the waterbed effect. *Nature Climate Change*. 9 (October), 736. [Online]. Available at: https://www.nature.com/articles/s41558-019-0580-z (Accessed: 25 April 2020).

Perino, G., Ritz R.A. and Van Benthem, A. 2019. *Understanding overlapping policies: Internal carbon leakage and the puncture waterbed*. EPRG Working Paper 1910. Cambridge Working Papers in Economics 1920. [Online]. Available at: https://www.

repository.cam.ac.uk/bitstream/handle/1810/291495/cwpe1920.pdf?sequence=1 (accessed: 25 April 2020).

Renner, J. and Wielgus, M. 2015. Improving and optimising the LoS of an airport. *International Airport Review*, 19(5) 47–50. [Online]. Available at: https://www.iata.org/contentassets/935670dbc80e40f3a35b85a71ddd368e/cons-apcs-los-article-iar-2015.pdf (Accessed: 1 May 2020).

Rogoff, K. 1996. The purchasing power parity puzzle. *Journal of Economic Literature*, 34 (June): 647–68.

Rosendhal, K.E. 2019. EU ETS and the waterbed effect. *Nature Climate Change*. 9 (October), 734–5. [Online]. Available at: https://www.nature.com/articles/s41558-019-0579-5 (accessed: 25 April 2020).

Squire, L. and van der Tak, H.G. 1975. *Economic Analysis of Projects. World Bank Research Publications*. Baltimore: The John Hopkins University Press.

Smit, H.T.J. and Trigeorgis, L. 2004. *Strategic Investment: Real Options and Games*. Princeton, NJ: Princeton University Press.

Taylor, M.P. 2010. Real exchange rates and Purchasing Power Parity: mean reversion in economic thought, in Taylor, Mark. (ed.) *Purchasing Power Parity and Real Exchange Rates*. London: Routledge.

Tica, J. and Druzic, I. 2006. *The Harrod-Balassa-Samuelson Effect: A Survey of Empirical Evidence*. Faculty of Economics and Business Working Paper 06–07. Zagreb: University of Zagreb. [Online]. Available at: http://web.efzg.hr/RePEc/pdf/Clanak%2006-07.pdf (accessed: November 2019).

Trigeorgis, L. 1996. *Real Options: Managerial Flexibility and Strategy in Resource Allocation*. Cambridge, MA: The MIT Press.

Tsafarakis, S. Kokotas, T. and Pantouvakis, A. 2018. A multiple criteria approach for airline passenger satisfaction measurement and service quality improvement. *Journal of Air Transport Management*, 68, 61–75.

U.S. Department of Transportation. 2016. *The Value of Travel Time Savings: Departmental Guidance for Conducting Economic Evaluations. Revision 2*. Washington D.C.: U.S. Department of Transportation. [Online]. Available at: https://www.transportation.gov/sites/dot.gov/files/docs/2016%20Revised%20Value%20of%20Travel%20Time%20Guidance.pdf (accessed 12 April 2020).

Ussinova, A., Laplace, I. and Roucolle, C. 2018. An analysis of the impact of larger aircraft (A-380) on flight frequency. *Energy Efficiency* 11, 701–12.

Varian, H.R. 1992. *Microeconomic Analysis*. 3rd Edition. London, UK: W.W. Norton & Co.

Vasigh, B., Fleming, K. and Tacker, T. 2008. *Introduction to Air Transport Economics: From Theory to Applications*. Farnham, UK: Ashgate.

Vose, D. 2008. *Risk Analysis: A Quantitative Guide*. 3rd Edition. Chichester, UK: Wiley.

Ward, W.A. 2019. Cost-benefit analysis theory versus practice at the World Bank 1960 to 2015. *Journal of Benefit-Cost Analysis*, 10(1), 124–44.

Ward, W.A. and Deren, B. J. and D'Silva, E.H. 1991. *The Economics of Project Analysis: A Practitioner's Guide. Economic Development Institute Technical Materials*. Washington DC: The World Bank. [Online]. Available at: http://documents.worldbank.org/curated/en/686191468766169340/The-economics-of-project-analysis-a-practitioners-guide (accessed 1 December 2019).

Wardman, M. Chintakayala, V.P.K. and de Jong, G.C. 2016. Values of travel time in Europe: review and meta-analysis. *Transportation Research Part A: Policy and Practice*, 94, 93–111.

Winston, C. and de Rus, G. (eds). 2008. *Aviation Infrastructure Performance: A Study in Comparative Political Economy*. Washington DC: Brookings Institution Press.

Woolley, P.K. 1972. A cost-benefit analysis of the Concorde project. *Journal of Transport Economics and Policy*, 6(3), 225–39.

World Bank 2005. *Treatment of Induced Traffic. Transport Note TRN-11*. Washington DC: World Bank. [Online]. Available at: http://documents.worldbank.org/curated/en/130181468176985963/Treatment-of-induced-traffic (accessed: 31 May 2020).

Index

Index. Aviation Investment, 2nd Edition. Doramas Jorge-Calderón, 15 November 2020

Printed in the United States
By Bookmasters